A Biographical Dictionary of Science Fiction and Fantasy Artists

A Biographical Dictionary of Science Fiction and Fantasy Artists

Robert Weinberg

Greenwood Press
New York • Westport, Connecticut • London

Library of Congress Cataloging-in-Publication Data

Weinberg, Robert E.
    A biographical dictionary of science fiction and
fantasy artists.

    Bibliography: p.
    Includes index.
    1. Science fiction illustrators—Biography—
Dictionaries.   I. Title.
NC961.6.W45   1988   741.6′092′2   [B]   87–17651
ISBN 0–313–24349–2 (lib. bdg. : alk. paper)

British Library Cataloguing in Publication Data is available.

Library of Congress Catalog Card Number: 87–17651
ISBN: 0–313–24349–2

First published in 1988

Greenwood Press, Inc.
88 Post Road West, Westport, Connecticut 06881

Printed in the United States of America

∞

The paper used in this book complies with the
Permanent Paper Standard issued by the National
Information Standards Organization (Z39.48–1984).

10 9 8 7 6 5 4 3 2 1

Contents

Introduction

During the past few years numerous books covering the history of science fiction have appeared. There have been several encyclopedias, a number of illustrated histories of the field, and personal memoirs by many top authors in the genre. However, all of these books suffer from one obvious blind spot. Each of them covers the important novels and stories written during the period of coverage; many of them devote a great deal of attention to the magazine editors responsible for shaping the course of modern science fiction; and numerous science fiction films, from the influential to the awful, have been analyzed again and again, covering the same territory with attention to the smallest possible detail. But none of these books pays much attention to science fiction and fantasy art or artists.

This is not to say that there have not been any books on SF art. Some years back, there was a brief flurry of trade paperbound books that touched on the subject. However, these mostly were picture books with the text seemingly added as an afterthought. Several were published with no text at all, representing merely a hodgepodge of illustrations on a variety of subjects. The only worthwhile art books were a limited number of collections, each focusing on the work of an individual artist. Books on Kelly Freas, Michael Whelan, Rowena Morrill, and Frank Frazetta are examples of some of the best volumes done in this tradition. For the serious student of science fiction interested in other artists, there was little else.

The Tuck and Nicholls SF encyclopedias do have more than fifty entries each on art and artists; however, many of the entries are based on incomplete data assembled from the pages of old pulp magazines. Unfortunately, little primary research was ever done in the period when many of the important artists in the formative days of science fiction were working. Thus neither book lists any real biographical information on Earle Bergey, Alex Ley-denfrost, Margaret Brundage, or a host of other important artists in the 1930s and 1940s. Other artists not as well known in the field but equally important, such as Peter Stevens and Rudolph Belarski, are completely ignored. Due to space limitations, there is no attention given to the many interesting but lesser artists who have worked in the genre.

This is the first book of any note to cover in depth the science fiction art field. It is not an art book but a book about *artists*. This work is aimed at those people interested in the history and state of science fiction art. It is the first comprehensive biographical dictionary ever done in the field and, I hope, will serve as a catalyst for future studies in the same area.

This volume is the result of years of work and a great deal of research. Although I tried to include as many artists as possible, size and time limitations made it impossible to include every artist who has ever done any work in science fiction. I began by preparing a basic list of artists to be included in the volume, and I circulated this list among several respected science fiction historians and noted artists who added other names. After a final survey of reference works I added a few more people, for a total of 279. Despite all precautions, however, a number of deserving artists may have been inadvertently omitted.

Among the criteria used for selection of artists were importance to the field, influence in the field, amount of work done in the field, and historical importance. Since so little has been written on early science fiction artists, less prolific artists from the period 1930–1950 generally were included even if it meant that a prolific new artist had to be left out. By and large, mainstream illustrators who worked in a fantastic vein but had not ever illustrated science fiction were not included. The same judgment also applies to children's artists and early fantasy artists, such as Arthur Rackham, whose names were primarily associated with children's literature. I hope that a revised volume some time in the future will correct any such oversights, and I am eager to learn of any suggested additions or corrections to this volume.

I tried to include not only the obvious but the obscure. For the first time in any study of science fiction art, artists have been included from the pulp field who, while not working for the science fiction magazines, created as much if not more science fiction art than many of the people normally included in such histories. I have also included mainstream artists who are adamant in their statements that they are not science fiction artists but whose work has appeared in the field. Even a few movie designers and important comic artists have been included.

No book of this size is the work of one individual. Thanks are due to a number of people without whose help this volume would never have been completed. Richard Dalby handled the British and French entries, with the assistance of Mike Ashley and Phil Harbottle. In the United States Jerry

Bails, Vincent di Fate, Alex and Phyllis Eisenstein, R. Alain Everts, Sam Moskowitz, and Doug Murray all provided a great deal of important information on artists, and without their help this book would have been much less complete. Nancy Ford did much of the necessary legwork, including making numerous telephone calls to insure the accuracy of many of our entries. Lois Horsky and Mary K. Coppens provided invaluable assistance on the bibliographical information, and my wife Phyllis, worked long and hard assisting me with all phases of the book, as well as putting up with my years of devotion to this project.

Finally, there are hundreds of artists who responded to my surveys, questions, letters, and telephone calls, without whose cooperation this book would never have been completed. To all of these people, I offer my heartfelt thanks.

How to Use This Book

This volume is divided into three parts. The first part is a brief history of modern science fiction art, concentrating on the economic and social history of the science fiction field and how these events shaped the growth of science fiction illustration. Major trends and important figures are noted as well as specific turning points in publishing that affected the art field. Although this historical discussion could stand by itself, it is meant to supplement the biographical entries in this volume by providing additional information about the field in general that would not be covered in specific biographies. As with all material in this book, it is meant to be used *with*, not independent of, the other parts.

The second part contains biographical sketches of more than 250 science fiction and fantasy artists, arranged in alphabetical order by artist. Each entry begins with the artist's name, last name first. Thus Rowena Morrill, who signs her art "Rowena," is listed under *Morrill.* However, in this case and similar situations, cross-references are entered from the first name or pseudonym. If known, the artist's birth (and if deceased, death) date is given; the notation *?* signifies that the date specified is in question. If no information on any date is available, a single question mark *(?)* is given. Following the date, the artist's nationality is listed. Next a biographical sketch is presented, using, whenever possible, information provided directly by the artist. All quotes in these sketches, unless noted otherwise, are in the artist's own words. Undocumented quotations usually are from my personal correspondence or interviews that I conducted. Biographies written by other contributors are signed at the end of the sketch; unsigned entries are my own.

Following each entry is a bibliographical listing of the artist's work in the science fiction and fantasy field. Artwork not relating to science fiction is not listed. These are working bibliographies, not the final word on the work of the illustrators. Although the magazine entries are fairly complete through the early 1980s, the book and paperback entries, by necessity, are not. Such bibliographical information would fill several volumes this size. Living artists were asked for bibliographical information, and whenever supplied, this information was used.

In the bibliographies, entries are listed first for hardcover appearances (HC); then for paperback or paperbound book format (PB); and, finally, for magazine appearances (each listed by magazine title). Paperbacks and hardcovers are listed alphabetically by title. Publication date, when known, follows each book listing. Using that information, it is hoped that a serious student of the genre will be able to find other necessary publication information about the books. In certain cases, when the bibliographical information is unique (as in the French illustrators of Jules Verne), more detailed information is included.

Magazine listings are for an appearance in the magazine, either a cover or interior illustration. Months are abbreviated by numbers (i.e., 6 = June, 9 = September). Bimonthly publications are listed by the first month's number (i.e., 1 = January/February). Quarterly magazines are listed by season. When magazines appeared as numbered, undated issues, an attempt was also made to list them in this manner. A full listing of abbreviations for magazine titles used in the bibliographies follows below. Researchers interested in the publication histories of the magazines are referred to the numerous detailed surveys of the science fiction and fantasy field published in the past few years. Particularly useful is *Science Fiction, Fantasy, and Weird Fiction Magazines*, edited by Marshall B. Tymn and Mike Ashley (see Bibliography).

The final part, following the artist biographies, consists of several appendixes. The first appendix surveys the fate of early original art in the science fiction field. It is followed by a chronological listing of the Hugo and World Fantasy Awards for Best Artist. A bibliography of some of the important books published on science fiction art concludes this third part.

Throughout the book, any unsigned material is my own work.

Abbreviations

The following *magazine* abbreviations are used in the lists of published work for each artist.

2CSAB	*Two Complete Science Adventure Books*
AA	*Amazing Stories Annual*
AKS	*Arkham Sampler*
AMF	*A. Merritt Fantasy*
AMZ	*Amazing Stories*
AQ	*Amazing Quarterly*
ASF	*Astounding* (later *Analog*)
ASF&FR	*Avon Science Fiction and Fantasy Reader*
ASFR	*Avon Science Fiction Reader*
ASH	*Astonishing*
AUTH	*Authentic Science Fiction*
AW	*Air Wonder Stories*
BEY	*Beyond*
CF	*Captain Future*
COM	*Comet Stories*
COS	*Cosmic Stories*
CSF	*Cosmos Science Fiction*
DEST	*Destinies*
DW	*Dream World*

DYN	*Dynamic Science Fiction*
EXT	*Extro*
F&SF	*Magazine of Fantasy and Science Fiction*
FA	*Fantastic Adventures*
FANTASY(BR)	*Fantasy* (British)
FB	*Fantasy Book*
FF	*Fantasy Magazine*
FFM	*Famous Fantastic Mysteries*
FgF	*Forgotten Fantasy*
FN	*Fantastic Novels*
FMSF	*Famous Science Fiction*
FSQ	*Fantastic Story Quarterly* (later *Magazine*)
FTC	*Fantastic*
FU	*Fantastic Universe*
FUT	*Future*
GAL	*Galileo*
GAM	*Gamma*
GXY	*Galaxy Science Fiction*
GXYN	*Galaxy Science Fiction Novels*
IASFA	*Isaac Asimov's Science Fiction Adventure Magazine*
IASFM	*Isaac Asimov's Science Fiction Magazine*
IF	*IF*
IMG	*Imagination*
IMGT	*Imaginative Tales*
Imp	*Impulse*
INF	*Infinity*
MIR	*Miracle Science Stories*
MOH	*Magazine of Horror*
MSS	*Marvel Science Stories*
NC	*Night Cry*
NEB	*Nebula*
NW	*New Worlds*
NWUS	*New Worlds* (U.S. edition)
ORB	*Orbit Science Fiction*
OTWA	*Out of This World Adventures*
OW	*Other Worlds*
PS	*Planet Stories*
RS	*Rocket Stories*

SAT	*Satellite Science Fiction*
ScF	*Science Fantasy*
ScS	*Science Stories*
SF	*Science Fiction*
SF+	*Science Fiction +*
SFA	*Science Fiction Adventures*
SFA (BR)	*Science Fiction Adventures* (British)
SFD	*Science Fiction Digest*
SFQ	*Science Fiction Quarterly*
SFYBK	*Science Fiction Yearbook*
SMS	*Startling Mystery Stories*
SpS	*Space Stories*
SpSF	*Space Science Fiction*
SpTr	*Space Travel*
SPWY	*Spaceway*
SRN	*Saturn*
SS	*Startling Stories*
SSF	*Super Science Fiction*
SSS	*Super Science Stories*
ST	*Strange Tales*
STAR	*Star Science Fiction Magazine*
STI	*Stirring Science Stories*
StrS	*Strange Stories*
SW	*Science Wonder Stories*
SWQ	*Science Wonder Quarterly*
TofW	*Tales of Wonder*
TOPS	*Tops in Science Fiction*
TRE	*Treasury of Great Science Fiction*
TSF	*10 Story Fantasy*
TWS	*Thrilling Wonder Stories*
TZ	*Twilight Zone*
UNC	*Uncanny*
UK	*Unknown* (later *Unknown Worlds*)
UNI	*Universe*
VAN	*Vanguard Science Fiction*
VEN	*Venture Science Fiction*
VofT	*Visions of Tomorrow*
VTX	*Vortex Science Fiction*

WB   *Worlds Beyond*
WC&S   *Witchcraft and Sorcery*
WOT   *Worlds of Tomorrow*
WQ   *Wonder Stories Quarterly*
WS   *Wonder Stories*
WSA   *Wonder Stories Annual*
WT   *Weird Tales*

Additional abbreviations used in this book:

HC   Hardcover book
PB   Paperback or paperbound book

A Biographical Dictionary of Science Fiction and Fantasy Artists

Science Fiction Art: A Historical Overview

Science fiction and fantasy, by the very nature of the material presented, is a visual medium. Illustration has always accompanied text from the earliest novels recognized as science fiction until the present. Unfortunately, although art has remained a common denominator in the field, it often has been considered almost unnecessary to the text. The fortunes of science fiction illustration have risen and fallen within the broader history of science fiction. Rarely, though, have the artists working in the field been given the credit they deserve.

Although science fiction is generally considered to be primarily of American (or British) origin, the earliest artists of note in the field were French. The most famous of these artists was Albert Robida whose work in the late 1800s is considered the first modern science fiction illustration. Robida produced a long saga of the midtwentieth century, *Voyages tres extraordinaires de Saturnin Farandoul*, which he wrote as well as illustrated. These stories first appeared in magazine form and then were reprinted in book form. Robida was particularly noted for his huge buildings, ironclad ships, submarines, and even flying machines. He was the first artist actively to predict the future of war in illustrated form.

At the same time, the fiction of Jules Verne was extremely important in the development of French science fiction art. Verne's long novels originally appeared as serials in leading French magazines, and all of the stories were published with numerous illustrations by leading French illustrators. Many of these artists would be forgotten if not for their work for Verne, which was reprinted in hardcover volumes published throughout the world. The best of these artists included Georges Roux, Alphonse Marie de Neuville, Leon Benett, Henri de Montaut, and Edouard Riou. The art done by these men, especially for the Hetzel editions of the Verne novels, endured until modern times. De Montaut's illustrations of the interior of the projectile used in *From the Earth to the Moon* are among the most famous in all science fiction. Jules Ferat's studies of the *Nautilus* are equally famous. Emile Bayard produced famous illustrations for *From the Earth to the Moon . . . and a Trip Around It*, including an oft-reprinted weightlessness engraving, a survey of the moon illustration, and a famous splashdown piece.

Modern students of science fiction history often fail to realize the popularity and influence of Verne's novels. One can grasp some measure of his importance by looking at the care given to the production of his books. Leon Benett was commissioned by Hetzel, Verne's publisher, for nearly two thousand engravings and illustrations for *Voyages extraordinaires*, and although he was the most prolific of all Verne illustrators, many other artists contributed work to the series as well. It was not unusual for one of Verne's books to contain more than a hundred illustrations.

Whereas Verne was the most popular and important science fiction author in Europe, H. G. Wells soon occupied that same position in England. Unfortunately, although most of Wells's early novels and stories appeared in magazine form, they were not as extensively illustrated as those by Verne. Much of Wells's work was printed in the *Strand*, and the illustrations by artists such as Alfred Pearse, Claude Shepperson, Edmund Sullivan, and Paul Hardy were less than spectacular. However, Henri Lanos produced eighteen very fine illustrations for *When the Sleeper Wakes* which appeared in the *Graphic Magazine*. These plates have been reproduced many times since their original appearance, usually without indication of the artist's name.

The most important and famous of all Wells's illustrators was Warwick Goble. A prolific artist who contributed to most of the English monthly magazines, he did sixty-six illustrations for the 1897 serialization of *The War of the Worlds* in *Pearson's Magazine*. His depictions of the Martian war machines were among the most famous science fiction illustrations ever to appear in print. Like many science fiction artists who followed him, Goble later abandoned the field for the more lucrative, fine-arts market.

Another important science fiction artist working in England at that time was Fred T. Jane. One of the major science fiction writers of that period, Jane was also an excellent illustrator who did work for both popular magazines and hardcover books. He illustrated a number of his own novels as well as George Griffith's best-selling epics, *The Angel of the Revolution* and *Olga Romanoff.*

However, after the flurry of activity at the turn of the century, science fiction illustration in England disappeared for nearly thirty years. Novels continued to be published, but due to rising costs and changing interests, lavishly illustrated science fiction hardcovers vanished.

In the United States early science fiction appeared in various newspapers and quality magazines. Often, these early stories, including reprints of British novels as well as new works, were published with attractive illustrations by technically competent artists. However, none of the art was particularly notable, and most of it was executed by staff artists who treated the work as just another assignment. No one specialized in science fiction or fantasy art.

However, popular publishing in America took a step in another direction in the late 1880s. Frank A. Munsey, publisher of *The Golden Argosy*, a fiction magazine aimed at children, came up with the concept of an inexpensive magazine aimed at mass readership. Until then, magazines were printed on glossy paper, featuring lots of illustrations and costing more than most blue-collar workers could afford. Instead, the common people were left with dime novels, which were adventure and detective novels usually featuring continuing series characters like Buffalo Bill or Nick Carter, printed in large-size newspaperlike format on the least expensive paper available. Munsey combined the two concepts. He used the least expensive paper available and stayed away from expensive reproduction of illustrations, using plain, heavy-stock covers. But he offered the magazine format, with a number of stories, including serialized novels, instead of one long juvenile adventure. He could keep the price per issue low because of the inexpensive paper. His renamed *Argosy* magazine became a tremendous success. This new-style magazine, dubbed "pulp" because of the inexpensive wood paper it used, revolutionized publishing in the United States. Within a few years, dozens of other pulp magazines were being published, and by the late 1920s hundreds of titles filled the newsstand racks.

The pulps, at first, rarely featured any artwork and used plain, unobtrusive covers. But as competition increased, the importance of a catchy cover illustration became obvious. At first, most pulp magazines featured covers designed to appeal to women, who were recognized as the largest group of buyers of such fiction magazines. However, as the magazines grew more specialized and adventure and action stories dominated the contents more and more, the covers changed to match the contents.

The arrival of Edgar Rice Burroughs helped change the pulp-art field even more. Burroughs' Tarzan and Mars novels were so popular that all of the major fiction publications soon started publishing material by Burroughs or by authors writing in a similar vein. These fast-paced scientific romances needed cover art that proclaimed their unusual nature to an eager buying market. As more and more covers in this vein were needed, certain staff artists working for the pulps became noted as specialists in such work. These men were specifically assigned covers based on their expertise. Thus the first true science fiction artists in the United States were born. Among these earliest pioneers in the field were P. J. Monahan, Clinton Peetee, Herbert Morton Stoops, and J. Allen St. John.

Hardcover publishing of science fiction and fantasy continued, but the books rarely matched the lavishly illustrated volumes of the late nineteenth century. A few artists became famous for their work in the fantastic fiction field, but in most cases they transcended the label of genre artist. These men included Frank Pape and Mahlon Blaine in America and Sidney Sime and Harry Clarke in England. But they were the exceptions, and most genre illustration was ignored by all but the readers.

Science fiction was not yet thought to be a distinct branch of modern fiction, and from time to time, novels in the field were published as original works in hardcover or reprinted from the pulp magazines. Often, when a serial was reprinted from *Argosy* (or its companion magazine, *All-Story*), the original cover illustration used for the serialization was also used for the book jacket.

In the case of Edgar Rice Burroughs, his work continued to gain in popularity throughout the teens and twenties, and nearly all of his novels appeared first as magazine serials and then as hardcover volumes. The first editions of the Burroughs novels often were illustrated with a number of interior plates commissioned especially for the volume. A number of artists worked on the Burroughs novels, but without a doubt, the most popular, prolific, and influential was Chicago artist J. Allen St. John. To this day, St. John is still considered the definitive Burroughs illustrator.

Because of the inexpensive wood-pulp paper used for the pulp magazines, interior illustrations rarely reproduced well. At first small story headings were all that appeared in the magazine to break the continual roll of print. However, as the battle to win readership continued, magazines strived for improvement, and interior art became a feature in many of the better pulps. *Bluebook* magazine used a slightly better quality of pulp paper and began running numerous illustrations in each issue. Halftones were impractical on pulp stock, but well-delineated line work reproduced fairly well if care was taken with the printing.

Many of the top pulp illustrators came from the newspapers, put out of a job when improvements in printing techniques made it possible for the daily papers to use photographs instead of line sketches of major news events. Newspaper artists, trained at producing accurate, crisp illustrations for reproduction on inexpensive paper, fit in perfectly with the requirements of the pulps. Probably the most famous artist for the pulps to emerge from the ranks of newspaper artists was Joseph Clement Coll. His fine line illustrations attracted enough attention so that often his art for serials was reprinted in hardcover editions of the works. Coll's art influenced a new generation of pulp-magazine illustrators.

Magazines grew more specialized as the reading market grew ever larger.

In 1919 there appeared *The Thrill Book*, a magazine devoted entirely to "different" stories. Although not actually a science fiction or weird-fiction magazine in content, it published a significant amount of both genres in its limited run. Due to limited distribution and a vague editorial policy, the magazine lasted for only sixteen issues.

Shortly after that, in 1923, *Weird Tales* appeared. A magazine devoted exactly to what the title proclaimed, it featured fantasy, horror, supernatural, and science fiction stories. Despite poor management decisions during its first year, the pulp continued publication and became a mainstay of the fantasy-fiction field. Unfortunately, to keep costs down, the earliest artists who worked for *Weird Tales* were mostly hack illustrators chosen not for their talent but for their willingness to work for little money. Among these artists were Andrew Brosnatch, Joseph Doolin, and Curtis C. Senf. It was not until the arrival of Hugh Rankin in the late 1920s that a fairly competent artist began working for *Weird Tales*.

Science fiction continued to be popular in the major pulp-fiction magazines. *Argosy All-Story* featured numerous science fiction serials by top-name writers, including A. Merritt, Ralph Milne Farley, and Edgar Rice Burroughs. Novels by these men always received the cover illustration, usually done by Paul Stahr or Robert Graef. Although forgotten today, Stahr and Graef were probably the most talented all-around science fiction illustrators working in the early days of magazine publishing.

Amazing Stories, the first magazine featuring only science fiction stories, appeared in April 1926. It was the creation of Hugo Gernsback, who had been publishing a number of other magazines on science and electronics for years. Gernsback ventured into the science fiction market encouraged by the popularity of similar stories he had been printing for years in his magazine *Science and Invention*. From that publication, Gernsback brought the artist who had been handling most of the fantastic illustrations, Frank R. Paul.

Born in Austria, Paul worked as a cartoonist for the *Jersey Journal* and did his science fiction illustrating as a sideline. Trained in architecture, he brought with him a strong feeling for huge buildings and complex machinery that perfectly fit the strongly scientific slant of the first all-science fiction magazine. *Amazing Stories* was published as a large eight-by-eleven-inch magazine, so the covers gave Paul plenty of room for work. His people were less than believable, but they were dwarfed by an array of bizarre machines, alien landscapes, and astonishing inventions. Paul also handled the interior illustrations for the magazine as well.

Although Paul was not as artistic a craftsman as Robert Graef or Paul Stahr, his often crudely done covers possessed a unique charm and flavor not shared by the slicker paintings. The term *sense of wonder* was used years later to describe the stories published in the early years of pulp science fiction, stories that thrilled and excited the imaginations of the readers. That same term applied equally well to Paul's covers. They may not have been art, but they worked, conveying the mystery and excitement of the stories they illustrated.

As an experiment, Gernsback had Paul paint a cover for the December 1926 *Amazing Stories* that did not illustrate any story. The artist came up with an unusual painting that showed a group of strange aliens on another world observing a spaceship transporting a modern ocean liner in some sort of force field. Gernsback invited his readers to base a story on the cover, offering a $250 prize for the best story. Astonishingly, more than 360 manuscripts were submitted, emphasizing the impact of cover art on science fiction readers.

In 1927, flushed with the success of *Amazing Stories*, Gernsback published the *Amazing Stories Annual*, a thick magazine featuring a complete novel and short stories, all illustrated by Paul. The annual sold out immediately and prompted Gernsback to publish *Amazing Stories Quarterly* beginning in 1928. Again, Paul did all of the art for this magazine. In the meantime, he continued to produce art for *Science and Invention*. Not only was Paul the first major star of science fiction magazine art, he was the busiest.

Major changes occurred in 1929 in the science fiction field and therefore in the science fiction art field. Gernsback lost control of *Amazing Stories* through an unusual bankruptcy suit pushed through by Bernarr MacFadden. Almost immediately, Gernsback began two new science fiction magazines, *Science Wonder Stories* and *Air Wonder Stories*. Within a short time, he began *Science Wonder Quarterly*. Again, the magazines were large size and featured covers and interior art by Paul.

Amazing, under its new publisher, Radio-Science Publications (later Teck Publications), found itself without a steady artist. Several magazine illustrators were used, most notably H. W. Wessolowski (Wesso), but after a short while the art assignment was given to Leo Morey. Although his paintings were not as colorful or imaginative as Paul's, Morey handled the cover and interior art for *Amazing* reasonably well. The magazine was produced at lower cost under the new publisher, and brightly colored covers were no longer used. A lesser grade of paper inside meant that the art reproduced poorly, and Morey never equalled Paul's intricately detailed black-and-white illustrations.

Paul's art for the Wonder group (as Gernsback's new magazines were called) equalled and often topped his earlier work for *Amazing Stories*. Again, machinery and giant spaceships dominated his paintings, and the people appearing in the art had a crude, stiff look. Bright colors dominated the art.

At the end of 1929 yet another science fiction magazine appeared on the newsstands. This was *Astounding Stories of Super Science*, a member of the Clayton chain of magazines and the first all-science fiction magazine to be published in pulp format. Instead of the larger sized magazines that had

appeared until then, the Clayton magazine was standard pulp size, approx-
imately seven by ten inches, and was printed on very inexpensive pulp
paper. Cover art was handled by Wesso and consisted of bright, imaginative
pieces painted in watercolors. Clayton specialized in magazines that featured
fast-paced adventure stories, and *Astounding Stories* was the first attempt to
publish a science fiction magazine in that category. Wesso was able to paint
people much better than Paul or Morey had done, and his covers featured
lots of action. The first cover for the new magazine depicted aviators fighting
against giant bugs. Future covers followed in the same vein, with conflict
between man and monster the primary theme. Interiors were well done by
Wesso and by several artists from outside the field, including John Fleming
Gould. Even Paul did some excellent interior artwork for the new magazine.

In late 1931 the Clayton chain added another magazine, *Strange Tales*.
Aimed at the same weird-fiction market that was served only by *Weird
Tales*, the new pulp featured excellent paintings by Wesso for the covers.
Most of the interior art was handled by Wesso, along with other artists
who worked for *Weird Tales* as well as the nonfantasy pulps of the time.

Farnsworth Wright, the editor of *Weird Tales*, realized that he had to
fight back. Not only was he hurt by *Strange Tales*, but the science fiction
magazines also cut into his sales. When *Amazing Stories* first began, it probably boosted the sales of *Weird Tales*. Fans looking for more science fiction
could find it only in the general adventure magazines like *Argosy* or in *Weird
Tales*. Wright ran science fiction very much in the same vein as that published in the early *Amazing Stories*, and for a while he even advertised his
magazine in the back pages of the other pulps. However, with the appearance of *Astounding*, *Strange Tales*, and *Wonder Stories* (a combined version
of the two earlier Wonder titles), Wright faced much greater competition.
No longer did fans have to search for science fiction. There were three
magazines totally devoted to the subject, as well as several quarterlies.

The Depression saw a huge rise in the number of pulp magazines published. Printers were eager to keep printing, and credit was easy to obtain.
Magazines were floated on little if any real cash. Titles often ran for only
a few issues; if they did not catch on with the reading public, they were
dropped. Long-running magazines found themselves fighting for space at
crowded newsstands. Covers became increasingly garish as each publisher
tried to attract new readers.

For years Wright had been using hack artists for interior and cover work
on his magazine. They worked for little money but rarely were worth even
the small sums they earned. Wright abandoned this policy in 1932 and
began paying higher prices for cover art, experimenting with the work of
two artists. He obtained several paintings by J. Allen St. John, who lived
and taught art in Chicago where *Weird Tales* was edited. St. John, who had
gained fame as illustrator for many novels by Edgar Rice Burroughs, was
looking for work since Burroughs also was experimenting with the work

of new artists. At the same time, Wright tried several covers by fashion designer Margaret Brundage, who had brought her portfolio of illustrations to his office some months earlier. St. John's paintings were fine pieces of fantasy art, but Brundage caught the readers' attention with voluptuous women clad in scanty garments. She was unable to paint a truly weird scene, but Brundage's near nude and totally nude women were a complete change from anything previously seen on a science fiction or fantasy magazine. She quickly became the premier cover artist for *Weird Tales*.

The Clayton chain went bankrupt in 1933. *Astounding Stories* and several other titles were bought by the Street & Smith publishing chain. Better financed, and with a new editor, the magazine soon established itself as a leader in the field. Howard V. Brown, an established illustrator who had been working the pulps for years doing covers for a variety of magazines, was brought in as principal cover artist. Brown was an excellent artist who was capable of painting believable people, interesting monsters, and the usual fantastic machinery that populated science fiction stories of the time.

Elliott Dold dominated the interiors. Dold had done some science fiction art for the only two issues of *Miracle Stories* in 1931 and soon became one of the most popular interior artists in the field. Brown also did a fair amount of interior work for *Astounding* and produced a number of interesting pieces.

Science fiction and fantasy spread beyond the genre magazines in 1933. Street & Smith began publication of *Doc Savage* as a monthly companion to its already popular magazine *The Shadow*. The *Doc Savage* pulp featured a complete novel about a superhero-style adventurer and his exploits around the world. Although it was basically an adventure magazine, the novels frequently drifted into science fiction. Cover art was well handled by Walter Baumhofer. The great success of these two Street & Smith "character pulps" spawned a vast number of imitations. Soon the newsstands were filled with magazines such as *The Spider*, *G-8 and His Battle Aces*, *Operator 5*, and *The Mysterious Wu Fang*. Most featured some pseudoscience as part of the story line, and many featured cover and interior art that ventured into the science fiction field.

In the fantasy genre, Popular Publications scored big with three magazines that featured fast-paced action stories with seemingly supernatural menaces that invariably turned out to be hoaxes or mad schemes. These "weird-menace" pulps rose in only a few months to the ranks of the best-selling pulp magazines on the strength of their bizarre stories and the superlative covers that illustrated them. *Horror Stories*, *Terror Tales*, and *Dime Mystery Magazine* all featured unbelievably gruesome covers by John Newton Howitt. A well-known landscape and portrait painter, Howitt had been forced by the Depression into magazine cover art. He did numerous covers for the pulps. Although he was never closely associated with the science fiction or fantasy fields, his covers for the "weird-menace pulps" were among the finest masterpieces of horror art published during the entire pulp era. Interior art for the magazines was capably handled by Amos Sewell and John Fleming Gould.

Changes in philosophy also took place in the 1930s. Originally, when a novel was serialized in a magazine, the cover painting normally illustrated some episode in the section of the novel appearing in that particular issue. Readers complained if the cover illustration revealed some detail of the novel that took place in a section of the story not immediately available. However, as serials became longer and covers more garish, publishers ignored this complaint. A cover painting illustrated a dramatic scene from the novel, not necessarily from a chapter appearing in that issue. As most serial novels were illustrated on the cover for the first issue of that serialization, and the most exciting parts usually were near the end, the cover often provided readers with clues to the most dramatic scenes to come.

Symbolic covers were featured on pulp magazines throughout their history. If an artist could not find a suitable scene for a cover (or if it might reveal too much about the story), he instead painted a cover capturing the feel of the novel instead of one particular scene. In the science fiction field, this soon became common, with contents-page listings stating "Cover illustration suggested by . . . " instead of implying that the art dramatized one particular event. This trend was accentuated in the 1930s.

Popular Publications magazines were among the first to feature covers with no tie-in to the stories in the issue. Many of the Howitt covers for *Horror Stories* and *Terror Tales* were symbolic of the contents of the magazines in general. Art became independent of the actual contents of the magazine, heralding even more unusual changes to come in the later part of that era.

In 1935 an important newcomer began illustrating for *Weird Tales*. Virgil Finlay was the first important artist of what might be termed the "second wave" of science fiction illustrators. When science fiction magazines began publication in 1926, artists were recruited from other magazines and pulps. Although a number of them had some previous experience with science fiction or fantasy, they were pulp illustrators first and science fiction illustrators second. They were the "first wave" of illustrators of the science fiction magazines. The "second wave" of illustrators were artists who emerged from the growing ranks of science fiction readers. They were fans of the magazines who believed they could do a better job of illustrating the stories than the men who were working for the pulps. Finlay was a reader of the science fiction magazines and *Weird Tales* and knew his art was better than anything appearing in that magazine. He was right, and within a short time, he became the sensation of the fantasy and science fiction field. For a change, an artist entered the field not as a general pulp artist but as a specialist in science fiction art. The field has remained a mix of the two waves—artists who begin as illustrators and then enter science fiction and artists who aim specifically at the science fiction field as their goal and have little interest in illustration outside the field.

Finlay brought a new excitement to science fiction and fantasy art. Frank R. Paul was popular with fans of science fiction, but his forte was giant cities and unusual spaceships. His people were crude and sticklike, and his aliens misshapen and grotesque. Finlay could not match Paul's vast scenarios, but he filled his art with beautiful women and heroic men. His monsters were suitably monstrous and yet had a bizarre sense of beauty. Finlay drew sensuous, desirable nudes and wonderfully menacing vampires and werewolves. Although he began his career in *Weird Tales*, it was not long before he was doing art for nearly all major science fiction magazines. Paul was the most popular artist of the 1920s. Finlay dominated the late 1930s and 1940s.

In the 1930s and early 1940s the magazine field *was* science fiction, and thus magazine art *was* science fiction art. A few hardcovers appeared from time to time, but they were rare exceptions and were not packaged as science fiction novels, which were considered juvenile pulp literature. So changes in the magazine field had an immediate effect on the science fiction art field.

Originally, the science fiction magazine industry was little more than a "ma-and-pa" operation. The Gernsback *Amazing Stories* and later *Wonder Stories* group were controlled by a small publisher with limited funds. When *Amazing Stories* was taken over by Teck Publications, nothing much changed. However, little by little, the small publishers in the pulps found themselves pushed out by competition from the large chains. Well financed and well distributed, the chains dominated sales. Science fiction buyers, while consisting of a strong core of loyal fans, were not a very profitable market when compared to that for mysteries, love stories, or general adventure. SF pulp publishing was only marginally profitable.

In 1936, bowing to the pressures of decreasing sales and lack of distribution, Gernsback sold *Wonder Stories* to the Standard Magazine chain. In 1938 *Amazing Stories* was bought by Ziff-Davis. *Astounding* was already published by the Street & Smith chain. Even *Weird Tales* was bought by the publisher of *Short Stories* and moved to New York City.

Chain ownership brought about more changes in the art field. The chains had more money and, in general, art rates went up. However, at the same time, the chains were run as one large business. Science fiction magazines received the same attention and treatment as any other pulp. Chains like Ziff-Davis had a full-time staff of artists working for their magazines. In a sense, the chains brought a return to the "first wave" of artists. Illustrators who were already working for pulp chains illustrating westerns, romances, and mysteries suddenly found themeselves responsible for science fiction art as well. When Ziff-Davis first took over publication of *Amazing Stories*, the first few issues featured photographic covers, until their house artists could start producing paintings.

Fortunately, most of the chain-magazine artists were strong craftsmen and handled their new assignments competently if not exceptionally. Some of the many artists who entered the science fiction field in this manner included H. W. Scott, Rod Ruth, Rudolph Belarski, Earle Bergey, Malcolm Smith, and Graves Gladney. At the same time, several very fine artists emerged from their ranks including Edd Cartier and Hubert Rogers.

Ziff-Davis publishers produced magazines through the use of a full-time staff. A group of writers on payroll created most of the stories for the pulps. Another group of artists did all of the artwork. Very little was done by outside help. Most story illustrations were done by the artists from a brief summary of the story or a quick reading of the manuscript. However, sometimes artists were told to produce a painting without any story behind it. Then the art was shown to an author and a story was written around the painting. Born of the desire to keep staff artists working continually, this unusual concept of having the cover before the story is still used in today's magazine field.

An interesting sidelight of this practice was the introduction of back-cover illustrations. Artists at Ziff-Davis were given free rein to paint a series of science fiction illustrations on a particular subject. These paintings were featured for a period of months on the back cover of the magazine, and a short article was printed inside the magazine, giving some background to what the cover represented. These paintings were published without any printing other than the title of the art and were an attractive addition to the magazine. Series on the back covers included "Men from Other Planets" and "Stories of the Stars" by Frank R. Paul, "Warriors of Other Worlds" by Malcolm Smith, and "Impossible but True" by James B. Settles. Some of the best art for the Ziff-Davis science fiction pulps appeared on their back covers. This practice was dropped in the late 1940s, probably due to the extra cost.

In the meantime, science fiction overseas remained barely alive. In the 1930s a weekly boys newspaper featuring science fiction stories, *Scoops*, ran for twenty-one issues before dying. Its illustrations could best be termed "forgettable." In 1937 Worlds Work Ltd. launched a new magazine, *Tales of Wonder*. This well-produced magazine featured some excellent covers during its sixteen-issue run. Unfortunately, wartime economics killed the publication. Science fiction publishing in Britain remained in a fairly dormant stage until 1946.

2

The war in Europe brought new prosperity to America, and in 1939 there was an explosion in the number of pulp magazines being published. Every major chain increased its line, and many new publishers entered the marketplace. In a few short months, the science fiction field suddenly went from only a few titles to nearly two dozen publications.

Street & Smith brought out *Unknown*. Standard Magazines issued *Startling Stories, Strange Stories*, and *Captain Future*. A companion magazine to *Amazing Stories*, titled *Fantastic Adventures*, was launched by Ziff-Davis. Red Star Publications, an offshoot of the original Munsey chain, entered the field with *Famous Fantastic Mysteries* and *Fantastic Novels*, two reprint magazines that used new artwork. Other magazines included *Super Science Stories, Astonishing, Cosmic, Comet, Future, Science Fiction Stories, Planet Stories, Marvel Stories*, and *Dynamic Science Stories*. Suddenly, a market existed for science fiction art.

Both new and veteran artists found work. Frank R. Paul, Leo Morey, Alex Schomburg, and a number of other artists from the 1930s found their work more in demand than ever before. Paul, hardly visible since the collapse of Gernsback's *Wonder Stories* in 1936, suddenly found himself in demand by a number of publishers, all looking for an artist whose name the fans would immediately recognize. Virgil Finlay, long a mainstay of *Weird Tales*, abandoned that magazine when a new publisher dropped the art rates. Other magazines wanted his art and were willing to pay competitive prices for it. Finlay soon became a fixture in *Famous Fantastic Mysteries* and continued to produce art for nearly all the major magazines in the field.

Finlay's replacement at *Weird Tales* was Hannes Bok. Samples of Bok's work were shown to Farnsworth Wright in 1939 by a young Ray Bradbury, who was attending the first World Science Fiction Convention in New York. Wright liked what he saw and began using Bok's work. The artist soon moved to New York and, within a short time, was doing work for most of the New York-based science fiction pulps.

Bok did not have the control and clarity of Finlay. However, his work was much more stylized and had a unique, distinct flair all its own. He soon became a favorite with many fans for his bizarre aliens and unusual people. Bok improved with each illustration, and his work grew more and more polished throughout the 1940s. Finlay brought beauty to science fiction. Bok brought style.

One other artist rivaled Bok and Finlay as the most popular craftsman for the science fiction pulps. Edd Cartier was a staff artist working for Street & Smith, originally one of the interior artists for *The Shadow* single-character pulp magazine. However, as was the custom with the chain publishers, Cartier was also given some assignments for their other magazines, including *Astounding Stories*. Cartier showed a flair for science fiction, and when the publisher began a new magazine featuring fantasy fiction, *Unknown*, Cartier was given a number of assignments.

It was a perfect match. Cartier possessed a clear, sharp line style that reproduced extremely well in the pulps. He had a fine eye for detail, but, more important, he could capture expressions as no other artist working in the pulp field could do. The faces of his characters often conveyed more emotion and feeling in a few lines than the writers put in their work. Cartier was especially skilled at humorous illustration, unsurpassed at drawing funny characters. His work was not cartoonish but actually funny. His illustrations were filled with whimsy and good humor and were unlike anything else being published in the pulp field. Along with Finlay's beauty and Bok's syle, Cartier added humor to the science fiction art field of the early 1940s.

The boom in science fiction magazine publishing did not spread to book form. Henry Holt Publishers experimented with reprinting several excellent fantasy novels from *Unknown* magazine in hardcover in the early 1940s, with a notable lack of success. Other science fiction and fantasy novels published during the war years were packaged as general fiction. The pulp field remained science fiction's ghetto. Unfortunately, editorial attitudes of many of the editors and publishers shaped the art as well as the story content of the magazines.

Many of the decision makers involved in the pulp field thought that science fiction appealed primarily to adolescents and slanted their magazines to that audience. This was particularly true of the Ziff-Davis chain, the Standard Magazine chain, and *Planet Stories*. Since the magazines were aimed at a juvenile, mostly male readership, covers were commissioned to appeal to the taste of such an audience.

Farnsworth Wright had instructed Margaret Brundage to use provocative nudes on the covers of *Weird Tales* in the 1930s to attract attention to his magazine. However, the covers did not accurately reflect the fairly high quality of fiction inside that pulp. In the 1940s, although covers were somewhat more subdued, they mirrored the contents of the magazines.

Street & Smith maintained a certain dignity about their pulps. Even the most action oriented did not feature the wild action scenes used on most other pulp magazines. At *Astounding Stories*, where editor John W. Campbell believed he was publishing a magazine aimed at an adult readership, art remained moderately low key. Hubert Rogers, a Canadian artist with a background in the pulps, did most of the prewar covers for *Astounding* from late 1939 on. Rogers paintings rarely featured violent action scenes but instead focused on one or more figures or a spaceship. A number of his covers were almost portraitlike in composition, the most famous of them being his painting of Kimball Kinneson, done for the serialization of "Grey Lensman." Rarely was there any major conflict on the cover. Inside illustrations were handled by Edd Cartier, the Isip Brothers, and Charles Schneeman. Again, the focus was on figures and setting, rarely on action scenes.

The early covers for *Unknown* were not overly violent, with a number of them symbolic. However, in an even more startling departure, in July

1940 *Unknown* switched from paintings to all print on the cover. Each issue featured a listing of the main stories in the issue along with a capsule summary (usually accompanied with a tiny illustration). It was an attempt to get away from the juvenile pulp image that was starting to haunt the science fiction genre.

However, the other chains did not seem bothered by the pulp label. Ziff-Davis started using the work of Robert Gibson Jones for covers for *Amazing Stories* and *Fantastic Adventures*. Jones, a particularly fine craftsman, was not noted for his subdued imagery. Women in peril and alien monsters dominated his work.

Planet Stories, a new magazine published by the Fiction House chain, experimented with a number of cover artists, including Paul and Finlay. However, the publisher finally settled on art by H. W. Ward and Parkhurst, two veteran pulp artists from outside the science fiction field. Both men contributed attractive but generic-style science fiction illustrations. Again, every issue usually featured a girl in peril, usually from a horde of alien monsters, with a heroic spaceman in the background. Later, comic artist Allen Anderson took over the cover responsibilities for *Planet* and maintained the same traditions. Anderson was another chain artist who produced art for western, adventure, and romance pulps for Fiction House as well as for its science fiction titles.

Earle Bergey, working steadily for *Startling Stories* and *Thrilling Wonder Stories*, produced carbon-copy cover paintings, each one featuring a threatened beautiful woman, clad in an impractical outfit including a cast-iron bra right out of Wagnerian opera. An accomplished artist, Bergey soon became so associated with this "girl-in-peril" style of cover that many fans later thought he was to blame for the juvenile approach to art that the magazines favored. It was the usual case of blaming the messenger for bad news. Bergey was only one of a number of artists who painted what the art directors wanted.

Entry of the United States into the Second World War changed the face of science fiction. The boom of 1939–1940 was already coming to an end. There were too many magazines, with most of them being published on extremely limited budgets. With rare exceptions, the stories matched their finances. Pulps began to die with increasing frequency. At the same time, the war mobilization forced cutbacks on paper. Chains were forced to reduce their numbers of magazines and frequency of publication. In 1940 and 1941 thirty-seven issues of science fiction magazines appeared on the stands. By 1944 only fifteen were available, and by 1945, only twelve.

Other changes came about as well. Finlay and Cartier were both drafted, and Rogers stopped working on American magazines. A number of other artists also found themselves in the service.

Astounding was hit the hardest in the art department. Working as Rogers's replacement, William Timmins did covers and most interiors for the magazine. Timmins produced uninspired art that rarely caused a stir. *Astounding*'s art sank into mediocrity. In late 1943, trying to escape the pulp stigma and bowing to paper requirements, *Astounding* shrunk from pulp size to five-by-eight-inch size, which became known as "digest-magazine" format. At the same time, *Unknown Worlds* (earlier *Unknown*) was quietly dropped.

Famous Fantastic Mysteries found itself without the services of Virgil Finlay. With full-page illustrations an integral part of the reprint magazine's format, the editors at Popular Publications quickly sought a replacement. They found him in Lawrence Sterne Stevens, an elderly artist on their staff, who had been trained as a newspaper artist. Stevens, who worked under the name "Lawrence," was an exceptionally fast artist who could produce detailed line illustrations in a style similar to Finlay's, although by no means a copy of it. Stevens soon was doing nearly all of the art for *Famous Fantastic Mysteries*. Although not as popular as Finlay, he was better than most of the artists working in the field at the time.

Covers for the other remaining pulps, including *Planet Stories*, *Amazing*, *Fantastic Adventures*, *Thrilling Wonder*, and *Startling Stories*, remained bright and colorful. However, interior art on all of the magazines suffered dramatically, with a horde of unknown artists dominating the inside pages.

However, the end of the war signaled a beginning of a new era for science fiction art. Ever since the publication of *Amazing Stories*, science fiction had been trapped in a ghetto of its own making. Artists interested in working in the SF field were bound by the narrow constraints and limited size of the pulp field. This all changed in the late 1940s. New markets opened for science fiction and thus for science fiction art. A rapidly expanding economy brought about rapid changes in the fiction marketplace, and science fiction sales were dramatically altered.

A thriving SF small-press movement started in 1946. In 1939 August Derleth and Donald Wandrei had begun Arkham House Publishers, in an effort to publish all of H. P. Lovecraft's fiction in book form. The two authors did so after most major publishers expressed no interest in such a project. Arkham House was successful enough with its first few ventures that in time it became a small but steady publisher of quality fantasy and weird fiction books. Virgil Finlay provided the art for the first Arkham House book, *The Outsider*, and later art was done by Ronald Clyne, Hannes Bok, and other well-known science fantasy illustrators. Unfortunately, Arkham had a very limited budget and modest illustration schedule. It never offered SF artists much in the way of a market.

However, the success of Arkham House was not unnoticed in the science fiction field. After the war, several groups of fans launched their own publishing ventures, modeled at least in part on Arkham House. Major publishing houses had ignored the pulps, so these new presses—Fantasy Press, New Collectors Group, Shasta Books, and Prime Press, among others—found themselves with a vast array of excellent material to draw upon.

Teenagers who had grown up with the pulps were now adults with money to spend on hardcover editions of their favorite novels. The books reflected the tastes of the organizers of the presses, which, in turn, reflected the general taste of science fiction fans of the period. E. E. Smith, A. E. Van Vogt, Jack Williamson, and other very popular authors of the time were soon appearing in hardcover editions that sold extremely well. The small presses flourished.

Although organized to make money, the small presses also worked hard to give their customers the full worth for their dollar. Not only did they publish the best available material from the magazines in book form, but the small presses issued them in attractive, illustrated format. Art always played an important role in all of the small-press editions. Early Fantasy Press hardcovers featured the jackets in one or two colors but also contained four or more full-page interiors, often done on coated stock. Later editions sometimes were published with illustrated endpapers, and many had full-color jackets.

Hannes Bok became a favorite artist of many of the small presses because of his adaptability to their needs. To help the publishers save money, Bok often did several renderings of his paintings, each in one particular color scheme, so that the printer did not have to do color separations. Working for Shasta Books, Bok produced some of the finest jacket art ever done in the field. Perhaps his greatest cover was for the novel *Kinsmen of the Dragon*, but his paintings for *Slaves of Sleep* and *The Wheels of If* were also exceptional.

Although the small presses tried hard to give the fans more, they usually worked on a limited budget. Color jackets were impressive but cost more money for separations and reproduction. As mentioned, Bok did multiple paintings to cut out the cost of separations. At Gnome Press, artists including Edd Cartier and Kelly Freas often did paintings in monochrome and provided the printers with color guides for the work. The extra color was added by the printer according to the artist's directions, producing a color cover from a monochrome painting. For *Travelers of Space*, a Gnome Press hardcover that featured sixteen pages of slick color illustrations, Cartier did the art as black-and-white illustrations and again the printer added basic colors. A color calendar was done by Gnome in the same manner.

Although Cartier did a great deal of work for Gnome Press, he also worked for Fantasy Press. Like Bok, he was extremely popular with the small publishers. Several new artists, including Ric Binkley and Mel Hunter, did outstanding work for the small-press field. Surprisingly, the most popular of all science fiction artists at the time, Virgil Finlay, did very little work for the small-press field. Finlay was capable of doing exceptional jacket work but was never called upon by the fan publishers. Some years later, he did a series of very good jackets for the Andre Norton young-adult science fiction novels published by World Publishing Co.

It was in part the success of the small-press hardcovers that motivated trade publishers to enter the science fiction hardcover field in the early 1950s. That occurrence, although a major step forward for the field, badly hurt the science fiction art market.

Another new area of growth for science fiction was in the paperback field. Paperback publishing started as an experiment by Pocket Books in 1939 and soon mushroomed into the biggest boom of the 1940s. The early paperback lines rarely published any science fiction other than an occasional H. G. Wells reprint. In 1944 Donald Wollheim edited the first science fiction paperback, *The Pocket Book of Science Fiction*, for Pocket Books. It was just a matter of time before science fiction became part of the paperback marketplace.

Wollheim became editor of Avon Books in the late 1940s and immediately started a science fiction line, reprinting old novels with pulp-style paperback art. Paintings were done by staff artists for the company, although at least one cover, for *The Lurking Fear*, was done by a *Weird Tales* magazine veteran, A. R. Tilburne.

However, it was not until the early 1950s that science fiction became a major force in paperback publishing. Avon remained alone as the only regular publisher of fantasy material in the 1940s.

The pulp magazine market literally erupted after the end of the war. With paper restrictions eased, magazines switched from quarterly to bimonthly to monthly schedules in a year or less. Better paper became available, providing better reproduction for interior as well as cover art. New magazines appeared. In 1948 Popular Publications revived *Fantastic Novels*, and in 1949, *Super Science Stories*. Their resurrection was merely a signal of the huge boom to follow.

Finlay was back, working for many of the science fiction pulps. Rogers returned to *Astounding*, as did Edd Cartier. Interior art improved noticeably in all of the science fiction magazines.

In England several fans and professionals banded together to start *New Worlds* and, later, *Science Fantasy*. The new magazines provided a small but steady market for English science fiction artists. It was a boom period for all of science fiction fandom.

3

The science fiction market experienced its second major boom at the end of the 1940s. Public interest in the field blossomed, and suddenly science fiction stories were appearing everywhere. In 1947 Robert Heinlein sold "The Green Hills of Earth" to the *Saturday Evening Post*. Other science fiction stories had appeared earlier in high-quality magazines (generally referred to as "the slicks" because of their slick coated paper, as opposed to the wood-pulp paper of the pulps) but were usually packaged as novelty items or borderline espionage-style fiction. There was no attempt at disguise this time. It was science fiction. Heinlein continued to sell to the slicks, as did Ray Bradbury, opening the way for a number of other authors. The field was gaining some measure of respect.

Hardcover anthologies appeared. Random House published a huge collection of science fiction, *Adventures in Time and Space*, edited by Healy and McComas. Crown Books soon followed with an entire series of thick anthologies edited by Groff Conklin. The books sold well, especially to libraries.

The pulp field continued to expand. New magazines included *Future*, *SF Quarterly*, *Marvel Stories*, *Space Stories*, *A. Merritt's Fantasy*, *Dynamic Science Fiction*, and *Two Complete Science Adventure Novels*.

At the same time, new digest magazines appeared. *Astounding* had been the first and only science fiction magazine in digest format until 1947, when Avon Books published the *Avon Fantasy Reader* edited by Donald Wollheim. Digests took up less space on the newsstand and were easier to handle. While the pulps continued to flourish, digests emerged as a new force in the science fiction field.

In late 1949 *The Magazine of Fantasy* (shortly changed to *The Magazine of Fantasy & Science Fiction*) and *Other Worlds* appeared as digests. In 1950 there appeared *Galaxy Science Fiction*, *Imagination*, and *Worlds Beyond*. In 1951 and 1952, *IF*, *Space*, *Galaxy Science Fiction Novels*, *Science Fiction Adventures*, and *Fantastic* came into being. The boom was on in both pulp and digest format.

In the paperback field, a number of companies began publishing science fiction. Bantam, Pocket Books, Dell, and Signet all started issuing paperback science fiction novels and collections. New companies were entering the paperback marketplace continually, and most were experimenting with a few science fiction novels as part of their lineup.

Science fiction art flourished as never before. Finlay and Bok were in constant demand and found themselves with more work than they could handle. Cartier continued to do a great deal of work for *Astounding* while branching out into the small-press field as well as to other magazines. Even Frank R. Paul returned for a short while in the pulps. Vincent Napoli, who had worked for *Weird Tales* in the 1930s, became a pulp regular, while Lawrence Sterne Stevens, Paul Orban, Earle Bergey, Allen Anderson, and Alex Schomburg continued to produce excellent work.

The pulps were not a closed market for new artists. They did not pay very high rates, but fresh faces and talent were always welcome. The slicks paid much better but wanted polished art and often employed staff artists who had been working at the publication for years. Breaking in with the major magazines was nearly impossible. The pulps served as a springboard for many artists just beginning their professional careers. Many went on to bigger and better things, but an equal number remained for years in the science fiction field. Advertising and commercial art offered more money, but the science fiction field offered greater freedom.

Ed Emsh, Frank Kelly Freas, and Ed Valigursky began working for the science fiction magazines in the early 1950s. All of them were exceptionally prolific, and their art attracted immediate fan attention. Each man was adept at both interior art and cover illustration. Within a few years, their work dominated the science fiction magazine scene.

Science fiction art split into two directions in the early 1950s. This was the direct result of the field itself experiencing growing pains. Ever since 1926 the genre had been labeled "pulp literature." Safe within this classification, the field had managed to evolve and grow as a distinct classification of fiction, like mysteries and westerns. However, in the early 1950s many writers and readers thought that the pulp label no longer fit. Science fiction was growing up. Not every story was juvenile pulp adventure. If SF was to be accepted as literature, it had to be packaged and presented in a new, more adult manner. Wild covers of women in metallic bras threatened by huge bug-eyed monsters no longer served any purpose. If anything, they served as a positive reminder of all that was wrong with the field. A new style of art was needed to match the more serious science fiction being written.

For years *Astounding Science Fiction* had been featuring much more dignified covers than any other magazine in the field. However, the art still remained firmly grounded in the pulp tradition. It was the *Magazine of Fantasy & Science Fiction* that broke the grip of action-oriented magazine art in 1949. *F&SF* was published by the Mercury Press, the publisher of *American Mercury* and *Ellery Queen's Mystery Magazine*. The new SF magazine was patterned after *Queen's* magazine, which had been appearing as a digest since 1943. It featured both new stories and reprints, all of high literary quality and not the least bit in the action-pulp tradition. Covers matched the contents. The first issue featured an attractive photo by Bill Stone. For the next few years, covers featured unusual surrealistic scenes by noted book designer George Salter, who served as the magazine's art director. From time to time, *F&SF* featured interplanetary landscapes by Chesley Bonestell.

Doubleday Books, Simon and Schuster, and several other major hardcover publishers entered the SF marketplace in the early 1950s. Genre hardcovers sold well to libraries, and the expanding science fiction field offered a new area of growth. However, librarians refused to buy books with garish, pulp-style covers. Gnome Press, one of the more aggressive small-press publishers, had discovered this when several Gnome Books were rejected by libraries because of their cover art. New, less pulplike covers were done for the books, and only then did the books sell. The major houses knew how to package their books from many years of experience. They bypassed popular science fiction artists and instead went with artists new to the field who could produce dignified, conservative covers without a trace of pulp influence.

Leading this group was the most influential science fiction artist of the 1950s, Richard Powers. Powers, more than any other artist, changed the perception of science fiction from space opera to real literature. He ranks as the most influential illustrator in science fiction in terms of setting a standard and style that many other artists, such as Vincent Di Fate, Paul Lehr, and Jack Gaughan, continued.

Although never honored by science fiction fandom with awards, Powers changed the face of science fiction art. He was one of the earliest of what can be considered a "third wave" of science fiction artists. Powers did not come from the pulp magazines into science fiction. He had no contact with pulp art and was not influenced by it. Nor was he a science fiction fan who moved into the SF art field. Instead, his influences were classical painters as well as Matta, Miro, Tanguy, and other European surrealists. Thus his work was entirely his own. It was surrealistic and symbolic, done in one or two colors due to the demands of the publishers.

Powers studied art at the School for Illustrators, run by Dan Content. Afterwards, he attended the New School, where he studied painting, and then worked with artist Jake Conoway in New England, studying landscape and marine painting. His earliest science fiction work came from Doubleday as part of a general assignment doing dust jackets for that company. Those paintings attracted the attention of Horace Gold, editor of *Galaxy* magazine, who was looking for new artists. Magazine assignments followed and then more jacket art. Powers found himself being offered science fiction assignments more frequently. Hardcover publishers did not want jacket art that reflected the pulps. They needed more respectable covers. Powers's art was much more commercial and practical. He soon became one of the most widely used artists in the fast-growing science fiction book field.

Often Powers was not even given the manuscript to read but was just given a title and the author's name. Art had little to do with the story but tried to catch the essence of the mood of science fiction. Powers's work was totally different from the usual straightforward illustrations that had been appearing until then in hardcover books and paperbacks. It set off science fiction from other works and yet did not give the books a garish, pulp appearance.

When Ian Ballantine began Ballantine Books, Powers was approached by an agent who promised that he could get the artist a great deal of work if he let the agent represent him. Powers agreed and soon was handling all of the covers for the important Ballantine SF series. Again, Powers got the assignment because there were few artists working in the paperback field who wanted to do science fiction covers all of the time. Powers himself stated in an interview published in *Algol* magazine: "If the number of good artists who are painting good SF now were working in the early 50's when Ballantine approached me to do the work, he might not have approached me, he might have approached somebody else and the competition would have been a hell of a lot stronger than it was."

Powers earliest pieces for Ballantine featured spacemen and spaceships done in the style of Chesley Bonestell but without the near photographic clarity of that artist's work. Instead, Powers combined his own surrealistic use of colors with the stock images of space travel. The covers were popular, and Ian Ballantine permitted Powers to experiment with more abstract pieces. His work for *Childhood's End* was much more symbolic and abstract but still was popular. After a while Powers was left on his own to create covers in his own style. Ballantine Science Fiction and Powers's covers became an accepted standard in the science fiction field.

The combination was extremely important. Ballantine's line stressed important, innovative works of science fiction. The emphasis was on modern, thoughtful literature instead of pulp action stories. The books were aimed at a more adult reading audience, and the Powers covers were an integral part of that package. More importantly, the art set science fiction off from other pulp-type literature as the realm of imagination. Although Powers's covers rarely reflected the actual contents of the books, they made it clear that they were works of imagination and the mind. It is impossible to conceive of a surrealist paperback western cover, but through Powers's influence, the combination of surrealism and science fiction seems natural.

At the same time, Signet Books began a short-lived but very influential science fiction paperback line. Among the books published were important works by Heinlein, Asimov, and A. E. Van Vogt. Again, the art director at Signet stayed away from pulp-style covers. Instead, covers were commissioned by Robert Schulz, Stanley Meltzoff, and Jack Farragaso, among others. All were artists new to the science fiction field, and again, all were members of this new "third wave" of science fiction artists—illustrators from outside the pulp or science fiction field who entered the field without any preconceived notions about style or substance of their paintings. Meltzoff was especially important because he taught at Pratt Institute, where he instructed both Paul Lehr and John Schoenherr. Covers done by Meltzoff for books by Robert Heinlein included *The Puppet Masters*, *The Green Hills of Earth*, and *Tomorrow the Stars*. Schulz and Faragasso both taught at the Art Students League, and although not as influential as Meltzoff, they also worked with a number of students who later went on to careers in the science fiction art field.

Paul Lehr, following Meltzoff's lead, became noted as a specialist in science fiction book illustration and has remained a prolific contributor to the field since the early 1960s. His earliest work, for *The Door into Summer*, *No Place on Earth*, and *The Deep Range*, shows the strong influence of Meltzoff's Signet paintings.

Signet published only a few books a year into the 1960s, but the books were widely distributed and presented an image of science fiction much different from mere pulp entertainment. The packaging of the books, primarily the cover art, strongly reinforced this image.

Pulp art was not dead, however. Ace Books maintained a strong science fiction line throughout the 1950s. Under the ownership of A. A. Wynn, once publisher of the Ace pulp line, and the editorial guidance of Donald Wollheim, Ace Books featured pulp-style fantasy with pulp-style covers. A number of artists from the pulps, including Paul Orban and Norman Saunders, did early covers for the Ace science fiction line. However, by the mid–1950s Ed Emsh and Ed Valigursky had taken over as the cover artists for the monthly books. Both illustrators were particularly good at producing polished art fast and painted literally hundreds of covers for both the paperback and magazine market.

As always, the boom in science fiction came to an abrupt end. There was no clear explanation: the field just began to shrink. Magazines died one after another, with the pulps going fast. Paperback lines were cut back or dropped entirely by publishers. The small presses, always run on a small margin of profit, could not compete with the large publishers and faded away. Then the major publishers cut back their lines, aiming what little science fiction they published at libraries. Many artists abandoned the shrinking field: Edd Cartier went into commercial art, and Hannes Bok pursued other interests. By the late 1950s science fiction was at a low ebb, causing one well-known fan to publish a survey entitled "Who Killed Science Fiction."

4

The late 1950s and early 1960s were a dismal time for science fiction. The small presses had come and gone. Magazine publishing was down to only a few regulars. *Analog* (a name change for *Astounding*) led the pack, with *Galaxy* and *The Magazine of Fantasy & SF* close behind. Farther back were *If, Amazing, Fantastic,* and *Fantastic Universe*. During the time, a number of other short-lived magazines came and went, victims of a flat market.

Art was handled by relatively few illustrators. In the late 1950s Kelly Freas and Henry Van Dongen were the workhorses for *Astounding*. In 1958 John Schoenherr began working for the magazine as an interior artist. He rose to prominence in the early 1960s when his work appeared on the cover of *Analog*. Another artist who came from outside the science fiction field, Schoenherr also painted a number of excellent covers for paperbacks, doing most of his work for Ace Books and Pyramid Books. His artwork for the serialization of Frank Herbert's epic *Dune* novels further enhanced his reputation in the science fiction community. Schoenherr left the SF field at the height of his popularity to concentrate on his nature paintings and rose to new heights of success in that specialty.

At *Galaxy* and *If* (both owned by the same publisher), art was handled by a number of artists including Ed Emsh, Virgil Finlay, Mel Hunter, and Jack Coggins. Covers rarely illustrated a particular story. They were often spaceship studies or humorous scenes. Emsh was the master of such "fun" art, and his series of Christmas paintings for *Galaxy* featuring a four-armed Santa Claus became one of the trademarks of the magazine. In the astronomical vein, Coggins, Dember, and John Pederson, Jr., produced the best work. On the inside, Wally Wood and Jack Gaughan were the two most prolific artists. As the 1960s began, Gaughan started to dominate the interiors of both magazines.

The Magazine of Fantasy & SF did not use any interior artwork. Covers were done primarily by Emsh and Hunter. From time to time, Chesley Bonnestel's paintings scheduled for book appearance were used as covers as well.

The Ziff-Davis magazines *Amazing* and *Fantastic* featured covers by Ed Valigursky. Alex Schomburg took on some of the cover responsibilities in 1960, sharing the duties with several other artists. Interiors were primarily handled by Leo Summers and Virgil Finlay.

In England, science fiction in paperback was nearly nonexistent. *New Worlds* and *Science Fantasy* were steady publishers of good science fiction, along with *Nebula* and *Science Fiction Adventures*. Art was not up to the level of American publications but was fairly well handled by Brian Lewis and Gerard Quinn.

In America most of the other magazines of the period, including *Infinity*, *Satellite*, *Science Fiction Stories*, and *Super Science Fiction* relied on Ed Emsh and Kelly Freas for most of their art. Both men were so talented and worked so fast that they were able to produce huge amounts of high-quality art for nearly every publication in the science fiction field.

Virgil Finlay was only one of many artists whose career went into a sharp decline with the fading fortunes of science fiction. Finlay's style was not suited for paperback book covers, nor was there any room for him as a hardcover jacket artist. Magazine rates were low, and Finlay normally took many hours to complete one illustration. The artist was forced to change with the times. He refined and revised his techniques, losing much of the fine detail for which he was famous, so that he could produce finished pieces at a faster rate. During the 1950s and 1960s Finlay did work for the Ziff-Davis magazines as well as for *Galaxy* and *If*. However, his most lucrative assignment was a series of covers for *Fantastic Universe* that appeared in the late 1950s. Unfortunately, the magazine folded in 1960. Finlay continued to work in the SF field but, like many other artists, looked for work elsewhere. He soon found a better paying market in the astrology magazine field.

Only a few artists were able to make a decent living as science fiction artists. Ed Emsh, Kelly Freas, and Ed Valigursky worked for both the magazine and paperback fields. Richard Powers continued to dominate much of the paperback and hardcover market. Mel Hunter produced work for both magazines and hardcovers. Most artists worked in other areas of illustration outside the science fiction genre. No one got rich as a science fiction artist.

The early 1960s brought more changes to the fantasy art world. Kelly Freas left science fiction illustration in 1960 and did not return until nearly five years later. Valigursky also left the field about this time, turning to the more profitable area of aviation illustration. Emsh retired from painting in 1964 to devote all of his time to experimental film making. In a few short years, the most prolific trio of artists of the 1950s were gone.

Other artists quickly filled the vacuum created by their departure. Most prolific was Jack Gaughan. Working in the surrealistic style of Richard Powers, Gaughan took over much of the cover work for Ace paperbacks, the leading SF publisher of the time. Alex Schomburg also did a number of fine covers for Ace. John Schoenherr, already popular at *Analog*, became a prolific paperback cover artist. Other artists including Ralph Brillhart and Gray Morrow produced creditable work.

It was a slow and steady period for science fiction. Magazine sales were stable while paperbacks sold to a fairly unchanging audience. Lancer Books, a new softcover publisher, started a science fiction line featuring attractive, colorful covers. Ace and Ballantine were still the major SF paperback lines, with the other major publishers maintaining small SF lists. Science fiction was genre literature and not considered a major market. Hardcover science fiction was aimed primarily at libraries. Science fiction art remained a dead-end proposition for most artists.

However, in 1962 the entire field changed. Several years passed before the true impact was felt, but from a quiet beginning, a revolution in science fiction publishing and science fiction art took place. In an odd quirk of fate, copyright law played a major role in revitalizing the entire field and changing the face of science fiction illustration.

An employee working for the Edgar Rice Burroughs estate forgot to renew copyrights on several of Burroughs's fantastic adventure novels. It seemed that the stories were in the public domain. Dover Books, a reprint house specializing in publishing public domain books, discovered the oversight and quickly issued trade paperbound reprints of the novels. Most of Burroughs's work had never appeared in paperback and all but a few of the Tarzan novels had been out of print for decades.

At Ace Books, Donald Wollheim saw the tremendous sales potential in the novels. Burroughs had been one of the most popular pulp authors of all time. His work had always appealed to teenagers and young adults looking for exciting fantasy adventure. The baby-boom generation fit right into that age group. It was perfect timing. The novels were available, and a huge audience existed for them. Ace started reprinting public-domain Burroughs novels in paperback.

To do the cover art, Wollheim selected Roy G. Krenkel, whose work he had seen in the fanzine *Amra*. Krenkel had been a Burroughs fan most of his life and produced cover paintings in the tradition of J. Allen St. John. His first cover, for *At the Earth's Core*, reproduced in color the same scene done by St. John as one of the lead illustrations for the first edition of the novel in hardcover many years earlier. Krenkel also did covers for *The Moon Maid* and *Pellucidar*. At the same time, Wollheim had Emsh paint one Burroughs cover for *The Moon Men*. Fan response favored Krenkel, and Wollheim wanted to maintain a St. John image on the covers. Ace continued using Krenkel for its reprint covers.

However, Krenkel was primarily a pen-and-ink illustrator. He did not have confidence in his own work and often found himself at a loss as to how to finish a piece. Krenkel soon asked his friend comic artist Frank Frazetta for some help. Frazetta, who had been ghosting the *Lil Abner* daily comic for nine years, had just left the strip and wanted to make his mark in the book field. Krenkel suggested to Donald Wollheim that Ace would be better served on the covers by Frazetta, a fast worker who captured all of the spirit of the Burroughs novels.

At first Wolheim was leary of using Frazetta's work because he was a "comics" artist. His first cover for Ace was for *Tarzan and the Lost Empire*. Krenkel and Frazetta continued to alternate on the covers and often worked together, with Frazetta finishing paintings Krenkel had started. Within a short time, fan reaction convinced Wollheim that Frazetta was attracting a large following and that he was much more than a mere comic-book illustrator.

The Burroughs paperbacks were tremendous sellers. A muddled copyright situation led Ace Books to settle out of court with Edgar Rice Burroughs, Inc., on the earlier reprints and to buy the rights to many more Burroughs books. Ballantine Books also signed contracts with the Burroughs estate and issued its own Tarzan and Mars reprints. All of the paperbacks sold extremely well. For several years the Burroughs books dominated softcover sales.

Frazetta continued to do covers for the Ace series. However, there was only a limited number of Burroughs books available for reprinting. By late 1964 Ace was at its limit on the Burroughs novels. But there were plenty of other old fantasy novels in a similar vein, and other authors could write Burroughs-style novels to feed the market. Ace soon began an ambitious line of other books in the Burroughs tradition. To help promote the books as Burroughs-style works, covers were by Frazetta. Early titles in this new series included *Warrier of Llarn* by Gardner Fox, *Gulliver of Mars* by E. L. Arnold, and *Swordsmen in the Sky*, an anthology edited by Wollheim. All of the books featured Frazetta covers. After a while, it became apparent that the books were selling not only because they were Burroughs imitations but also because they featured Frazetta artwork.

Frazetta was never happy with Ace. He thought they had little respect for his art and paid him low rates because of his background from the comics. Lancer Books, noting Frazetta's popularity, hired him at a better rate to do covers for its line. His first work for the smaller company was *The Reign of Wizardry* by Jack Williamson published in late 1964. The cover, one of Frazetta's finest, attracted a great deal of attention. However, Lancer offered Frazetta little work until 1966. He continued to do paperback covers for a number of other companies, as his reputation as an artist whose paintings sold books continued to grow.

In late 1966 Lancer called on him again. His first new assignment was for *Phoenix Prime* by Ted White. A science fiction adventure novel with swords-and-sorcery trappings, the book did exceptionally well, at least in part due to the Frazetta cover. His next book had a much greater impact. Again, Frazetta was the right choice for the right series of books at the right time.

For years the Conan Books by Robert E. Howard had been tied up in an involved copyright suit. Lancer Books finally obtained rights to the novels in 1966. *Conan the Adventurer* was published late that year, with a superb cover by Frazetta. It was followed shortly in 1967 by *Conan the Warrior*, *Conan the Conqueror*, *Conan the Usurper*, and *Conan*. All of the books had spectacular sales. Each featured a tremendous Frazetta cover. Although Howard's writing obviously had something to do with the books' great reception, the cover art played a major part in selling the paperbacks. The Conan novels helped thrust Lancer into the limelight as one of the leading publishers of fantasy and science fiction paperbacks in the late 1960s. The success of the Howard books brought forth a huge flood of imitations. Science fiction entered a swords-and-sorcery boom.

Already, Frazetta commanded top dollar for his work. It was obvious to everyone in the field that a painting by Frazetta, if not guaranteeing success for a book, definitely helped its chances a great deal. When Lancer refused to pay a higher price for his work and used another artist on several Conan paperbacks, cries of outrage from the fans greeted the move. Frazetta was brought back despite his cost. But even for more money, Frazetta could produce only so many paintings. Other artists quickly entered the field, working in the "Frazetta style." Most popular was Jeffrey Jones, whose early paintings were very much in the Frazetta tradition, with their heroic muscular heroes and beautiful, near-naked heroines. Over a period of years, Jones developed much more of his own look, and now his paintings are uniquely his own.

Boris Vallejo was another artist whose work was strongly influenced by Frazetta, and his early art was often compared with Frazetta's. The same was true of Ken Kelly. As with Jones, both artists have since their earliest days forged their own claim to fame, though often the Frazetta influence still shows in some of their paintings.

The world of science fiction was expanding and changing, and so was the science fiction art marketplace. The huge Edgar Rice Burroughs and swords-and-sorcery explosions had created ripples that spread among all of the major publishers. At the same time, other books created big waves in a somewhat different area.

The infamous "baby-boomer" generation was just entering college in the 1960s. Here was a vast buying market that had been raised in a world where the advances of science were not looked upon with the same amazement as was the case twenty or thirty years before. It was a market ripe for science fiction. However, even more so, it was a restless group of young adults that embraced values and ideas different from those of the past. The "counterculture" movement of the 1960s provided a huge boost to science fiction and fantasy. Fueling the interest in science fiction as an alternative to "safe" reading was Robert A. Heinlein's novel *Stranger in a Strange Land*. The controversial story was embraced by the hippie movement and became a campus best-seller.

At the same time, Ace Books discovered that Tolkien's *Lord of the Rings* trilogy was in public domain due to a copyright slip by the publisher. Both Ace and Ballantine brought out editions of the novels. Ace did the books without permission of Tolkien, while Ballantine published authorized versions. Both sets did very well, with the Ballantine books becoming huge best-sellers. The success of Tolkien led Ballantine to experiment with other novels in the same adult-oriented fantasy market. The books also sold well, and Ballantine shortly began its Adult Fantasy Series.

Science fiction in paperback experienced a flurry of activity. Every major publisher had a line of science fiction or fantasy novels. Emsh, Valigursky, and Freas no longer dominated the market. Powers was still working, but even he could not keep up with all of the books being issued. In the late 1960s John Schoenherr all but left the market, leaving another gap to be filled. Attracted by the freedom of expression and the openness of the market, a number of new artists entered the field.

Book covers split into two main categories. As already mentioned, swords-and-sorcery and high-adventure SF novels had a distinct Frank Frazetta flavor. Beautiful unclad women and extremely muscular heroes dominated the paintings, with one or more monsters in the background.

At the same time, the surrealist movement strongly entered the science fiction art field. The "third wave" of artists—men who were not originally science fiction fans and thus worked without any preconceived notions of what science fiction art should be—brought unusual and exciting new imagery to the field. Artists like Powers, Paul Lehr, and John Schoenherr had cleared the way for symbolic, surrealistic paintings. In science fiction writing, there was a new emphasis on character development over plot. Many writers explored subjects and notions rarely considered in traditional, conservative science fiction. Since this "new wave" sweeping through the field was aimed at a much more sophisticated reading audience, books were packaged to appeal to that audience. Pulp-style science fiction illustration was out. Swords-and-sorcery art did not work on books by Harlan Ellison or Michael Moorcock.

Foremost among the artists who emerged as leaders in the SF illustration field were Don Ivan Punchatz, Leo and Diane Dillon, Robert Lo Grippo, Gervasio Gallardo, Gene Szafran, and Robert Pepper. For several years, this new wave of surrealism held sway over the science fiction paperback marketplace. Then reality intruded.

Science fiction entered a recession of sorts, and a number of publishers dropped or cut back their science fiction lines. Although the new wave of SF writing might have been controversial and more adult in approach, it didn't sell very well. Surrealistic art, strongly linked with the new wave style of writing, shared the blame when the books stopped selling. Whether valid or not, the perception existed that the covers had turned away buyers. Many of the artists who had entered the field during the brief fling at surrealism left it soon after.

At the same time, in England, Christopher Foss broke into the science fiction paperback art market with a remarkable series of paintings. Foss's work was obviously strongly influenced by the 1968 film *2001—A Space Odyssey*. His paintings featured huge spaceships that were complex, bizarre creations unlike any seen before in the field. The paintings were done in near photographic detail and featured numerous tiny portholes and lettering that emphasized the immense size of the machinery. Foss was equally adept at painting huge buildings, alien landscapes, and gigantic machines, giving them all a clarity and size that was never before realized in science fiction artwork. Other science fiction artists, from Paul to Bonnestell, had done space scenes featuring spaceships, but none had painted ships that totally dominated the landscape in the way that Foss's creations did. The slick, metallic look of airbrush art immediately took over the covers of British paperback science fiction. Covers for science fiction books were done either by Foss or by artists painting in the "Foss style." In many ways, Chris Foss became the Frank Frazetta of the early 1970s.

The same wave of "heavy-metal" hardware art soon reached America. Spaceships no longer looked as if they were new, perfectly made vehicles. Instead, they were battered and beaten, showing all of the details of years in service. John Berkey rose to prominence as the American master of science fiction hardware art. Fortunately, most American artists kept away from the absolute totality of giant ships that filled Foss's work and instead produced excellent space scenes. Among the notable artists who began work during this period were Dean Ellis, Vincent di Fate, and Rick Sternbach.

Science fiction publishing ebbed and flowed in the 1970s, with a number of new markets opening. Donald Wollheim left Ace Books and formed his own publishing house, DAW Books, printing four science fiction titles a month. Ballantine Books, noting the success of the DAW imprint, created Del Rey Books, with Lester and Judy-Lynn Del Rey in charge of a large science fiction and fantasy line. Ace continued to publish a large number of paperbacks, and the programs at Berkley, Dell, and several other publishers remained competitive.

While the magazines faded quietly into the background, Stephen Fabian, a fan artist who made the transition from fan to professional without the benefit of formal art training, became a popular black-and-white as well as cover artist. A number of other new interior artists entered the field, as the low rates paid by most magazines attracted only talent willing to work for little money to gain exposure.

Hardcover publishing in science fiction remained constant, with most books still aimed at the library market. Cover art did improve as publishers used the same artists who did most paperback art.

5

Change came to the science fiction art field almost unnoticed. Hardware science fiction art lost its appeal in the middle 1970s, and traditional illustration again returned to most covers. Laser Books was born, an extension of Harlequin Romances, featuring fast-action science fiction novels. In an unusual move, Laser commissioned Kelly Freas, always popular and dependable for good cover art, to do all of its cover art. The paintings were done by strict guidelines, giving the paperbacks a uniform look. Unfortunately, the packaging made the books look too similar, and the novels themselves reflected the low payment rates paid by the publisher. Laser did not last.

DAW Books continued to publish entertaining science fiction featuring covers by almost every artist working in the field. Gaughan and Freas were prominent among artists working for the company, but Wollheim was not hesitant about using new artists. Michael Whelan, who began his career at Ace Books, soon became a regular at DAW.

The 1976 World Science Fiction Convention in Kansas City was a watershed in modern science fiction art history. At that convention, Laser Books mounted a huge display of its books and the matching Freas covers. There was a *Star Wars* display, heralding the new movie that brought life and believability to Chris Foss's art. George Barr, a popular fan artist who had become an equally popular professional, was the art guest of honor. Michael Whelan and his wife, Audrey, set up the first major display of his work at a world convention.

The Freas art was well regarded, but the interest in Laser Books was negligible, foreshadowing the coming collapse of its series. The *Star Wars* exhibit and slide show generated some excitement, but no one suspected the impact that the movie would have on science fiction. One of Barr's paintings sold for $450 at the art auction, a near record price and an indication of the intense fan interest in science fiction art. Whelan's art was the hit of the show, attracting widespread attention from both publishers and fans. Within a short time, Whelan's career was on a swift rise that still has not peaked.

Whelan was the first of a new group of science fiction artists who remain dominant in the field today. His art had a polished, slick look rarely seen before on covers. Whelan combined all of the best features of preceding science fiction art. His people were larger than life but did not have the exaggerated muscles and barbarian features of the typical Frazetta painting. At the same time, Whelan's faces had all of the character of the best of Kelly Freas's work. Detail was not neglected. Machinery was done with the same technical skill of Chris Foss and others of the heavy-metal science fiction school. More importantly, Whelan worked hard on every detail of his background. The main figures were technically brilliant, and the surroundings in which they interacted were equally detailed. There was no skimping on detail.

An excellent science fiction illustrator, Whelan also excelled at fantasy art or science fiction art with a fantastic element. His covers for DAW reissues of the Elric novels by Michael Moorcock in late 1976 were immediately hailed as the definitive version of that tragic hero. His paintings done for the Dragonriders of Pern series by Anne McCaffrey received the same praise. His cover paintings for the Little Fuzzy Books by H. Beam Piper were hailed by critics and fans alike as perfectly capturing the spirit of the novels.

As if spurred on by Whelan's success, a new wave of artists flooded the science fiction field. The only problem with such an influx of talent was that there were not enough books being published for each artist to be fully appreciated. Rowena Morrill became a fixture at Timescape Books. Darrell Sweet took over much of the work at Del Ray paperbacks. Don Maitz did a great deal of work for Popular Library, as did Carl Lundgren.

In England, Peter Jones rose to the top of the field with covers that showed the Foss influence but were not slavish imitations. Jones's distinctive style featured stylish humans and sinuous, snaky aliens. Like most of the British artists, he was a master at a hard, finished look. Equally good, with work again featuring a polished, almost metallic look, was Jim Burns. In the swords-and-sorcery market, Chris Achilleos painted a number of fine pieces featuring larger-than-life heroes and heroines but with more style and less photographic realism than his American counterparts.

The impact of this new breed of artists who came into prominence in the 1970s is still being felt today. New artists, influenced by the art of the past decade, are regularly entering the science fiction art marketplace, making this era the most exciting ever for science fiction illustration. Important talents such as Whelan, Rowena, Boris Vallejo, Don Maitz, and Carl Lundgren are serving not only as artistic influences but as role models for new artists. The artists of the late 1970s proved that cover art could be challenging and rewarding for those willing to work at perfecting their craft.

In the late 1980s the science fiction art field is in a state of transition. By and large, experimental, unusual art is out; there is little surrealism or experimentation. Paintings are done to tell a story or illustrate a scene and nothing else. Just as the "new wave" has merged back into science fiction, so has new-wave art vanished into the mainstream of genre art. Without any question, Whelan is the most dominant force in modern science fiction illustration. He is a favorite with both the fans and editors alike. One measure of his popularity is that advertisements for hardcovers and paperbacks often highlight the fact that the cover art is done by Michael Whelan. As was the case with Frank Frazetta earlier, fans are collecting books because the cover art is by Whelan.

Whelan is constantly striving to produce better and better art and has succeeded again and again in topping his own previous best. In this respect, it seems doubtful that his position as the most highly regarded science fiction illustrator of today will be seriously challenged in the immediate future. His work remains on the cutting edge of modern science fiction artwork.

Artist Biographies

ACHILLEOS, CHRIS (b. 1947) British artist. Born in Famagusta, Cyprus, Achilleos moved to England with his mother and three sisters in 1960, his father having died several years earlier.

Achilleos attended school in London, feeling very much an outsider due to his foreign upbringing. He became a fan of the comics, with a special interest in the art of Frank Bellamy. Achilleos soon found himself concentrating on art, a field in which his mastery of a foreign language was not very important.

Unable to get into college because of required academic qualifications, Achilleos instead attended Hornsey College of Art in 1965 and studied technical and scientific drawing. While at Hornsey, Achilleos collected American comics and was strongly influenced by the dynamism of the graphics in them. At the same time, he added the strong technical control from his main courses of study.

In 1968 he illustrated *The Moon Flight Atlas* by Patrick Moore, which gave him a head start on most other beginning artists. In 1969 he graduated and began work as a science fiction and fantasy artist. He also married his girlfriend, Angie, and began working for Brian Boyle Associates. At that studio he learned a great deal about the various aspects of design, layout, and lettering of covers. After a while, he joined the Arts of Gold Studio in Covent Garden. By this time he was also the father of a daughter, Esther.

Working for Arts of Gold, Achilleos did numerous paperback covers as well as advertising art and illustrations for British men's magazines. It was during this period that he began doing the cover paintings for the highly popular novelizations of the Dr. Who television series, published by Target Books. In 1975 the founder of Arts of Gold was killed, and the company disbanded. Achilleos started to freelance, specializing in science fiction. His main work was with the Dr. Who novels, which were published monthly.

In 1977, the year his second daughter, Anna, was born, Achilleos was approached by Dragon's World about publishing a collection of his work in book form. *Beauty and the Beast* was a full-color collection of many of Achilleos's paintings and has sold more than one hundred thousand copies throughout the world. However, the book seemed to have a negative impact on his career. In retrospect, the artist thought that due to the book's success, he began painting on a much grander scale, producing art that was much more difficult to use for book or paperback illustrations. At the same time, the British SF market went into a long slump, and many artists found themselves without much work.

During the late 1970s Achilleos found himself doing more art for men's magazines as well as working for the film world, doing cover art for novelizations of films and promotional work for the movies themselves. He worked extensively for the film *Heavy Metal*.

In the 1980s Achilleos worked mostly outside the science fiction field, doing advertising art and pinup illustrations. However, the revival of fantasy art in England, primarily due to role-playing game books, led Achilleos back to the fantasy art field. He recently did work on a portfolio of Dr. Who illustrations, as well as more work in the film community.

The artist's style is based on strong attention to detail. He works exclusively on commission, paints by daylight, and devotes one to four weeks for each painting. Achilleos works first with a pencil rough and then develops these drawings into full paintings using inks, watercolors, and fabric dyes. To obtain the necessary finish in his graphic work he uses an airbrush, but for large paintings he uses acrylics on canvas.

Achilleos's work is larger than life, and as an artist he is primarily interested in paintings with heroic heroes, humanoid monsters ("the most effective monster is something you can relate to") and larger-than-life, perfect women, the stuff that dreams are made of. Achilleos's style is perfectly suited to the swords-and-sorcery field, and most of his best pieces are in that genre.

PUBLISHED WORK:

HC: *Beauty and the Beast* (78), *Sirens* (86)

PB: *All Our Yesterdays, Almuric* (76), *Amok King of Legend* (76), *Assassin of Gor* (77), *Back to the Stone Age* (74), *Balance of Terror, The Belgariad Vol. 1, The Belgariad Vol. 2, Black Moon* (77), *Bull and the Spear* (75), *The Cabal* (77), *Captive of Gor* (77), *Chariots of Fire* (74), *A Circus of Hells* (78), *The City on the Edge of Forever, Conquest of the Amazon* (76), *The Corbomite Maneuver, Darkness Weaves* (77), *The Doctor Who Monster Book 2* (77), *Dr. Who and the Abominable Snowman, Dr. Who and the Ark in Space* (75), *Dr. Who and the Carnival of Monsters, Dr. Who and the Claws of Axos* (76), *Dr. Who and the Curse of Peladon, Dr. Who and the Dinosaur Invasion* (75), *Dr. Who and the Genesis of the Daleks* (75), *Dr. Who and the Ice Warriors, Dr. Who and the Sea*

Devils, Dr. Who and the Space War (75), *Dr. Who and the Three Doctors, Dr. Who and the Web of Fear, Dr. Who and the Zarbi, Dragonquest, Elric and the End of Time, The Evangelist, The Eve of Midsummer* (76), *Fearless Master of the Jungle, The Final Quest, Firefloods, A Frozen God* (77), *The Ginger Star, The Grail War, The Hanadu Talisman, The Hounds of Skaith, Hunters of Gor* (77), *King Kull* (76), *Kuldesak* (76), *The Land Leviathan* (75), *Land of Terror* (74), *Lords of the Shadows, Lost Valley of Iskander* (75), *The Making of the Five Doctors, Marauders of Gor* (77), *Monsters and Medics* (76), *Moorcock's Book of Martyrs* (75), *Nightwinds, Nomads of Gor, Out of the Pit, The Passion of New Eve, Priest Kings of Gor* (78), *Raiders of Gor* (77), *Raven* (77), *The Reavers of Skaith, The Rebel Worlds, Robert E. Howard Omnibus* (75), *The Shadow Kingdom* (75), *Skull Face* (75), *Slave Girl of Gor* (77), *Star Trek 9, Star Trek 10, A Storm of Wings, The Strickland Demon* (76), *A Story of the Days to Come* (75), *Swords of Shahrazar* (75), *Swordships of Scorpio* (74), *Tanar of Pellucidar* (74), *Tanith* (77), *Temple of Terror, A Time of Dying* (77), *A Time of Ghosts* (77), *To Die in Italbar* (76), *To Ride Pegasus, The Unbidden* (71), *The Valley of the Worm* (78), *The War Hound and the World's Pain, The War of the Powers Vol. 1, The War of the Powers Vol. 2, War of the Wing Men* (76), *Warriors of Scorpio* (74), *Will o the Wisp* (76), *The World Set Free* (75), *Worms of Earth* (75)

ADDAMS, CHARLES SAMUEL (b. Jan. 7, 1912) American artist. Born in Westfield, New Jersey, Addams became famous for his bizarre and macabre cartoons running in *The New Yorker* since 1935. He was the first modern artist to successfully blend humor and horror together. Most of his cartoons are sight gags with little need for dialogue or a punchline. The picture and the story it tells without words provide all of the humor.

Addams succeeded in taking the monstrous and making it funny. In many ways, his work predated the theme of *Unknown* magazine, that is, logical fantasy for adults. Addams's monsters were creatures trying to cope with the modern world. They lived lives and enjoyed simple pleasures—albeit somewhat different ones than did normal families—as did other suburbanites. The characters from Addams cartoons would have been perfectly at home in a Robert Bloch story, and in many ways, some of Ray Bradbury's finest short stories seem like they were inspired by Addams's work.

PUBLISHED WORK:

HC: *Addams and Evil* (47), *Black Maria* (60), *Charles Addams Mother Goose* (67), *Dead Dead Days* (59), *Drawn and Quartered* (42), *The Groaning Board* (64), *Homebodies* (54), *Monster Rally* (50), *Nightcrawlers* (57)

ADKINS, DAN L. (b. 1937) American artist. Adkins, who worked for a short time in the science fiction field during the early 1960s, was one of a number of artists hired by the Ziff-Davis chain in its attempt to upgrade the quality of its science fiction line from 1961 to 1965. Adkins also did work for Marvel Comics, and with the sale of the Ziff-Davis magazines, he devoted his full attention to comic art. He was influenced by Wallace Wood★ and John Schoenherr★.

PUBLISHED WORK:

AMZ: 1961 (1, 8, 9, 10, 11, 12); 1962 (1, 2, 3, 6, 7, 10); 1963 (2, 7, 12); 1964 (1, 2, 5); 1968 (9, 11); 1969 (1, 3, 5, 7, 9); 1970 (9); 1971 (7, 9)

FTC: 1961 (2, 3, 4, 6, 7, 8, 9, 10, 11, 12); 1962 (2, 4, 5, 6, 7, 8, 10, 12); 1963 (2, 3, 4, 6, 7, 9); 1964 (1, 2, 6); 1968 (12); 1969 (4); 1970 (8, 10); 1971 (6)

GXY: 1966 (8); 1968 (4, 11); 1969 (7)

IF: 1965 (11); 1966 (1, 3, 5, 6, 9, 10, 11, 12); 1968 (2, 3, 4, 8, 9, 10); 1969 (4, 5, 7)

INF: 1958 (10, 11)

OW: 1957 (1, 3)

ADRANGA, ROBERT (?) American artist. Adranga first began working in the science fiction field in the early 1960s, when Ziff-Davis tried to revive *Amazing Stories* and *Fantastic*. He was one of several new artists, including Lloyd Birmingham★ and Vernon Kramer★, who worked for the two magazines, giving them a sharper, less pulplike look. After the magazines were sold, Adranga left science fiction. He returned in the late 1970s to do a number of paperback covers, most notably for Ace Books.

PUBLISHED WORK:

PB: *Lord Darcy Investigates* (81), *Too Many Magicians* (79), *Murder and Magic* (79)

AMZ: 1963 (3); 1964 (1, 8, 9, 10, 11, 12); 1965 (3)

FTC: 1962 (12); 1964 (3, 4, 6, 7, 9, 10, 11)

ALEJANDRO. See CANEDO, ALEJANDRO.

ALEXANDER, PAUL R. (b. Sept. 3, 1937) American artist. Born in Richmond, Indiana, Alexander graduated from Wittenberg University (Ohio) in 1967 and later from the Art Center College of Design, Los Angeles. He first found work in the art field with architectural firms and then moved into advertising, concentrating mostly on still-life and men-and-machines subject matter. In 1976 he began working with an art representative in New York who brought his work to the attention of Ace Books. Impressed by his command of hardware and machinery illustration, Ace gave Alexander some assignments. His first published cover was illustrated for Ace's *Best from F&SF* anthology (1977). Although Alexander has become proficient at illustrating people as well as machines, he is still known best for his high-tech illustrations. All work is done in gouache on illustration board. Concept sketches are done after reading the complete manuscript. He prefers to submit his own ideas for covers rather than having an art director select the scene. While still doing some SF art, Alexander primarily concentrates on advertising and corporate art.

PUBLISHED WORK:

PB: *After Things Fell Apart* (77), *Best from F&SF* (77), *Get Off the Unicorn* (77), *Hostage of Zir* (82), *Night of Kadar* (80), *Prisoner of Zhamanak* (83), *Virgin of Zesh/ Tower of Zanid* (83)

IASFA: 1978 (fall)

IASFM: 1978 (1)

ANDERSON, ALLEN (?) American artist. A prolific artist for the Fiction House magazine chain, Anderson worked on both its comic books and its pulp magazines. He painted numerous covers for all of the pulps published by this company, including many covers for western and detective magazines. Reference volumes often confuse Anderson with interior artist Murphy Anderson★, who worked for Fiction House for a short time during World War II. Allen Anderson was the regular cover artist for *Planet Stories* for the late 1940s through the early 1950s.

Anderson worked with vivid colors, usually using acrylics. The poor reproduction methods used by the pulps rarely captured the brightness and intense colors of his work. Most of his paintings featured a beautiful woman as the centerpiece, but Anderson was equally adept at portraying monsters or heroic figures.

PUBLISHED WORK:

2CSAB: 1950 (winter); 1951 (spring, summer, winter); 1952 (spring, summer, winter)

PS: 1942 (winter); 1947 (spring, summer, fall, winter); 1948 (spring, summer, fall, winter); 1949 (spring, summer, fall, winter); 1950 (spring, summer, fall); 1951 (1, 3, 5, 9, 11); 1952 (1, 3, 7, 11); 1953 (1, 3, 5)

ANDERSON, DAVID LEE (b. July 29, 1953) American artist. Born in Norman, Oklahoma, Anderson received a BA in commercial art from Central State University in Edmond, Oklahoma, in December 1984. However, he had already been working in commercial art some ten years. He helped pay for his schooling by working in the commercial art field and selling art at science fiction conventions. He was a one-man art department for several printing companies and did freelance book design for the Johns Hopkins Press.

Anderson originally wanted to be a comic-book artist but quickly grew disillusioned with that field. He got into science fiction illustration indirectly. Interested in science fiction, he took some writing classes with SF author C. J. Cherryh without realizing that she was a professional author. When Anderson showed Cherryh a piece of his art, she encouraged him to display his work, telling him it was as good as most seen at science fiction conventions.

Anderson is a fan of SF hardware artists, and his work has been described as "Maxfield Parrish gone High-Tech." Major influences include Robert McCall*, Syd Mead*, N. C. Wyeth, Roger Dean*, and the Brandywine Illustrators. When executing an assignment, Anderson tries to do as literal an interpretation of a work as possible. After a test painting, he lets the art editor make the final decision on changes, but he rarely has to make changes. As an artist who is both a reader and a writer, he tends to see the writer's viewpoint and tries to remain fathful to the writer's intentions. He works in acrylics and with air brush and likes to do "custom" work. His favorite work has been an L–5 poster, "Manned Station, " which has received a great deal of attention in and out of the SF community.

Active in science fiction fandom as well as the professional field, David has done the art programming for the World SF Convention in 1984, the North American SF Convention in 1985, and the World Fantasy Convention in 1985. He is married to Carolyn Novotny and is the father of three children.

PUBLISHED WORK:

PB: *Strangers* (87)

ANDERSON, MURPHY (b. July 9, 1926) American artist. Born in Asheville, North Carolina, Anderson moved with his family to Greensboro, North Carolina, at age eight. After graduation from high school in 1943, he attended the University of North Carolina for two quarters. Predicting that he would not be a civilian for long, he traveled to New York to become an artist. He landed a job as a staff artist at Fiction House, working on several of its comic books as well as its pulp line, including *Planet Stories*. Primarily an interior artist for the pulps, Anderson was often confused by science fiction fans as the artist who did the covers for *Planet Stories*, Allen Anderson*. While living in New York, Murphy Anderson attended the Art Students League at night in 1944.

In early November 1944 Anderson was drafted into the navy. Stationed in the Chicago area, he met his future wife, Helen. After his discharge in late 1945, he rejoined the art staff at Fiction House. However, after a short time, he decided to freelance and moved to Chicago. At first he attended the Art Institute School there, but the huge size of classes due to the postwar boom made him abandon hopes for further education.

In Chicago, Anderson found himself in the right place at the right time. In 1947 he took over art chores on the syndicated *Buck Rogers* comic strip. In 1948 he and Helen were married. They eventually had three children, Sophie, Mary, and Murphy Anderson III.

In 1949 Anderson left *Buck Rogers* to freelance once again. Concentrating on comic books in the early 1950s, he became one of the mainstays for DC Comics. A minor science fiction pulp artist, Anderson nevertheless was influential through his science fiction work done for the DC series such as *Adam Strange* and *Atomic Knights*. His crisp, sharp line work helped make the science fiction comics of the 1950s and 1960s memorable. Many young fans of that period who had never seen work by classic comic-strip illustrators like Alex Raymond★ or Hal Foster were influenced by Anderson's science fiction comic-book art.

Anderson now owns a company that specializes in doing four-color separations for comic-book companies. Although successful with that work, Murphy still produces some comic art for DC Comics.

PUBLISHED WORK:

AMZ: 1949 (6, 7); 1950 (5, 7); 1951(7)

FA: 1947 (10); 1949 (4, 10); 1950 (1, 4); 1951 (7)

PS: 1944 (winter); 1945 (spring, summer); 1946 (fall)

ARFSTROM, JON D. (b. Nov. 11, 1928) American artist. Arfstrom was born in Superior, Wisconsin, the son of Swedish parents, but his parents soon moved to Minnesota, where he has lived most of his life. He was always interested in fantasy art and was largely self-taught. He studied with Birney Quick, Zalton Szabo, Robert Wood, and Milford Zornes. In the late 1940s he became involved in science fiction fandom, contributing to numerous fanzines. He corresponded with another fan artist of the time, Jack Gaughan★, and the two young men even collaborated on several pieces. Arfstrom worked in a factory and submitted art to pulps in his spare time. In 1950 he got a job as a full-time commercial artist and worked in that field thereafter. Having succeeded in selling an unsolicited cover piece to *Weird Tales* magazine in 1951, he worked for that magazine, doing both color work and interior pieces, until it folded in 1954.

Since his early work for the pulps, Arfstrom has become a major midwestern artist, having more than thirty one-man shows, winning numerous awards, and placing art in many institutions and private collections. He also has served as president of the Northstar Watercolor Society and is an associate of the American Watercolor Society.

PUBLISHED WORK:

OW: 1951 (10); 1952 (6)

WT: 1952 (1, 3, 5, 7, 9, 11); 1953 (1, 3, 5, 7, 9, 11); 1954 (3, 5)

ARISMAN, MARSHALL (b. Oct. 14, 1938) American artist. Born in Jamestown, New York, Arisman attended Pratt Institute from which he received the BFA in 1960. He began working as a freelance illustrator in advertising, his first published piece being a promo ad for Time-Life. Magazine clients have included *Penthouse, Rolling Stone, Playboy,* and *Time,* for which he created the cover for their issue on violent crime. Most of the book covers he has painted have been psychoanalytical case histories.

Arisman got into the science fiction art field when some of his personal paintings were picked up by *Omni* magazine. The paintings were of large heads with metal fragments, a combination of metal and flesh, with both human and robot qualities. Artist and art scholar Vincent Di Fate* called Arisman "a major art talent who does primarily easel art of a surreal/ impressionistic nature who has come to be associated with SF through his work in *Omni*."

The artist prefers to paint illustrations in oils on paper or canvas. Most of his assigned work deals with sociological phenomena, mostly violent. Major artistic influences include Francis Bacon, Velazquez, Goya, and El Greco.

Married, with no children, Arisman has won numerous awards for his work from American Institute of Graphic Arts (AIGA), Graphis, and the Society of Illustrators.

ARTZYBASHEFF, BORIS (1899–1965) American artist. A highly regarded artist who did more than two-hundred cover paintings for *Time*, Artzybasheff was born in Kharkov, Russia. He graduated from the Prince Tenisheff School in St. Petersburg. After the Revolution, he escaped on a freighter and, several years later, went to America. There he found work in an engraving shop and soon was working as a book illustrator. Artzybasheff illustrated more than forty books, some of which he also edited. This led to assignments for cover art and advertising illustrations. He painted more than two-hundred covers for *Time*. Among many awards, he won the Newberry Medal.

Much of his work, especially for magazines, had a fantastic flavor to it, but he is primarily remembered in the fantasy field for his unusual illustrations for *The Circus of Dr. Lao* by Charles Finney. Due to the fantastic leanings of his art, Artzybasheff was also used as cover artist for a number of science fiction novels published by mainstream concerns including *The Incomplete Enchanter* and *Land of Unreason* by L. Sprague de Camp and Fletcher Pratt, both published by Holt in the 1940s. Artzybasheff also did a series of fine illustrations in the fantastic vein for *Life* during the early days of World War II.

PUBLISHED WORK:

HC: *The Circus of Dr. Lao* (35), *The Incomplete Enchanter* (41), *Land of Unreason* (42)

ASHMAN, WILLIAM (?) American artist. A prolific interior artist, Ashman prepared art for most of the major science fiction magazines from 1952 through 1956. He had a murky, surrealistic style, often achieved by using a grease pencil and large patches of blacks and grays. Many of his figures were done with thick black lines and exaggerated features. His style worked better with fantasy than hard science fiction, and the best of his work appeared in *Beyond Fantasy Fiction*.

PUBLISHED WORK:

AMZ: 1952 (10); 1953 (4, 6, 8); 1954 (3); 1967 (6)

BEY: 1953 (7, 11); 1954 (1, 7, 9); 1955 (10)

FA: 1952 (7, 9)

FTC: 1952 (11); 1953 (1, 3, 7, 11); 1954 (4)

GXY: 1952 (8, 9, 10, 11, 12); 1953 (1, 2, 3, 4, 7, 8, 12); 1954 (3, 4, 5, 6, 8, 9); 1955 (3, 4, 6, 7, 8, 9, 11); 1956 (1, 3)

AUSTIN, ALICIA (b. Nov. 24, 1942) American artist. The first of three children in an army family, Austin was born in Providence, Kentucky, but traveled to a number of locations including Germany and Japan when she was young. She attended Sacred Heart Dominion College in Houston, Texas, on an art scholarship but changed to a biology major in her third year and completed training in cytology at M. D. Anderson Hospital in Houston. She then moved to Canada and soon was involved in Canadian fandom. The World SF Convention in St. Louis was also the first place she had displayed art.

In 1970 Austin moved to Los Angeles, where she lived with fans John and Bjo Trimble for several years before moving out on her own. She won a Hugo Award for best fan artist during this time and soon made the jump from fan to professional artist. Much of her finest artwork has been done for Donald Grant Publications. In recent years, she has worked in collaboration with George Barr* and has continued to produce artwork on her own. Like many artists who came from the ranks of fandom, Austin has discovered a strong market for her art (and prints, cards, and so on using her art) at SF conventions, and much of her art does not see publication outside this market.

PUBLISHED WORK:

HC: *Age of Dreams* (78), *Black God's Shadow* (78), *Echoes from an Iron Harp* (72)

PB: *Mask of Circe, Voorloper* (80)

AMZ: 1981 (5, 7, 9); 1982 (1)

DEST: 1979 (8, 10); 1980 (2, spring)

IASFM: 1981 (8, 11); 1982 (3)

AUSTIN, HENRY (?) British artist. A British maritime artist, Austin illustrated several books by Jules Verne for London publisher Ward Lock at the turn of the century. These novels included *The Adventures of Captain Hatteras, The Mysterious Document,* and *Among the Cannibals.* His magazine illustrations in the fantasy field include work for George Griffith's "From Pole to Pole" (*Windsor*, October 1904) and Winston Spencer Churchill's "Man Overboard" (*Harmsworth*, December 1898).

Richard Dalby

BALBALIS (?) American artist. A prolific illustrator, Balbalis did interesting work for *Galaxy* throughout the 1950s and 1960s and produced artwork for the magazine's short-lived fantasy companion publication *Beyond*.

PUBLISHED WORK:

BEY: 1953 (7, 9); 1954 (5)

GXY: 1953: (6, 8, 9); 1956 (2, 3, 4, 5, 6, 7, 8, 9, 10, 11, 12); 1957 (1, 4, 5, 6, 7, 8, 9, 10, 11, 12); 1958 (1, 2, 3, 4, 5, 6, 7, 8, 9, 10, 11, 12); 1959 (2, 4, 6, 8, 10, 12); 1960 (2, 4, 6, 8, 10, 12); 1961 (2, 4, 6, 8, 10, 12); 1962 (2, 4, 6, 8, 10, 12); 1963 (2, 4, 6, 8, 10, 12); 1964 (2, 4, 6, 8, 10, 12); 1965 (2, 4, 6, 8, 10, 12)

BAMA, JAMES ELLIOTT (b. Apr. 28, 1926) American artist. Born in New York City, Bama studied for four years with Frank Reilly at the School of Art and Design in that city and later attended the Art Students League for three years. He got into paperback cover art in 1950 with *A Bullet for Billy the Kid* for Avon Books. During the next few years he drew interior illustrations for *The Saturday Evening Post*, *Argosy*, and *Reader's Digest*. From 1955 through 1971 he worked primarily for Bantam Books, doing 450 cover paintings. He also produced some artwork for Avon, Signet, and Berkley Books and served as the official artist for the New York Giants as well as doing work for the Baseball Hall of Fame.

A trip to a friend's ranch convinced Bama to move West, and he now lives and works at a Wyoming studio on his ranch, twenty miles from the nearest town. Since 1971 Bama has specialized in scenes of the American West. He is recognized as one of the leading artists in this very popular American art field. Many of his paintings are in major museum collections including the Cowboy Hall of Fame and the Whitney Museum of Western Art.

Bama's fame in the Science Fiction field rests on a series of sixty-two cover paintings he did for the Doc Savage paperbacks published by Bantam Books. His covers for this series featuring a bronze superhero reprinted from 1930s pulp magazines were credited with establishing the books as major sellers in the crowded superhero field. Bama used Steve Hullen, a close friend and one-time actor, as his model for Savage. A conscious decision was made by Bama and Bantam art director Len Leone to update the look of Doc Savage. This new paperback look for Doc Savage sold the series. Of the first sixty-seven novels, Bama did all but the covers for Books 3, 4, 5, 6, and 8; marriage to his wife, Lynette, and their honeymoon were the reasons Bama was not able to do those covers.

Virtually every artist who has illustrated Doc Savage books since Bama has followed his style of portraying the lead character, described by one critic as "a cross between a Nazi Storm Trooper and the Jolly Green Giant, but in bronze."

PUBLISHED WORK:

PB: *Annihilist* (68), *Cold Death* (67), *Czar of Fear* (68), *Dagger in the Sky* (69), *Deadly Dwarf* (68), *Death in Silver* (68), *Devil on the Moon* (70), *Devil's Playground* (68), *Dust of Death* (69), *The Evil Gnome* (R) (76), *Fantastic Island* (66), *Fear Cay* (66), *Feathered Octopus* (70), *Flaming Falcons* (68), *Fortress of Solitude* (68), *Freckled Shark* (72), *Giggling Ghosts* (71), *Gold Ogre* (69), *Golden Peril* (70), *Green Death* (71), *Green Eagle* (68), *Haunted Ocean* (70), *He Could Stop the World* (70), *Hex* (69), *Land of Always-Night* (66), *Land of Long JuJu* (70), *Living Fire Menace* (71), *The Lost Oasis* (65), *Mad Eyes* (69), *Mad Mesa* (72), *Merchants of Disaster* (69), *Majii* (71), *The Man of Bronze* (64), *Man Who Shook the Earth* (69), *Man Who Smiled No More* (70), *Mental Wizard* (70), *Midas Man* (70), *Motion Menace* (71), *Munitions Master* (71), *Murder Melody* (67), *Mystery Under the Sea* (68), *The Mystic Mullah* (65), *Other World* (68), *The Phantom City* (66), *Pirate of the Pacific* (67), *Pirate's Ghost* (71), *Poison Island* (71), *The Quest of Qui* (66), *Red Skull* (67), *Red Snow* (69), *Resurrection Day* (69), *Saragasso Ogre* (67), *Sea Angel* (70), *Sea Magician* (70), *Secret in the Sky* (67), *Spook Legion* (67), *Squeaking Goblin* (69), *Submarine Mystery* (71), *Terror in the Navy* (69), *The Thousand Headed Man* (64), *Vanisher* (70), *World's Fair Goblin* (69), *Yellow Cloud* (71).

BARLOWE, WAYNE DOUGLAS (b. Jan. 6, 1958) American artist. Born in Glen Cove, New York, Barlowe was the son of Sy and Dorothea Barlowe, both well-known natural history artists. He studied at the Art Students League when he was eleven and later attended Cooper Union in New York. Along with his instructors, Wayne was strongly influenced by Zdenek Burian, a Czech painter known for his work of dinosaurs and cavemen. Other influences included Pyle, Ingres, Parrish, and the Wyeths. A longtime SF reader, Barlowe naturally gravitated to the field that held his interest. His first published piece was painted for *Cosmos* for a story by Michael Bishop. He soon began producing artwork for Berkley Books and, shortly thereafter, all of the major SF magazine and book publishers. His art collection, *Barlowe's Guide to Extraterrestrials* (1979), has more than ninety-thousand copies in print.

Because of the success of his "aliens" book, Barlowe has developed a reputation as being the perfect artist for rendering unusual creatures. As a result of his natural history background, he has had no problem coping with such demand and finds organic creatures easier to paint than hardware. Like many other modern SF artists, Barlowe likes to read the manuscript of the work to be illustrated. He takes notes on all details and then does several sketches. From there, a formal finished sketch is shown to the art director. Sketches are done with much detail so as to deal with problems at this stage of work instead of on the finished painting level. Barlowe works on Bainbridge 172 illustration board and uses acrylics exclusively.

Barlowe's work has been exhibited at the New Britain Museum of American Art, the Bronx Museum of the Arts, The Society of Illustrators, and the Hansen Gallery. In 1983 he created and designed PowerLords, a line of toys produced by Revell. Among his personal favorites of his paintings are *Lightfall*, *Black Easter*, and *Vagabond Prophet*, all paperbacks from Avon Books; the June 1984 cover for IASFM; and *Barlowe's Guide to Extraterrestrials*. He currently lives in New York and is married to Shawna McCarthy, editor of IASFM.

PUBLISHED WORK:

HC: *Barlowe's Guide to Extraterrestrials* (79), *Beyond the Blue Event Horizon* (80)

PB: *Barlowe's Guide to Extraterrestrials* (79), *Battle of Forever* (82), *Black Easter* (82), *Dr. Mirabilis* (82), *Mission to the Heart Stars* (82), *Narrow Land* (82), *The Silkie* (82), *Welcome to Mars* (83)

ASF: 1980 (12); 1981 (3/2, 3/30, 7, 8, 9, 11); 1982 (1, 5, 11)

COS: 1977 (1)

FTC: 1980 (7)

IASFM: 1980 (11); 1981 (3, 10, 11); 1982 (12)

BARR, GEORGE (b. 1937) American artist. Born in Arizona, Barr was raised in Salt Lake City, Utah, and attended commercial art school there. As with many SF fans interested in art, Barr's first artwork was done for fanzines. His first published artwork was prepared for *Fantastic* in 1961, and he also did early work for *Amazing* and *Galaxy* during this period. Barr quickly moved on to cover art, starting with Ace Books and then moving to DAW Books when that company began. He now produces a great many interior illustrations for *Isaac Asimov's Science Fiction Magazine*.

Barr is very careful in constructing his cover paintings. He reads the book to be illustrated very thoroughly and takes notes on characters, locales, and every description given by the author. He tries to make his illustrations as accurate as possible—anything else he believes would be "cheating: false advertising."

Barr's style was influenced by Maxfield Parrish and Arthur Rackham, and much of his art has a grace and style that fits fantasy much better than hard SF. Barr's color work is done primarily in watercolor, and he is a master of using colored pens for illustration. He was nominated for the Hugo Award for best fan artist five times and won the award in 1968. He was artist guest of honor at the World Science Fiction convention in Kansas City in 1976.

PUBLISHED WORK:

HC: *Dying Earth* (76), *Green Magic* (79), *Red Nails* (75), *Upon the Winds of Yesterday* (76), *Whispers* (77)

PB: *At the Narrow Passage* (79), *The Birthgrave*, *Broken Sword* (71), *Clockwork Traitor* (77), *Darkover Landfall* (72), *Elidor*, *The Eye of the Zodiac*, *Forest of Forever* (71), *Games Psyborgs Play*, *Getaway World* (77), *Golden Gryphon Feather* (79), *Heritage of Hastur* (75), *How Are the Mighty Fallen* (74), *Hunters of the Red Moon* (73), *Imperial Stars* (76), *The Metallic Muse*, *Night's Master* (78), *The Not-World* (75), *Perilous Dreams* (76), *Quest for Simbilus* (74), *The Shattered Chain* (76), *The Spell Sword*, *Star*, *Strangler's Moon* (76), *The Weathermonger*, *Wildings of Westron* (77), *The Witling*, *The Years Best Fantasy Stories #1* (75), *The Years Best Fantasy Stories #2* (76), *Zothique* (70).

AMZ: 1961 (5); 1965 (8); 1981 (11); 1982 (11)

FgF: 1970 (12)

FTC: 1961 (3, 5); 1962 (4, 6, 8, 11); 1963 (7)

GXY: 1969 (4)

IASFA: 1979 (spring, summer, fall)

IASFM: 1978 (1, 3, 7, 9, 11); 1979 (2, 4, 6, 7, 9, 10, 11); 1980 (2, 3, 4, 5, 7, 9, 11); 1981 (1, 2, 8, 9, 10, 11, 12); 1982 (3, 4, 6, 7)

IF: 1969 (3, 7)

POSTERS: "Flesh Gordon," "The Middle-Earth Songbook"

BARR, KENNETH JOHN (b. 1933) American artist. Born in Glasgow, Scotland, Barr worked six years from age fourteen as an apprentice sign painter. He served in the British army in North Africa. After his tour of duty, he moved to London and started working in commercial art. He painted his first SF cover for *Nebula*, a British SF magazine, in 1958. Barr liked the field very much because of the lack of restrictions on his imagination.

Barr immigrated to the United States in 1967 and has continued to be prolific in both advertising and science fiction art. Major influences include Alex Raymond*, Burne Hogarth, and Norman Rockwell.

PUBLISHED WORK:

HC: *The Many Colored Land* (81)

PB: *Beast Master (81)*, *Brave Dragon* (69), *City Outside the World* (77), *Kyric Fights the Demon World* (75), *No Brother, No Friend* (79), *The Power of the Serpent* (76), *The Seedbearer (76)*, *Star Rangers* (81), *Vestiges of Time* (79).

NEB: 1958 (32, 33, 34, 35, 36, 37); 1959 (38, 39, 41)

BARTH, ERNEST K. (?) American artist. A prolific interior artist, Barth worked for the digest science fiction magazines in the early 1950s. Like many of the artists of this era, his art was competent but uninspired.

PUBLISHED WORK:

AMZ: 1953 (3, 8, 12); 1954 (3, 7, 9, 11); 1955 (1); 1956 (7); 1957 (4)

BEY: 1953 (7, 9); 1954 (1)

FA: 1953 (1)

FTC: 1953 (5, 9, 11); 1954 (1, 8, 10, 12); 1955 (2); 1956 (12); 1957 (2, 6); 1966 (11); 1967 (5); 1968 (1)

GXY: 1953 (9); 1954 (3, 9, 10, 12)

IF: 1953 (5); 1955 (1, 7); 1957 (12)

BAUMAN, JILL (b. 1942) American artist. One of a growing number of successful women artists in the fantasy field, Bauman did not set out to be an artist. She received her art education at Adelphi University and Queens College and then worked as an art teacher in junior high school for five years. After that, she shifted directions and for the next ten years ran a successful antique business. During this time she also brought up two daughters.

Dealing in rarities strengthened Bauman's confidence in herself as a businesswoman but did not completely satisfy her artistic yearnings. She finally left the antique business to become an artist. But with no contacts in the art world and some rough edges on her work, Bauman found that she could not break into the tough world of commercial art. It was then that she met Walter Velez★. Bauman became Velez's agent—work that she was eminently suited for with her business background—and Velez helped her with her art. Both benefited. Bauman succeeded in selling Velez to many new markets, and with Velez's tutoring, Bauman finally broke into the art field. She is now considered one of the best fantasy artists working in the field and has been nominated several times for the World Fantasy Award for Best Artist. In addition to doing her fantasy art, Bauman has contributed work to *Heavy Metal, Epic, High Times*, and *Scholastic* and has done advertising work and several videodisc album covers.

PUBLISHED WORK:

HC: *Cast a Cold Eye, Perpetual Light*

PB: *Attack of the Giant Baby, The Auction, Buried Blossoms, Carlisle Street, Cast a Cold Eye, A Cold Blue Light, Eye of the Tarot, Fall into Darkness, A Glow of Candles, The Green Millennium, Incarnate, The Kill, Journey from Flesh, Last Communion, The Magic Grandfather, Native Tongue, A Quiet Night of Fear, Perpetual Light, Pole Shift, Rensime, Sardonyx Net, Sinister Twilight, Something Answered, Stand and Deliver*

BAYARD, EMILE-ANTOINE (Nov. 2, 1837–1891) French artist. Born in La Ferte-sous-Jouarre, France, Bayard was a distinguished French portrait painter. He also was a busy illustrator for *Journal des Voyages, Journal pour Rire, Cassell's Magazine*, and many other publications. He illustrated many of Erckmann-Chatrian's fantasy tales, including "Hugeus-le-Loup," "Une nuit dans les bois," "L'Heritage de l'oncle Christian" and "L'Illustre Docteur Maltheus."

But it is for his classic illustrations drawn to accompany Jules Verne's *Autour de la Lune* in 1872 that Bayard will always be remembered. His engravings showing the effects of weightlessness upon the pioneer astronauts; the survey of the moon's surface; and, above all, the "splashdown" picture are among science fiction's most famous illustrations. The latter piece, showing the American flag securely fixed above the module, proved to be amazingly prophetic when Frank Borman of the Apollo 9 moon expedition landed in the Pacific, one hundred years later, only two or three miles from the point mentioned in the book. Unfortunately, Bayard did not become a regular Verne illustrator. He died in Cairo in 1891.

PUBLISHED WORK:

(In science fiction; all to books in Jules Verne's Voyages Extraordinaires series, first published by Hertzel in Paris and later in England.)

HC: *Autour de la Lune* (1872), forty-five illustrations, in collaboration with de Neuville; *Dr. Ox's Experiment and Other Stories* (1874), *Une Fantasie du Docteur Ox* (1874), *From the Earth to the Moon . . . and a Trip Around It* (1873)

Richard Dalby

BEECHAM, THOMAS (?) American artist. Born in Colorado, Beecham served as a corpsman in the South Pacific in the navy. He attended the St. Louis School of Fine Arts, Washington University. Like many artists who worked in the science fiction field for a short time, he entered the field during the boom years of the early 1950s when New York publishers were looking for artists who would work for little money and could prepare art quickly.

PUBLISHED WORK:

AMZ: 1951 (11); 1952 (5, 7, 8, 9, 10, 12); 1953 (1); 1955 (3, 5, 7, 9, 12); 1956 (2, 4, 7); 1969 (3)

DYN: 1954 (1)

FA: 1951 (12); 1952 (1, 4, 6, 10)

FF: 1953 (6)

FSQ: 1954 (spring)

FTC: 1952 (fall, 11); 1953 (1); 1955 (2, 6, 8, 10); 1956 (4); 1966 (7); 1969 (8)

FUT: 1953 (3, 5, 9, 11)

GXY: 1953 (2)

IF: 1953 (11); 1953 (1, 3, 7, 9)

PS: 1952 (5)

RS: 1953 (4, 7)

SFA: 1953 (5)

SFQ: 1953 (5, 8)

SS: 1953 (4)

BEEKMAN, DOUGLAS L. (b. Nov. 29, 1952) American artist. Born in Findlay, Ohio, Beekman exhibited some early talent in the creative areas—drawing, music, and writing. He attended the Columbus College of Art and Design in Columbus, Ohio, on a full scholarship from 1971 through 1972. By then, he had grown disenchanted with the program there and moved to New York. While working in New York City, he attended the Art Student's League. There he studied with James Bama★ and Carl Hantman, both students of Frank Reilly. He also studied briefly with Robert Schulz★ and Jack Faragasso★. He continued studying Reilly's methods with Michael Aviano.

Beekman took a science fiction-based portfolio to several publishers and received a number of assignments. His first art assignment was for "Sierra Maestra" by Norman Spinrad, published in *Analog* in 1975. Beekman has produced artwork for that magazine ever since. In paperbacks, he began producing illustrations for some of the smaller publishers and soon found assignments with the larger chains. He has painted more than one hundred book and magazine covers and has produced advertising art for various national clients as well as doing movie work for *The Spy Who Loved Me*.

In 1980 Beekman decided to take a break from commercial illustration. He spent two years developing his own projects and executing a number of paintings for his own pleasure. During this time he moved to Vermont, where he now lives.

After the long break, the artist returned to commercial illustration but at a much more casual pace. He has been careful not to overbook his schedule or accept assignments that do not have the potential of becoming visually absorbing. He has found that this more leisurely pace has resulted in better work for each subject.

As to Beekman's philosophy toward illustrating, he believes that "it is important not just to visually describe the way things look in a story, but to understand and communicate how that environment smells, how it tastes, how it sounds; getting inside the characters and bringing them to life. They should live and breathe in that picture. Everything contributes to that effect. . . . If a world is brutal and harsh, populated by vicious characters, my painting should exude those qualities. If the subject is beautiful and lyrical, the illustration should emphatically convey the sumptous rhythms and colors of it. Every time I sit down to work up a science fiction or fantasy painting, I'm creating a world no one has really seen before, so it needs to be as rich and fascinating as I can make it."

As to influences, Beekman was influenced by Rembrandt, Sargent, N. C. Wyeth, Remington, Lindsay, and Heinrich Kley. A modern influence was Harold Foster, creator of *Prince Valiant*.

In 1982 Beekman formed Buckhorn Studios, whose members include Jeffrey Potter★, Richard Bober★, Dan Horne★, Bob Eggleton★, and Linda Burr★.

PUBLISHED WORK:

HC: *Beyond Sanctuary, Beyond the Veil, Beyond Wizardwall*

PB: *Cascade Point, Crossroads, The Death God's Citadel, Drawing of the Dark, Greybeard, Hands of Glory, Imperial Stars, Motherlines, The Source of Magic, Time Is the Simplest Thing, Walk to the Ends of the Earth*

AMZ: 1976 (9)

ASF: 1975 (10, 12); 1976 (7, 8); 1977 (1, 2, 3, 8, 9, 11); 1978 (1, 4, 5, 6, 7, 11); 1979 (4, 6)

COS: 1977 (7, 11)

FTC: 1976 (11)

BELARSKI, RUDOLPH (Mar. 27, 1900–1983) American artist. As a twelve-year-old, Belarski was working in a Dupont, Pennsylvania, coal-processing plant as a slate picker. A picture he drew on a whitewashed wall was seen by one of his bosses who thought enough of it to give Belarski the job of painting safety posters for the company. Belarski was self-taught, learning from books during what little free time he had. At age twenty-one he put himself through Pratt Institute in Brooklyn by working at odd jobs. His painting instructor at Pratt was Max Hermann, and he won a number of prizes in art competitions while at Pratt. In 1929, several years after he graduated, Belarski was invited back to teach specialized subjects in commercial art. During the same period he began a long and succcessful career as a freelance illustrator. He sold material first to Delacorte, including a number of paintings for its war pulp magazines. He soon was involved in doing air-war covers as well.

Belarski divided his time between New York, Maine and Canada. An avid outdoorsman, he would get sketches approved in New York and then go to the woods to stay in a cabin and do the paintings. Along with his war paintings, Belarski did a number of fine covers for the Munsey chain, publisher of the best-selling pulp *Argosy*. It was for *Argosy* in the late 1930s that Belarski did many of his finest science fiction paintings, illustrating novels including *The Red Star of Tarzan, Lords of Creations, Minions of the Moon, The Synthetic Men of Mars, Carson of Venus*, and *Escape on Venus*.

During the Second World War, Belarski joined the USO and was sent overseas to entertain troops in the London hospitals. He did sketches and portraits of soldiers during this period. After the war he began working for Pines Publications (Standard Magazines), one of the larger pulp publishers, and moved from New York to New Rochelle, New York, where many artists were then living. In the late 1940s Belarski met and married Gladys Bell, who served as the model for many of the women in his paintings during the next few years. But the marriage was not successful, and they were divorced in the 1950s.

The art editor at Pines was Churchill Ettinger, a former illustrator who Belarski thought was the best in the business. In 1948 Belarski expanded his market from pulps to paperbacks and became well known as one of the leading paperback cover artists of the 1950s, doing nearly all of his work for Ettinger for Pines' Popular Library. When Ettinger was fired suddenly, Belarski left shortly afterward. He did a few more paperback covers and then went to work for men's adventure magazines. Tiring of the hectic life of a freelance artist, he joined the staff of the Famous Artists School in 1957 and dropped out of the cover market. He taught courses in commercial art and figure illustration. In 1960 Belarski married Barbara Holzhausen. In 1972 he was let go due to a staff reduction at the school. Belarski died in retirement in 1983, just as there was a revival of interest in his art in the paperback field.

PUBLISHED WORK:

CF: 1942 (summer, fall)

FUT: 1955 (28)

SS: 1941 (5, 7, 9, 11); 1942 (1, 9); 1943 (1); 1947 (3)

StrS: 1939 (2); 1940 (4)

TWS: 1941 (8, 10); 1942 (2, 8, 12)

BELLAMY, FRANK ALFRED (May 21, 1917–1976) British artist. Born in England, Bellamy followed a career primarily in the comic field although he did a number of science fiction illustrations for weekly magazines in Britain.

Bellamy's first comic artwork was an advertisement for a toothpaste company and was called "Commando Gibbs vs. Dragon Decay." From 1948 through 1955 he drew comic strips for *Mickey Mouse Weekly*. After that he did numerous features for Eagle Comics for more than ten years. In 1959 and 1960 he completely designed the hardware of the famous science fiction comic strip *Dan Dare*, originally conceived by Frank Hampson. His work for that comic made him a great favorite among British science fiction fans. From 1971 to his death in 1976 Bellamy worked on the newspaper adventure strip *Garth*.

Much of Bellamy's best art was done for weekly television magazines published in England and has never been collected. In 1985 *Timeview*, a complete collection of all *Doctor Who* illustrations done by Bellamy for *Radio Times*, was published, with commentary by his son David Bellamy.

PUBLISHED WORK:

PB: *Timeview* (85)

Richard Dalby

BENETT, LEON (Mar. 2, 1839–1917) French artist. The professional name used by Hippolyte Leon Benet. Benett was born in Orange, southern France. During the 1860s he acted as an official registrar and made several trips to the French colonies including IndoChina, Martinique, New Caledonia, and Algeria. He assembled an invaluable collection of sketches and notebooks on his travels, which formed a useful source of inspiration during his long and distinguished career working for the French publisher Hetzel from the early 1870s to the outbreak of the First World War in 1914.

Benett illustrated many of the best fantasy stories of the writing duo Erckmann-Chatrian including *La Comete* and *L'Oeil invisible*. He also prepared art for the fantasies of Andre Laurie including *Le tour du globe d'un bachelier* and *L'Heritier de Robinson*. However, it is for his brilliant and vast range of artwork for twenty-five of Jules Verne's *Voyages extraordinaires* that Benett is best known. He was the most prolific of all of the great Verne illustrators, contributing nearly two thousand engravings and drawings to the series. Some of his best work appeared in *Hier et demain* (including some SF shorts) and *Robur le conquerant/The Clipper of the Clouds*. Benett portrayed the "Albatross" machine perfectly in this heavier-than-air SF fantasy.

The artist always signed his work "L. Benett," a slight variation on the true spelling of his surname. He died in Toulon in 1917.

PUBLISHED WORK:

(All are part of Verne's Voyages Extraordinaires series. The Paris edition published by Hetzel is listed first, with the number of illustrations noted. The London edition from Sampson Low of the title is given afterwards.)

HC: *Bourses de voyage* (1903), 72 illustrations; *Claudius Bombarnac* (1892), 55 illustrations: *Claudius Bombarnac* (1894); *Clovis Dardentor* (1896) 47 illustrations: *Clovis Dardentor* (1897); *Deux ans de vacances, ou Un pensionnat de Robinsons* (1888), 90 illustrations: *Two Years Holiday* (*Adrift in the Pacific* and *Second Year Ashore*) (1889); *Face au Drapeau* (1896) 42 illustrations: *For the Flag* (1897); *Hier et demain* (1910) illustrated in collaboration with Myrbach and Roux*; *Keraban le tetu* (1883), 101 illustrations: *Kerban the Inflexible* (1884 and 1885); *La jangada* (1881), 95 illustrations: *The Giant Raft* (1881; *La Maison a vapeur* (1880), 101 illustrations: *The Steam House* (1881); *L'Agence Thompson* (1907); *L'Archipel en feu* (1884), 51 illustrations including three color plates: *The Archipelago on Fire* (1886); *Le chateau des Carpathes* (1892), 50 illustrations: *Castle of the Carpathians* (1893); *Le rayon vert* (1882), 44 illustrations: *The Green Ray* (1883); *Le tour du monde en quartre-vingt jours* (1874), 80 illustrations in collaboration with de Neuville*: *Around the World in Eighty Days* (1874); *Les cinq cents millions de la Begum* (1879), 48 illustrations including three color plates: *The Begum's Fortune* (1880); *Les revoltes de la Bounty* (1879): *The Mutineers of the Bounty* (1880); *Les tribulations d'un chinois en Chine* (1879) 52 illustrations, including three color plates: *Tribulations of a Chinaman* (1880); *L'Ecole des Robinsons* (1882), 51 illustrations: *Godfrey Morgan* (1883); *L'Etoile du sud* (1884), 63 illustrations including 3 color plates: *The Vanished Diamond* (1885); *L'Ille a helice* (1895), 81 illustrations: *The Floating Island* (1896); *L'Invasion de la mer* (1905), 43 illustrations; *Mathias Sandorf* (1885), 113 illustrations: *Mathias Sandorf* (1886); *Mistress Branican* (1891) 83 illustrations: *Mistress Branican* (1892); *Nord contre sud* (1887), 86 illustrations including six color plates: *North against South* (1888); *P'tit bonhomme* (1893), 85 illustrations: *Foundling Mick* (1895); *Robur le conquerant* (1886), 45 illustrations including three color plates: *The Clipper of the Clouds* (1887); *Un drame en livonie* (1904), 33 illustrations

Richard Dalby

BENNET, HARRY (?) American artist. One of the major paperback cover artists of the 1950s, Bennet was born in Lewisboro, New York, in the 1920s, and he studied at the Art Institute and the American Academy of Art in Chicago. He began painting paperback covers in the early 1950s and did 650 covers for Fawcett, 475 for Pocket Books, 250 for Berkley, 65 for Dell, and 5 each for Ace and Ballantine. His fantasy and SF covers were largely impressionistic. He often used a razor blade to create special effects for his paintings.

PUBLISHED WORK:

PB: *Monsters Galore* (65)

BERGEN, DAVID (b. 1947) British artist. Bergen studied at the Western Australian Institute of Technology and traveled widely in Peru and Mexico. His interest in the artifacts of ancient cultures is shown in his science fiction paintings, most notably the Great Pyramid in *Laser Beams from the Stars.* Six of his paintings are included in *The Flights of Icarus* (1977).

Richard Dalby

BERGEY, EARLE KULP (Aug. 26, 1901- Sept. 30, 1952) American artist. More than any other science fiction magazine cover artist, Bergey was associated with the term *pulp science fiction*. He achieved fame for his numerous paintings featuring scantily clad women, usually wearing tiny outfits and brass breastplates. His space scenes often featured women in transparent, and highly unbelievable, spacesuits.

The seventh of eight children of A. Frank and Ella (Kulp), Bergey was born in Phildelphia. His father was a well-known musician and conductor of the Philadelphia Municipal Band. Bergey's talent, though, was in art, and he attended Northeast High School, graduating in 1919, and shortly thereafter entered the Academy of Fine Arts in Philadelphia, where he studied art from late 1921 until 1926, winning a European Competition while there.

After graduating, Bergey started working for the *Philadelphia Ledger* in the art department. About then he also entered the pulp field, preparing artwork primarily for the Fiction House chain.

After Bergey's marriage in early 1935, he left the *Ledger* and worked as a freelance artist for the rest of his life. He produced many illustrations and covers for the pulps but also did some work for *The Saturday Evening Post*, in 1935, as well as many other slick magazines. However, it was his pulp artwork that supported him. Shortly after his marriage, Bergey and his growing family moved to rural Bucks County, Pennsylvania, while maintaining an apartment in New York City. He used many of the local people for models for his cover art.

Bergey was noted for his pinup-style art but did not do science fiction art until 1939, when he began doing the artwork for covers for the Standard magazine chain—*Strange Stories*, *Startling Stories*, *Thrilling Wonder*, and *Captain Future*. Burgey was brought in with Rudolph Belarski* to help pep up the covers of the Standard publications. Until then covers had been done by Howard Brown*. Brown did exceptional work with aliens and space ships, but his covers were not slanted to attract the typical newsstand buyer; they appealed primarily to the longtime science fiction fan. With the increase of competition during the early 1940s, Standard slanted its magazines to a younger audience. Heroic figures and beautiful women seemed one way to attract such a readership. Bergey's earliest covers featured monsters much like those of Brown, but this quickly changed, and after a short time, the cover paintings invariably featured a beautiful woman in some sort of terrible danger.

Bergey did a number of paperback covers for Popular Library. In the early 1950s it was owned by Standard publications, the same company that owned Standard magazines. Belarski, who had been brought in with Bergey in 1940 to help the magazine line, was also brought in with Bergey to help spice up the paperback line, which had been noted for its tastefully done symbolic covers. With Bergey and Belarsky working, Popular Library soon was filled with beautiful, half-clad women in perilous situations.

In the early 1950s Standard, in a switch in editorial policy, tried to upgrade its magazines when faced with the more sophisticated challenge of publications such as *Galaxy* and *The Magazine of Fantasy* and *SF*. Among other changes it made, it dropped the girls on the covers. However, Bergey met the challenge, and his last few covers showed that he could paint other science fiction illustrations with the same talent.

Bergey died suddenly in September 1952, while visiting a doctor's office. It is ironic that today he is primarily remembered for his "brass-brassiere"-style art, since he was starting to break away from that image when he died.

R. A. Everts and Robert Weinberg

PUBLISHED WORK:

PB: *Behind the Flying Saucers* (51), *The Big Eye* (50), *Dragon's Island* (52), *Revolt of the Triffids* (51), *Space Platform* (53)

ASFR 1952 (3)

CF: 1940 (summer, fall); 1941 (winter, spring, summer); 1943 (winter, summer); 1944 (winter, spring)

FSQ: 1950 (spring, summer, fall); 1951 (winter, spring, summer); 1952 (11); 1953 (1)

FUT: 1940 (5, 7)

SFA: 1953 (2)

SpS: 1952 (12)

SpSF: 1952 (9, 11)

SS: 1940 (7, 9, 11); 1941 (1, 3); 1942 (3, 5, 7, 11); 1943 (3, 6, fall); 1944 (winter, spring, summer, fall); 1945 (winter, spring, summer, fall); 1946 (winter, 3, spring, summer, fall); 1947 (1, 5, 7, 9, 11); 1948 (1, 3, 5, 7, 9, 11); 1949 (1, 3, 7, 9, 11); 1950 (1, 3, 5, 7, 9, 11); 1951 (1, 3, 5, 9); 1952 (1, 2, 3, 6, 8)

StrS: 1939 (8, 10, 12); 1940 (2, 6, 8, 10, 12); 1941 (2)

TWS: 1940 (9, 10, 11, 12); 1941 (2, 3, 4, 12); 1942 (4, 6, 10); 1943 (2, 4, 6, 8, fall); 1944 (spring, summer); 1945 (winter, spring, summer, fall); 1946 (winter, spring, summer, fall, 12); 1947 (2, 4, 6, 8, 10, 12); 1948 (2, 4, 6, 8, 10, 12); 1949 (2, 4, 10); 1950 (6, 8, 10, 12); 1951 (6, 8); 1952 (2, 6, 10)

BERKEY, JOHN (b. 1932) American artist. Born in Edgley, North Dakota, Berkey attended a Minneapolis art school after becoming interested in painting in high school. He then began working for Brown & Bigelow doing calendar art. He is married and lives in a quiet town in Minnesota where he has his studio in the basement of his home. Berkey is highly regarded by his peers in the SF art field and is noted for his skill at depicting future hardware.

PUBLISHED WORK:

PB: *Dream Millenium* (74), *Humanoid Touch* (81), *I Robot* (70), *Lifeboat* (72), *Lucky Star on Moons of Jupiter* (78), *Mindwarpers* (72), *Star SF 3* (72), *Star SF 5* (72), *Star SF 6* (72), *The Way Back* (78), *Worlds Best SF #1* (72)

BERRY, D. BRUCE (b. Jan. 24, 1924) American artist. Born in Oakland, California, Berry was a self-taught artist, using art books and constant practice as his only guides. At seventeen he began working as a draftsman for the U.S. Engineering Department. At eighteen he was working as an editorial cartoonist for a California paper. During the Second World War he painted signs at an air base in England. Afterwards, Berry entered the advertising business, drawing machinery and merchandise and retouching photos for ads. During this period he moved to Chicago, where he lived for the next twenty years. A science fiction fan most of his life, Berry encountered William Hamling's Greenleaf magazines and began working for them, illustrating *Imagination, Imaginative Tales,* and *Space Travel.* Unfortunately, the magazines were already on the way out, and soon after Berry began working for them, they were cancelled.

Berry changed career directions and became a writer. Unfortunately, in a major fall he broke his arm and shoulder and ripped the muscles in his chest and back. Fortunately, since it took only one hand to draw, he went back to illustration. He returned to California and entered the comic field as a letterer and an inker. Married, with a young daughter, Berry has recently been assisting noted comic-book artist Jack Kirby, who began his career doing several illustrations for *Marvel Stories* in the late 1930s.

PUBLISHED WORK:

IMG: 1958 (4, 6, 8, 10)

IMGT: 1958 (1, 5)

OW: 1951 (10)

SpTr: 1958 (7, 9, 11)

BINDER, JACK (JOHN) R. (b. Aug. 11, 1902) American artist. The elder brother of Earl and Otto Binder (who collaborated on science fiction stories as Eando Binder), Jack Binder was born in Austria-Hungary but immigrated to the United States when he was eight years old. He attended the Art Institute of Chicago and later studied with J. Allen St. John★. He later did art research at the Field Museum in Chicago. Married, with three children, Binder worked at a number of odd jobs, including lumberjack, miner, blacksmith, boxer, and wrestler, before settling down as an illustrator. He primarily worked as an interior artist for *Thrilling Wonder Stories* and *Startling Stories* in the late 1930s. During this period, he also worked for the Harry Chesler Studio as art director in the comic field.

In 1940 Binder opened his own shop, producing thousands of pages of art for all of the major comic books. After years of doing this, he went to work for C. C. Beck, who produced *Captain Marvel.* He stopped working for Beck in 1946 and in 1953 retired completely from the comic book field. He returned to the commercial-art field and started a studio to produce commercial outdoor sculptures.

PUBLISHED WORK:

ASF: 1936 (12); 1937 (4, 6, 11, 12); 1938 (1, 2, 3, 5, 6, 8, 10, 11, 12); 1939 (1, 2, 3, 4); 1941 (2, 4)

ASH: 1940 (2)

CF: 1940 (summer)

DYN: 1939 (2, 4)

FUT: 1939 (11)

SFQ: 1940 (Summer)

SS: 1939 (1, 3, 5, 7, 9, 11); 1940 (1, 3, 5, 7, 9, 11)

StrS: 1939 (6)

TWS: 1937 (1, 6, 8, 10, 12); 1938 (2, 4, 6, 8, 10, 12); 1939 (2, 4, 6, 8, 10, 12); 1940 (1, 2, 3, 4, 5, 6, 7, 8, 9); 1941 (2)

BINKLEY, RIC (?) American artist. Binkley began his career in the fantasy field when he found that no regular publisher would look at his portfolio because he had nothing published. His earliest work appeared on jackets done for Fantasy Press. He later moved to New York City, where he prepared a number of paintings for Gnome Press and Avalon Books. According to Fantasy Press founder Lloyd Eshbach, Binkley died young.

PUBLISHED WORK:

HC: *Aliens from Space* (58), *Assignment in Eternity* (53), *Ballroom of the Skies* (52), *Black Star Passes* (53), *Blue Barbarians* (58), *Children of the Lens* (54), *Conquest of Earth* (57), *Edge of Time* (58), *Fire in the Heavens* (58), *Flight into Yesterday* (53), *Foundation* (51), *Future Tense* (52), *Galactic Patrol* (50), *Gray Lensman* (51), *Heads of Cerberus* (52), *Hidden World* (57), *Iceworld* (53), *Immortality Delivered* (58), *Invisible Barriers* (58), *Islands of Space* (57), *Languages of Pao* (58), *Lost Continents* (54), *Mixed Men* (52), *Mutant* (53), *Out of This World* (58), *Robot and the Man* (53), *Robots Have No Tails* (52), *Second Stage Lensman* (53), *Seeds of Life* (51), *Sentinels from Space* (53), *Shambleau* (53), *Solomon's Stone* (57), *Space Egg* (58), *Space Lawyer* (53), *Starhaven* (58), *Starmen* (52), *Tower of Zanid* (58), *Troubled Star* (57), *Twice in Time* (57), *Tyrant of Time* (55), *Wasp* (57)

BIRMINGHAM, LLOYD P. (b. Aug. 23, 1924) American artist. Birmingham was one of several artists who had a short but productive career in the SF field due to an effort by the Ziff-Davis publishing chain to improve its science fiction magazines *Amazing* and *Fantastic*. In October 1960 the two magazines were completely reworked to make them competitive with better-selling SF publications. To this end, editor Cele Goldsmith brought in many authors who had never before written for the magazines and changed the entire art focus. Top-name artists including Ed Emsh★ and Alex Schomburg★ shared the art assignments with newcomers, including Birmingham, Vernon Kramer★, and George Schelling★.

Birmingham was trained in painting and illustration at the Parsons School of Design and the School of Art Studies in New York. He became a freelance illustrator specializing in aerospace and industrial artwork. A client recommended that he try *Flying Magazine*, a Ziff-Davis magazine, for assignments. The editor there explained that *Flying* did not use illustrations but referred him to *Amazing* since Cele Goldsmith was looking for new artists.

During this time, writing and cover paintings often overlapped. Many cover paintings were done to illustrate specific stories. However, in many cases, artists were told to do a painting, and then authors were asked to create a story based on the painting. Birmingham's first cover, "The Hatchery of Dreams," was a concept painting done by the artist for which Fritz Leiber wrote a story.

Birmingham worked in tempera on illustration board about twice the size of the printed cover. Preliminary sketches were done the size of the actual cover and were detailed in full color. When a story was to be based on a painting, a photostat was sent to the author as soon as the painting was completed. Birmingham took three to five days on a painting. Editorial freedom allowed him to vary style and technique. The cover for "It's Magic, You Dope" was done entirely in pen and ink, with a transparent color overlay.

In 1965 Ziff-Davis sold its SF magazines to Sol Cohen. The new publisher was interested in only reprint art for his covers. With an increase in assignments in scientific illustration, Birmingham left the science fiction field.

PUBLISHED WORK:

PB: *Envoy to the Dog Star* (65)

AMZ: 1961 (12); 1962 (3, 4, 7, 8, 9, 10, 12); 1963 (1, 3, 8, 9, 10)

ASF: 1962 (1, 2, 4)

FTC: 1961 (11, 12); 1962 (1, 3, 9, 11, 12); 1963 (2); 1964 (12)

BLAINE, MAHLON (1894–1970) American artist. Born in California, Blaine was an elusive figure for most of his life. A major illustrator of horror and fantasy fiction in the 1920s, he was completely forgotten by the time of his death. Some recent reprintings of his erotic and macabre illustrations have contributed to a small revival of interest in his work.

Blaine believed in keeping his personal life private. A biographical sketch appearing in 1927 evidently consisted of tall tales told to an interviewer who never realized his subject was making up details as he went along. Blurbs on books illustrated by Blaine gave conflicting information on everything from his birthplace to his education to his age. Other than the fact that Blaine's art was strongly influenced by Aubrey Beardsley, little is known about his early life.

Blaine worked in both oils and pen and ink. His reputation rested on his interior illustrations. A major book illustrator in the 1920s, he fell on hard times when illustrated books virtually disappeared during the Depression. He made a living doing private commissions. Late in life, he illustrated a series of reprints of Edgar Rice Burroughs hardcovers from Canaveral Press, work for which his unusual style was completely unsuited.

PUBLISHED WORK:

HC: *A Fighting Man of Mars* (62), *Alraune* (27), *The Art of the Fantastic* (78), *At the Earth's Core* (62), *Fantasy Collectors Annual* (74), *Fantasy Collectors Annual* (75), *The Land That Time Forgot* (62), *Limehouse Nights* (26), *The Monster Men* (62), *The Moon*

Men (62), *Pellucidar* (62), *Salambo* (27), *The Sorceror's Apprentice* (27), *Tanar of Pellucidar* (62), *Vathek* (28), *The Wolf Leader* (50)

PORTFOLIOS: *Venus Sardonica* (29), *Nova Venus*

BOBER, RICHARD (b. 1943) American artist. Bober studied under Lee Gaskins and won a scholarship to Pratt Institute. At Pratt, he studied under a series of "Jackson Pollack clones" and was expelled in 1966, holding the school record for cutting classes. He later studied at the Art Students League with Lennart Anderson.

Bober worked as a freelance medical illustrator for Roche and Upjohn. Since the 1970s he has prepared paperback cover art for Dell, Avon, Berkley, and New American Library (NAL), among other publishers. He painted many of the covers for the Alfred Hitchcock paperback reissues from Dell in the 1970s and for *The Guardians of the Flame* series and the *Silver Call* series for NAL during 1984–1987. Bober also has undertaken numerous private commissions including portraits and landscape paintings. He won the Isaac N. Maynard Prize for Portraiture from the National Academy of Design. The painting is in the Academy's permanent collection.

Influences include the Dutch Masters, as well as Joseph M. W. Turner. Bober tries everything in his paintings, using intermediary layers of varying paints, finishing with oil paint and alkyd resin. He is a member of the Buckhorn Studio.

BOK, HANNES (1914–1964) American artist. Born Wayne Woodard, the artist used the name Hannes Bok for most of his life. One of the few stylists in the pulp magazine field, Bok was also one of the unique personalities of early SF and fantasy illustration. Born in Duluth, Minnesota, the child of a broken home, he moved to Seattle, Washington, after high school and became friends with science fiction fans in the area. A self-taught artist, Bok was a strong admirer of Maxfield Parrish and considered himself a student of the Parrish school of illustration, although he never actually studied with that illustrator.

Bok moved from Seattle to Los Angeles and soon was involved in the active science fiction fan community there. His close friend Ray Bradbury showed some samples of Bok's work to Farnsworth Wright, the editor of *Weird Tales* magazine, during a trip to New York in 1939. Wright liked what he saw, and Bok soon moved to New York to work for the pulp. His first professionally published painting was the cover for the December 1939 *Weird Tales*.

Although Bok did a great deal of work for *Weird Tales*, he soon was working for other science fiction pulps as well. His major problem was a lack of discipline in both his professional and private life. He lived the way he wanted with little worry about convention. He never let editors dictate to him what he should do in terms of illustration, and this lost him a number of assignments during his career. When Farnsworth Wright was fired as editor of *Weird Tales*, Bok tried to organize a boycott of that magazine even though the publication was his main source of income at the time. He never broke into the pages of *Astounding Science Fiction*, which was not surprising since he could not depict machinery or people realistically. More surprising was the fact that Bok, like Virgil Finlay★, was able to sell very little to *Unknown* (later *Unknown Worlds*), the major fantasy market of the early 1940s, which was published by the same chain as was *Astounding*, Street & Smith. Bok's lack of success was probably due more to his inability to meet deadlines and satisfy rigid requirements than to any artistic failings.

When the Science Fiction Small Press publishers started publishing after World War II, Bok found a new market. His imaginative paintings worked well as jacket art. He did some of his finest work for Shasta Books. Many of the small-press publishers could not afford expensive color separations and had the artists do paintings in monochrome to which the printers added color. Bok went a step further. He supplied acetate overlays for many of his paintings with specific colors for each overlay—in effect, doing four color separations himself to insure that the painting would turn out the way he intended. Some of the finest jacket art in the fantasy field was done by Shasta Books for Bok paintings for *Sidewise in Time*, *Slaves of Sleep*, and *Kinsmen of the Dragon*. Bok also did exceptional work for Arkham House and Fantasy Press.

Bok got involved in the publishing field, joining with several other fans to form the New Collectors Group. A lifelong fan of A. Merritt, Bok finished two incomplete Merritt novels, which the house published in hardcover editions with Bok's illustrations. Some questionable business activities by one of the other members of the group caused the company to cease publication, with Bok losing money in the deal; it was his first and last taste of the publishing end of science fiction.

Meanwhile, Bok continued to work for the many science fiction magazines in the field. His art was in demand by all of the smaller companies, but he never seemed to be able to sell to the best markets. Again, his lack of discipline and fannish habits worked against him. When the market suffered major reversals in the 1950s, Bok left illustration and became an astrologer, maintaining only a few contacts in the SF community.

Bok was the first major stylist in the pulp science fiction market. He was never a master craftsman and was primarily concerned with horror and fantasy art. His pieces were free flowing and stylized and in no way realistic. Lush curves and exaggerated detail ruled. His humans were not photographic but pixiesh. His monsters were creatures of nightmare, bizarre and unusual but rarely frightening. Along with Virgil Finlay★, Bok was considered the greatest SF artist of the 1940s. But he has gained little recognition outside the field since his death of a heart attack at the age of fifty.

PUBLISHED WORK:

HC: *Alien Minds* (55), *And Flight of Angels* (68), *Beyond Infinity* (51), *The Black Wheel* (47), *The Blind Spot* (51), *Bok* (74), *The Castle of Iron* (50), *The Checklist of Fantastic Literature* (48), *The Crystal Horde* (52), *The Fox Woman & The Blue Pagoda* (46), *The Green Man of Graypec* (50), *The Hounds of Tindalos* (46), *The House on the Borderland* (46), *Kinsmen of the Dragon* (51), *Lest Darkness Fall* (49), *The Moon Is Hell* (51), *Out of Space and Time* (42), *Out of the Storm* (75), *The Secrets of Dr. Taverner* (62), *Seven Out of Time* (49), *Sidewise in Time* (50), *Skullface and Others* (46), *Slaves of Sleep* (48), *The Sphinx Child (48), Stardrift* (71), *The Titan* (52), *Under the Triple Suns* (55), *The Wheels of If* (48), *Who Goes There?* (48)

ASH: 1940 (4, 6, 8, 12); 1941 (4, 9, 11); 1942 (3, 6); 1943 (4)

COS: 1941 (3, 5, 7)

F&SF: 1963 (11)

FF: 1953 (3, 6, 8, 11)

FFM: 1941 (2); 1943 (9, 12); 1947 (8, 10); 1949 (8); 1950 (2, 4, 6); 1951 (12); 1952 (6, 12); 1953 (4)

FN: 1940 (11); 1941 (1); 1950 (11); 1951 (1, 6)

FU: 1956 (10, 11, 12); 1957 (1)

FUT: 1940 (11); 1941 (4, 8, 10, 12); 1942 (2, 4, 8, 10, 12); 1943 (2, 4, 7)

IF: 1968 (12)

IMG: 1950 (10); 1951 (6, 9)

MSS: 1951 (8, 11)

OW: 1950 (7, 10, 11); 1951 (5); 1952 (4); 1953 (1, 3, 6); 1956 (2, 6)

PS: 1940 (winter); 1941 (spring, summer, fall, winter)

ScS: 1953 (10)

SF: 1941 (3, 6, 9)

SFQ: 1941 (spring, summer); 1942 (winter, spring, fall); 1943 (winter)

SpSF: 1953 (3)

SS: 1941 (5)

STAR: 1941 (2, 4, 6); 1942 (3)

StrS: 1940 (6, 8)

TSF: 1951 (spring)

2CSFA: 1954 (spring)

UK: 1942 (12)

WT: 1939 (12); 1940 (1, 3, 5, 7, 9, 11); 1941 (1, 3, 5, 7, 9, 11); 1942 (1, 3, 5, 7, 11); 1943 (7, 9, 11); 1944 (1, 3, 5, 7, 11); 1951 (1, 3)

WS: 1972 (8)

PORTFOLIOS: *Blind Spot & Spot of Life* (51), *Bokanalia Foundation Folio # 1, 2, 3, Fantasy Folio # 1, The Powers Lithographs* (45), *Sketchbook* (67), *Utopia Publications* (48)

MISC: Fantasy Calendar 1949 (seven plates), Fantasy Calendar 1950 (five plates), Fantasy Press Bookplates—three different (51)

BONESTELL, CHESLEY (Jan. 1, 1888–June 11, 1986) American artist. Born in San Francisco, Bonestell attended St. Ignatius College and George Bates University in that city. He attended Hopkins Art Institute in the evenings and later entered Columbia University as an architecture major. After three years he left, intending to return after gaining some practical experience, but he never received a degree. He worked as a designer for prominent San Francisco architect Willis Polk and helped design many famous landmarks.

Bonestell married Mary Hilton in November 1911 and was separated in 1918. In 1918 he moved to New York, where he again worked as an architect and collaborated with Rockwell Kent on an eighty-foot mural of the early history of Maine.

In 1922 Bonestell married Ruby Helder, an English concert singer, and moved to London, where he worked for *Illustrated London News*. He returned to the United States some years later and continued working on major architectural projects, including the designing of the Golden Gate Bridge. In 1938 he began working as a matte artist for the motion-picture industry. In 1939 his second wife died, and in 1940 he remarried his first wife.

In the early 1940s Bonestell began painting a series of space illustrations, most of which were published in *Life*. These major paintings combined technical realism and stunning photographic technique. Bonestell specialized in astronomical art for the rest of his career. His most notable achievements were illustrations for ten books on space science, including the influential *Conquest of Space*, done between 1949 and 1972. Many of these paintings were printed as covers for science fiction magazines before their inclusion in these books. Bonestell also painted a number of huge murals for major institutions depicting outer space scenes as they might be seen from off-Earth locations.

In 1950 Bonestell worked on the backgrounds for the first realistic science fiction film *Destination Moon*. He later prepared all the backgrounds for the important SF films *When Worlds Collide* (51), *War of the Worlds* (53), and *The Conquest of Space* (53). In 1967 Bonestell moved back to California. Winner of numerous art awards, Chesley Bonestell was awarded the special Achievement Hugo in 1974.

Bonestell's wife died in 1961, and in the fall of 1962 he married Hulda von Neumayer Ray. He died at age ninety-eight, perhaps the most respected and famous space artist ever, whose career spanned the whole history of manned air flight.

PUBLISHED WORK:

HC: *Across the Space Frontier* (52), *Best from F & SF #1* (52), *Best from F&SF #2* (53), *Best from F&SF #3* (54), *Beyond Jupiter* (72), *Beyond the Solar System* (64),

Complete Book of Outer Space (53), *Conquest of the Moon* (53), *The Conquest of Space* (49), *The Exploration of Mars* (56), *Man and the Moon* (61), *Mars* (64), *The Solar System & Rocket to the Moon, The World We Life In* (55)

ASF: 1947 (10); 1948 (4, 7); 1949 (6); 1950 (1); 1951 (11); 1954 (12).

F&SF: 1950 (12); 1951 (8); 1952 (2, 10, 12); 1953 (3); 1954 (2, 10, 11, 12); 1955 (4, 9, 12); 1956 (2, 4, 7); 1957 (9); 1959 (2); 1960 (10); 1961 (10); 1962 (12); 1963 (10); 1964 (10); 1965 (10); 1966 (7); 1967 (2, 10); 1968 (9); 1969 (9, 10); 1970 (4, 10); 1971 (11); 1972 (3); 1974 (8); 1975 (3); 1976 (10); 1977 (10); 1978 (3)

GXY: 1951 (2, 5)

BORIS. See VALLEJO, BORIS.

BOWMAN, WILLIAM R. (?) American artist. An excellent black-and-white illustrator, Bowman worked primarily for the smaller science fiction magazines for a brief period from 1956 through 1958. He served as art associate for *Infinity* and *Science Fiction Adventures* from August 1956 through October 1957.

PUBLISHED WORK:

AMZ: 1957 (7)

GXY: 1957 (8, 9, 11, 12)

INF: 1957 (2, 4, 9, 10, 11); 1958 (1, 3, 6, 8)

SAT: 1958 (10)

SFA: 1956 (12); 1957 (2, 4, 6, 8, 9, 10, 12); 1958 (1)

SFA(BR): 1958 (1, 4)

SSF: 1957 (6, 8, 10, 12); 1958 (2, 4, 6, 8, 10, 12); 1959 (2)

BRANDT, ROLF A. 1906-Jan. 30, 1986) British artist. A British subject, Brandt was born in Hamburg, Germany, and moved to England after Hitler's rise to power in 1933. He is best remembered by collectors of bizarre and fantasy illustration for his artistic contributions to a number of books published in London during the 1940s. His art appeared under the byline of R. A. Brandt and included *Come Not, Lucifer,* an anthology of horror stories; *The Devil's Heir, and Other Tales from "Les Contes Drolatiques"* by Honore de Balzac; and *Gargantua and Pategruel* by Rabelais. His artwork was reminiscent of both Sidney Sime★ and Mervyn Peake★. It was noteworthy for its powerful imagery and strong overtone of the macabre. Among his later commissions were drawings done for *The Earth-Owl and Other Moon-People* by Ted Hughes (now the British poet-laureate). A collection of his most recent fifty weird and fantastic drawings entitled *Apparitions* was published in 1984.

Brandt had several one-man shows of his paintings and drawings in the Paris Gallery, as well as the Institute of Contemporary Art in London and the Pater Gallery in Milan. His style in later years became increasingly obscure and abstract. He died in London in January 1986.

PUBLISHED WORK:

HC: *Apparitions* (84), *Come Not, Lucifer* (45), *The Devil's Heir and Other Tales from "Les Contests Drolatieques"* (45), *The Earth-Owl and Other Moon-People* (63)

Richard Dalby

BRAUTIGAM, DONALD P. (b. Sept. 12, 1946) American artist. Born in Paterson, New Jersey, Brautigam began his professional career while attending the School of Visual Arts with the sale of a piece to "Sesame Street." He is married, with two sons, James and Daniel, and works as a freelance illustrator. Influences include Gilbert Stone; Doug Johnson; Norman Rockwell; J. C. Leyendecker; Maxfield Parrish; the art director at New American Library, James Plumeri; his art teacher in high school; and his father.

Brautigam works in acrylics on boards, with airbrush and brush mixture. He has prepared advertising art, magazine covers, record-album covers, hardcover and paperback book illustrations, and many other works. His cover for *The Stand* was awarded Cover of the Year by Marketing Best-sellers, and he has won numerous other awards and commendations.

PUBLISHED WORK:

HC: *The Stand*

PB: *Dark Companions, Donors, Family Trade, Feral, Green Ripper, Heads, Killer Flies, The Man Who Would Not Die, Nightshift, Nightwalker, Pain, The Playground, The Ritual, Robots, Sargasso of Space, The Stand, The Surrogate, Threat, Time Gate, Winter Lord.*

BRILLHART, RALPH (?) American artist. A prolific paperback cover artist, Brillhart produced competent but unexciting artwork for Monarch's short-lived science fiction line. He also prepared a scattering of science fiction covers for other paperback publishers including Belmont Books and Pyramid.

PUBLISHED WORK:

PB: *Colors of Space* (63), *D–99* (63), *Day the Earth Froze* (63), *Day the Machines Stopped* (64), *Day the Oceans Overflowed* (64), *Memory Bank* (62), *Mr. George and Other Odd Persons* (64), *Planet Big Zero* (64), *Rest in Agony* (63), *Running Man* (63), *Space Prison* (62), *Ten from Infinity* (63), *Unending Night* (64), *Witch House* (62), *World Grabbers* (64)

BROSNATCH, ANDREW (1896-?) American artist. An early illustrator for *Weird Tales* magazine, Brosnatch illustrated many famous horror and fantasy stories in the 1920s and proved to be unequal to the task. His mediocre covers were surpassed only by his equally terrible interior illustrations. Brosnatch worked for *Weird Tales* in a period when the magazine was on shaky financial ground and payment to artists was among the lowest of all pulp magazines. He was, according to the editor of the publications, "a bargain artist," that is, one who would work for much less than the going rate for magazine illustrations. But his art was not a bargain at any price. Fortunately, the magazine prospered, and Brosnatch disappeared from its pages.

Originally from Pennsylvania, he lived in Indiana during the time he worked for *Weird Tales*. Once he lost his market for illustration with that magazine, he left the pulp field.

PUBLISHED WORK:

WT: 1924 (11, 12); 1925 (1, 2, 3, 4, 5, 6, 7, 8, 9, 10, 11, 12); 1926 (1, 2, 3, 4)

BROWN, HOWARD V. (July 5, 1878-?) American artist. One of the most popular early science fiction magazine illustrators, Brown was born in Lexington, Kentucky, and studied at the Art Institute in Chicago. A member of many professional art societies during his life, Brown was a prolific artist with his science fiction art representing only a small part of his total output.

His earliest science fiction art was done not for the science fiction magazines (*Amazing* being the only magazine published, and it was completely dominated by the work of Frank R. Paul*) but for *Argosy*, which published a great deal of science fiction in the late 1920s. Brown painted covers for science fiction stories such as "Darkness on Fifth Avenue" (29), "Rain Magic" (28), and "The Girl in the Moon" (28).

Brown was a prolific cover artist and was noted for his striking use of colors and willingness to portray fantastic monsters. When *Astounding Science Fiction* was bought by Street & Smith, Brown was brought in to handle the covers, displacing Hans Wesso*. Brown was one of the greatest of the BEM (bug-eyed monster) painters for the pulps. His interiors, done in charcoal pencil, were much more subdued but equally well done. From 1933 through 1937 Brown dominated the covers of *Astounding*. In 1936 he prepared a series of highly acclaimed illustrations for two H. P. Lovecraft novels, *The Shadow Out of Time* and *At the Mountains of Madness*. However, when John W. Campbell became editor of the magazine, he wanted a different look, something less garish: Brown's wild covers were out. Almost immediately, Brown began painting covers for *Thrilling Wonder Stories* and *Startling Stories*, published by Standard magazines. The Standard pulps were aimed at a somewhat more juvenile audience than *Astounding*, and Brown's art matched the contents perfectly. Many of the artist's finest monster covers were painted for these magazines.

PUBLISHED WORK:

ASF: 1933 (11, 12); 1934 (1, 2, 3, 4, 5, 6, 7, 8, 9, 10, 11, 12); 1935 (1, 2, 3, 4, 5, 6, 7, 8, 9, 10, 11, 12); 1936 (1, 2, 3, 4, 5, 6, 7, 8, 9, 10, 11, 12); 1937 (1, 2, 3, 4, 5, 7, 8, 10, 12); 1938 (2, 4, 5, 6, 7, 10, 11); 1939 (2)

SS: 1939 (1, 5, 7); 1940 (1, 5)

TWS: 1936 (8, 10, 12); 1937 (2, 4, 6, 10, 12); 1938 (2, 4, 6, 8, 10, 12); 1939 (2, 4, 6, 8, 10, 12); 1940 (1, 2, 3, 4, 5, 6, 7, 8)

BRUNDAGE, MARGARET (1900–1976) American artist. In a field dominated until just a few years ago by men Brundage was one of the few women to make an indelible mark. She was the leading cover artist for *Weird Tales* during the height of the pulp's popularity and strongly influenced the style and content of the work of many other artists who followed.

Born Margaret Johnson, the artist was a lifelong resident of Chicago. A student early in her life at the Art Institute, she received her formal training at the Chicago Academy of Fine Art but never obtained a degree. She was married in 1927 to Myron Brundage, and a son, Robert, was born in 1929. Her marriage led to her art career since a wandering husband who disappeared for weeks at a time, a baby son, and an invalid mother forced her to work as an agency artist and fashion designer. But the Depression made fashion jobs scarce so she sought magazine work.

The only publishing house with an office in Chicago was *Weird Tales*. Brundage had no knowledge of the contents of the pulp and was not familiar with fantasy or science fiction. However, a Far East female art study in her portfolio caught the eye of Farnsworth Wright, editor of both *Weird Tales* and a companion magazine, *Oriental Stories*. Brundage was signed to paint a cover for the latter magazine. The art proved so popular that Wright gave Brundage a *Weird Tales* cover assignment. Soon she crowded all other artists from the cover of the magazine and became the only woman who was an important science fiction pulp cover artist.

Brundage's earliest covers showed the strong influence of fashion design, featuring a prominent female figure, usually partially clothed, with a vague menace hinted at in the background. She was very good at painting women but was not very good at portraying menaces or monsters. Since she could not afford models, she used magazine photos instead. Farnsworth Wright, picking up on his artist's strong points, soon had the women with less and less clothing, and the erotic aspects of the pictures increased. Even in the pulp magazines of the 1930s sex sold.

Brundage used pastel chalks for her paintings, and the colors gave her work a soft beauty that was unlike anything else being published in the magazine field. Whereas the powerful covers by Hans Wesso★ for *Strange Tales* offered supernatural thrills, Brundage's chalk work promised the thrill of beautiful women and unspeakable threats to their virtue.

At first the covers were well received, with many readers writing in enthusiastic praise. However, as the nudes grew bolder, reader sentiment began to change. When Wright revealed that the covers were being done by a woman, complaints filled the letter column of *Weird Tales*: it was all right to feature nudes on the cover but not nudes that were painted by another woman.

Wright continued to use Brundage despite the complaints. During the height of the Depression, magazines competed bitterly for readers. Cover illustrations sold magazines, and Wright knew that his regulars would buy his publication regardless. Moreover, the nudes attracted one-time buyers who otherwise never would have looked at his magazine.

Several authors, seeing the slant that Brundage covers had taken, made sure that their stories featured at least one scene with a nude woman in jeopardy. Seabury Quinn freely admitted that he aimed his stories for the cover of *Weird Tales* by featuring naked women in his work no matter what the main theme of the tale was. When Virgil Finlay★ first began illustrating covers for *Weird Tales*, many of his paintings showed a strong Brundage influence. Wright thought that Brundage-style nudes sold his magazine, and no matter who did the cover, the illustration had to remain the same.

When *Weird Tales* was sold in late 1938 and its editorial offices moved to New York City, Brundage found herself without a job. Her pastel paintings had to be kept under glass at all times, and shipping glass to New York was expensive. In addition, Brundage used to visit Wright at his office every week to discuss cover ideas, but now editor and artist conferences were impossible. Therefore, Virgil Finlay, who lived on the East Coast, took over cover assignments for *Weird Tales*.

Brundage found little market in Chicago for her pastel nudes and left the fantasy art field, although she did sell a few more paintings to *Weird Tales* in the 1940s. By this time she was divorced from her husband and was forced to take various low-paying art jobs. Forgotten by most science fiction and fantasy fans, she died in near poverty after a long illness.

Brundage's nudes brought sex to the covers of science fiction and fantasy magazines. Most covers before hers had featured either giant machinery, spaceships, or monsters. Brundage's work proved that the same type of cover that sold many other pulp magazines would also work for the SF-fantasy lines. She was the first of many artists to become known for women-in-peril-style covers.

PUBLISHED WORK:

FA: 1945 (4)

WT: 1932 (9, 10); 1933 (3, 6, 7, 8, 9, 10, 11, 12); 1934 (1, 2, 3, 4, 5, 6, 7, 8, 9, 10, 11, 12); 1935 (1, 2, 3, 4, 5, 6, 7, 8, 9, 10, 11, 12); 1936 (1, 2, 3, 4, 5, 6, 7, 8–9, 11); 1937 (1, 3, 5, 6, 8, 9, 10, 11); 1938 (1, 3, 5, 6, 8, 9, 10); 1940 (3, 7, 11); 1941 (3, 7, 9); 1942 (7); 1943 (5, 9); 1944 (5); 1945 (1); 1953 (11)

Robert Weinberg and R. A. Everts

BULL, REINA M. (?) British artist. Bull had a brief flourish with fame for her distinctive covers painted for John Carnell's *New Worlds* and *Science Fantasy* in 1951–52. Called "one of the most remarkable artists to enter the British field" by Brian Aldiss, Bull's art could not be called attractive, but her paintings were full of action, power, and menace and carried (as Aldiss observed in *Science Fiction Art*), "high sexual charges." Perhaps these qualities were stoo strong for the modest English readership or perhaps Bull found commitments elsewhere; in any case, her work ceased to appear after 1952. Her paintings were signed "RMB."

PUBLISHED WORKS: (All British magazines).

NW: 1951 (fall); 1952 (11)

ScF: 1951 (winter); 1952 (spring)

Mike Ashley

BURNS, JIM (Apr. 10, 1948) British artist. Born in Cardiff, Wales, Burns was obsessed from an early age with flying machines and airplanes. A devoted fan of Frank Hampson's★ *Dan Dare* comic-strip series in *Eagle* magazine, Burns entered the Royal Air Force as a trainee pilot in 1966. After two years of this, he joined the Newport School of Art. From 1969 through 1972 he attended the St. Martin's School of Art, from which he received a diploma in art and design.

Since graduation, Burns has painted numerous book and paperback covers. He specializes in historical romances and science fiction and is equally adept with gouache, acrylic, watercolor, and oil. A collection of his work, featuring one hundred color illustrations, was published by Dragon's World in 1986.

PUBLISHED WORK: (All British publications).

PB: *The Anome, The Asutra, Best of SF 8, Beyond Bedlam, The Brave Free Men, The Fifth Head of Cerberus, The Ice Schooner, Kalivide* (82), *The Sirens of Titan, Year's Best Fantasy Stories #10* (84)

IF: 1966 (9, 12); 1967 (1, 2)

Richard Dalby

BURR, LINDA (b. Jan. 6, 1951) American artist. Burr attended the Memphis College of Art and the University of Tennessee in Knoxville. She has worked as a visual coordinator for the Missouri Mines Historical Site and an art instructor for the Mineral Area College. She was influenced by the Impressionists, particularly Claude Monet, and by John Millais, William Holman Hunt, and Hieronymus Bosch. Other artists whose work she considers important to her own include Max Ernst and Salvador Dali. She works with oil on canvas, frequently done over air-brushed acrylic underpainting. In black-and-white work, she uses pencil.

As to her philosophy in art, she believes that "art is the continuous remixing of the imagination and observation, to the result of expressing the vision that exists in my mind's eye. To do this successfully is the greatest of satisfactions."

Burr has worked for the Science Fiction Book Club, St. Martins Press, Arbor House, and many of the science fiction magazines. She is a member of Buckhorn Studios.

PUBLISHED WORK:

HC: *5000 BC* (82), *Blood of Amber* (86), *Worlds End*

BURROUGHS, JOHN COLEMAN (Feb. 28, 1913–1979) American artist. The third child of Edgar Rice Burroughs, John Burroughs was trained as an artist and illustrator and graduated Phi Beta Kappa from Pomona College in 1934. He illustrated thirteen of his father's books, beginning in 1937 and continuing until Edgar Rice Burroughs's death in 1950. He also wrote several science fiction stories in collaboration with his brother Hulbert Burroughs. After the death of his father, Burroughs turned to fine art and became a painter of scenes of the Southwest. He did many character studies of Indians and cowboys and had many successful one-man shows and gallery exhibits throughout the West.

PUBLISHED WORK:

HC: *Back to the Stone Age* (37), *Carson of Venus* (39), *The Deputy Sheriff of Comanche County* (41), *Escape on Venus* (46), *The Lad and the Lion* (38), *The Land of Terror* (44), *Llana of Gathol* (48), *The Oakdale Affair & The Rider* (37), *Synthetic Men of Mars* (40), *Tarzan and the Forbidden City* (38), *Tarzan and the Foreign Legion* (47), *Tarzan the Magnificent* (39)
SS: 1941 (9)

CALDWELL, CLYDE (?) American artist. Caldwell received the MFA from the University of North Carolina in Greensboro. His artwork has appeared both as science fiction and fantasy covers as well as for fringe magazines such as *Heavy Metal* and *The Dragon and The Savage Sword of Conan*. Much of his recent work has been for TSR Hobbies, illustrating various Dungeons and Dragons games. Caldwell and his wife, Susan, are parents of a daughter, Kelly.

PUBLISHED WORK:

HC: *Celestial Steam Locomotive* (83)
PB: *Night Fear* (79), *Oron* (78)

CALLE, PAUL (b. 1928) American artist. Born in New York City, Calle attended Pratt Institute in Brooklyn and sold his first illustration to *Liberty* magazine at the age of nineteen. He began working for the pulps in the late

1940s and, after a few years, moved on to better paying markets. Calle illustrated for *McCalls*, *The Saturday Evening Post*, *National Geographic*, and *Fortune*, among others. He was selected as official artist for the NASA Fine Arts Program and designed the "First Man on the Moon" stamp for the Post Office, one of thirteen stamps he has designed for that service. He also served as the official artist covering the Apollo-Soyuz training for NASA. Calle now does historical paintings, which have won him a large following. His works are in the permanent collections of many museums as well as in the NASA collection.

PUBLISHED WORK:

HC: *Star Seekers* (53)
AMF: 1949 (12); 1950 (4, 7, 10)
GXY: 1953 (3)
GXYN: 1950 (2)
IMG: 1953 (7); 1954 (3)
SSS: 1949 (11); 1950 (1, 3, 5, 7, 9, 11); 1951 (8)
WB: 1950 (12)

CANEDO, ALEJANDRO (?) American artist. Canedo contributed a number of striking, somewhat surrealistic covers to *Astounding Science Fiction* in the late 1940s using the pen name Alejandro.

PUBLISHED WORK:

ASF: 1946 (12); 1947 (9, 12); 1948 (2, 5, 8, 9); 1949 (3, 10); 1952 (9); 1954 (7)

CANTOR, ANN (?) American artist. Cantor was a staff artist for Avon paperbacks during the 1940s and early 1950s. During this period, art was not credited on covers, but a search of copyright records by paperback collector Michael Barson uncovered Cantor as one of the mainstays of the Avon line. The publishing house printed many of the earliest science fiction paperbacks, and Cantor was responsible for the art in several important books in that line. Since many of the Avon covers were not credited even in the copyright registrations, it is likely that Cantor did many other books in the Avon science fiction line; covers such as *The Green Girl*, *Princess of the Atom*, and *Perelandra* feature art very similar to those definitely identified as Cantor's work.

PUBLISHED WORK:

PB: *The Daughter of Fu Manchu* (50), *The Girl with the Hungry Eyes* (49), *Out of the Silent Planet* (50)

CANTY, THOMAS (?) American artist. Working in a variety of media from graphite to watercolor to oil, Cantry is known for his delicate line work and meticulous detailing. He looks at art as augmenting or illuminating a mood, rather than as the story itself. In the *1982 World Fantasy Program Book* Canty stated, "By illustrating the mood of a book, allowing the subject a knowledge of the viewer, and combining texture and style in the drawing or painting, I always try to move toward a harmony between what's written and implied, between picture and print."

Canty was nominated as Best Artist for the 1981 World Fantasy Awards. His work is included in the permanent collection of the New Britain Museum of American Art.

PUBLISHED WORK:

HC: *The Changing Land*

CARTIER, EDD (b. Aug. 1, 1914) American artist. One of the most influential artists in the science fiction pulps, Cartier helped establish humor as one of the major ways to illustrate a science fiction or fantasy story.

Born as Edward Daniel Cartier in North Bergen, New Jersey, he attended Pratt Institute in Brooklyn, where one of his teachers was pulp artist H. W. Scott★. Cartier graduated with a three-year certificate from Pratt in 1936 and was immediately hired by the Street & Smith publishing chain. The artist was put to work illustrating love, western, and detective stories in the various Street & Smith pulp magazines. Soon after starting work for the company, Cartier found himself providing illustrations for the biweekly single-character detective pulp *The Shadow*.

At first Cartier followed the lead of previous artists who had illustrated that pulp and produced dark and murky drawings, tying in with the theme of the novels, that of a mysterious crime fighter who stayed in the shadows. However, Cartier began developing a style of his own for the magazine and by 1937 had changed the focus of the art in the pulp. Light replaced dark, and instead of mood pieces, action dominated. Strong characterization pieces for all of the major players were used. Using a brush and lithographic pencil, Cartier became the Shadow's definitive illustrator, producing more than eight hundred illustrations for that magazine.

John W. Campbell, Jr., who edited *Astounding Stories* for Street & Smith, recognized Cartier's talents and approached him with an assignment for a new Street & Smith magazine. *Unknown* was an innovative new pulp, a fantasy magazine printing logical fantasy stories, often with strong humorous elements. Cartier illustrated *Sinister Barrier*, the lead novel in the first issue of *Unknown*, as well as "The Trouble with Water," an influential short humor story. A perfect match had been formed. Cartier's illustrations became an integral part of the magazine. His exceptional cover paintings were masterpieces of fantasy artwork, and authors and fans alike lavished praise on his black-and-white interiors. His *Shadow* characterizations had shown that he could give life and depth to the most bizarre criminals. Therefore, Cartier was given full range to show what he could do with a vast array of fantastic beings. Subtle nuances became full-blown whimsy. His gnomes, elves, goblins, and bemused humans perfectly fit the stories they illustrated. For the first time in the history of science fiction, an artist had emerged who specialized in humor. In the thirty-nine issues of *Unknown* (later retitled *Unknown Worlds*) Cartier contributed more than two hundred illustrations.

Cartier entered the army in 1941 and was sent overseas shortly after he met and married his wife, Georgina, in 1943. He was gravely wounded at the Battle of the Bulge and did not return to illustrating until 1946. Back at Street & Smith, Cartier found *Unknown* had been dropped in 1943, due to a combination of poor sales and the paper shortage, but that *Astounding SF* was still being published. Cartier had done a few illustrations for that magazine before the war, although his style was less suited for the straight-forward science fiction printed in that pulp. During the war, *Astounding* had shrunk from pulp to digest size. By late 1946 paper quality had improved, and Cartier's illustrations reproduced better in this form.

Cartier's postwar art featured a tighter style and greater concentration on fine detail. More humorous fiction began appearing in *Astounding*, and Cartier was given total control over such stories. Editor Campbell made sure that any story featuring animals, mutants, robots, or bizarre extraterrestrials was given to Cartier.

The Shadow had been cut back from a biweekly to a monthly magazine during the war. To make up for the loss of work, Cartier contributed art work for another Street & Smith pulp, *Doc Savage*, for which he did more than one hundred illustrations. Looking to expand his markets, Cartier also went outside the Street & Smith chain and produced a number of illustrations for other science fiction magazines, including *Fantastic Adventures*, *Other Worlds*, *Planet Stories*, and *Universe SF*. *Astounding*, however, remained his major magazine market.

Among the science fiction small-press publishers, Cartier found another market. The publishers of these hardcover reprints from the SF magazines were all fans of Cartier's work, and they knew that other science fiction fans closely identified the artist with *Astounding* and *Unknown*. He was the top choice to illustrate books reprinting stories from those magazines. His broad, sharp strokes and sweeping line work produced dramatic and striking cover art. Cartier became one of the leading cover artists for the small-press field, creating a number of fine pieces for Fantasy Press and Gnome Press. He also prepared some fine black-and-white interior pieces for Fantasy Press. When Gnome Press published a series of fantasy calendars, Cartier was their choice for artist for most of the illustrations. Later, he designed a series of bookplates for Fantasy Press that were very popular.

Increased work did not seem to mean greatly increased revenue for Cartier. With his wife and two sons, Dean and Kenn, born in the 1950s, to support, Cartier returned to Pratt part time and obtained a degree in fine arts in 1953. He left the science fiction field for the more lucrative field of graphic art and design.

Cartier was the first science fiction artist to demonstrate that there was a place for humorous illustration in the field, and in this he set the standard by which all others were to be judged. More important, in larger terms, Cartier along with Virgil Finlay★ and Hannes Bok★ brought about a revolution in science fiction and fantasy. Before this trio began working in the late 1930s, art in science fiction magazines was considered a waste of paper by most readers. SF art rarely contributed to the stories illustrated. The spectacular art of Finlay, Bok, and Cartier, however, convinced fans and authors alike that illustrations would enhance stories and improve the magazines in which they appeared. Their work generated the first fan mail for artists. It was their contributions that changed magazine science fiction from a print medium to a more graphic form.

PUBLISHED WORK:

HC: *Bridge of Light* (50), *The Cometeers* (50), *Cosmic Engineers* (50), *Darker Than You Think* (49), *Dreadful Sanctuary* (51), *Genus Homo* (50), *Earthman's Burden* (57), *Masters of Time* (50), *Sinister Barrier* (48), *I Robot* (50), *Foundation and Empire* (52), *Journey to Infinity* (51), *Men against the Stars* (50), *Minions of the Moon* (50), *Pattern for Conquest* (49), *Seetee Ship* (51), *Sixth Column* (49), *Travelers of Space* (51), *Vortex Blaster* (62)

PB: *Unknown* (63), *Unknown Five* (64)

ASF: 1939 (6, 8); 1940 (8, 10, 11); 1941 (2, 12); 1942 (2); 1947 (1, 2, 3, 5, 6, 7, 8, 9, 10, 11, 12); 1948 (1, 3, 4, 5, 6, 7, 8, 9, 10, 11, 12); 1949 (1, 2, 3, 4, 6, 7, 8, 9, 10, 11, 12); 1950 (1, 2, 3, 4, 5, 7, 8, 9, 10, 11, 12); 1951 (1, 2, 3, 4, 5, 6, 7, 8, 9, 10, 11, 12); 1952 (1, 2, 3, 4, 5, 6, 7, 8, 9, 10, 11, 12); 1953 (1, 2, 3, 4, 5, 6, 7, 8, 9, 10, 11, 12); 1954 (1, 2, 3, 4, 5, 6, 7, 8, 9, 10, 11, 12); 1955 (1, 2, 3, 4, 5, 6, 7, 8, 9, 10, 11, 12)

FA: 1951 (9)

OW: 1951 (5, 7, 9); 1952 (1, 3, 4, 7); 1953 (6); 1956 (2)

PS: 1951 (3, 5)

UK: 1939 (3, 4, 5, 6, 7, 8, 9, 12); 1940 (2, 3, 4, 5, 6, 7, 8, 9, 10, 11, 12); 1941 (2, 4, 6, 8, 10, 12); 1942 (2, 8, 12); 1943 (2, 8)

UNI: 1953 (3)

From Unknown Worlds. Published in 1948, this was a one-shot reprint collection from *Unknown* that featured a new color cover and all new black-and-white interiors by Cartier.

MISC: Gnome Press Calendars 1949, 1950, 1952, Fantasy Press Bookplates 1952 (four designs)

CAWTHORN, JIM (b. Dec. 21, 1929) British artist. Active in science fiction fandom since 1953, James (Jim) Cawthorn has worked as both an amateur and a professional artist. His first illustrations were done for the

English fanzine *Satellite*, drawing straight onto the stencils before duplication.

Cawthorn is noted as a lifelong devotee of the works of Edgar Rice Burroughs. Many of his black-and-white illustrations appeared in *Tarzan Adventures*. Since the early 1960s he has contributed to *New Worlds*. There is some resemblance between his vigorous and entertaining style and that of Mervyn Peake★ and Burne Hogarth. A friend and sometimes collaborator with noted science fiction author Michael Moorcock, Cawthorn did jacket illustrations for a number of Moorcock's swords-and-sorcery novels. He also collaborated with Moorcock on the script of Burrough's fantastic adventure *The Land That Time Forgot*, filmed in 1974 by Amicus Productions.

PUBLISHED WORK:(All British publications).

HC: *The Jewel in the Skull, The Mad God's Amulet, The Runestaff, Sword of the Dawn*
Richard Dalby

CHAYKIN, HOWARD (b. Oct. 7, 1950) American artist. Born in Newark, New Jersey, Chaykin attended Columbia College in Chicago for eight months, majoring in radio broadcasting, but he felt he was a terrible student and quit. Having been a science fiction fan ever since reading *Space K'at* at age eight, Chaykin gravitated to the SF field because it was easy to get work there. He later took art courses at the School of Visual Arts in New York. A comic art fan, his first professionally published work as an illustrator was in DC Comics, featuring a science fiction hero, Iron Wolf. He then prepared art for Atlas Comics for a short time as well as *National Lampoon*. Chaykin worked for Marvel Comics after this, rendering the comic version of *Star Wars*, which proved to be among the best-selling comic-book series of all time.

In the late 1970s Chaykin turned to science fiction. Working with packager Byron Preiss, Chaykin illustrated a number of science fiction novels published in trade paperbound form with his first work for *Empire* by Samuel Delany and *The Stars My Destination* by Alfred Bester. While acclaimed for their artwork, the books were commercial failures.

Chaykin continued to produce comic art as well as to freelance in the science fiction field. His first paperback cover was painted for *Coils* from TOR books. He contributed a number of covers for TOR paperbacks and seemed to be concentrating more on science fiction than comics when First Comics was organized. A new comic-book publisher, First gave Chaykin a free hand in developing his own comic and characters. Chaykin devoted himself almost entirely to "American Flagg," the character he developed for First, winning numerous awards for his creation. Since that time, Chaykin has moved on to other graphic projects, leaving science fiction behind. At present, he and his wife, Leslie Zahler, also an artist, live in New York City.

Chaykin has a different approach to painting a cover than have many science fiction artists. "I try to sell the book. You have to convince a person to buy the book, and you only have a three-by-four-inch cover to do it. I try to keep my fannish desires and impulses away from the book." Chaykin strongly believes that a cover should not synopsize the book, just sell it. Chaykin wishes that "science fiction art was as interesting as the writing. There is a tremendous desire to reduce the sense of wonder to television terms."

He works in mixed media, using a lot of acrylics, but often using markers, pens, and so on in the same piece.

PUBLISHED WORK:

HC: *The Stars My Destination* (79)

PB: *Empire Star* (78), *Greatheart Silver* (82), *The Purple Book* (82), *The Stars My Destination* (79)

AMZ: 1974 (8)

CHERRY, DAVID A. (b. Dec. 14, 1949) American artist. Born in Lawton, Oklahoma, Cherry was raised in Oklahoma City, where he has lived ever since. He received the BA in Latin with honors and, in 1975, the JD from the University of Oklahoma. He worked for six years with Morgan & Brown, a law firm specializing in interstate transportation law. Always interested in science fiction and science fiction art, he attended his first SF convention with his sister, author C. J. Cherryh, in 1976. Seeing the art show brought home the fact that people could and did make a living illustrating science fiction. It was a mental turning point in his career.

Several years later, he was asked to illustrate *Ealdwood*, a novel written by his sister being published in hardcover by Donald Grant Publishers. The art for that book was his first published work. Soon the desire to become a full-time artist was in conflict with his legal work. However, one of his firm's partner's left for other pursuits, and the other died shortly after. Cherry was able to work out an arrangement with another attorney to do legal work part time at his own convenience and devote the rest of his time to art.

Being allergic to oil paints and turpentine, Cherry uses acrylic underpainting, overpainted with alkyds. He tries to make his covers as realistic as possible, and his interiors he treats as fine-art pieces, suitable for display.

PUBLISHED WORK:

HC: *Ealdwood, Daughter of Regals (Deluxe edition)*

PB: *The Dreamstone, Timescoop*

CHRISTENSEN, JAMES C. (b. Sept. 26, 1942) American artist. Born in Culver City, California, Christensen attended the University of California, Los Angeles, and Brigham Young University; he received the MFA from Brigham Young. A member of the faculty at Brigham Young, Christensen first taught for five years in the California secondary schools and then at Alan Hancock College. He works as a freelance artist on the side and has illustrated book interiors and covers and has handled editorial illustration. Christensen lives in Orem, Utah, with his wife, Carole Larsen, and his five children.

PUBLISHED WORK:

HC: *Lyonesse* (83)

CLARKE, HARRY (Mar. 17, 1889–1931) British artist. Clarke was one of a select group of artists from the golden age of book illustration in the distinguished company of Arthur Rackham, Edmund Dulac, and Kay Nielsen, whose works have become very highly prized by collectors. Often called "the outstanding Symbolist of Ireland" and considered the greatest stained-glass artist of his generation, Clarke is best remembered today both for his exceptionally detailed and imaginative horror-fantasy style and for his beautiful illustrations for the fairy tales of Andersen and Perrault.

Born on St. Patrick's Day in Dublin, Ireland, Harry Patrick Clarke became a stained-glass apprentice at age fourteen and during the next decade spent much of his time reading, drawing, and studying graphic art. He traveled extensively in Ireland, Britain, and France. In 1914 he married art teacher Margaret Crilley.

His five great series of book illustrations were all commissioned by the London publisher George Harrap. For the juvenile market, there were the delightful *Hans Andersen's Fairy Tales* in 1916, *The Years at the Spring* in 1920, and *The Fairy Tales of Perrault* in 1922. In the weird-horror market, Clarke composed the brilliant illustrations for Poe's *Tales of Mystery and Imagination* in 1919 and Goethe's *Faust* in 1925. His work in this genre has never been equaled.

It is now generally acknowledged that Clarke was the greatest and most successful of all artists who have attempted to illustrate the stories of Edgar Allan Poe. Even the later fine work by Arthur Rackham pales in comparison. The eminent art critic Malcolm Salaman, writing in *The Studio* in 1923 and 1924, stated that Clarke's "tremendous imagination vitalizing pictorially with amazing power and invention, the *Tales of Mystery and Imagination*. Never before, I think, have these marvelous tales been visually interpreted with such flesh-creeping, brain-haunting, illusions of horror, terror and the unspeakable. In black and white, Mr. Clarke sets pictures before us that glimpse for us fresh meanings in the tales and at the same time give us artistic satisfaction."

The book was so well received that a completely new and reedited version was produced in the autumn of 1923. This edition had eight new plates in color, tipped in on grey paper. The first edition of 1919 was illustrated in black and white. Many further reprints have appeared in the past sixty years including a pirated edition by the Tudor Company of New York in 1933 and the latest British edition of 1985. It has remained the most popular edition of Poe's *Tales* ever printed.

Clarke's last book for Harrap, Goethe's *Faust*, was considered by many critics to be his graphic masteriece, even greater than the work for Poe's *Tales*. One thousand signed copies were produced for the United States, with another thousand for Britain. The edition was bound in quarter vellum, and the illustrations comprise eight color plates, eight wash drawings, six full-page line drawings, and fifty text decorations on hand-made paper.

There is a magical combination of horror, drama, and humor in these brilliant illustrations, especially in the characters of the semifemale Mephistopheles and the rejuvenated Faust. The features of the latter are definitely based on those of Clarke himself, and there is an enigmatic parallel between the wistful Margaret, who in the story knows her lover Faust as Henry (Clarke's original name), and the real life Clarkes: Margaret and Henry.

The leading Irish writer George Russell commented that in the sheer imaginative genius of portraying the "fabulous incubi or succubi of medieval wizardry living beyond the grave . . . Clarke is not the artist of men and women but the seer of forms which their passions and imaginations assume." The nightmarish drawings of Walpurgis Night and the Witches on the Brocken are especially unforgettable.

A major exhibition of Clarke's work was opened by President Cosgrave in Dublin on August 3, 1925. It marked the peak of the artist's career. The intensity and long hours of his work led to agonizing headaches and a severe eye infection. Clarke suffered recurrent bouts of tuberculosis, and this resulted in his premature death in Coire, Switzerland, in January 1931, two months before his forty-second birthday.

Clarke's eight stunning black-and-white drawings for Coleridge's *Rime of the Ancient Mariner*, executed in 1913, were long thought to be lost. They were discovered in Dublin seventy years after their execution and were published for the first time in 1986, alongside the poem as originally intended.

The influence of Clarke on later twentieth-century fantasy, horror, and science fiction illustrators was monumental. Virgil Finlay★, Lawrence Sterne Stevens★, Vincent Napoli★, and Wallace Smith★ were a few of the many artists whose work showed a strong Clarke influence. His strong line work and masterful black-and-white illustrations were so popular and well known that virtually every major modern artist after him was exposed to Clarke's works. Nearly seventy years after their publication, his illustrations for Poe's short stories are still considered the definitive art for these works.

PUBLISHED WORK:

HC: *Faust* (25), *The Rime of the Ancient Mariner* (86), *Tales of Mystery and Imagination* (19), *Tales of Mystery and Imagination* (23)

Richard Dalby

CLOTHIER, ROBERT (?) British artist. The first regular cover artist for *New Worlds Magzine*, starting with the fifth issue in 1949, Clothier painted ten covers for that magazine as well as six for *Nebula*, along with many interior illustrations.

Clothier was not a particularly talented artist. His portrayal of people was crude, and the picture relied mostly on the depth and breadth of his imagination to bring them alive. He concentrated predominantly on simple scenes of spaceships on alien landscapes, but he had a tendency to spoil his paintings by incorporating too much in them. It became a feature of Cloth-ier's covers for him to hide his name somewhere in the painting—on the side of a vehicle or on a hoarding.

Of Clothier, *New Worlds* editor John Carnell wrote: "In Britain, where fantasy art has not been developed at all in the past, it is extremely difficult to find artists with any flair for the medium at all. Both Clothier and (Alan) Hunter★ are improving, but, like authors, need practise and guidance before they produce their best."

Clothier's work did steadily improve, and his best covers were done for *Nebula* in which his simple stark portrayal of a rocket on the moon for issue 9 (August 1954) was considered to be his best work. However, the rising popularity of Gerald Quinn★ soon resulted in his replacement of Clothier as the regular cover artist, and Clothier disappeared from the magazines.

PUBLISHED WORK:

NEB: (3, 4, 5, 6, 7, 8, 9, 10, 12)

NW: (5, 6, 7, 8, 9, 10, 11, 12, 13, 14, 16, 18, 19, 20, 21)

ScF: 1952 (winter, spring, fall); 1953 (spring); 1954 (7)

Mike Ashley

CLYNE, RONALD (b. 1925) American artist. One of the few fantasy artists who made the leap from the narrow confines of the genre to major success as a commercial artist, Cline was a Chicago fan in the early 1940s and contributed to a number of fanzines published in the Midwest. His popularity in fanzines prompted him to submit artwork to the SF pulps, and he began selling art to *Famous Fantastic Mysteries*. It was in 1945 that Clyne believed his true art career began. Encouraged by his success in the pulp field, the artist submitted a sample of his work to August Derleth, editor and publisher of Arkham House Books, the only specialty press printing weird and fantasy fiction. Derleth liked what he saw and com-missioned Clyne to paint a cover for the press. Clyne's first painting was for *Something Near*, a collection of Derleth short stories. During that same year, Clyne did four more dust-jacket illustrations. Also, Clyne was commissioned to design a colophon for a new imprint published by Arkham, Mycroft and Moran, which specialized in Sherlockian type works but also published fantasy.

In 1946 Clyne continued to work for Arkham House, illustrating another five jackets. One of those jackets was for the book *Fearful Pleasures*, a collection of A. E. Coppard ghost stories. The jacket was seen by an art director, and Clyne was offered a commission to illustrate a book of Voltaire's short stories. It was Clyne's first venture into the commercial-art field. Later that same year, Clyne's illustration for the book *This Mortal Coil* was listed as one of the fifty best jackets published during that year. The honor helped push him further into the commercial-art field. He continued to prepare artwork for Arkham House, but his interest in fantasy fiction declined as his career in commercial design continued to increase. Clyne illustrated a few Arkham House books throughout the years, with his last work being for *The Abominations of Yondo* in 1960. Never paid more than about fifty dollars for his art, Clyne considered his work for Arkham House to be a labor of love.

Now a very successful commercial artist, Clyne lives in a two-story brownstone apartment, which he designed, filled with an exceptional collection of primitive and modern art. In an interview published in *Xenophile* #18 (1975), Clyne made it clear why he abandoned fantasy art: "because I didn't want to end up doing hack work for five to ten dollars for the rest of my life."

PUBLISHED WORK:

HC: *The Abominations of Yondo* (60), *Beachheads in Space* (52), *The Clock Strikes Twelve* (46), *The Curse of Yig* (53), *The Doll and One Other* (46), *Fearful Pleasures* (46), *The Fourth Book of Jorkens* (48), *Green Tea and Other Ghost Stories* (45), *The Lurker at the Threshhold* (45), *Night's Black Agents* (47), *Not Long for this World* (48), *The Opener of the Way* (45), *Revelations in Black* (47), *Something about Cats* (49), *Something Near* (45), *The Survivor* (57), *Tales from Underwood* (52), *This Mortal Coil* (47), *The Throne of Saturn* (49), *West India Lights* (46), *Witch House* (45), *Worlds of Tomorrow* (53)

AKS: 1948 (winter, spring, summer, fall); 1949 (winter, spring, summer, fall)

AMZ: 1943 (7, 11); 1944 (1); 1948 (4)

FA: 1941 (11); 1943 (8); 1945 (7); 1949 (3)

FFM: 1944 (9, 12); 1945 (12); 1946 (4); 1948 (10)

PS: 1944 (spring, summer)

WT: 1944 (3); 1946 (5)

COBB, RON (b. 1937), American artist. Born in Echo Park, Los Angeles, Cobb grew up in the Burbank area. He attended Burbank High School and graduated in 1955. From 1955 through 1957 he worked as an in-between-er and break-down-artist at the Disney Studios. Cobb had always wanted to do animation and had applied to Disney right out of high school. His main work at the studio was on the cartoon feature "Sleeping Beauty."

In 1957 Cobb left the Disney studio, thinking that animation work was too tedious. From 1960 to 1963 he served in the U.S. Army, spending a year in Vietnam with the Signal Corp. When he left the army, Cobb decided to become a freelance artist, and he had an exhibit at the Encore Theater, where he showed all kinds of work, including art, photos, and cartoons. During this stage of his career, Forrest J. Ackerman, who served as his agent, introduced him to Ray Bradbury, who helped Cobb with his advice and connections. Also at this time, Cobb painted a number of covers for *Famous Monsters of Filmland* magazine to help pay the bills.

In 1966 and 1967 Cobb worked for the *Los Angeles Free Press* as a political cartoonist. In 1972 he moved to Australia, where he worked as a political cartoonist for *The Digger*, a paper in Sidney, Australia. While he was over-seas, Cobb met Robin Love and was married.

In 1973 Cobb began work as a film designer, with his work on *Dark Star*. He soon became one of the most important and innovative workers in the science fiction film-design field.

In 1982 Cobb was one of the ten official artists chosen by NASA to document the launch and landing of the STS4. Two of these paintings are on exhibit in the Smithsonian Aerospace Museum.

Cobb served as art director for Digital Productions in 1982–1983, when he soon became captivated by his current medium, the computer. In 1984 he designed the alien spaceman for the Los Angeles Olympics Closing Ceremony.

Science Fiction film design is the area in which Cobb has made his greatest mark in the art field. He has worked on many of the major films in the genre during the past decade. He helped design some of the elaborate aliens in the Cantina scene in *Star Wars*. For *Alien*, he came up with the concept for the Nostromo and designed about two-thirds of the ship. He designed everything for *Conan the Barbarian*. For *Close Encounters of the Third Kind, Special Edition*, he helped design the Mother Ship. For *Real Genius* he created all of the laser technology. In *My Science Project* he designed the UFO device found by the heroes. He also did design work on *Back to the Future*, *Amazing Stories*, *Raiders of the Lost Ark*, and *Aliens*. Cobb even designed the spaceship used in a music video by ZZ Top.

During the past twenty years, film design has greatly influenced art, and art has greatly influenced film design in the science fiction field. Every new concept shown on the movie screen has been quickly translated into book covers, and most major artists' work has found some expression on the movie screen. In this respect, Cobb's influence in the science fiction art field has been tremendous and pervasive.

Of his career, Cobb believes it has been so varied because of his boundless enthusiasm for the world and his impressions of it. He cannot bear to get stale or recycle ideas. When he senses that the same things keep coming up, he moves to a new medium. At present, he is working with the new computer technology, although he finds it somewhat crude for everything he would like to do. He also likes acrylic, rapidograph, and prismacolor.

To Cobb, the medium is never the important thing in his life; it is the expression of his views. He enjoys having new areas to learn in, and if he can make a living along the way, so much the better.

PUBLISHED WORK:

F&SF: 1959 (7)

CoCONIS, TED (b. 1927) American artist. Born in Chicago, Illinois, Constantinos (Ted) CoConis attended the American Academy of Art in that city for a year and spent three months at the Art Institute of Chicago. Before starting to sell art to magazines, CoConis worked as a studio artist in New York and also taught at the San Francisco Academy of Art. His first published illustration was in *Sunset* magazine in 1954 His artwork includes record album covers, book covers, travel-campaign art, and motion-picture posters. He recently spent several years in Europe and now concentrates primarily on fine-arts work while still doing some story illustrations and movie-poster art. CoConis also owns and drives Formuala race cars.

PUBLISHED WORK:

PB: *Camber of Culdi* (76)

COGGINS, JACK (b. July 10, 1911) American artist. Born in London in a military family, Coggins moved with his family to the United States while still a child. He studied at the Grand Central School of Art and the Art Students League and first specialized in marine painting. During World War II, he did many war illustrations for *Life* and produced commercial art. He served as a U.S. Army correspondent in Europe from 1943 until the end of the war.

Starting in the early 1950s, Coggins painted a number of science fiction magazine covers for *Galaxy* and *Fantasy & SF*. He specialized in paintings of spaceships and astronomical art. He also worked with Fletcher Pratt on several books about space travel.

After his science fiction work, Coggins wrote and illustrated books on military and naval history. He is a member of the National Defense Association and is on the Advisory Committee of the Philadelphia Maritime Museum.

PUBLISHED WORK:

AMZ: 1953 (4)

F&SF: 1953 (3, 8, 9); 1954 (5)

FSQ: 1954 (spring, fall)

GXY: 1952 (5, 7, 9, 11); 1956 (7, 9); 1957 (2, 4, 8)

SFQ: 1953 (11)

SS: 1952 (10)

TWS: 1953 (2, 4, 8); 1954 (winter, summer, fall)

COHEN, RICHARD L. (?) American artist. Described by art historian and critic Vincent Di Fate★ as a "terrific glaze artist in the tradition of Maxfield Parrish," Cohen worked for a number of years for Dell Books on its science fiction line. In recent years, he contributed some fine pieces of art to *Omni* magazine.

PUBLISHED WORK:

PB: *Count Brass, Quest for Tanelorn, The Champion of Garathorm*

COLL, JOSEPH CLEMENT (1881–1921) Called American's greatest virtuoso in the use of pen and ink (in *The Illustrator in America*, 1984), Cole was an excellent illustrator who had a superb command of his medium. Many of his finest illustrations were done for science fiction and fantasy stories.

Coll was born in Philadelphia, the son of Irish immigrant parents. His father was a bookbinder, so Coll was exposed to books and illustrations all of his life. Born during a period when pen-and-ink illustration was at one of its highest points, Coll was most strongly influenced by the Spanish artist Daniel Vierge. He also thought highly of American illustrators Edwin Austin Abbey, Howard Pyle, and A. B. Frost. All of these men worked for the leading magazines of the day, such as *Harpers, McClures,* and *The Century Magazine.* Coll studied their excellent examples closely and attempted to work in a similar fashion. Vierge used strong contrasts with the white of the paper to offset strong, bold, black lines, and this technique was to highlight much of Coll's work as well.

Coll graduated from Boys Central High School with no formal art training but managed to obtain a job as an apprentice newspaper artist for the *New York American.* Before the advent of inexpensive newspaper photo techniques, the newspaper artist had to do quick sketches of events as they were happening. Coll covered all sorts of stories for which he had to draw quickly and accurately. He learned fast and was sent to the Chicago paper owned by the *American* to further his training.

In 1901 Coll returned to Philadelphia, where he joined the staff of the new *North American.* His editor there, J. Thomson Willing, recognized

Coll's quickly maturing talents and gave him special assignments. He and Coll remained friends long after the artist left the paper.

One of Coll's greatest gifts was that of an exceptional imagination. Although he later would use models, much of his work was based on his own ideas and feelings. He had a strong sense of the dramatic, and his newspaper work gave him plenty of background for composing convincing and believable pictures.

Coll moved on from newspaper work in 1905 and began working for magazines. His artwork for Conan Doyle's novel *Sir Nigel* for the *Associated Sunday Magazines* immediately announced his presence in the illustration field. His primary market was *Collier's*, which at that time was a weekly magazine, for which he illustrated work by Sax Rohmer, Conan Doyle, and Edgar Wallace. Coll also did illustrations for *Everybody's* pulp magazine owned by Street & Smith. Many of the stories Coll illustrated had a strong fantasy element, and he was the perfect artist for them. Among these works were serial versions of "The Lost World" by Sir Arthur Conan Doyle, the first several Fu Manchu stories (published as a series of short stories instead of a novel), "Fire Tongue" also by Rohmer, "King—of the Khyber Rifles" by Talbot Mundy, and "The Messiah of the Cylinder" by Victor Rousseau.

Advertisers, seeing the effect of his work, also used him to illustrate important magazine ad campaigns. Married, with a daughter, Eleanor, Coll died suddenly from appendicitis at age forty-one. Since most of his work was done for magazines that have long been forgotten, his work has drifted into obscurity. Only among illustrators is his name still remembered as one of the greatest of all American pen-and-ink geniuses, and his influence is still being felt in illustration. For example, in the 1920s and 1930s nearly all of the art in *Bluebook* magazine, one of the most prestigious of all pulps, resembled Coll's work. Many of the top pen-and-ink illustrators such as Austin Briggs and J. R. Flanagan★ worked very much in the Coll style, and their work was to influence those who followed them. Thus Coll's illustrations helped mold an entire generation of artists that followed him long after he had died. In fact, his influence on artists like Vincent Napoli★ and Charles Schneeman★ and on many other illustrators in the science fiction field was enormous.

PUBLISHED WORK:

HC: *King—of the Khyber Rifles* (16, 80), *The Magic Pen of Joseph Clement Coll* (78), *The Moon Pool* (19)

CORBEN, RICHARD (b. Oct. 1, 1940) American artist. Born in Anderson, Missouri, and brought up in Sunflower, Kansas, Corben always wanted to be an artist. A comic-book fan, Corben was a loner, and when he moved with his family to Kansas City, he spent much of his time drawing the comics he liked most. He attended the Kansas City Art Institute and became interested in animation art, making his own animated short films. His art training and amateur films helped him get a job with Calvin productions, an industrial film company in Kansas City, where he worked in the animation department from 1963 through 1972.

While working days, Corben also began doing artwork for underground comics, continued his film making, and did science fiction paintings, submitting the art to the few magazines that were published then. His first professional sale was to *Fantasy and Science Fiction*, a spaceship painting that was used for the September 1967 cover. Shortly after that he began doing cover work for Warren Publishing Company for the illustrated horror magazines *Creepy* and *Eerie*. His paintings at the World SF Convention in St. Louis caught the eye of the art director of Doubleday Books, and Corben soon found himself getting assignments from Doubleday. Many of his science fiction paintings were done for the Science Fiction Book Club.

Corben was becoming a major force in the underground comic field. His first published piece of comic art was published in *Voice of Comicdom*, a fanzine, in 1968, and his first work for the underground comics appeared in 1970. As his stature in the underground comic field grew, Corben found his art in greater demand. He was able to quit his film job and become a full-time freelance artist. While still continuing his comic work, primarily in magazines such as *Heavy Metal*, Corbin has branched out into film posters, record album covers, and illustrated books. He is married and lives with his wife and daughter in Kansas City.

PUBLISHED WORK:

HC: *The 1977 Annual World's Best SF, A Feast Unknown, The Day of Their Return* (73), *Llana of Gathol & John Carter of Mars* (77), *Ox* (76), *Spaceling, The Best of L. Sprague de Camp* (78),

PB: *Flashing Swords #5, Demons and Daggers* (81)

F&SF: 1967 (9)

COYE, LEE BROWN (July 24, 1907–Sept. 5, 1981) American artist. Born in Syracuse, New York, Coye discovered while in medical school that he could make more money as a medical illustrator than as a doctor during the Depression. He soon moved into all types of illustration, from medical works to children's books. His first fantasy art was for his own Gothic tale, "The Seventh Ogre," in 1932.

In 1944 he was commissioned by Farrar & Rinehart to illustrate a series of horror-fiction anthologies edited by August Derleth. Not having copies of the stories, Coye went to the offices of *Weird Tales* magazine, from which many of the stories were selected. He met Lamont Buchanan, art director of the pulp, who was impressed by Coye's art and asked him to illustrate for *Weird Tales*. The exposure in the horror anthologies and his work for *Weird Tales* soon had Coye in the forefront of fantasy illustrators.

When *Weird Tales* fell on hard times, Coye returned to fine art and illustration. He worked with oils, sculpture, silverwork, watercolors, and scratchboard. He had exhibits at the Whitney and the Metropolitan Museum of Art. Then, when Ziff-Davis publications revamped *Fantastic* magazine in the early 1960s, Coye was lured back to the horror field. His work for that magazine was among the best ever done in macabre illustration.

The years had taken the rough edges off Coye's art. His pictures were stark, powerful images, making good use of black splotches of color, with an inclination toward fat, dangerous-looking rats and decaying corpses. But his art was not for everyone. One fantasy editor returned a number of pieces with the comment that it was "too horrible to be published in a mass market book." With his return to the fantasy field, Coye painted a number of fine dust jackets and produced interior illustrations for small hardcover houses devoted to horror and fantasy fiction. He twice won the World Fantasy Award for Best Artist. In 1977 he suffered a major stroke from which he never full recovered, and he died in 1981.

PUBLISHED WORK:

HC: *At the Mountains of Madness* (64), *Dagon* (65), *The Dunwich Horror* (63), *Far Below* (74), *Murgunstruum* (77), *The Night Side* (46), *Sleep No More* (44), *Tales of the Cthulhu Mythos* (69), *Three Tales of Horror*, *Whispers 1* (77), *Whispers 2* (79), *Whispers 3* (81), *Who Fears the Devil* (63), *Who Knocks* (46), *Worse Things Waiting* (73)

AMZ: 1963 (4)

FTC: 1962 (12); 1963 (1, 2, 3, 4, 8, 10, 11, 12); 1964 (1, 4)

SAT: 1959 (3)

WT: 1945 (3, 7, 9, 11); 1946 (3, 7, 9, 11); 1947 (1, 3, 5, 7, 9, 11); 1948 (1, 3, 5, 7, 9, 11); 1949 (1, 3, 5, 9, 11); 1950 (1, 3, 7, 11); 1951 (3, 5, 7, 9, 11); 1952 (7)

CRANDALL, REED (b. 1917) American artist. Crandall attended the Cleveland School of Art from 1935 to 1939 and later the Art Students League. After graduation, he first illustrated children's books but soon turned to the comic-book field. He worked for the Iger-Eisner shop, starting in 1940, and did advertising art later in his career.

In the 1960s Canaveral Press began a series of reprints of Edgar Rice Burroughs novels in hardcover. After beginning with unusual art by Mahlon Blaine that was universally condemned by both fans and critics, Canaveral turned to Roy Krenkel★ and Frank Frazetta★, who were painting Burroughs covers for Ace paperbacks. In a continuing search for other artists, Richard Lupoff, editor of the Canaveral line, contacted comic artist Al Williamson. When Williamson was too busy to complete his assignments for Canaveral, he suggested Crandall. Crandall was living in Wichita, Kansas, at the time and did his assignments by mail. His sharp, clean line work made interesting and attractive illustrations for the Burroughs novels. In addition to illustrating these books, Crandall had contacts to illustrate *The*

Gods of Mars, A Fighting Man of Mars, and *The Moon Men* when Canaveral suspended publication of the Burroughs titles. Most of the art was later published in fanzines, as were a number of Burroughs-style illustrations done as samples for the publisher.

Influences on Crandall include Joseph Clement Coll*, Herbert Morton Stoops*, and Howard Pyle.

PUBLISHED WORK:

HC: *Edgar Rice Burroughs: Master of Adventure* (63), *John Carter of Mars* (63), *Tarzan and the Madman* (64)

CTEIN (b. 1949) American artist. An artist without an art degree, Ctein entered the science fiction art field in a roundabout way. Born in New York City in 1949, he moved with his family to California in the late 1950s. A science fiction reader all of his life, he attended Cal. Tech, where he majored in both English and physics, although art had always been one of his hobbies. Since there was no art program at the college, the students created one with Nobel Prize winner Richard Feynman serving as the advisor. This was the only way to get any art classes at the school, so Ctein joined. In about two years, he was running the program. However, when he looked at what he was learning, he decided art would make an interesting hobby but not a profession, so he decided to become a photographer.

In 1968 he was recruited in the "Save Star Trek Campaign." He organized a march on the studios in Burbank, California. Through this effort, he met Bjo Trimble, a well-known Star Trek fan who also was involved in the science fiction art field. Through her Ctein met George Barr* and Alicia Austin*. He discovered science fiction fandom in 1974.

Ctein works primarily as a professional photographer, doing occasional work in the science fiction and science fact field. His favorite medium is photography followed by acrylics. He "paints things he can't photograph," with his work ranging from very realistic to impressionistic. He is visually oriented—reading a piece usually brings to mind how something would work or look. He also finds puns a good source of ideas.

Ctein has contributed artwork to *Future Magazine, Sky and Telescope, American Photographer, Starlog, Minus 10 and Counting,* and *Songs of the Space Age,* as well as to several of the science fiction magazines. When he discovered how little money was being paid artists in the SF industry, Ctein helped form the Association of Science Fiction Artists.

Influences on his work include Ray Bradbury, Richard Feynman, Frank Kelly Freas*, Bjo Trimble, Alicia Austin, and George Barr. Personal favorites in the art field include Freas, Rick Sternbach*, Tim Kirk*, and Janet Aulisio.

PUBLISHED WORK:

ASF: 1983 (1)

D'ACHILLE, GINO (b. 1935) American artist. Born in Rome, Italy, D'Achille studied at the Liceo Artistico in Rome and spent three years studying architecture at the university there. He moved to Milan afterwards, where he started work as a freelance illustrator. In 1964 he moved to London, where he continued his career as an illustrator. He primarily worked as a jacket artist and has done hundreds of paintings for books in both England and the United States. Along with performing cover work, he has done some children's books and advertising art.

PUBLISHED WORK:

PB: *Avengers of Carrig* (80), *The Face* (79), *Killing Machine* (78), *Lucifer's Comet* (80), *People Beyond the Well* (80), *Pursuit of the Screamer* (78), *Quest for the White Witch* (78), *Storm Lord* (76), *Time Slave* (75), *Tribesmen of Gor* (76), *Uller Uprising* (83), *Warlord of the Air* (78)

DAVIES, GORDON C. (?) British artist. Davies began painting science fiction paperback covers in 1952, when he was working for an art studio. He was given free hand to dream up cover subjects and produced a stream of imaginative paintings ranging from the acme of bad taste in bug-eyed monsters such as *Chloroplasm* (1953), which showed a hideously deformed yellow dwarf alien torturing a woman in a glass bottle, to the highly amusing *Bio-Muton* (1953), which showed an intelligent lobster holding a wristwatch, and including beautiful sleek spaceships and astronomical detail, as in *Cosmic Echelon* (1952).

Like Frank R. Paul★, Davies created human figures that were initially unconvincing, and so his covers tended to feature monsters, machines, and alien landscapes. His art was in constant demand from several publishers, including Hamiltons and John Spencer, until he became the mainstay of Curtis Warren. Unlike most regular cover artists of the time, Davies was rarely given a manuscript to read and then illustrate—he created his own covers. Curtis Warren's mainstay author, Dennis Hughes, was producing atrociously banal space operas in 1950 and 1951, based on Ray Theobald★ covers. In 1952 Hughes was asked to write a science *fantasy* novel based on Davies's more bizarre paintings. Hughes's work improved greatly, and the floundering Curtis line prospered until the end of the British paperback boom in 1954.

Davies's talents were too good to be ignored, and quality publishers such as Pan Books employed him throughout the late 1950s, often on their lead science fiction title, usually by Robert A. Heinlein. When Heinlein was acquired by other publishers, Davies's art went with him, and he was called upon to illustrate covers for New English Library into the 1970s. He painted most of these works from his home in Lyminge, Kent, where he lived with his wife.

Davies's early work was characterized by crowded action and pulp cliches, but his later covers for better quality publishers were beautifully air-brushed space and astronomical scenes. Unfortunately, while at the height of his creative powers, Davies's output dwindled due to serious illness. Several of his Heinlein paintings are still in print on later paperback editions, with his credit line misspelled as "Gordon C. Davis." This is ironic, since Davies deserves to be credited as one of the most important and finest British science fiction artists.

PUBLISHED WORK:

HC: *History of the SF Magazines, 1956–65* (78)

PB: *'A' Men* (52), *Amateurs in Alchemy* (53), *And the Stars Remain* (52), *Asteroid Forma* (53), *Atom-War on Mars* (52), *Beyond Geo* (52), *Beyond These Suns* (52), *Beyond This Horizon* (78), *Bio Muton* (52), *Biology 'A'* (52), *Blue Asp* (52), *Blue Peril* (53), *Brain Palaeo* (53), *Challenge* (54), *Childhood's End* (56), *Chloroplasm* (52), *Cosmic Conquest* (53), *Cosmic Echelon* (53), *Cybernetic Controller* (52), *Destination Alpha* (52), *Dread Visitor* (52), *Dwellers in Space* (53), *Earthlight* (57), *Encounter in Space* (53), *Ferry Rocket* (54), *Flight into Space* (52), *From What Far Star?* (53), *Gamma Product* (52), *The Green Hills of Earth* (56), *House of Many Changes* (52), *Ionic Barrier* (53), *Lost Aeons* (53), *Lost World* (53), *Mammalia* (53), *The Menacing Sleep* (52), *The Mortals of Reni* (53), *The Mutant Rebel* (53), *Operation Orbit* (53), *Organic Destiny* (53), *Out of the Silent Places* (52), *Overlord New York* (53), *Pacific Advance* (54), *Photomesis* (52), *Pre-gargantua* (53), *Research Opta* (53), *Satellite B.C.* (52), *Solar Gravity* (53), *Space Family Stone* (71), *Space Salvage* (53), *The Seventh Dimension* (53), *Space Treason* (52), *Suns in Duo* (53), *The Third Mutant* (53), *Time and Space* (52), *To the Ultimate* (52), *Tri-planet* (53), *Twenty-Four Hours* (52), *Underworld of Zello* (52), *Valley of Terror (53), War of Argos* (52), *World of Gol* (53), *Zenith-D* (52)

AUTH: (21, 22, 23, 27)

FUTSS: 1953 (summer)

TofT: (8, 9, 10)

WofS: 1952 (11)

WofF: 1953 (summer); 1954 (spring)

Philip Harbottle

DAVIS, PAUL (?) American artist. One of the founders of the famous Push-Pin Studio, Davis is a surrealist in the Magritte vein. He has done a great deal of science fiction cover art for the hardcover SF market during the past twenty-five years.

DAVIS, ROGER (?) British artist. A very talented artist, Davis appeared briefly in the science fiction field in the mid–1950s. His color work had a bold simplicity, but his black-and-white illustrations, often executed on scratchboard, were pleasantly intricate and comparable to the best art in the field. Unfortunately, his work was not taken up by any of the better publishers. Instead, Davis drifted in to "gangster" covers, and he was lost to the science fiction field.

PUBLISHED WORK (All British publications).

PB: *Decreation* (52), *The Time Trap* (52)
WEIRD WORLD: (1, 2)

Philip Harbottle

DE MONTAUT, HENRI (?) French artist. A celebrated French cartoonist and caricaturist for nearly half a century (1860–1905), Montaut was one of the most important contributors to the humorous journals *Le Rire*, *L'Art et la Monde*, and *Journal Amusant* (from 1863 onwards). Very little is known about him, but he is known to have illustrated two books: the nonfantasy *Mere de famille* by Manceau and the science fiction classic *De la terre a la lune* by Jules Verne. De Montaut illustrated the 1872 edition of the latter work, which appeared seven years after the original and has been reprinted with his illustrations countless times since then. De Montaut's fine illustrations of the interior and exterior of the projectile are among the best known in all science fiction. The most popular French caricaturist of the 1860s, "Nadar" (pseudonym of Gaspard Felix Tournachon, a friend of both Verne and de Montaut), served as the model for de Montaut's illustrations of the astronaut Michel Ardan.

PUBLISHED WORK:

HC: *De la Terre a la Lune* (1872), forty-three illustrations; *From the Earth to the Moon Direct in 97 Hours 20 Minutes, and a Trip Around It* (1873)

Richard Dalby

DE NEUVILLE, ALPHONSE MARIE (May 31, 1835–May 18, 1885) French artist. Born in Saint-Omer, France, de Neuville was a pupil of Eugue Delacroix and a distinguished French painter especially celebrated for his battle scenes and pictures of military life. His full power was not reached until after the war of 1870, episodes of which he depicted in a famous series of paintings including "The Last Cartridges" and "Surprise at Daybreak." At the same time he supplied 309 plates for Guizot's *Histoire de France* (1872–1875) and more than 100 illustrations for three of Jules Verne's most popular *Voyages extraordinaire*. His classic "Nautilus" illustrations for *Vingt mille lieues sous la mer* in 1870 are his best remembered works. He did illustrations in collaboration with Edouard Riou★ for *Twenty Thousand Leagues under the Sea*. For *From the Earth to the Moon . . . and a Trip Around It* he did 45 illustrations in collaboration with Emile Bayard★. For *Around the World in Eighty Days* he did 80 illustrations in collaboration with Leon Benett★.

In 1881 de Neuville was made an officer of the Legion of Honour for his works "The Company of Saint-Privat" and "The Despatch-Bearer." He died in Paris in May 1885.

PUBLISHED WORK:

(All for Jules Verne's *Voyages extraordinaires*; French Hetzel edition listed first with number of illustrations, followed by English edition).

HC: *Autour de la lune* (1872), 45 illustrations in collaboration with Bayard: *From the Earth to the Moon . . . and a Trip Around It* (1873); *Le tour de monde en quatre-vingt jours* (1874), 80 illustrations in collaboration with Benett: *Around the World in Eighty Days* (1874); *Vingt mille lieues sous la mer* (1870), 111 illustrations in collaboration with Riou: *Twenty Thousand Leagues under the Sea* (1873)

Richard Dalby

DE SOTO, RAPHAEL (b. Feb. 18, 1904–1987) American artist. Born in Spain in 1904, De Soto moved to Puerto Rico with his family when he was seven years old. He went to high school in Puerto Rico and decided to attend Columbia University, with hopes of becoming an archaeologist. De Soto liked art very much, but his father, a typically practical parent, believed that no one could make a living as an artist, so De Soto settled for architecture. When his family lost everything in the Depression, he found himself living in New York without funds. He had his bachelor's degree but little else.

In 1930 he began illustrating interiors for *Top-Notch*, a pulp published by Street & Smith, and that was his first actual training in art. He illustrated interiors for two years and then began doing paintings. At first he did one painting a month and lived on that one payment. He continued to work for Street & Smith for several years, producing mostly western art. In the middle 1930s he began branching out and did artwork for Pines Publications and Ace magazines. In the late 1930s he began preparing art for Popular Publications. John Howitt* had recently left Popular, and De Soto and Peter Stevens* helped fill the void that his departure had created.

For the next sixteen years, De Soto painted hundreds of covers for Popular, primarily in the mystery and adventure fields. He sometimes painted two covers a week. Like Howitt, De Soto was not thought of as a science fiction artist, but many of his covers had a strong science fiction element. He painted some covers that were for science fiction stories in adventure pulps, such as his cover for *Earth's Last Citadel* published in *Argosy* in 1943. His covers for *The Spider* pulp magazine often featured science fiction elements, which reflected the fantastic nature of the stories themselves. He was a fine artist capable of fast work, a necessary skill to make it as a pulp artist. De Soto estimated that he did more than eight hundred cover paintings in a period of just under twenty years. Also, during the 1940s he created numerous covers for "slick" magazines like *Colliers*, *Argosy*, and *American Weekly*.

When the pulps died, De Soto easily moved on to the paperback field and painted numerous covers for most of the major paperback publishers. He also created hundreds of magazine covers and interiors in the men's adventure field, but he left that field in 1960 to concentrate on fine art. De Soto became well known as a portrait painter and numbered among his commissions the official painting for the governor of Puerto Rico. Semi-retired, he has taught artwork in college in New York State for the past few years.

PUBLISHED WORK:

PB: *Haploids* (53), *Human?* (54), *The Island of Dr. Moreau* (59)

FFM: 1950 (10)

FN: 1950 (11; 1951 (1)

DEAN, MALCOLM FRED (April 15, 1941–1974) British artist. Dean was equally well known in science fiction and the jazz world, and he made his mark in the latter field with his illustrations in *Melody Maker* magazine. Dean illustrated several books by Michael Moorcock, and his work was especially associated with the Jerry Cornelius stories. He also painted a series of memorable covers for *New Worlds* in the late 1960s and early 1970s. His style was vivid, strong, and surrealist. He preferred to work in black and white and often in a satirical vein. His very promising career was cut short by cancer early in 1974, and he was only thirty-two when he died.

Richard Dalby

DEAN, ROGER (b. Aug. 31, 1944) British artist. Born in Ashford, Kent, England, Dean studied industrial design (first silversmithing and then furniture design) at the Canterbury School of Art from 1961 to 1964. He then spent three years at the Royal College of Art. After leaving college in 1968, he designed the seating for "Upstairs" at Ronnie Scott's jazz club in London. The manager of a rock group called Gun saw a drawing by Dean (at the club) that he thought would make a good jacket for their album, "Race with the Devil." This record "sleeve" launched Dean's prolific career as the foremost illustrator of record-album covers in Britain. His first sleeve to attract major attention was his design for the first "Osibisa" album (in spring 1971), which featured a flying elephant that later became characteristic of the band.

Dean's versatility has been extraordinary. In addition to illustrating record covers and book dust jackets, he has designed exhibitions, posters, furniture, houses, hotels, office towers, and a toy space station. The 1970 *Daily Telegraph* Design for Living Exhibition featured his Teddy Bear Chairs, and five years later, Dean had an exhibition of his work at the New York Cultural Center.

With his brother Martyn, Dean formed the Dragon's Dream company to publish his book *Views* in 1975. The company name came from the fact that the year was the Chinese "Year of the Dragon." Since *Views* featured primarily Dean's record-sleeve paintings, with much fantasy and science fiction content, it was designed to match the size and shape of a record sleeve, with the same cost of an album. Aiming to produce the most technically perfect picture book possible, the brothers spent fifty times more than a normal publisher would have invested on a book with a £3.95 cover price, packing it with hundreds of color plates. The Christmas rush helped put *Views* straight to the top on the *Sunday Times* best-seller list, and the book went on to sell half a million copies all over the world. It was a unique phenomenon in the publishing field.

In 1976 Dean set up a second company (with Hubert Schaafsma) to publish books under the Paper Tiger imprint. The Deans gave credibility to the work of fantasy illustration by commissioning books by the best artists available, including Chris Foss★, Patrick Woodroffe★, and Frank Hampson★. These books from Paper Tiger helped create a much greater demand for such artists and their work.

In 1979 Dean became a director of Magnetic Storm, the design company he formed with his brother and Robert Fitzgerald to specialize in product research and development, theatrical construction, architectural design, illustrated books, posters, and film production.

This company gave its name to the successor to *Views*. Published in October 1984, the book *Magnetic Storm* was a compilation and retrospective of the art and designs of Roger and Martyn Dean. It covers album covers, rock stages, starcodes, architecture, video pods and games, and publishing. The book articulates the innovative use of timeless principles such as Chuku Jujitsu, the Martial Art of Fortress Design, used as a foundation for the Dean designs for domestic architecture.

PUBLISHED WORK:

PB: *Magnetic Storm* (84), *Views* (75)

Richard Dalby

DEMBER (?) American artist. An excellent cover artist who specialized primarily in astronomical paintings, Dember had all of his work published in *Galaxy* or its companion magazines.

PUBLISHED WORK:

GXY: 1958 (3, 4, 7, 9, 10); 1961 (12); 1962 (12); 1963 (10); 1964 (4)

IF: 1961 (7); 1964 (5), with John Pederson★

WOT: 1963 (8)

DI FATE, VINCENT (b. 1945) American artist. Born in Yonkers, New York, Di Fate has lived most of his life in the New York area. He received his art training from the Manhattan Center of Pratt Institute in the middle 1960s. Upon graduation, he began working as an animator for Ralph Bakshi, doing television work. When that show was cancelled, he switched to illustration. His first illustrations were published in *Analog* in August 1969. Since that time, he has worked exclusively in the science fiction field.

At first Di Fate produced both black-and-white interiors and cover paintings, but over the years he dropped the interior work to concentrate entirely on color work. He participated as a NASA artist in the Apollo/Soyuz program and has done many aerospace illustrations. In 1979 he was awarded the Hugo for Best Professional Artist. Di Fate has won numerous other art-show awards including the Frank R. Paul award in 1978.

Di Fate studied under the renown American glaze painter Peter Hopkins. When he first began working in the science fiction field, he did not realize the limits of reproduction used by most paperback markets, and for the first few years of his career, Di Fate found that many of his paintings did not reproduce as well as he would have liked. He soon modified his glaze style, combining the glaze with opaque applications to give the paintings greater brightness when reproduced.

In 1976 Di Fate began a column on science fiction art, which he called "Sketches," in *Algol* magazine. This interesting look at the art field by an insider has consistently featured important interviews and observations on the history of science fiction illustration as well as offering detailed analysis of the strengths and weaknesses of modern science fiction art. In his role as a science fiction art historian, Di Fate has lectured at the Smithsonian, Columbia University, New York University, and other colleges.

PUBLISHED WORK:

HC: *Cemetary World* (73), *Windhaven* (81)

PB: *1984 Annual Worlds Best SF* (84), *Adventures of Jules de Grandire* (76), *Black Legion of Allisto* (72), *Blue World* (77), *Casebook of Jules de Grandin* (76), *Ceres Solution* (84), *Children of Dune* (77), *Combat SF* (80), *Dark Design* (78), *Devil's Bride of Jules de Grandin* (76), *Dune Messiah* (70), *Endless Frontier* (79), *Hellfire Files of Jules De Grandin* (75), *Horror Chambers of Jules de Grandin* (77), *Jandar of Callisto* (72), *Lankar of Callisto* (75), *Mad Empress of Callisto* (75), *Manna* (83), *Mind Riders* (76), *Mind Wizards of Callisto* (75), *Search for the Sun* (83), *Skeleton Closet of Jules de Grandin* (76), *Sky Pirates of Callisto* (73), *Star Search* (84), *Supermind* (77), *Thongor and Dragon City* (76), *Thongor and Wizard of Lemuria* (76), *Tyrant of Hades* (83), *Warrior at World's End* (74), *World's Desire* (72)

AMZ: 1981 (7)

ASF: 1969 (8, 10, 11, 12); 1970 (1, 3, 4, 5, 6, 8, 11, 12); 1971 (1, 2, 4, 7, 8, 9); 1972 (3, 4, 9, 10, 12); 1973 (2, 3, 4, 8, 10); 1974 (3, 4, 10); 1975 (1, 5, 10, 11); 1976 (1, 3, 4, 10, annual); 1977 (1, 3, 4, 5, 6, 7, 10, 11, 12); 1978 (2, 3, 4, 5, 7); 1979 (10, 11, 12); 1980 (3, 4, 5, 10); 1981 (2); 1982 (3, 9, 11)

COS: 1977 (5, 7, 11)

DEST: 1980 (spring, fall)

F&SF: 1971 (9); 1972 (9)

GXY: 1977 (3, 4)

IASFM: 1977 (fall, winter); 1978 (3, 5); 1979 (1, 5, 8, 9, 11); 1980 (5); 1982 (12, mid–12)

DILLON, LEO and DIANE (b. Mar. 1933) American artists. Leo and Diane Dillon were both born in March 1933 but came from opposite coasts and different races. They met at Parsons School of Design and the School of Visual Arts and married a year after graduation, in 1957. They have one son, Lee, born in 1965.

At first the Dillons worked separately, but soon they decided to blend their two styles into one, to avoid problems of professional jealousy. Their earliest work was primarily done in the magazine field, illustrating for whatever markets were available, which included the numerous men's magazines of the late 1950s and the science fiction magazine and book field. Using a woodcut style of art, the Dillons provided a number of dust-jacket illustrations for Gnome Press as well as interiors for *Galaxy* magazine. As their career flourished, their markets expanded. They began producing jackets for numerous juvenile novels, artwork for Caedmon records, and illustrations for Time-Life Books. Outside the book field, they created movie posters, advertising art, greeting cards, and corporate logos.

In the late 1960s the Dillons were given the cover assignments for a new series of major novels to be done by Ace Books. These Ace "specials" included a number of important works that won many major awards in the science fiction field. The Dillon covers gave that series a distinctive look and firmly established them as major artists in the science fiction field, even though they had begun working in the genre more than ten years earlier. Nominated for the Hugo Award as best science fiction artists, the Dillons won in 1971, primarily because of their work on the Ace specials.

During the same period, the Dillons began working on a series of illustrated children's books, including *The Ring and the Praire, Gassier's Lute, Whirlwind Is a Ghost Dancing*, and *The Hundred Penny Box*. In 1976 they received a Caldecott Medal for their book *Why Mosquitoes Buzz in People's Ears*. In 1977 their next picture book, *Ashanti to Zulu*, won them an unprecedented second Caldecott Medal. Along with the Hamilton King Award from the Society of Illustrators in 1976, these awards firmly established them as major modern American illustrators.

The Dillons work in many mediums, using woodcuts, pochoir, stencils, air brush, typography, and Bourgess overlays in their work. They taught classes in art technique at the School of Visual Arts from 1969 through 1977. Diane served as president of the Graphic Artists Guild from October 1981 through October 1983. The Dillons have also lectured at art schools throughout the country.

Although not as heavily involved in science fiction as they once were, the Dillons still do some work in the field. In 1981 Ballantine Books published *The Art of Leo and Diane Dillon*, one of the most highly acclaimed art collections of the year.

PUBLISHED WORK:

HC: *Art of Leo and Diane Dillon* (83), *Deathbird Stories* (75), *Dangerous Visions*, *Methuselah's Children* (58), *San Diego Lightfoot Sue*, *Seedling Stars* (57), *Snow Queen* (80), *Two Sought Adventure* (57)

PB: *After Things Fell Apart* (70), *And Chaos Died* (70), *Barefoot in the Head* (72), *Black Corridor* (69), *Canary in a Cat House* (61), *Chronocules* (70), *Demon Breed* (68), *Eclipse of Dawn* (71), *Eleventh Commandment*, *Firebug* (61), *Fourth Mansions* (69), *Furthest* (71), *Island under the Earth* (69), *Isle of the Dead* (69), *Jagged Orbit* (69), *Left Hand of Darkness* (69), *Lincoln Hunters* (68), *Mechasm* (69), *Nine Hundred Grandmothers* (70), *One Million Tomorrows* (70), *Palace of Eternity* (69), *Past Master* (68), *Pavane* (68), *Phoenix and the Mirror* (70), *Picnic of Paradise* (68), *Preserving Machine* (69), *Revolving Boy* (68), *Ring* (68), *Rite of Passage* (68), *Silent Multitude* (69), *Some Will Not Die* (61), *Steel Crocodile* (69), *Synthajoy* (68), *Torrent of Face* (68), *Traveler in Blace* (71), *Two Timers* (68), *Why Call Them Back from Heaven* (67), *Witches of Karres* (68), *Wizard of Earthsea* (70), *Year of the Quiet Sun* (70)

F&SF: 1972 (8); 1973 (3)

DOLD, ELLIOTT (?) American artist. One of the forgotten artists of science fiction, Dold at one time was considered one of the SF magazine field's most important contributors. He attended William and Mary College in Virginia and after graduation received a scholarship to the Art Students League of New York, where he studied with George Bridgeman. He started his career in advertising art and after the First World War began painting magazine covers. Dold was doing air and western pulp paintings for Harold Hersey in the early 1930s and pressed Hersey to start a science fiction magazine (according to an interview with Dold published in *Fantasy Magazine* in 1934). Thus was born *Miracle Science and Fantasy Stories*, which Dold edited. He also painted the covers for both issues of that magazine and produced the illustrations; his brother Douglas, also a Hersey employee, wrote the lead novel for one issue. The magazine died when Dold was not able to continue working for it due to a serious illness.

Dold later began working for *Astounding SF* when it was purchased by Street & Smith. During the period from 1934 through 1937 he was the leading artist for that magazine. Although Dold was not very good at illustrating people, he was a marvelous detailer of machinery. His work was done with strong contrasts between blacks and whites with no greys. Pieces were prepared double the size of the actual illustration on illustration board. Dold's last illustration in the field was a black-and-white illustration for the cover of *Cosmic Stories* in 1941.

PUBLISHED WORK:

ASF: 1934 (3, 4, 5, 6, 7, 8, 9, 10, 11, 12); 1935 (1, 2, 3, 4, 5, 6, 7, 8, 9, 10, 11, 12); 1936 (1, 2, 6, 7, 8, 9, 10, 11, 12); 1937 (1, 2, 3, 4, 5, 6, 7, 8, 9, 10, 11, 12); 1938 (1, 2, 3, 4, 5, 6, 7, 8, 9, 10); 1939 (1)

COS: 1941 (7)

MIR: 1931 (4, 6)

STI: 1941 (6)

DOLGOV, BORIS (?) American artist. Dolgov was a New York City fan and friend of Hannes Bok★, who did some fine illustrations for the pulp magazines edited in the New York area. Dolgov and Bok collaborated on several interior pieces and signed them "Dolbokgov." Dolgov produced a large number of black-and-white interiors for *Weird Tales* as well as several excellent covers, and he was one of the better artists to work for that magazine during its long decline in the 1940s.

PUBLISHED WORK:

HC: *Destination Universe* (52)

ASH: 1942 (12)

COS: 1941 (7)

FUT: 1941 (8, 10, 12); 1942 (2)

SSS: 1943 (2)

STI: 1941 (6) 1942 #(3)

WT: 1941 (9, 11); 1942 (1, 3, 5, 7, 9, 11); 1943 (1, 3, 5, 7, 9, 11); 1944 (1, 3, 5, 7, 9, 11); 1945 (1, 3, 5, 7, 9, 11); 1946 (1, 3, 5, 7, 9, 11); 1947 (1, 3, 5, 9, 11); 1948 (1, 3, 7, 9, 11); 1949 (1, 3, 7, 11); 1950 (1, 3, 5, 9); 1951 (3, 7); 1952 (1, 3, 11); 1954 (1, 7)

DOLLENS, MORRIS SCOTT (b. 1920) American artist. One of the best-known semiprofessional fan artists, Dollens was born in Indiana in 1920 but moved to Minnesota in 1922. He first discovered science fiction reading Buck Rogers comic Sunday pages and then discovered SF magazines in 1932. He studied art and photography at the Minneapolis School of Art for a year and then began working for a commercial photographer.

Dollens moved to California in the 1940s and became active in science fiction circles. He worked for several years at MGM studios, and early in the 1950s he began selling paintings at science fiction conventions. Most of his work is astronomical.

PUBLISHED WORK:

COS: 1941 (5)

F&SF: 1957 (11)

FTC: 1959 (11)

GAM: 1963 (spring, fall); 1964 (only issue)

SF+: 1953 (4)

SPWY: 1953 (12)

VEN: 1958 (5)

DONNELL, A. J. (?) American artist. One of the four founding members of Fantasy Press, Andrew Julian Donnell worked for Glidden Paint in the 1940s as the staff artist for *The Whilhelm Ambassador*. When Lloyd Eshbach, science fiction author and fan, as well as a Glidden employee, began Fantasy Press, Donnell was one of his associates at the office who helped start the firm. Donnell served as an artist for the early Fantasy Press hardcovers and produced some excellent pieces of art, although he had no interest in science fiction. In 1950 Eshbach bought out his partners, and Donnell was finished with the small-press field.

PUBLISHED WORK:

HC: *A Martian Odyssey* (49), *Beyond This Horizon* (48), *Black Flame* (48), *Book of Ptath* (47), *Darker Than You Think* (49), *Divide and Rule* (48), *First Lensman* (50), *Forbidden Garden* (47), *Incredible Planet* (49), *Legion of Space* (47), *Of Worlds Beyond* (47), *Seven Out of Time* (49), *Sinister Barrier* (48), *Skylark of Valeron* (49), *Skylark Three* (48), *Spacehounds of IPC* (47), *Triplanetary* (50)

DOOLIN, JOE (b. 1902) American artist. A New York artist who worked for many years illustrating the pulp magazines and, later, comic books, Doolin was a friend of Seabury Quinn and consulted Quinn on his illustrations featuring that author's character, Jules de Grandin. He worked for Fiction House Comics in the 1940s.

PUBLISHED WORK:

PS: 1942 (winter); 1943 (3, 5, fall); 1944 (spring, summer, fall, winter); 1945 (spring, summer, fall winter); 1946 (spring, summer); 1947 (spring)

SS: 1940 (3)

StrS: 1940 (4, 6, 12); 1941 (2)

WT: 1925 (12); 1926 (12); 1931 (10, 11, 12); 1932 (1, 2, 3, 4, 5, 6); 1935 (3, 4, 5, 6); 1938 (11)

DOWLING, STEVE (Mar. 19, 1904–Mar. 19, 1986) British artist. Born in Liverpool, England, Stephen (Steve) Dowling studied at the Liverpool and Westminster schools of art. After graduation, he worked with his brother Frank, originating first *Belinda Blue Eyes* (modeled on the American *Little Orphan Annie*) and then *Ruggles*, a strip mirroring contemporary family life.

Dowling's important contribution to the British science fiction art scene was the superhero Garth. Interviewed in 1965 as to the origins of his most famous strip, Dowling recalled: "Back in 1943, the editor at the time wanted a new approach to the cartoon strips in the *Daily Mirror*. The idea for Garth came from Gordon Boshell, who was working at the paper at the time. Garth was modelled on Superman—however, we had Garth as a human being. . . . I only wrote Garth for the first three or so weeks, but I also had to write and draw the 'Ruggles' strip at the same time." The writing was farmed out to his originator, Boshell. After him, Don Freeman and later Peter O'Donnell both took on the writing duties. O'Donnell left the strip in 1965 to concentrate on writing his own famous creation, *Modesty Blaise*, and he was succeeded by Jim Eager.

The strip opened with Garth on a raft without memory. Aided by his mentor, the scientific genius Professor Lumiere, Garth continues to this day to search for his destiny, forty-three years after his first appearance. The greatest years of the strip were between 1953 and 1965, when O'Donnell wrote the scripts and Dowling was at the height of his powers. *Garth* gradually evolved from a "lost-lands" scenario into imaginative adult science fantasy. Dowling's versatility was extraordinary and covered the whole spectrum of science fantasy; his creations ranged from malign supernatural villains to galactic empires. Particular attention was given to visual accuracy, be it geographical, architectural, or technical machinery. Dowling frequently used cross-hatching to induce a weird somber atmosphere perfect for stories of the supernatural.

Dowling retired from the strip in 1968, after a twenty-five-year run. He then ran a farm and riding school. Dowling died on his eighty-second birthday in March 1986.

Richard Dalby and Philip Harbottle

DRIGIN, SERGE R. (?) British artist. A Russian-born artist, Drigin illustrated many boys' action stories in British magazines of the 1920s and 1930s. He was a sailor before moving to London. After joining the staff of Pearsons (London), Drigin had the distinction of illustrating all twenty covers for Britain's first science fiction magazine, *Scoops*, published weekly from February to June 1934. The magazine was done as a tabloid newspaper. Covers were line drawn, tinted usually in red. In retrospect, Drigin's work was routine and unimpressive. It featured wooden people and unrealistic robots and monsters. The lack of quality is not surprising: Drigin once admitted in an interview that he never had an art lesson in his life. However, *Scoops* was an important landmark in the science fiction field in Britain, and today all issues are rare collectors items.

Four years after *Scoops* folded, Drigin was commissioned to illustrate the three issues of *Fantasy*, published by Newnes during 1938 and 1939. Unlike *Scoops*, these color designs were in color. Drigin also did interior artwork for the magazines. His paintings for the first and third issues were typical of his mediocre work. The cover of the second issue, featuring giant insects attacking Piccadilly Circus, as described in "Winged Terror," was highly effective and easily the best thing he ever did.

Drigin also contributed to other boys' magazines published by Newnes and Pearson Magazines in the 1930s, including *Boy's World of Adventure*, *Chums*, and *Pearson's Weekly*.

PUBLISHED WORK: 148 (All British publications).

FANTASY: 1938, 1939

SCOOPS: Twenty issues weekly from February 10 to June 23, 1934

EBEL, ALEX (b. Nov. 14, 1932) American artist. The son of German parents, Alex Ebel was born in Mexico City, where his father, a bridge engineer, was working on assignment and had brought his wife with him. Soon another job brought the family to Houston, Texas, and it was there that Alex first started to draw, his first remembered picture that of a locomotive done on the sidewalk in front of his house for almost a half block. The Ebel family settled in Mexico City, where Alex grew up surrounded by books and good music. The *Buck Rogers* comic strip in the Mexican Sunday paper soon had him constantly sketching science fiction. A copy of *Amazing Stories* prompted him to perfect his command of English just to be able to read the magazine.

Ebel attended the Fine Art Academy and Graphic Arts School in Mexico City and came in contact with the famous Mexican artists Diego Rivera and Gonzalez Camarena. He first worked for printing firms and then advertising agencies and did freelance illustration. In 1951 he got his first job in the United States, working for a printing company in Illinois. He soon moved to New York City and became established as a successful commercial artist. In 1956 he became an American citizen.

His first science fiction illustration was for *Esquire* magazine in March 1953. He followed this with covers for SF magazines and then moved on to paperback art, working for major companies including Ace, Avon, and Fawcett. He has also done illustrations for most major magazines including *Playboy*, *Penthouse*, *Science Digest*, and *Boy's Life*.

Ebel works in inks and dyes and believes his best works are those done when he has complete freedom of expression. He has won numerous awards from important artist groups including The Art Directors Club, Society of Illustrators of Los Angeles, and The American Institute of Graphics Arts.

Alex and Bertha Ebel live in the New York suburbs in a house he designed and built. They have three children, Xenia, Roldk, and Eldryk.

PUBLISHED WORK:

PB: *Ability Quotient, Galactic Empires* (79), *Planet of Exile, Planet Wizard* (77)

FF: 1953 (2, 6, 8, 11)

FSQ: 1954 (winter)

RS: 1953 (4, 7, 9)

SFA: 1953 (2, 3, 5, 7, 9); 1954 (2, 4)

SpSF: 1952 (11); 1953 (2, 3, 5, 9)

EBERLE, JOSEPH R. (?) American artist. Eberle was another of the prolific interior artists who entered the science fiction field during the boom years of the early 1950s, when the pulps and digest magazines were looking for artists to work at low cost. Like the work of Ernest Barth★ and William Bowman★, Eberle's work was competent but uninspired.

PUBLISHED WORK:

FF: 1953 (6,8)

IF: 1953 (9)

OW: 1953 (7)

PS: 1953 (9); 1954 (5, summer, fall); 1955 (winter, spring, summer)

RS: 1953 (7, 9)

ScS: 1954 (2)

SFA: 1953 (5, 7)

SpSF: 1953 (7)

UNI: 1953 (3); 1954 (4)

EGGLETON, BOB (b. Sept. 13, 1960) American artist. Eggleton, who attended Rhode Island College, was influenced by Ron Cobb★, Ralph McQuarrie★, Syd Mead★, and comic artist Mobius. He works in acrylic and with air brush for paintings, scratchboard for black and white. He believes that "I don't practice what I preach because I'm not the kind of person I preach to. Live, paint, have fun, make money—a secret, silly person." He has been actively working in the science fiction field since 1984, his earliest work being done for Baen Books. Since then he has worked for *Analog* and *Asimov's SF Magazine*, as well as TOR Books and a number of other publishers. He believes that "in painting space scenes, accuracy and substantial detail is very important, but no more so than a sense of scope, scale and perspective." Eggleton is a member of Buckhorn Studios.

PUBLISHED WORK:

PB: *Babylon Gate, Fall of Winter, October the First Is too Late*

ELLIS, DEAN (b. Dec. 25, 1920) American artist. Born on Christmas Day, 1920, in Detroit, Michigan, Ellis graduated from high school in Cleveland and then attended the Cleveland Institute of Art, where he received the BFA. He then did some postgraduate work at the Boston Museum School of Fine Art. All of his training was aimed at his becoming a fine artist and not an illustrator. However, when Ellis returned to Cleveland, he took a job in a commercial studio to gain some experience in the art field.

His first ties with the science fiction field came from Bantam Books. He had already produced some trade-book and mystery covers for that publisher and was asked by Bantam to create some covers for their Ray Bradbury books. That assignment consequently led to his working with many other publishers in the science fiction field.

In doing an assignment, Ellis always tried to elicit from the publisher exactly what was wanted in an illustration. His personal preferences have little to do with what he paints. He works in all mediums, although he prefers opaque gouache and acrylic. He often uses acrylic for underpainting, with oil for fine touches.

To Ellis, the science fiction field was never extremely important. As a prolific and popular artist, he "never depended on it for a livelihood." In the past five years, he has done very little science fiction work, concentrating instead on advertising work. He has done editorial work for *Popular Science* and *Popular Mechanics*. Ellis has paintings for a number of U.S. stamps including the "Flag over the Supreme Court," the "Navigation of the Arkansas river," the "American Hospitals," "Natural History," and the "Jefferson Memorial." He also has created a number of stamps for foreign governments. Ellis is currently working on a series of portraits of sixty prominent people for first-day covers done by the Wyoming Co.

Ellis is married and lives with his wife, Lois, and daughter Tracey in New York City. His favorite piece of his science fiction work is the cover painted for Ray Bradbury's *Illustrated Man*.

PUBLISHED WORK:

PB: *All Judgment Fled* (70), *Ambulance Ship* (79), *Best of Fritz Leiber* (74), *Best of Stanely G. Weinbaum* (74), *Han Solo at Star's End* (79), *Han Solo's Revenge* (79), *Lost Continent* (72), *Major Operation* (71), *Neutron Star* (68), *People of the Mist* (73), *Ringworld* (70), *Tar Aiym Krang* (72), *Tomorrow Is too Far* (71)

ELSON, PETER (1947) British artist. One of the numerous excellent British science fiction artists specializing in space hardware, Elson studied at Ealing Art School and later won a *Science Fiction Monthly* art competition in 1975. His work is very much in the tradition of Chris Foss★. A book of thirty-one of his best paintings was published in 1981 by Dragon's Dreams Press.

PUBLISHED WORK:

PB: *The Best of Isaac Asimov, The Big Sun of Mercury, Derelict 2, The Early Williamson, The Fall of the Tower, Get Out of My Sky, A Martian Odyssey, The Moons of Jupiter, Naked to the Stars, Nova 4, Oceans of Venus, Operation Ares, The Outposter, Parallel Lines* (81), *Pebble in the Sky, Pirates of the Asteroids, The Power of Blackness, Reach for the Stars, The Rings of Saturn, Space 1, Tomorrow and Tomorrow, Trader to the Stars, Up the Line, Venus Plus X, Vulcan's Hammer, Welcome to Mars*

Richard Dalby

EMSH, ED. See EMSHWILLER, EDMUND ALEXANDER.

EMSHWILLER, EDMUND ALEXANDER (b. Feb. 16, 1925) American artist. One of the most prolific and popular artists ever to work in the science fiction field, Emshwiller, along with Kelly Freas* dominated the science fiction art field throughout the 1950s.

Emshwiller was born in Lansing, Michigan, and grew up in Big Rapids, Michigan; Chicago; Washington D.C.; and Richmond, Virginia. He served in the army from 1943 through 1946. He then attended the University of Michigan, majoring in painting and illustration, receiving a bachelor of design degree in June 1949. He married Carol Fries on August 30, 1949, and they soon moved to Paris, where they both continued to study art at the Ecole des Beaux Arts. In 1950 they returned to New York, where he studied graphics at the Art Students League.

In 1951 Emshwiller sold his first science fiction illustration to *Galaxy* magazine. He then sold the same magazine a cover painting and soon became one of the most prolific artists ever to work in science fiction. During the next thirteen years, he did more than four hundred science fiction cover paintings for magazines, paperbacks, and hardcovers. He also did many hundreds of black-and-white illustrations for all of the science fiction magazines of the period. During this time, the Emshwillers moved to Levittown, Long Island. She stopped painting and began writing science fiction, some of which he illustrated. They had three children: Eve in 1955, Susan in 1957, and Peter in 1959. Emshwiller did so much work in so many different styles that he used several names including Emsh, Ed Emsler, Ed Alexander, Ed Emsch, EAE, Ensh, Harry Gars, and Willer. Nominated for the Hugo Award as best SF artist eight times, Emshwiller won five statues, in 1953, 1960, 1961, 1962, and 1964.

While working on science fiction art, Emshwiller continued to do fine-art graphics and paintings, exhibiting at several group shows and one one-man show. His show was largely abstract expressionism. Also during this time, Emshwiller began making 16mm films. This interest in film making would drastically change the direction of his career.

In 1964 Emshwiller received a grant from the Ford foundation to make his film *Relativity* and a commission from the government to make the film *Faces of America*. The artist told SF publishers that he was taking a year off from illustration work to make these films. The year became much more than that, and he never returned to painting other than for a few paintings he did as favors for friends. He continued to make experimental, underground, and documentary films until 1973, receiving numerous awards at film festivals, as well as grants from state and federal arts agencies and private foundations.

In 1971 he made his first videotape. In 1972 he became artist-in-residence at the Television Laboratory WNET/13 in New York. He made a number of videoart tapes during this period, receiving more awards. In 1978–1979 he made his first computer-animated videotape, *Sunstone*, at New York Institute of Technology.

Since that time, Emshwiller has moved to Newhall, California, and has become dean of the School of Film and Video at California Institute of the Arts, Valencia, California. In 1981 he took on the additional job as provost (academic vice-president). As of late 1984 he was working on various multimedia projects at CalArts.

In all of his science fiction work, Emshwiller was a conscientious craftsman, striving to do the best possible work for every story he illustrated. He read the material given to him by the art director and editor, usually in galley form. The style of his cover paintings was done very much within the character of the magazine as well as the content of the story. Some magazines preferred action-oriented covers, others were open to the more abstract or symbolic paintings. Emshwiller preferred the latter but did whatever was best suited for the publication. Most of all, he enjoyed the freedom he had found in science fiction that was not available in most other illustration of the time.

Many of his magazine covers were strictly products of his imagination. He would show sketches to the art directors, and often writers were then assigned to write stories around the cover illustration. Other times, paintings were published with no tie-in of the cover with the inside of the magazine. *Galaxy* featured a number of such covers, stunning paintings that told a story in themselves, with just the title of the work given on the contents page.

Color work was done in gouache, casine, or designer colors. A very fast worker, Emshwiller did most of his paintings in one or two days. He usually did not use oils, often because they took too long to dry. He did use oils a few times, however, as well as dyes, colored inks, pastels, photographs, and even the air brush.

Interiors were done in black and white on scratchboard using india ink, with both pen and knife. He also used photographic techniques and some zipatone.

A typical schedule was for Emshwiller to travel into New York once a week. He would bring in cover sketches and finished artwork, and he would then pick up stories and discuss what sketches would be done as finished paintings. Then he would return to Long Island and spend the next day reading the new stories he had been given. A day or two would be spent doing sketches and doing mattes, taking pictures of the models when used for a piece, and sketching out final cover painting layouts. A typical work week after finishing all of his final details was often seventy hours long.

Emshwiller had no particular style that made him memorable, although all of his work was top quality. He had a flair for humor but did not resort to exaggeration for effect. Instead, his humor was that of situation, showing characters in humorous occurrences or bizarre circumstances. Probably, the best known of all of his humorous paintings were his series of paintings done for *Galaxy SF* each December featuring a four-armed Santa Claus in traditional Christmas scenes with alien carolers, robot reindeer, and the like. He also did some fine humorous covers for *Astounding SF* including several Christmas scenes.

His action paintings were smooth and colorful; his people were lifelike and his alien monsters believable. His black-and-white illustrations, with strong blacks, were equally striking; his lines were strong and rough, and his pictures featured people with character in their faces. In retrospect, one can only marvel at the speed at which he worked, since his covers and interiors never featured artistic shortcuts to make the work easier to do. Every picture was done in complete detail—nothing was hidden. His art was so distinctive that it was impossible to mistake it for that of any other artist. He was one of the major forces in the science fiction art field, and when he retired, he left a major void in the magazine and paperback marketplace.

PUBLISHED WORK:

HC: *Across Time* (57), *Address: Centauri* (55), *Alien Dust* (57), *All about the Future* (55), *Armageddon 2419 AD* (62), *Believer's World* (61), *Big Planet* (57), *Bridge to Yesterday* (63), *City on the Moon* (57), *Collision Course* (61), *Conan the Barbarian* (54), *Cybernetic Brains* (62), *Dark Destroyers* (59), *Day of the Giants* (59), *Deathstones* (64), *Destiny's Orbit* (61), *Drums of Tapajos* (61), *Duplicated Man* (59), *Encounter* (59), *Exile of Time* (64), *Five Galaxy Short Novels* (58), *Forgotten Planet* (54), *Full Circle* (63), *Giants from Eternity* (59), *Glory That Was* (60), *Golden Ape* (59), *Hand of Zei* (63), *Have Space Suit—Will Travel* (58), *Highways in Hiding* (56), *Hunter of Space* (60), *Infinite Brain* (57), *Interplanetary Hunter* (56), *Involuntary Immortals* (59), *Island in the Sky* (61), *Little Men* (60), *Lords of Atlantis* (60), *Lost in Space* (59), *Martian Missile* (58), *Mel Oliver and Space Rover on Mars* (54), *Mission to a Star* (64), *Next Door to the Sun* (60), *Other World* (63), *Outlaws of Mars* (61), *Outposts in Space* (62), *Plague Ship* (56), *Planet of Death* (64), *Planet of Peril* (61), *Prelude of Space* (54), *Prince of Peril* (62), *River of Time* (63), *Sargasso of Space* (55), *Search for Zei* (62), *Secret People* (56), *SF 56* (56), *SF Terror Tales* (55), *Star Ways* (56), *Swordsman of Mars* (60), *Tales of Conan* (55), *Tam, Son of Tiger* (62), *Three to Conquer* (56), *Tomorrow's World* (56), *Troyana* (61), *Undersea Fleet* (56), *Undersea Quest* (54), *Virgin Planet* (59), *Wall of Serpents* (60)

PB: *And Then the Town Took Off* (60), *Armageddon 2419 AD* (62), *Atlantic Abomination* (60), *Best from F&SF 3rd Series* (60), *Best from F&SF 4th Series* (60), *Best from F&SF 6th Series* (62), *Beyond the Silver Sky* (61), *Big Planet* (58), *Bow Down to Nul* (60), *Brigands of the Moon* (58), *Cache from Outer Space* (62), *Castle of Iron* (62), *Catseye*

(62), *Celestial Blueprint* (62), *Conquest of Earth* (64), *Crashing Suns* (65), *Currents of Space* (63), *Darker Than You Think* (63), *Defiant Agents* (63), *Door through Space* (61), *Dreadful Sanctuary* (63), *Dying Earth* (69), *Earth in Peril* (57), *Earth's Last Fortress* (60), *Earthman Go Home* (60), *Edge of Time* (59), *End of Eternity* (63), *End of the World* (56), *Envoy to New Worlds* (63), *Eye of the Monster* (62), *First Flight* (63), *First to the Stars*, *Galactic Derelict*, *Golden Blood* (64), *Great Explosion*, *Great SF Adventures* (63), *Greatest Adventure*, *Hand of Zei*, *Hidden Planet*, *Humanoids* (63), *Incomplete Enchanter* (64), *I Speak for Earth*, *I Want the Stars*, *Invaders Are Coming*, *Invaders from Earth*, *Joyleg*, *King of the 4th Planet*, *Lest Darkness Fall*, *Let the Spacemen Beware*, *Light of Lilith*, *Macabre Reader*, *Man with Nine Lives*, *Mars Monopoly*, *Masters of Evolution*, *Mind Spider*, *Moon Men* (62), *Naked to the Stars* (64), *Naked Sun* (64), *No Man's World* (61), *One against Herculum*, *One of Our Asteroids Is Missing*, *Outlaws of Mars*, *Pawns of Null-A*, *People Minus X*, *People of the Talisman* (64), *Perfect Planet* (63), *Planet Savers*, *Psionic Menace*, *Puzzle Planet*, *Rebels of the Red Planet*, *Recalled to Life* (62), *Recruit for Andromeda*, *Regan's Planet* (64), *Rendezvous on a Lost World*, *Sargasso of Space*, *Search for Zei*, *Secret of Sinharet* (64), *Secret of Zi* (58), *Seven from the Stars* (62), *Shadow Girl* (62), *Six Worlds Yonder* (58), *Slavers of Space* (60), *Slaves of the Klau* (57), *Space Station #1* (57), *Spacial Delivery*, *Star Born*, *Star Gate*, *Star Hunter*, *Stars Like Dust* (63), *Stepsons of Terra*, *Storm over Warlock*, *Sun Smasher*, *Sword of Alsones*, *Swordsman of Mars*, *This Fortress World*, *Time to Teleport*, *Time Traders*, *Towers of Toron*, *Transit* (64), *Trial of Terra*, *Troubled Star* (59), *Twenty-Second Century* (62), *Valley of Creation* (64), *Valley of the Flame* (64), *Vanguard from Alpha*, *Variable Man*, *Void Beyond*, *Voodoo Planet*, *Vulcan's Hammer*, *War of the Wingmen*, *Warlord of Kor*, *When the Sleeper Wakes*, *World without Men*, *World of Null-A*

AMZ: 1952 (1, 2, 3, 6, 7, 8, 9, 10, 11, 12); 1953 (2, 4, 8, 12); 1960 (8, 10, 11); 1961 (8); 1962 (1); 1963 (6, 7, 12); 1964 (3, 5, 7, 10); 1967 (6); 1969 (1)

ASF: 1955 (10, 11, 12); 1956 (2, 3, 4, 7, 8); 1957 (5, 6, 10); 1958 (5, 6, 12); 1959 (3); 1960 (6)

BEY: 1953 (7, 9, 11); 1954 (2, 3, 7, 9)

F&SF: 1952 (6, 9, 10, 11); 1953 (2, 4, 5, 6, 7, 10, 11, 12); 1954 (1, 2, 3, 4, 8, 11, 12); 1955 (1, 4, 6, 8, 11); 1956 (5, 6); 1957 (2, 9, 10); 1958 (2, 5, 8, 9, 10, 12); 1959 (1, 3, 4, 6, 8, 10, 11); 1960 (1, 2, 4, 6, 8, 9, 11); 1961 (1, 2, 4, 5, 7, 9, 11, 12); 1962 (2, 4, 5, 6, 7, 9, 10, 11); 1963 (1, 3, 4, 6, 7, 8, 9, 12); 1964 (1, 5, 6, 7, 11); 1965 (3); 1966 (10); 1968 (1); 1969 (7, 12); 1972 (11); 1974 (4); 1976 (11); 1979 (2)

FA: 1952 (1, 2, 4, 5, 8, 9, 10, 11, 12); 1953 (1)

FF: 1953 (2)

FSQ: 1952 (9); 1953 (5, 7); 1954 (winter, summer, fall); 1955 (winter, spring)

FTC: 1952 (summer, fall, 11); 1953 (1, 11); 1960 (9, 11); 1961 (4); 1962 (7, 10); 1963 (10); 1964 (1, 2, 5, 7, 8, 9); 1965 (1, 9, 11); 1966 (1); 1968 (5, 8)

FU: 1956 (1, 5, 6); 1959 (12); 1960 (3)

FUT: 1954 (3, 6, 8, 10, 29, 30, 31, 32, 33, 34, 35); 1959 (2, 4, 6, 8, 10, 12); 1960 (2, 4)

GXY: 1951 (5, 6, 7, 8, 9, 10, 11, 12); 1952 (1, 3, 4, 5, 6, 7, 8, 9, 10, 11, 12); 1953 (1, 2, 3, 4, 5, 6, 7, 8, 9, 10, 11, 12); 1954 (1, 2, 3, 4, 5, 6, 7, 8, 9, 10, 11, 12); 1955

(1, 2, 3, 4, 5, 6, 7, 9, 10, 11); 1956 (1, 2, 3, 4, 5, 6, 7, 8, 10, 11, 12); 1957 (1); 1958 (1); 1959 (6, 10, 12); 1960 (2, 4, 6, 8, 12); 1961 (2, 8); 1963 (2, 4, 10, 12); 1964 (2)

IF: 1953 (3, 5, 7, 9); 1954 (4, 5, 6, 7, 8, 9, 10, 11); 1955 (1, 2, 3, 4, 5, 6, 8, 10, 12); 1956 (4, 6, 8, 10, 12); 1957 (2, 4, 6, 8, 10, 12); 1958 (2, 4, 6, 8, 10, 12); 1959 (2, 7, 11); 1960 (1); 1963 (7, 9, 11); 1964 (11, 12)

INF: 1956 (2, 6, 8, 10, 12); 1957 (2, 4, 6, 7, 9, 10, 11); 1958 (1, 3, 4, 6, 8, 10, 11)

PS: 1952 (3, 5, 7, 11); 1953 (3, 5, 9, 11); 1954 (5, summer, winter); 1955 (spring)

RS: 1953 (4)

SAT: 1956 (10); 1957 (4)

SF: (2); 1955 (1, 3, 5, 7, 9, 11); 1956 (3, 5, 7, 9, 11); 1957 (1, 3, 5, 7, 9, 11); 1958 (1, 5, 7, 9, 11); 1959 (1, 2, 3, 5, 7, 9, 11); 1960 (1)

SFA(BR): 1958 (1, 2, 3, 5); 1960 (15)

SFA: 1953 (3); 1956 (12); 1957 (4, 6, 8, 9, 12); 1958 (3, 4, 6)

SFQ: 1954 (5, 8, 11); 1955 (5, 8, 11); 1956 (2, 5, 8, 11); 1957 (2, 5, 8, 11); 1958 (2)

SpS: 1952 (10, 12); 1953 (2, 4, 6)

SpSF: 1952 (11); 1953 (2, 3)

SS: 1952 (6, 7, 8, 10, 12); 1953 (1, 2, 3, 4, 5, 6, 8); 1954 (spring, summer, fall); 1955 (winter, spring, summer, fall)

SSF: 1956 (12); 1957 (2, 4, 6, 8, 10, 12); 1958 (2, 4, 6, 8, 10, 12); 1959 (2, 4, 6, 8, 10)

TOPS: 1953 (fall)

TRE: 1964 (1)

TWS: 1952 (4, 8); 1953 (4, 6, 8, 11); 1954 (winter, spring, summer, fall); 1955 (winter)

VAN: 1958 (6)

VEN: 1957 (1, 5, 7, 9, 11); 1958 (1, 3, 7)

WSA: 1953

FABIAN, STEPHEN E. (b. Jan. 3, 1930) American artist. Fabian did not start out to be a science fiction artist. He attended several schools before joining the U.S. Air Force in 1949. He served as a teacher in Advanced Radio and Radar School at Scott Air Force Base, Belleville, Illinois, for the next four years. In 1953 he left the air force and began working for a number of electronic firms, including Dumont TV Labs, Curtiss Wright Electronics Division, and Simmons Precision Products. He was working as an associate engineer at Simmons in Vermont when the Arab oil boycott of 1973 brought about a major layoff in the industry, and he found himself out of work.

A science fiction reader since the early 1950s, Fabian had always been a fan of the art featured in the pulps, especially the work of Hannes Bok★, Edd Cartier★, and Virgil Finlay★. He had always been interested in art of all kinds since childhood and had assembled a huge library on all types of art as well as a large section of instructional books on how to illustrate. Entirely a self-taught artist, he studied and practiced drawing and painting on his own, putting thousands of hours of study into his interest before ever attempting to sell a piece. In the late 1960s he began submitting pieces to fanzines and become a well-known fan artist. The day he was laid off from Simmons, he came home to find letters from Sol Cohen, publisher of *Amazing Stories*, and Jim Baen, editor of *Galaxy Magazine*, inviting him to submit work to their magazines. Fabian made the switch from electronics engineer to full-time artist immediately.

Fabian's first year of freelance illustration was difficult, but with the help of his family, friends, and editors, he was able to adjust to his new lifestyle. Since that time, he has remained one of the busiest and most popular illustrators in the science fiction field.

Fabian does both color and black–and–white work, although he is known more for his interiors than for his cover paintings. He often used textured (coquille) board for many of his earlier black and whites, giving these pictures much of the texture of a Finlay illustration. Fabian is also one of the few science fiction artists who can create a good humorous illustration, and he has done some fine cover paintings with humorous themes. Since the market for interior illustration is limited in the professional science fiction field, Fabian has also done a great deal of work in the semipro publishing field as well. His work for *Weirdbook, Crypt of Cthulhu*, and other fanzines is as good as his regular magazine work and has helped to maintain his status as a fan favorite. Fabian also has become a regular illustrator for many of the small-press publishers, and he has become a specialist in doing elaborately illustrated hardcover editions for publishers such as Underwood-Miller and Donald Grant Books.

Before working on any assignment, Fabian takes several factors into consideration. Art direction is minimal in science fiction, and artists are expected to know how to handle their work. Among the important non-story essentials that Fabian takes into consideration is whether the editors have any taboos on things such as nudity or violence. How the art will be reproduced is also a factor. Some publishers want only line work for interiors to keep costs down. Deadlines, too, must be considered with every assignment.

Fabian reads every manuscript that he will illustrate. The number of illustrations required for the work determines how detailed his note taking is for the story. He focuses his notes on character descriptions, interesting scenes and backgrounds, and any unique details the author has included in the work. Afterwards, he reviews his notes and lays out blank sheets of paper for the number of illustrations to be done. He then selects key characters and scenes to be illustrated. Fabian gives some consideration to spacing out drawings so that they will all not be clustered from one area of the story. He also avoids revealing any secrets or dramatic scenes the author builds into the work. Fabian believes that illustrations should complement a story but not give away major points of the work.

Married for thirty years, Fabian is the father of two sons, Stephen, Jr., and Andy. He has won numerous awards in the science fiction and fantasy field and has been nominated as best artist for seven Hugo Awards and four World Fantasy Awards.

PUBLISHED WORK:

HC: *Dragon of the Ishtar Gate* (82), *Dream of X* (78), *Eyes of the Overworld* (77), *Far Future Calling* (79), *For a Breath I Tarry* (80), *Golden Blood* (78), *Golden Torc* (82), *Green Magic* (79), *Nonborn King* (83), *Out of the Storm (75), Rhialto the Marvellous, Seventeen Virgin and Bagful of Dreams* (79), *Superluminal* (83), *Vultures* (73), *Whispers* (77), *Whispers 2* (79), *Whispers 3* (81), *Whispers 4* (83)

PB: *Raum* (77), *Survey Ship* (81)

AMZ: 1974 (12); 1975 (3, 5, 7, 9, 11); 1976 (1, 3, 6, 9, 12); 1977 (3, 7, 10)

FTC: 1975 (2, 4, 8, 10, 12); 1976 (2, 5, 8, 11); 1977 (2, 6, 9, 12)

GXY: 1971 (8, 9)

IF: 1974 (10)

FAGG, KENNETH (?) American artist. When it first began publishing, *IF* magazine featured a number of cover artists new to the science fiction field. Most of these artists produced one or two covers and then disappeared. The best of them was Fagg, who remained as the regular cover artist for the magazine for nearly two years. Fagg worked with bright colors and produced some outstanding covers for the digest magazine. He was a capable artist who did attractive renderings of aliens as well as believable humans. Many of his best paintings were wraparound covers for *IF* that propelled that magazine into the forefront of the science fiction field at the time. Unlike many of the new artists entering the science fiction field right out of college, Fagg came to the science fiction field from the slick magazines, and his experience showed in his well executed covers.

PUBLISHED WORK:

HC: *Attack from Atlantis* (53), *Battle on Mercury* (53), *Mystery of the Third Mine* (53)

IF: 1953 (3, 5, 7, 9, 11); 1954 (1, 3, 4, 6); 1955 (5)

FARAGASSO, JACK (b. Jan. 23, 1929) American artist. Born in Brooklyn, New York, Faragasso was one of numerous New York students who studied under Frank Reilly at the Art Students League, attending that school from 1949 through 1953. He sold his first paperback cover in 1952 and has done artwork for Pocket Books, Popular Library, Signet, Lancer, and many other paperback publishers. He works in oil, tempera, and watercolor and does photographic covers as well. In 1979 he wrote the highly regarded *Student Guide to Painting in Oils.* Like a number of other graduates of the

Art Students League, Faragasso has returned to the school as a teacher and has worked with a number of younger artists who have since entered the science fiction field, including James Warhola*.

PUBLISHED WORK:

PB: *Ensign Flandry* (67), *Secret of the Runestaff* (69), *Sword of the Dawn* (68), *The Time Masters* (54)

FECK, LOU (1925-Nov. 4, 1981) American artist. Like many other New York-based artists, Feck attended Pratt and graduated in 1950 from the School of Art and Design. He was a steady contributor to the paperback cover art market for a number of years, working primarily for Berkley Medallion books and Bantam. Feck worked in a wide range of style and did two gothic covers a month for most of the 1970s. He was a versatile artist who used bright, naturalistic colors as well as direct brush strokes. Feck died of a heart attack at age fifty-six.

PUBLISHED WORK:

PB: *A Canticle for Leibowitz, Kull* (78), *Mockingbird, The Beyonders*

FEIBUSH, RAY (b. Jan. 22, 1948) British artist. Born in Liverpool, England, Feibush immigrated with his family to the United States in 1955, and he lived there for eleven years. He sold his first artwork to a horror magazine shortly before returning to England in 1966.

After failing to qualify for a grant to enter art school, Feibush became a technical illustrator for a science magazine. His record cover for Milhoud's *La creation du monde* won a Music Week design award.

Feibush's first science fiction commission was the cover for Ronald Hall's *Open Cage* published by Panther Books in 1971. This was followed by a long run of science fiction covers for New English Library.

Feibush's preferred medium is acrylic and gouache, and his style is strongly influenced by surrealism.

PUBLISHED WORK: 149 (All British).

PB: *Chessmen of Mars* (73), *The Far Out Worlds of A. E. Van Vogt* (74), *The Godmakers, Podkayne of Mars, A Second Isaac Asimov Double* (73)

Richard Dalby

FERAT, JULES-DESCARTES (Nov. 28, 1819–1889?) French artist. Born in Ham (Somme), France, Ferat was a French painter who exhibited regularly at the Paris Salon from 1857 to 1878. He illustrated many books from Sue's *Mysteres de Paris* in 1857 to Poe's *Contes* in 1884, but he is chiefly remembered for his artwork done for seven titles by Jules Verne, most notably his 154 illustrations for *L'Ile mysterieuse* in 1875, which included several fine studies of one of Verne's most famous creations, the submarine

Nautilus. His illustrations were signed "J. Ferat." He disappeared from view in the late 1880s, and no definite date is known for his death.

PUBLISHED WORK: 168 (A checklist of his Jules Verne illustrations. The original Hetzel French publication is given first, with the number of illustrations. The Sampson Low British hardcover edition and date follow.)

Adventures de trois russes et de trois anglais (1872), 52 illustrations: Meridiana: The Adventures of Three Englishmen and Three Russians in South Africa (1873); Le Chancellor (1877), 58 illustrations in collaboration with Riou: Survivors of the Chancellor (1877); Le Pays des Fourrures (1873), 105 illustrations in collaboration with de Beaureppare: The Fur Country (1873); Les Indes Noires (1877), 45 illustrations including three color plates: Child of the Cavern—or, Strange Doings Underground (1877); L'Ile Mysterieuse (1875), 154 illustrations: The Mysterious Island (1875); Michel Strogoff (1876), 95 illustrations: Michael Strogoff (1876–1877); Une ville flottante (1872), 44 illustrations: A Floating City (1876)

Richard Dalby

FERNANDES, STANISLAW (b. May 8, 1945) American artist. Born in Uganda, East Africa, Fernandes moved to London in 1954. He graduated from St. Bonaventure School in London in 1961 and was awarded a major scholarship and a place at St. Martin's School of Art, London, to study fine art (he later switched to illustration and graphic design). In 1966 he graduated from St. Martin's with a BA (with honors). He was awarded a special postgraduate diploma in cinematic production and photography from St. Martin's in 1967.

Between 1968 and 1971 Fernandes worked as an art director for a large paperback publishing house in London. He became interested in science fiction art when he discovered it to be an area in illustration in which the artist had the most freedom of expression, and imagination could flourish boundlessly. He started to experiment with some visual concepts of his own, which were published as paperback covers. The psychedelic period of the sixties combined with the thoughts of the dadaists and the surrealists triggered many of his ideas, and he began to use the air brush since it seemed better suited to his visions of the future.

In 1974 the artist moved from London to New York City. He established himself as a freelance illustrator and did a number of paperback covers for Ballantine Books, Avon, and other publishers.

Most cover illustration ideas came from reading the books to be illustrated. Where there was no imagery to derive from the writing, Fernandes would look for a symbolic feeling for the story and illustrate the work that way. During the past few years, he has been doing paintings based entirely on his own thoughts and ideas. The finished work is sent to clients who then buy reproduction rights. He has illustrated a number of covers for Omni magazine in this fashion.

Fernandes also created the movie poster for *Star Trek II—The Wrath of Khan*. He has done futuristic paintings for advertising and record albums as well. Now working on a number of different types of projects, Fernandes believes he has gone beyond the traditional science fiction genre, with his work in the SF field representing only a small portion of his total output.

PUBLISHED WORK:

PB: *Appointment at Bloodstar* (78), *Eclipsing Binaries* (83), *The Omicron Invasion* (84), *Planet of Treachery* (82), *The Purity Plot* (80), *Revolt of the Galaxy* (85)

FINLAY, VIRGIL WARDEN (July 23, 1914–Jan. 18, 1971) American artist. Perhaps more than any other artist, Finlay changed the course of science fiction illustration. Before he began working for the pulp magazines of the 1930s, art was considered little more than a filler by most readers of the publications. Even the popular artwork by Frank R. Paul★ was disliked by many fans as taking away valuable space that could be used for more fiction. Finlay raised the level of interior art from illustration to fine art and became the most popular interior artist ever to work in the science fiction field. He served as a source of inspiration for a generation of artists who followed and helped keep alive interior art in the science fiction field. Finlay was one of the "big three" of the science fiction pulp artists, the others being Edd Cartier★ and Hannes Bok★. Each man contributed something special to the science fiction art field. Cartier demonstrated that illustrations could be done with humor. Bok added style to science fiction art. Finlay, the greatest of the three, brought beauty to the science fiction magazines.

The artist was born in Rochester, New York, the son of Warden Hugh Finlay and Ruby Cole. His father was a woodworker who had a difficult time making ends meet during the Depression. Finlay had a younger sister, Jean Lily, born four years after him.

In high school Finlay was interested in two things—sports and art. He was an accomplished athlete but also enjoyed writing poetry and painting. He studied art primarily through the use of books in the library and received his first professional art instruction in high school.

Artists who influenced Finlay included Gustave Dore, Aubrey Beardsley, Harry Clarke★, Winsor McKay, Norman Lindsay, Heinrich Kley, and Wallace Smith★; he was also a great admirer of Pablo Picasso. Finlay was especially influenced by Dore, and in trying to master Dore's black-and-white style, Finlay came up with his own detailed technique. He used a 290 lithographic pen and india ink to construct a detailed illustration through the use of stipple art. For each dot, he dipped his pen in the india ink, wiping the pen-top clean after each marking. His best illustrations were the results of hundreds of precise groupings of tiny black dots by which he achieved a beautiful, near photographic reproduction. The stipple technique, which was old, being popular during the turn of the century, was a time-consuming method of work, and the artist needed great patience to achieve the desired results. Finlay was a master of this technique.

During the Depression Finlay took free night courses at the Mechanics Institute. He later took classes in anatomy, landscape, and portraiture from the WPA during the Depression. After graduation, he worked in a stockroom, on a radio assembly line, and as a house painter. He also did some portrait work, but such jobs during the Depression were rare.

Finlay had been interested in science fiction and fantasy ever since his first exposure to *Amazing Stories* in 1927. He preferred fantasy over science fiction and was a regular reader of *Weird Tales* from 1928 on. However, like most of the readers of the pulp, Finlay thought very little of its interior illustrations, so in 1935 he decided to submit a small portfolio of illustrations to the magazine.

Farnsworth Wright, editor of *Weird Tales*, immediately recognized Finlay's talent. Not only were the illustrations far superior to anything done in the pulps of the time, but Finlay also had a superb imagination and used it in his work. However, Wright had misgivings about the reproduction of stipple work on pulp paper and bought only one illustration from Finlay. However, when the art was printed and reproduced well, Wright immediately commissioned Finlay for numerous other illustrations.

Along with editing (and owning a small part of) *Weird Tales*, Wright dreamed of publishing other magazines. In late 1935 he experimented with a pulp reprint of Shakespeare's *A Midsummer Night's Dream*, evidently aimed to tie in with the release of the Warner Brothers film. To help dress up the magazine, Wright commissioned Finlay to provide twenty-five illustrations for the play. Unfortunately, the publication was a dismal flop. The only volume in the Wright's Shakespeare Library is remembered today primarily for the large number of Finlay illustrations.

Finlay's art had an amazing impact on fantasy fans. For the first time in the field, letters of praise flooded *Weird Tales* not about the stories but about the Finlay art. Even the authors raved about Finlay's art, and one of the most enthusiastic was H. P. Lovecraft, who wrote a sonnet about one of Finlay's illustrations for a Robert Bloch story.

Finlay was paid eight to eleven dollars an illustration for his work in *Weird Tales* in the 1930s. Although this was not a huge amount, he usually contributed five or six illustrations per issue, so it provided a reasonable income during the Depression. By 1937 Wright was using Finlay on the covers of *Weird Tales*, alternating his work with that of the popular Margaret Brundage★. Finlay was paid one hundred dollars a cover, which, combined with his money for interiors, made him one of the highest paid monthly pulp illustrators.

Finlay's work for *Weird Tales* paid off handsomely in late 1937. Impressed by the art he saw in the pulp, Abraham Merritt, the editor of *The American*

Weekly, offered Finlay a job on the magazine's staff. At that time, the *Weekly* was the largest circulation magazine in the world, serving as the Sunday supplement to the entire Hearst line of newspapers. Merritt was a famous science fiction and fantasy author who had gone on to better things. However, he still was a fan and reader of the pulps and recognized Finlay's spectacular artistic talent. He invited the young artist to move to New York and work on his paper for the excellent salary of eighty dollars a week.

Finlay immediately accepted Merritt's offer and moved to New York City. While working for *The American Weekly* he continued to do art for *Weird Tales* and thus did quite well financially. However, during this time Finlay continued to support his mother and sister, and life in New York proved to be a series of ups and downs. He was fired after six months at *The American Weekly* for taking two-hour lunch breaks. But soon he was hired again, and for the next few years Finlay continued to work off and on for the publication, either as a staff artist or by contributing freelance art.

At the same time, Finlay's popularity with *Weird Tales* fans did not go unnoticed by other publishers. When *Weird Tales* cut its rates for art as a result of a change in publishers, Finlay found his art in demand by many other science fiction and fantasy magazines. He continued to prosper, contributing art to *The American Weekly* as well as to *Amazing Stories*, *Fantastic Adventures*, *Captain Future*, *Strange Stories*, *Thrilling Wonder Stories*, and a number of other publications.

In 1939 Munsey Magazines began publishing reprint magazines using the early fantasy fiction published in *Argosy* and *All-Story Magazine*. Merritt was instrumental in having Finlay illustrate many of his stories that were reprinted by *Famous Fantastic Mysteries* and *Fantastic Novels*. Finlay's name soon became closely linked with the reprint publications, and he was a reader favorite.

In 1938 Finlay converted to Judaism and married his longtime girlfriend, Beverly Stiles, in New York City at a ceremony presided at by Rabbi Dr. Clifton Harby Levy, a leader of the Jewish Reform Movement.

Finlay continued to work in the science fiction field until he was drafted in 1943. After training as a combat engineer, he served as a corporal in the United States before being sent to Okinawa in April 1945. During his time overseas, he was involved in a number of combat missions. He remained overseas until 1946, rising to the rank of sergeant.

During the time Finlay was in the army, *Famous Fantastic Mysteries* was without his services. Desperate for an artist who could attract readers in the same fashion as Finlay, the publisher commissioned Lawrence Sterne Stevens★ to produce art in the Finlay style. Stevens, who had been trained as a newspaper illustrator, did not work in exactly the same manner as Finlay, but his exceptionally detailed line work was very much in the same tradition as Finlay's delicate, detailed illustrations with stunningly beautiful women. Readers wanted Finlay but settled for Lawrence. Stevens's work proved popular enough so that after the war, when Finlay returned, the two artists shared the work for *Famous Fantastic Mysteries* and *Fantastic Novels*.

In the late 1940s Finlay rode the crest of the wave of science fiction publishing. A major boom among magazine publishing took place after World War II, and Finlay found plenty of work. He produced hundreds of fine illustrations, all done in his meticulous style. He often worked sixteen hours a day, seven days a week. In 1949, Beverly Finlay gave birth to their only child, Lail, and in 1950 Finlay was able to buy a house in Westbury, Connecticut, where he lived for the rest of his life.

Although Finlay was known primarily as an interior artist, he also did attractive cover art and produced a number of popular paintings for the science fiction magazines. However, his work did not seem suited for the hardcover field, and he did not sell any work to the small-press publishers, as did many of the other artists of the time.

Unfortunately, all booms come to an end, and Finlay's difficulty with the book market came back to haunt him when magazines began to fold and Finlay's work was not particularly suited to paperback covers. Although he did some hardcover jacket paintings, numerous other artists like Ed Emshwiller* and Richard Powers* were more popular with publishers. Finlay even tried some work for the comics, but his meticulous, detailed style was not particularly suited for this market, and he could not meet the short deadlines so common in the comic-art field.

Finlay managed to earn his living doing interior illustrations for astrology magazines. He contributed a steady stream of new pieces for *Everyday Astrology* and *Astrology—Your Daily Horoscope* for the rest of the 1950s and during the 1960s. He also continued to do artwork for the remaining science fiction magazines, even though payment was minimal.

A new area of art opened up to Finlay in the late 1950s when he began working on large abstract paintings on canvas. These pieces became popular and sold well through galleries, something he had never been able to achieve with any of his interior illustrations. Some of Finlay's canvas work was hung at the Metropolitan Museum of Art, the New York Center Art Gallery, the Library of Congress, and other prestigious art centers.

In 1970, while experiencing a financial resurgence, Finlay learned he had cancer, and the painful operations made it difficult for him to work. Fortunately, unlike most artists for the pulps, Finlay had asked for most of his originals to be returned. Working with longtime friend and art collector Gerry de la Ree, Finlay began selling many of his originals; these sales generated a substantial amount of money, which helped pay most of his medical bills.

The pain grew worse, and Finlay returned to the hospital for further tests. He then learned that he had serious liver trouble and died soon after, on

January 18, 1971, of cirrhosis of the liver. After his death, it was discovered that he also had suffered from advanced lung cancer.

It is impossible to overestimate Finlay's importance to the science fiction art field. He entered the field during a period when the magazines featured mediocre art and poor reproduction; his work brought about a renaissance in science fiction illustration. A new group of fans emerged: people who were interested in the art despite the story. In fact, Finlay was capable of producing fine illustrations for the worst stories, and a number of fans bought and collected magazines not for the fiction but for his art.

Finlay was a dedicated artist who devoted his life to his art. Among science fiction artists, he stands supreme as the most popular interior illustrator ever to work in the field. He was one of the most prolific illustrators as well, doing more than twenty-five hundred interior illustrations and more than two hundred cover paintings. His career served as a watershed for modern science fiction illustration, and his influence in the field is still being felt today.

PUBLISHED WORK:

HC: *The Book of Virgil Finlay* (75), *Bullard of the Space Patrol* (51), *The Complete Book of Space Travel* (56), *Dwellers in the Mirage* (50), *The Far Place* (49), *The Fifth Book of Virgil Finlay* (79), *Five against Venus* (51), *The Fourth Book of Virgil Finlay* (79), *From off This World* (49), *The Kid from Mars* (49), *Marginalia* (44), *One against the Moon* (56), *The Outsider* (39), *Roads* (48), *The Second Book of Virgil Finlay* (78), *The Ship of Ishtar* (49), *The Sixth Book of Virgil Finlay* (80), *Space Pioneers* (54), *Space Police* (56), *Space Service* (53), *Star Born* (57), *The Stars Are Ours* (54), *The Third Book of Virgil Finlay* (79), *The Time Traders* (58), *Virgil Finlay* (71), *Virgil Finlay: An Astrological Sketchbook* (75), *Virgil Finlay Remembered* (81), *The Winged World* (49)

PB: *Gods for Tomorrow* (67), *The Million Cities* (63), *The Spell of Seven* (65), *Swords and Sorcery* (63), *Two Complete Novels by Lester Del Rey* (63)

AMF: 1950 (2, 7, 10)

AMZ: 1942 (1); 1943 (1, 2, 3, 7); 1944 (3); 1945 (3, 6); 1946 (10); 1947 (5); 1951 (1, 5, 9, 12); 1952 (3, 5, 8); 1953 (10); 1955 (3); 1956 (5, 10, 11, 12); 1957 (1, 2, 3, 4, 8, 12); 1958 (1, 8, 9, 10, 11, 12); 1959 (1, 2, 3, 4, 5, 6, 7, 8, 9, 10, 11, 12); 1960 (1, 2, 3, 4, 5, 6, 7, 8, 9, 10, 11, 12); 1961 (1, 2, 3, 5, 6, 7, 9, 10, 11, 12); 1962 (1, 2, 3, 4, 5, 6, 7, 8, 9, 10, 11, 12); 1963 (1, 2, 3, 4, 5, 6, 8, 9, 11, 12); 1964 (3, 4, 6, 7, 8, 9, 10, 11); 1965 (1, 5); 1967 (6)

ASF: 1939 (8)

ASH: 1942 (6)

DW: 1957 (5, 8)

FA: 1942 (3, 4, 12); 1943 (7, 8, 10); 1944 (4, 6, 10); 1945 (1, 4); 1946 (2, 9); 1947 (5, 9, 10, 11, 12); 1948 (2, 3, 6, 7, 12); 1949 (2); 1951 (3, 5, 7, 8, 10, 11, 12); 1952 (1, 3, 8)

FFM: 1939 (11, 12); 1940 (1, 2, 3, 4, 5, 8, 9, 12); 1941 (2, 4, 6, 8, 10, 12); 1942 (2, 4, 6, 7, 8, 9, 10, 11, 12); 1943 (3, 9, 10); 1946 (12); 1947 (2, 4, 6, 8, 10, 12); 1948

(2, 4, 6, 8, 10, 12); 1949 (4, 10, 12); 1950 (2, 4, 6, 8, 10); 1951 (7, 10, 12); 1952 (2, 4, 6, 8, 10, 12); 1953 (2, 4, 6)

FMSF: All reprints (1, 2, 3)

FN: 1940 (7, 9, 11); 1941 (1, 4); 1948 (3, 5, 9, 11); 1949 (1, 3, 5, 7, 9, 11); 1950 (3, 5, 7, 11); 1951 (1, 6)

FSQ: 1950 (spring, summer); 1952 (winter, summer, 9, 11); 1953 (3, 7, 9); 1954 (winter, spring, summer, fall); 1955 (winter, spring)

FTC: 1952 (summer, fall, 11); 1953 (1, 3); 1955 (4); 1956 (6, 10, 12); 1957 (2, 3, 4, 5, 6, 10, 11); 1958 (1, 2, 3, 5, 6, 7, 8, 11, 12); 1959 (1, 2, 3, 4, 5, 6); 1961 (3, 8, 9, 10); 1962 (1, 3); 1963 (2, 3, 7, 9, 11, 12); 1964 (1, 2, 3, 5, 8); 1965 (11); 1966 (1, 7); 1967 (5); 1968 (8); 1969 (6); 1971 (8); 1973 (2)

FU: 1957 (3, 4, 5, 6, 7, 8, 9, 10, 11, 12); 1958 (1, 2, 3, 4, 5, 6, 7, 8, 9, 10); 1959 (1, 3, 7, 10, 11); 1960 (1, 2, 3)

FUT: 1950 (7, 9, 11); 1951 (1, 3, 5, 9, 11); 1952 (1, 3); 1958 (12); 1959 (6)

GXY: 1956 (7, 8, 10, 12); 1957 (1, 2, 5, 8, 9); 1958 (3, 4); 1959 (12); 1960 (12); 1961 (2, 3, 8, 10, 12); 1962 (4, 10); 1963 (2, 4, 6, 8, 10); 1964 (2, 8, 10, 12); 1965 (2); 1966 (2, 10, 12); 1967 (6, 8, 10); 1968 (10)

IF: 1953 (7); 1954 (8, 9, 11); 1956 (8); 1957 (2, 4, 6, 8, 10, 12); 1958 (2, 4, 6, 8); 1960 (5); 1961 (11); 1962 (1, 3); 1963 (5, 7, 9, 11); 1964 (1, 10); 1966 (8, 9, 10, 12); 1967 (5, 6, 7, 9, 10); 1968 (1, 3, 10, 12); 1969 (3)

MOH: All reprints (15, 16, 17, 18, 19, 20, 21, 22, 23, 24, 25, 26, 27, 29, 31, 33)

OW: 1953 (12); 1954 (84); 1956 (4, 6, 9, 11); 1957 (7)

PS: 1941 (summer)

SF: 1943 (7); 1959 (1, 2, 3, 4)

SF+: 1953 (10, 12)

SFQ: 1951 (8, 11); 1955 (11)

SFYBK: 1967 (1); 1968 (2); 1969 (3, all reprints)

SMS: All reprints (3, 4, 5, 6, 7, 8, 9, 10, 11, 12, 14)

SpS: 1952 (2)

SS: 1939 (9); 1940 (1, 5, 9); 1942 (5); 1943 (6, fall); 1944 (spring, summer); 1947 (3, 9); 1948 (3, 5, 7, 9, 11); 1949 (1, 3, 7, 9, 11); 1950 (3, 7, 9); 1951 (1, 9); 1952 (1, 2, 3, 5, 7, 8, 9, 10, 12); 1953 (1, 2, 3, 5, 6, 10); 1954 (1, spring, summer, fall); 1955 (winter, summer, fall)

SSS: 1942 (5, 9); 1943 (2, 5); 1949 (1, 7, 11); 1950 (1, 5, 9, 11); 1951 (1, 4, 8)

StrS: 1939 (4, 6, 8, 12)

TWS: 1939 (4, 6, 8, 12); 1940 (1); 1941 (4, 8, 10); 1942 (6, 8); 1943 (8); 1944 (winter); 1945 (spring); 1946 (fall); 1947 (2, 8, 10); 1948 (2, 4, 6, 8, 10, 12); 1949 (2, 4, 6, 10, 12); 1950 (2, 4, 8); 1951 (12); 1952 (2, 4, 6, 8, 10, 12); 1953 (4, 6, 8, 11); 1954 (winter, spring, summer, fall); 1955 (winter); 1957 (annual); 1963 (annual)

UNI: 1953 (12); 1954 (3)

UK: 1940 (2)

WOT: 1963 (4, 6, 8, 10, 12); 1964 (6); 1965 (1, 11)

WSA: 1950, 1951, 1952, 1953

WT: 1935 (12); 1936 (2, 3, 4, 5, 6, 7, 8, 10, 11, 12); 1937 (1, 2, 3, 4, 5, 6, 7, 8, 9, 10, 11, 12); 1938 (1, 2, 3, 4, 5, 6, 7, 8, 9, 10, 12); 1939 (1, 2, 3, 4, 5, 6, 7, 8, 9, 10, 11, 12); 1940 (1, 3, 5); 1941 (1); 1942 (3); 1944 (7); 1945 (1, 3); 1951 (11); 1952 (5, 7, 9, 11); 1953 (1, 3, 5, 7, 9, 11); 1954 (1, 3, 5, 9); 1973 (summer)

MISC: *Famous Fantastic Mysteries* printed three Finlay portfolios, which were offered as premiums for subscribers. They were done in 1941, 1942, and 1948 and were later reprinted by the National Fan Federation. Another portfolio of Finlay art was published by Nova Press in 1953. Finlay also did an original that was used as the back of a deck of cards sold at the Thirteenth World SF Convention in 1955, and he did numerous illustrations for *Times to Come*, the flyer of future releases of the SF Book Club.

In 1971 well-known art collector Gerry de la Ree began an ambitious program of reprinting booklets and portfolios of unpublished Finlay art. These included *Virgil Finlay: A Portfolio of His Unpublished Illustrations* (71), *Klarkash-ton and Monstro Ligriv* (73), and *Finlay's Lost Drawings* (75).

FLANAGAN, JOHN RICHARD (1895–1964) American artist. Born in Sydney, Australia, Flanagan apprenticed to a lithographer at age twelve and entered art school at the same time. After he finished school, he immigrated to the United States. His first illustration work was for a Chinese story in *Every Week* magazine. This art and several pieces following established him as an expert on the Orient, something he never claimed to be. His pen-and-ink art was very much in the tradition of Joseph Clement Coll★. This was aptly demonstrated, when, after the death of Coll, *Colliers* needed another artist to illustrate Sax Rohmer's stories. Flanagan was chosen as the perfect artist to illustrate the Fu Manchu novels, since his work resembled that of Coll's so closely. Flanagan's name became so associated with oriental villains that when Popular Publications published several magazines featuring Fu Manchu imitations—*The Mysterious Wu Fang* and *Dr. Yen Sin*—Flanagan was brought in to do the interior art to give the magazines the proper style.

Flanagan was one of the premier illustrators for *Bluebook* pulp for which he did the art for many of its borderline fantasy and science fiction stories, including "The Cave of the Invisible" (39), "The Serpent People" (39), and "The Wolf Woman" (39). Flanagan also worked in color as well as on scratch board, along with his pen-and-ink illustrating. He later designed stained-glass windows. From 1954 until his death, he served as an instructor at the York Academy of Arts in Pennsylvania.

FOGLIO, PHIL (b. May 1, 1956) American artist. Born in Mt. Vernon, New York, Foglio attended the Chicago Academy of Fine Arts, from which he received the BFA in cartooning. He had originally planned to enter the computer field, but when he discovered that one had to know math, that career choice was no longer an option. He had been drawing since he was very young, so when he considered what he would like to do for a living, art came first.

Influences include Kelly Freas★, Vaughan Bode, and Charles Schulz. Foglio originally planned to be an illustrator like Freas, but it soon became clear that "cartoonists were making all the money," so he became a cartoonist instead.

Foglio was well known as a science fiction fan artist long before he sold any professional work. He won two Hugo Awards for Best Amateur Artist in 1977 and 1978, helping to bring his art to the attention of major publishers. His first professionally published art was for "Taking the Fifth," a story in *Isaac Asimov's Science Fiction Magazine.*

In deciding what to illustrate, Foglio looks for the action or a humorous happening in the story. He tries to find "something I would like to see illustrated." He works in pencil or acrylic. His favorite work is for the comic adaptation of *Mythadventures* by Robert Asprin, which he is doing for WarP Graphics and Donning Books, since it offers him the most freedom to do his own work the way he wants.

PUBLISHED WORK:

HC: *Sex Life on the Planet Mars*

PB: *Another Fine Myth, Myth Directions, Myth Inc. Link* (86)

FOSS, CHRISTOPHER (b. Mar. 19, 1946) British artist. One of the most prolific and highly acclaimed British science fiction artists of the modern era, Foss has hundreds of covers in the genre to his credit. He was born in Devon, in the southwest of England, and as a child loved to build models of railway lines and steam engines, which he soldered together from scraps of metal. His art teacher persuaded him to enter a scholarship course, which won him a place at a public school in Dorset. During this period he often sketched the semiderelict shipyards at Poole Harbor and rebuilt car wrecks to create new working machines. At an early age, he was obsessed with color, speed, and technology.

Foss's earliest ambition was to be an artist, but at his family's insistence, he went to Cambridge University in 1964 to study architecture. His first science fiction work was a six-page adult comic strip done in the style of Barbarella, which he sold to *Penthouse* magazine.

Foss spent three difficult years after school, first working for an architectural sculptor and then driving cars for hire. Publishers began showing an interest in his work in 1970, when an intricate line drawing by Foss depicting a futuristic city was published in *Nova.* The first of numerous commissions quickly followed. His first cover was for the Panther paperback edition of Arthur C. Clarke's *Coming of the Space Age.* Within three years, Foss had become an international success. Many authors specifically asked for him to illustrate the British editions of their books, most notably Isaac Asimov and his *Foundation Trilogy*.

Foss was increasingly sought after for his air-brushed scenes of future warfare, which featured ships and planes but, most usually, fantastic starships. His asymmetrical structures were totally unlike the streamlined shapes that had been used in science fiction illustrations before him. From Foss's in-depth studies of twentieth-century mechanics, he had strong ideas about the role of machinery in the future. The recurrent theme of transportation in space characterized all of his work, with acrylic gouache color used to achieve the clear lines in his paintings.

In 1975 Foss became even better known when he visited Paris to work with Alejandro Jodorowsky on the never-completed version of Herbert's *Dune*. However, this work led to assignments on both *Superman* and *Alien*. The success of his paintings was so great that a whole school of new British artists has developed with Foss as their model. Nearly all British science fiction hardware covers owe their development to Foss's style. Many of the modern science fiction films, beginning with *Star Wars*, feature spacecraft that look as though they came out of a Foss painting. Since that film was one of the most influential of all modern science fiction movies, the Foss style of spaceships has become a permanent feature of the cinematic landscape.

PUBLISHED WORK:

PB: *21st Century Foss* (79), *Aliens, Exiles, Novellas X 3* (74), *Ancient My Enemy* (76), *The Best of Arthur C. Clarke Vol. 1* (73), *The Best of Arthur C. Clarke Vol. 2* (73), *Catchworld* (76), *The Caves of Steel* (71), *Cities in Flight* (72), *City of Illusions* (72), *The Coming of the Space Age, Crash* (73), *Currents of Space* (72), *Dramaturges of Yan* (74), *The Drought* (77), *The Early Asimov Vol. 1* (72), *End of Eternity* (73), *Foundation Trilogy* (73), *Frederick Pohl Omnibus* (71), *The Gods Themselves* (73), *The Grain Kings* (76), *Grey Lensman* (72), *The Humanoids* (76), *Kronk* (71), *Mandelov Conspiracy* (78), *The Masters of the Vortex* (71), *Mindbridge* (76), *The Naked Sun* (73), *The Ophinchi Hotline* (77), *Patterns of Chaos* (74), *Perry Rhodan 13* (75), *Planets for Sale* (77), *The Radiant Dome* (70), *Rebels of Tuglan* (75), *Recalled Conscience* (75), *The Reproductive System* (76), *Science Fiction Art* (76), *The Shephard* (75), *Skylark Three* (75), *The Space Machine* (76), *Venus Equalateral Vol. 1* (78), *Venus Equilateral Vol. 2* (78), *Visitors from Outer Space* (74), *Voyage of the Space Beagle* (72), *We Can Build You* (86), *Who Needs Man?* (70)

                                                                    Richard Dalby

FOWKE, ROBERT GREGORY (b. July 24, 1950) British artist. Known as "Bob" Fowke, the artist studied at Eastbourne School of Art and Somerset College of Art. A contributor to *Science Fiction Monthly* in the mid–1970s, he also designed posters and record covers. Among his best works were paintings for Robert Heinlein's *Man Who Sold the Moon* and *The Puppet Masters* and Ray Bradbury's *Golden Apples of the Sun*.

Fowke achieves brilliant colors through the use of gouache and water on white card paper. His work contains much mythical imagery.

Richard Dalby

FOX, MATTHEW (b. 1906) American artist. A commercial artist who entered the fantasy field through the comics medium, Fox had a background in advertising art and lithographs. His fantasy art was first published in 1941, when he was in his middle thirties. Although he worked in woodcuts, watercolors, etchings, and other mediums, his fantasy work was done in oils. Fox was not afraid to make unbelievably bizarre creatures the center of his paintings. Unfortunately, most of his work had a rough, cartoon look. Many of his paintings featured the devil or demons locked in combat, and he filled his canvas with loathsome creatures, rarely leaving any empty space in the pictures.

PUBLISHED WORK:

ASH: 1940 (4, 6, 8)

FFM: 1944 (6)

FUT: 1943 (2)

PS: 1942 (winter)

SSS: 1940 (3)

WT: 1943 (3, 5, 11); 1944 (3, 5, 7, 9, 11); 1945 (1, 3, 9); 1946 (3, 5, 7); 1947 (1, 3, 5, 11);1948 (5, 7, 9); 1949 (3, 5, 7, 11); 1950 (1, 3, 5, 7, 11); 1951 (5, 7)

FRANCIS, RICHARD D. (?) American artist. Another one of the prolific interior artists who entered the science fiction field during the boom years of magazines in the early 1950s, Francis worked for several magazines when he first began illustrating science fiction, but after a short while, he concentrated mainly on illustrating for *Galaxy*. He was a reasonably good artist who drew fairly believable people and kept away from alien monsters in his illustrations.

PUBLISHED WORK:

AMZ: 1952 (10, 11,); 1953 (2, 3, 8); 1966 (6)

BEY: 1954 (1, 3, 5, 9), (9); 1955 (10)

FA: 1952 (11); 1953 (1, 2, 3)

FSQ: 1955 (winter)

FTC: 1953 (3); 1961 (6)

GXY: 1953 (1, 5, 7, 9, 11); 1954 (2, 6, 7, 8, 9, 11, 12); 1955 (3, 4, 6, 7, 9); 1956 (4, 5, 6, 8, 9, 10, 11); 1957 (1, 4, 5, 6, 7, 10, 11, 12); 1958 (1, 2, 4, 5, 6, 9, 11, 12);

1959 (2, 4, 8, 10, 12); 1960 (2, 4, 6, 8, 10, 12); 1961 (4, 6, 8, 10, 12); 1962 (2, 4, 6); 1963 (2, 6)

IF: 1960 (1, 3, 7, 9, 11); 1961 (1, 3); 1962 (1, 9); 1963 (5)

SS: 1954 (summer); 1955 (winter)

TWS: 1954 (fall)

FRAZETTA, FRANK (b. Feb. 9, 1928) American artist. Frazetta is probably the most important artist in the science fiction field since Virgil Finlay★. In many ways, a strong argument can be advanced that Frazetta is the most important and influential artist ever in the genre. Unlike Finlay, whose name is known only to a few outside the science fiction field and who is now forgotten by many modern fans, Frazetta is a well-known artist in mainstream America whose fans include movie producers and actors and whose paintings command fabulous prices.

The artist was born Frank Frazzetta (he later dropped one of the z's) in Brooklyn, New York. He began drawing before he was three years old and was an accomplished amateur artist within a few years. When he was eight years old, he began studies at the Brooklyn Academy of Fine Arts, working with the classic Italian artist Michael Falanga for the next eight years. But his education came to an abrupt end with the death of Falanga.

Frazetta entered the professional art field at the age of sixteen as an assistant to John Giunta★ doing comic-book art. From 1944 until he began producing science fiction cover art in 1964, Frazetta worked on comic books or comic strips. He did work for a number of comic companies including Magazine Enterprises, Famous Funnies, DC Comics, and EC Comics. In the early 1950s, Frazetta worked on his own comic strip, *Johnny Comet*, but the strip was dropped after a year. Afterwards, Frazetta was offered a job on Al Capp's staff, and he worked on *Lil Abner* for the next nine years.

Frazetta then wanted to do something else; however, he soon discovered that his comic-book style was considered too old-fashioned and that the comic market had shrunk to a few companies. There was not much work to go around. A number of magazine publishers also turned down Frazetta. Again, "too old-fashioned" was the reason he was given. Frazetta was reduced to doing some illustrations for men's magazines and men's paperbacks.

However, Frazetta's fortune soon changed. He was approached by Canaveral Books, which was reprinting several Edgar Rice Burroughs books in hardcover as well as printing for the first time several uncollected stories. Frazetta did illustrations for several of these books. In 1964 Ace Books began an ambitious program reprinting many of the Burroughs novels. Roy Krenkel★, a longtime friend of Frazetta from his comic-book days, was given the assignment to do the covers for two of the books. Since he was not sure he could do both covers, he asked Frazetta to do one. Donald

Wollheim, editor of Ace Books, was not overly impressed by Frazetta's work, but the artist was given some Burroughs cover assignments.

Frazetta was unhappy with his treatment by Ace—he thought the pay was low, and the company kept his artwork. His early paperback covers for the company were rush jobs that often were done in a day or two. But the art was well received by fans. Then Frazetta was approached by Lancer Books, which offered him more money for his paintings and returned his art. He quickly left Ace and began working for Lancer and, soon after that, other companies. Years later, Frazetta returned to Ace to do a new series of Burroughs cover paintings, but this time payment was much better, and there was no mention of his art being too old-fashioned.

It was Frazetta's work for Lancer Books that vaulted him into the forefront of fantasy illustrators. Lancer had just bought the Conan series of heroic fantasy stories by Robert E. Howard for publication, and Frazetta was given the cover assignments. His cover paintings were superb renderings of the barbarian hero and helped make the books among the best-selling paperbacks of the 1960s and 1970s. Collectors began buying paperbacks just for the Frazetta covers. In a situation similar to what had been done for science fiction magazine covers, companies began buying Frazetta paintings and then having authors write novels to go with the art. A Frazetta cover soon became a status symbol for fantasy paperbacks, guaranteeing sales.

At the same time, Frazetta did a series of horror and fantasy covers for the Warren black-and-white comic horror magazines, *Creepy* and *Eerie*, which also attracted a great deal of attention. His paintings *Egyptian Princess* and *Sea Witch* were extremely popular both in and out of the comic field.

When posters of Frazetta paintings were published by several companies, the artist and his wife quickly realized how popular his work had become. They started their own poster company, working from the original art, most of which Frazetta had managed to keep. Frazetta continued to do artwork for paperback houses while also doing album covers, movie posters, and some advertising art. In 1966 he was awarded the Hugo Award for Best Science Fiction artist of the Year and was nominated four other times for the same award. His name was everywhere. Interviews and articles about him were appearing in both the science fiction and the comic-book fields.

By the 1970s Frazetta was becoming well known outside the science fiction field. In illustration, nothing attracts attention as much as success, and Frazetta was very successful. With that success, came increased attention. He received the Award of Merit from the Society of Illustrators. Interviews with and articles about the artist began appearing in magazines like *American Artist* (May 1976) and *Esquire* (June 1977). Frazetta was able to pick and choose his assignments, and his originals, when sold, were going for thousands of dollars.

Frazetta's art was so popular that there were many collectors who collected books with his paintings without knowing the contents of the books. In 1975 came the final breakthrough. Bantam Books published a collection of Frazetta's art, *The Fantastic Art of Frank Frazetta*. A number of Frazetta's finest pieces were reproduced from the original art using high-clarity reproduction and fine color printing. An introduction at the beginning of the book gave fans outside the comic or science fiction field information about the artist, and a brief notice on the copyright page informed collectors of posters available from Frazetta's poster company. The Frazetta boom became a craze.

Four more collections of his art followed, as did a number of calendars. Frazetta had little time for paperback art since new and more elaborate projects took up his time. He continued to do a few paintings from time to time but by the 1980s had stopped producing art in the fantasy field. However, constant reprints of his work keep his name in the forefront of fantasy illustrators.

Frazetta works on wood, masonite, or canvas panel. He does paintings in oils, using raw umber for both line and areas of tone. He works in what is known as the "classic" approach, starting with bristle brushes to lay in transparent color washes and then finishing with sable brushes for blending. He uses color glazes for certain areas and constantly adds highlights to the painting as needed. In his pen-and-ink pieces, Frazetta also never does preliminary work but instead begins working with pen, letting the drawing flow for itself around the action part of the scene.

Frazetta and his wife, Eleanor, have four sons, who help with the poster business and various other Frazetta enterprises. Most recently, they opened a Frank Frazetta museum in Pennsylvania, featuring most of the artist's originals on display.

Frazetta is probably among the best-known artists working in the United States today. His work long ago left the narrow science fiction and fantasy field and is seen on everything from record album covers to the sides of vans. Frazetta helped sell swords and sorcery and Robert E. Howard, and although the material might have succeeded without Frazetta, there is no question that his art was a tremendous boost in the right direction. More so, Frazetta's influence on modern science fiction art is incalculable. Numerous young artists admit that Frazetta was a major influence on them, and even older artists are unreserved in their praise of his art. Frazetta demonstrated that there is no barrier to success by being a genre artist. He proved that to be successful, an artist does not have to abandon illustration and become a "fine" artist to achieve fame and financial success. Long after many of the fine artists of today are forgotten, Frank Frazetta's work probably will still be collected and admired.

PUBLISHED WORK:

HC: *1972 Annual Worlds Best SF* (73), *Dancer from Atlantis, Downward to Earth* (70), *Dracula/Frankenstein, Edgar Rice Burroughs: Master of Adventure, Flashing Swords I* (73), *Flashing Swords 2* (73), *The Girl from Farris's, Gods of Mars and Warlord of Mars* (71), *Master Mind of Mars and Fighting Man of Mars* (73), *Night Images, Orn, A Princess of Mars* (70), *Red Moon and Black Mountain, Swords of Mars and Synthetic Men of Mars, Tarzan Alive, Tarzan and the Castaways* (65), *Tarzan at the Earth's Core* (62), *Thuvia Maid of Mars and Chessmen of Mars* (72)

PB: A number of the Edgar Rice Burroughs books illustrated by Frazetta were published in several editions, with new covers by Frazetta for each printing. Such reprints are indicated by the words "new edition."

The Amsirs and the Iron Thorn, Ardor on Aros, At the Earth's Core, Atlan, The Autumn People, Back to the Stone Age (new edition), Back to the Stone Age, Beasts of Tarzan, Beyond the Farthest Star (new edition), Beyond the Farthest Star, The Black Star, Bloodstone, Brak vs. the Sorceress, Bran Mak Morn, Carson of Venus (new edition), Carson of Venus, Conan, Conan the Adventurer, Conan the Avenger, Conan the Buccaneer, Conan of Cimmeria, Conan the Conqueror, Conan the Usurper, Conan the Warrior, Creature from Beyond Infinity, Danger Planet, Dark Crusade, The Dark Gate, Death's Angels Shadow, Devils Generation, Edgar Rice Burroughs: Master of Adventure, Escape on Venus, Fantastic Art of Frank Frazetta (75), Fighting Man of Mars, Flashing Swords 1, Flashing Swords 2, Frank Frazetta Book Four (80), Frank Frazetta Book Three (78), Frank Frazetta Book Two (77), The Godmakers, Gulliver of Mars, Into the Aether, Jongor Fights Back, Jongor of the Lost Land, Jungle Tales of Tarzan, Kavin's World, King Kong, Land of Hidden Men, Land of Terror (new edition), Land of Terror, Lost Continent, Lost on Venus, Luana, Mad King, Mastermind of Mars, Maza of the Moon, Monster Men, Monster Out of Time, Moon Maid, Moon Men, The Mucker, Night Winds, The Oakdale Affair, Outlaw of Torn, Outlaw World, Pellucidar, People That Time Forgot, Phoenix Prime, The Reassembled Man, Reign of Wizardry, The Return of Jongor, Return of the Mucker, The Rider, Savage Pellucidar (new edition), Savage Pellucidar, Secret People, The Serpent, The Solar Invasion, Son of Tarzan, Swords against Darkness, Swordsmen in the Sky, Tales from the Crypt, Tales of the Incredible, Tanar of Pellucidar, Tarzan and the City of Gold, Tarzan at the Earth's Core, Tarzan the Invincible, Tarzan and the Jewels of Opar, Tarzan and the Lion Man, Tarzan and the Lost Empire, Tarzan the Triumphant, Thongor in the City of Magicians, Thongor against the Gods, Time War, The Tritonian Ring, The Vault of Horror, Warrior of Llarn, Witch of the Dark Gate, Witherwing, Wolfshead, Wonderful World of Oz.

FREAS, FRANK KELLY (b. Aug. 27, 1922) American artist. Freas has the distinct honor of being the most popular artist in the science fiction field for the longest time. Although other artists' fame has sometimes eclipsed Freas's accomplishments, in the long view no other artist can match his achievements in the world of science fiction illustration. For more than thirty years he has remained a favorite of both fans and professionals. No other artist in science fiction has consistently matched quality and quantity of art for such an extended period. Freas is one of the most prolific artists ever to work the science fiction field, and his output is matched only by the excellence of his work.

Freas was born in New York but was brought up in Canada. He attended Cooper Union for engineering and later Georgetown as a premed student. He was a lifelong science fiction fan and reader, with a particular fondness for the stories published in *Astounding Science Fiction* during the early 1940s.

Freas served for four and a half years in the air force in the Pacific Theater in World War II as a photographer. He returned after the war to continue as an advertising artist. He had already been working as a freelance illustrator doing advertising art as well as having served as an art director for Curtis-Wright's *P.R.O.* in Columbus, Ohio, before the war. He served a year as art director for the Pittsburgh *Bulletin Index* and enrolled at the Art Institute of Pittsburgh, continuing his freelancing while in school.

Freas studied under John Jellicoe at Pittsburgh. Another student and friend, Charles Kennedy, sold a cover painting to *Weird Tales* magazine and suggested that Freas send them a painting of Pan that Freas had done as a class project. The tip led to his first published painting, used for the November 1950 issue of *Weird Tales*.

After his first success, Freas slowly began submitting more art to the New York science fiction publishers. At the same time, he continued to work as an advertising illustrator in Pittsburgh, doing art for television and working with one of the best ad agencies in the city. Despite the steady income, Freas decided to move to New York. He gave up his advertising work in November 1952 and became a full-time illustrator.

About this same time Freas married science fiction fan Polly Bussard, who has been both his partner and researcher ever since. Within a short time Freas was working for many of the science fiction publishers as well as doing jacket art for Gnome Press.

In 1953 Freas began working for *Astounding Science Fiction*, long considered the leading magazine in the field. He soon became the leading interior artist for the magazine and shared cover responsibilities with H. R. Van Dongen. John W. Campbell, Jr., editor of *Astounding* also had Freas provide a series of small cover inserts, used at the top of each cover during the 1950s, to distinguish *Astounding* from the other science fiction magazines being published during that period. The symbols ranged from "Hex Signs Circa 1960" to "The Nonconformists." All were simple but witty little illustrations that added something extra to the magazine.

While contributing to nearly every science fiction magazine in the field, Freas continued to do work outside the science fiction field. He was a frequent contributor to *Mad* magazine and is credited with doing the first Alfred E. Neuman illustration. He also did numerous religious illustrations for the Franciscans during this period.

Except for a break from science fiction while living in Mexico for several years, Freas has continued to produce quality science fiction year after year into the 1980s. He has always been a fan favorite—winning ten Hugo Awards for Best Science Fiction Artist, five of the awards in a row. He and his wife have been guests at numerous conventions as well as guests of honor at the World SF Convention.

NASA selected Freas's design for a shoulder patch for the astronauts on Skylab I. As part of his own interest in space travel, he designed five posters for the space program. They were originally printed in the graphics department of the Virginia School system. These posters were so popular that NASA used them in its own educational program. The five illustrations were done on negatives, and no actual paintings exist of the art. Copies of each of the posters are displayed in the Smithsonian.

Freas was hired by Laser books to produce all of the covers for its science fiction line. These covers were done to an exact formula, with an action illustration and a large head always in the forefront of the picture. The books were published by Harlequin Books and were aimed to appeal to the same readers who bought the Harlequin Romances. However, sales were never what the publisher expected, and the line was dropped after two years. Freas did fifty-seven covers for Laser Books, perhaps being the only artist ever to do every cover for a paperback line.

Freas works primarily in acrylics for his paintings, although he has done some work in watercolors. He rarely uses oils due to an allergic reaction. His black-and-white interior illustrations are done in a variety of styles, although primarily with crisp india-ink line work on white illustration board.

One of the first artists to offer prints of his paintings for sale, Freas also was one of the first artists to collect his best work in book form. His *Frank Kelly Freas—The Art of Science Fiction* not only reprinted many of the artist's finest illustrations, but the accompanying text gave Freas an opportunity to describe intelligently his feelings and thoughts about science fiction art.

According to Freas, "An illustrator, whether science fiction or otherwise, is essentially a story-teller who can't type. . . . A feeling of conviction in a picture comes from a solid grounding in reality, no matter how far out the situation may be. To explore the unknown, you range outward from the known, and successful pioneers always move out from solidly established advance bases. Actually, being an artist is a bit like being a pioneer. Your real goal, like his, is freedom."

More than any other artist in the science fiction field, Freas draws character. As the artist himself put it, in *The Art of Science Fiction*, "One of the things I brought to science fiction art was people. Not always well painted, but still real, understandable, believable *people*, whether they were rock-jawed, bristle-headed Terran topkicks or blue-furred aliens with three eyes and a prehensile tail."

Freas brought wrinkles to science fiction—his illustrations show real people with bags under their eyes and wrinkles in their faces. His characters had expressions, and most of all, they had depth. They were not always beautiful, although he was capable of doing beautiful people when he wanted to, but they were always human. More than any other artist ever working in science fiction, Freas captured emotion. "I always tried to say in my drawings and paintings something the *author* would have said had *his* medium permitted, and it was usually a human reaction which would have taken pages to describe" (*The Art of Science Fiction*).

Emerging as a direct consequence of his mastery of human emotion is Freas's other great talent: humor. He is one of the few artists in science fiction who can create humorous illustrations. A lifelong admirer of Edd Cartier★, Freas is a master of the same type of art. His characters' expressions reveal the same frustrations, annoyances, and surprise that are an essential part of any humorous illustration. He draws people who are real but, at the same time, are larger than life. His wrinkled old men are incredibly wrinkled—his muscular supermen are filled with bulging muscles—his beautiful women are too good to be real. His aliens are dreadful creations of fangs and teeth. Such a style readily lends itself to humor, and even the most serious of Freas's art seems to be laughing gently behind its back. There is a twinkle in the eye of most characters in Freas's illustrations, and one suspects it lurks in the eyes of its creator as well.

PUBLISHED WORK:

HC: *Against the Fall of Night* (53), *Children of the Atom* (53), *City* (52), *Coming of Conan* (53), *Five SF Novels* (52), *Judgment Night* (52), *Second Foundation* (53)

PB: *1985 Annual Worlds Best SF* (85), *Arsenal Out of Time* (67), *The Beast* (83), *Beyond Capella*, *Birth of Fire* (76), *Birthright* (75), *Black Roads* (76), *Blake's Progress* (75), *Brain Machine* (68), *Brandyjack* (76), *But What of Earth?* (76), *Caravan* (75), *Carnelian Cube* (67), *Catch the Star Winds* (69), *Cemetary World*, *Conscience Interplanetary* (74), *Crash Landing on Iduna* (75), *Cross of Empire* (76), *Currents of Space* (66), *Dance of the Apocalypse* (76), *Dark Dimension*, *Day of Timestop* (68), *Day of Wrath* (71), *Dinosaur Beach* (72), *Dreadful Sanctuary* (67), *Dreamfields* (76), *Ecolog* (77), *End of Eternity* (66), *Epitaph in Rust* (76), *Extraterritorial* (77), *Eye in the Sky*, *Falling Toward Forever* (75), *Finish Line* (76), *Future Sanctuary* (76), *Galactic Invaders* (76), *Gates of the Universe* (75), *Gift of the Manti* (77), *Girls from Planet Five* (67), *Hard to be a God* (74), *Hard Way Up* (72), *Hawk of Arcturus* (75), *Hellquad* (84), *Hell's Gate* (70), *Herds* (75), *Hierarchies* (73), *The Horde* (76), *Hunters of Jundagai*, *I Aleppo* (76), *Ice Prison* (66), *In the Kingdom of the Beats* (71), *Into the Slave Nebula* (68), *Invasion* (75), *Iron Rain* (76), *Jeremy Case* (76), *Kane's Odyssey* (76), *Keeper* (76), *Key to Venudine*, *King of Eolim* (75), *Law for the Stars* (76), *Legacy* (76), *Lion Game* (73), *Man of Many Minds* (59), *Man Who Wanted Stars* (68), *Mankind under the Leash*, *Marauders of Gor* (75), *Martians Go Home*, *Master of the Stars* (76), *Meddlers* (76), *Mindwipe* (76), *Mister Justice* (73), *Moniter found in Orbit* (74), *Naked Sun* (66, 69), *Nebula Alert* (67), *Needle* (69), *Off Worlders*, *Operation Chaos* (72), *Out of Their Minds* (83), *Owl Time* (84), *Pandora's Planet* (73), *Pity about Earth*, *Rebels of Merka* (76), *Recoil*, *Redbeard* (69), *Renegades of Time* (75), *River and the Dream* (77), *Ruler of the World* (76), *Scavenger Hunt* (76), *Seas of Ernathe* (76), *Seeds of Change* (75), *The Seeker* (76), *Seeklight* (75), *Serving in Time*

(75), *Shadow on the Stars* (77), *Shepherd* (77), *Siege Perilous* (66), *Skies Discrowned* (76), *Slaves of Sleep* (67), *Somewhere a Voice* (67), *Space Barbarians* (69), *Space Trap* (76), *Spawn* (76), *Star Web* (75), *Stardroppers* (72), *Stars Like Dust* (66), *Stone That Never Came Down* (73), *Tactics of Mistake* (70), *Telzey Toy* (73), *Then Beggars Could Ride* (76), *This Side of Infinity*, *Tiger in the Stars* (76), *Time Gladiator* (69), *To Renew the Ages* (76), *Tonight We Steal the Stars*, *Tower of Medusa* (69), *Toyman*, *Treasure of Tau Ceti*, *Unknown Shore* (76), *Unteleported Man*, *Unto the Last Generation* (75), *Walls within Walls* (75), *Warriors of Dawn* (75), *West of Honor* (76), *Who?* (68), *Winds of Darkover* (71), *Wizards of Senchuria* (69), *World Jones Made*, *World Wreckers* (71), *Zen Gun* (83)

2CSAB: (spring, summer, winter); 1954 (spring)

AMZ: 1965 (10)

ASF: 1953 (9, 10, 11, 12); 1954 (1, 2, 3, 4, 5, 6, 7, 8, 9, 10, 11, 12); 1955 (1, 2, 3, 4, 5, 6, 7, 8, 9, 10, 11, 12); 1956 (1, 2, 3, 4, 5, 6, 7, 8, 9, 10, 11, 12); 1957 (1, 2, 3, 4, 5, 6, 7, 8, 9, 10, 11, 12); 1958 (1, 2, 3, 4, 5, 6, 7, 8, 9, 10, 11, 12); 1959 (1, 2, 3, 4, 5, 6, 7, 8, 9, 10, 11); 1960 (2, 4, 5, 6); 1964, (7, 8, 9, 11, 12); 1965 (1, 4, 7, 8, 9, 10, 11, 12); 1966 (1, 2, 3, 4, 5, 6, 7, 8, 9, 10, 11, 12); 1967 (1, 2, 3, 4, 5, 6, 7, 8, 9, 10, 11, 12); 1968 (1, 2, 3, 4, 5, 6, 7, 8, 10, 11, 12); 1969 (1, 2, 3, 4, 5, 7, 9, 10, 11, 12); 1970 (1, 2, 3, 4, 5, 6, 7, 8, 9, 10, 11, 12); 1971 (1, 2, 3, 4, 5, 6, 7, 8, 9, 10, 11, 12); 1972 (1, 2, 4, 5, 6, 7, 8, 9, 10, 11, 12); 1973 (1, 2, 4, 5, 6, 7, 9, 11, 12); 1974 (1, 3, 5, 6, 7, 8, 9, 10, 11, 12); 1976 (2, 4, 5, 6, 7, 8, 9, 12, annual); 1977 (1, 3, 8); 1978 (6, 8); 1980 (2); 1982 (8, 9, mid–9)

BEY: 1953 (9)

F&SF: 1954 (9, 10); 1955 (2); 1956 (9, 10, 11, 12); 1957 (3, 5, 12); 1958 (4); 1977 (7)

FF: 1953 (2, 6, 8)

FU: 1955 (4, 6, 8, 10); 1956 (2, 4); 1957 (2)

FUT: 1954 (3, 6, 8, 10); 1956 (29, 30); 1957 (31, 32, 33, 34); 1958 (3, 5, 10); 1959 (2); 1960 (2)

GAL: 1979 (9)

GXY: 1952 (10); 1954 (3); 1977 (8)

IASFM: 1977 (summer, fall, winter); 1978 (1, 7.9) 1979 (4, 10)

IF: 1953 (1, 3, 5, 7, 22); 1954 (1, 3, 4, 5, 6, 7, 8, 9, 10, 11, 12); 1955 (2, 3, 5, 6, 8, 10, 12); 1956 (2, 4); 1958 (10, 12); 1959 (2)

IMGT: 1956 (3, 5, 7)

NWUS: 1960 (3)

PS: 1952 (5, 7, 9, 11); 1953 (3, 5, 7, 9, 11); 1954 (1, 3, 5, summer, fall); 1955 (spring, summer)

RS: 1953 (7, 9)

SAT: 1956 (12)

SF: 1954 (2); 1955 (1, 3, 5, 7, 9, 11); 1956 (1, 5, 7, 9, 11); 1957 (1, 3, 5, 7, 9, 11); 1958 (1, 3, 5, 6, 7, 8, 9, 11); 1959 (3)

SFA: 1953 (2, 5, 7)

SFQ: 1954 (5, 8, 11); 1955 (2, 5, 8, 11); 1956 (2, 8, 11); 1957 (2, 5, 8)

SpSF: 1953 (3, 5, 7)

SS: 1955 (spring, summer)

SSF: 1956 (12); 1957 (2, 4, 8, 10); 1958 (2, 6, 8, 12); 1959 (6)

TOPS: 1953 (spring, fall)

TWS: 1953 (11); 1954 (spring); 1955 (winter)

VAN: 1958 (6)

WT: 1950 (11); 1951 (11); 1952 (12); 1953 (1, 3)

FUQUA, ROBERT. See TILLOTSON, JOSEPH WIRT.

GALLARDO, GERVASIO (b. 1934). Spanish artist. Born in Barcelona, Spain, Gallardo studied art for a number of years and worked for several Spanish art agencies before moving to Munich in 1959. After a short time, he spent four years working for the Delpire Agency in Paris.

In 1963 Gallardo moved to the United States for a short period. He then returned to Paris, where he freelanced as an artist, traveling back to the United States for a number of New York exhibitions. He finally settled in Barcelona, where he set up his own studio.

By this time, Gallardo was well known in the commercial art field for his advertising illustrations. He also worked in the fine-art field, doing paintings for collectors and museums. His art was a blend of surrealism and humor and revealed the strong influence of Magritte but with a uniqueness all his own.

In 1969 Ballantine Books began using Gallardo for its adult fantasy series. His unique covers helped define the series and establish its identity among the books published during that period. Even though other artists of note contributed to the adult fantasy line, it was Gallardo's name that was firmly linked with the books. Unfortunately, when the surrealist movement in science fiction and fantasy died in the middle 1970s, Gallardo's work was rarely seen again in the genre. He has continued his career as a popular artist in both the fine-art and commercial-advertising field and has recently begun to do some art for new fantasy hardcovers from mainstream publishers.

Gallardo was the winner of a number of Gold Medal Awards from the Society of Illustrators as well as some European Art awards. His work was done in nearly all popular mediums—acrylics, oils, gouache, pen and ink, and colored pencils, and he often used combinations of techniques and mediums in a single work. He also used glazing on his paintings to give them a strong, vivid color.

PUBLISHED WORK:

PB: *Aliens 4* (74), *Beyond the Fields We Know* (72), *Beyond the Golden Stair* (70), *The Charwoman's Shadow* (73), *The Doom That Came to Sarnath* (72), *Double Phoenix* (72),

The Dream Quest of Unknown Kadath (70), *Evenor* (72), *Excalibur* (73), *The Fantastic World of Gervasio Gellardo* (76), *A Fine and Private Place* (69), *The Forgotten Beasts of Eld* (74), *Great Short Novels of Adult Fantasy 1* (72), *Great Short Novels of Adult Fantasy 2* (73), *Imaginary Worlds* (73), *Khaled* (71), *The Last Unicorn* (69), *A Look Behind the Cthulhu Mythos* (72), *Lud-in-the-Mist* (70), *The Man Who Was Thursday* (71), *Merlin's Ring* (74), *Over the Hills and Far Away* (74), *Phantastes* (70), *Poseidonis* (73), *Spawn of Cthulhu* (71), *The Sundering Flood* (73), *Water of the Wondrous Isles* (71), *Well at the Worlds End 1* (70), *Well at the Worlds End 2* (70), *Xiccarph* (72)

GAUGHAN, JACK (Sept. 24, 1930–1985) American artist. Born in Springfield, Ohio, Gaughan attended the Dayton Art Institute in Dayton, Ohio. Interested in science fiction most of his life, he sold his first published piece to Fantasy Publishing Company, Inc., (known as FPCI Publishers) while still in school. He majored in commercial art and, after obtaining his degree, went on to graduate work until drafted in 1952. After service at Fort Eustis, Virginia, he returned to civilian life and used the GI bill to continue his studies at Dayton Art Institute. Gaughan then went to Philadelphia to illustrate a children's book and from there traveled to New York, where he stayed with Hannes Bok★ for a short while. He started working for an art studio in New York, worked as an art director for some small ad agencies, and then went into commercial filmstrip art as an art director. During this time, he married and had a son, Brian.

Gaughan had remained active in science fiction, doing freelance illustrations since the middle 1950s. Since he was not happy with his occupation, his wife, Phoebe, encouraged him to freelance as a full-time SF artist. An exceptional series of interior illustrations for the Jack Vance story "The Dragon Masters" in *Galaxy*, August 1962, had caused a great deal of excitement in the SF field and had vaunted Gaughan into the front rank of SF illustrators. Even with his new-found popularity, however, Gaughan remained active as a fan artist. Later, he became the only artist ever to win Hugo Awards for the best professional and best fan artists in the same year (1967).

Gaughan illustrated his first paperback cover for Donald Wollheim at Ace Books and, with its sale, became a full-time science fiction artist. His entry into the paperback-cover field was well timed since it happened when Ed Emshwiller★ was getting involved in other mediums and Kelly Freas★ was not doing much work. So there was a void that Gaughan helped to fill. He did a great number of covers for Ace Books and most other paperback publishers in the 1960s, usually in a simple, abstract style. At the same time, his black-and-white illustrations dominated the pages of *Galaxy* and *If* magazines, which were increasingly important during that same decade. His domination of the art field at that time is noted in the fact that Gaughan won the Hugo Award for Best Artist in 1967, 1968, and 1969. From 1969 through 1972 he served as art director for *Galaxy*.

Gaughan continued to be active in the field into the 1970s. However, the slow but steady decline in magazine science fiction during the previous fifteen years hurt Gaughan's career: there were not many markets for black-and-white illustrations. Although he was an able cover artist, a new generation of artists including Michael Whelan★ and Rowena Morrill★ provided a great deal more competition than he had experienced in the 1960s. As the market in the paperback field expanded, so did the number of artists looking for work. Tastes in art changed, and abstract art like Gaughan's and Richard Powers★ was not in demand as it had been in earlier times. Poor health also forced Gaughan to cut back on his art, and for the last few years of his life he contributed very little to the SF art field. He died of cancer in 1985.

PUBLISHED WORK:

HC: *After 12,000 Years* (50), *Damnation Alley* (69), *Hidden Universe* (50), *People of the Comet* (48), *Planets of Adventure* (49), *Radium Pool* (49), *Rat Race* (50), *Toymaker* (51), *Triton* (49), *Works of M. P. Shiel* (48)

PB: *2nd Book of Fritz Leiber* (75), *Almuric* (64), *Arsenal of Miracles* (64), *Beachhead Planet* (70), *Best of John Jakes* (77), *Beyond the Stars* (63), *Book of Andre Norton* (75), *Book of Fritz Leiber* (74), *Brains of Earth* (66), *Brass Dragon* (69), *Children of the Lens* (66), *Closed Worlds* (68), *Cradle of the Sun* (69), *Crystal Gryphon* (73), *Darkover Landfall* (72), *Day the World Ended, Dragon Masters, Einstein Intersection* (67), *Exile of Xanadu* (64), *Exiles of the Stars* (72), *Exiles of Time* (65), *Fantastic Swordsman* (67), *The Fellowship of the Ring, The First Lensman* (64), *Five Gold Bands, Flight from Yesterday* (63), *Forerunner Fray* (80), *Fury from Earth* (63), *Galactic Patrol* (64), *Game Players of Titan* (63), *Garan the Eternal* (72), *Gather in the Hall of Planets* (71), *Ghosts of Manacle* (64), *Golden People* (64), *Gray Lensman* (65), *Green Millenium* (69), *Harvest of Hoodwinks* (70), *Here Abide Monsters* (74), *Houses of Isam* (64), *Karchee Reign* (66), *King in Yellow, King Kobold* (71), *King of the Worlds Edge, Last Castle* (67), *Legion of Space* (67), *Legion of Time* (67), *Limbo, Many Worlds of Magnus Ridolph* (66), *Masters of the Lamp* (70), *Masters of the Vortex* (68), *Monsters in Orbit* (67), *Night Monsters* (69), *Night of Light* (66), *One against the Legion* (67), *One Million Centuries* (67), *The Other Log of Phileas Fogg* (73), *Planeteers* (66), *Prism, Quag Keep* (78), *The Return of the King, Rogue Dragon* (65), *Second Book of Fritz Lieber* (75), *Second Stage Lensman* (65), *Silverlock, Slave Planet* (63), *Son of the Tree* (64), *Spell of the Witch World* (72), *Stealer of Souls* (67), *Stormbringer* (67), *The Sun Destroyers* (73), *Swordsmen in the Sky* (64), *Tales in a Jugular Vein* (65), *Three against the Witchworld, Three Worlds to Conquer* (64), *Time Tunnel* (64), *Triplanetary* (65), *The Twisted Men* (63), *The Two Towers, The Unholy City* (68), *Warlock in Spite of Himself* (69), *Warlock of Witchworld* (67), *Weapon from Beyond* (67), *Witch World* (63), *World Between* (67), *World of the Sleeper* (67), *World of the Starwolves* (68), *Wrath of Fu Manchu* (73), *Yank at Valhalla* (73), *Yurth Burden* (78), *Web of the Witch World* (64)

AMZ: 1961 (11); 1965 (12); 1982 (11)

ASF: 1949(1); 1972 (3, 8, 10, 11, 12); 1973 (1, 2, 5, 6, 7, 9, 10, 11); 1974 (1, 2, 3, 4, 5, 6, 9, 10, 11, 12); 1975 (1, 3, 4, 5, 7, 8, 9, 11, 12); 1976 (1, 3, 5, 6, 10, 11, 12, annual); 1977 (1, 2, 4, 5, 7, 8, 9, 10, 11, 12); 1978 (1, 2, 3, 4, 5, 6, 8, 12, yearbook);

1979 (2, 3, 5, 7, 9, 10, 11); 1980 (6); 1981 (2, 3, 4, 5, 6, 7, 8, 9); 1982 (2, 3, 3/29, 7, 8, 9)

COS: 1977 (5, 7, 9, 11)

F&SF: 1964 (2, 4, 12); 1965 (2, 7); 1966 (1, 4, 9); 1967 (3, 7, 12); 1968 (7, 12); 1969 (5, 11); 1970 (6, 11); 1971 (2); 1973 (6); 1976 (3); 1980 (2)

FB: 1950 (6)

FTC: 1962 (9); 1963 (3)

GXY: 1956 (8, 9, 10, 12); 1957 (1, 2, 3, 4, 5, 7, 8, 11, 12); 1958 (1, 12); 1961 (2, 4, 6, 12); 1962 (2, 4, 6, 8, 12); 1963 (2, 12); 1964 (4, 6, 8, 10); 1965 (2, 4, 6, 10, 12); 1966 (2, 6, 10); 1967 (2, 4, 8, 12); 1968 (2, 4, 8, 9); 1969 (1, 2, 3, 4, 5, 8, 9, 10, 11, 12); 1970 (1, 2, 3, 4, 5, 6, 7, 8, 10, 12); 1971 (1, 2, 3, 4, 5, 7, 9, 11); 1972 (1, 3, 4, 5, 7, 9, 11); 1973 (1, 3, 5, 7, 9, 10, 11, 12); 1974 (1, 2, 3, 4, 5, 6, 7, 8, 9); 1977 (3, 4)

IASFM: 1977 (summer); 1978 (1, 3, 5, 7, 9, 11); 1979 (1, 2, 3, 4, 5, 6, 7, 8, 9, 12); 1980 (1, 3, 5, 11, 12); 1981 (2, 3, 4, 5, 6, 7, 8, 9, 10, 11, 12); 1982 (1, 2, 3, 4, 6)

IF: 1960 (3, 7, 9, 11); 1961 (3, 5, 11); 1962 (1, 5, 7, 9, 11); 1963 (7, 11); 1964 (3, 7, 8, 10); 1965 (1, 2, 3, 4, 6, 7, 8, 9, 10, 11, 12); 1966 (1, 2, 3, 4, 5, 6, 7, 8, 9, 10, 11, 12); 1967 (1, 2, 3, 4, 5, 6, 7, 8, 9, 10, 11, 12); 1968 (1, 4, 5, 6, 7, 8, 9, 10, 11, 12); 1970 (1, 2, 4, 5, 7, 9, 11); 1971 (1, 3, 6, 8, 12); 1972 (2, 4, 6, 8); 1973 (6); 1974 (10, 12)

INF: 1957 (4)

OW: 1950 (3)

WOT: 1963 (4, 6); 1964 (2, 6, 8); 1965 (1, 3, 5, 7, 9)

GEARY, CLIFFORD (?) American artist. A children's book artist, Geary is remembered in the science fiction field for his illustrations in the Scribner hardcover editions of Robert Heinlein's juvenile novels. Since the Heinlein books were among the most important and widely read science fiction books aimed at teenagers and young adults in the 1950s, Geary's illustrations must be considered particularly influential in the growth and development of the modern science fiction community.

PUBLISHED WORK:

HC: *Farmer in the Sky* (53), *Red Planet* (49), *Rolling Stones* (52), *Space Cadet* (48), *Starman Jones* (53)

GIUNTA, JOHN (1920-Nov. 6, 1970) American artist. An active fan in the 1930s, Giunta started illustrating for fanzines in that period. He began his professional career in comics, working for the Chesler shop in 1938–1939 as a letterer and colorist. In the early 1940s he broke into the science fiction field preparing artwork for the Popular Publications science fiction pulps. Soon Giunta was doing artwork for *Weird Tales* as well. He later worked as a comics editor for Magazine Enterprises in 1948–1949. His art was strongly influenced by comic-book artist Will Eisner. In the late 1950s he served as art director for the short-lived *Saturn Science Fiction* magazine. Along with his SF and comic art, Giunta also did cartoons for *Quick Frozen Food* magazine, edited by SF historian Sam Moskowitz. Giunta never married.

PUBLISHED WORK:

AMZ: 1955 (11); 1956 (4, 6, 10, 12)

ASF&FR: 1953 (1, 4)

F&SF: 1958 (11)

FA: 1952 (8)

FTC: 1955 (10); 1956 (8)

FU: 1960 (3)

GXY: 1962 (12); 1963 (2, 12); 1964 (2, 4, 6, 12); 1965 (8, 12)

IF: 1962 (11); 1963 (1, 3, 5, 6, 9, 11); 1964 (3, 5, 11, 12); 1965 (1, 3, 4, 5, 6, 7, 8, 9, 10, 11, 12); 1966 (1)

INF: 1955 (11); 1956 (6); 1957 (2)

SAT: 1956 (2, 4, 6, 10, 12); 1957 (2, 6)

SRN: 1957 (3, 5, 7, 10); 1958 (3)

SFA: 1956 (12)

SSS: 1941 (1); 1942 (11); 1943 (5); 1949 (4)

TSF: 1951 (spring)

VEN: 1957 (1, 3, 5, 7, 9, 11); 1958 (1, 3, 5, 7)

WOT: 1963 (6); 1964 (2, 4 11); 1965 (3, 5, 7, 11)

WT: 1942 (11); 1943 (1, 3 7, 9, 11); 1944 (3, 7, 9); 1947 (5, 7, 9); 1948 (1, 3, 5, 7, 9, 22); 1949 (1, 5, 7, 9); 1950 (1, 5); 1954 (9)

GIUSTI, ROBERT G. (b. 1937) Born in Zurich, Switzerland, Giusti attended the Tyler School of Fine Art. He later studied at the Cranbrook Academy of Art until 1961. His first sale was to *American Girl* in 1956, and since that time, his art has appeared in numerous magazines including *McCalls*, *Redbook*, *Fortune*, and *Penthouse*. He also has painted numerous dust-jacket covers as well as poster art.

GLADNEY, GRAVES (Dec. 10, 1907–Mar. 24, 1976) Born in St. Louis, Gladney wanted to be a painter since early childhood. He attended Amherst College and graduated with a BS degree. He traveled to Europe and studied at L'ecole des Beaux Arts and the Slade School of the University of London. Gladney married in Europe, and when he returned to the United States with a wife and two children, he moved to New York to earn a living. After failing to get a job illustrating for *The New Yorker*, he was advised by several other artists to try pulp art. He sold his first cover to Fiction House in the mid–1930s and worked for most of the big pulp publishers from then on. Gladney was typical of many pulp painters in that almost anything would provide inspiration for his work. A glance at his writing table in his studio gave rise to a cover for *Dime Mystery* in 1937, a bizarre horror painting showing a madman and his assistant about to cut off the legs of a woman by using a giant paper cutter. He joined the staff of Street & Smith Publications in 1939. There his primary job was painting covers for *The Shadow* pulp magazine, but he also did covers for other Street & Smith pulps, including *Unknown* and *Astounding*. He painted more than 275 covers during a span of six years of painting for the pulps.

Gladney was drafted in 1942 and served with the 82nd Division Airborne gliders during World War II, which put an end to his pulp painting. After the war, however, he returned to art, producing some calendar art and preparing art for several comic strips. However, after the real violence of the war, Gladney found himself unable to deal with the false violence of comic art. Therefore, he took a post teaching at Washington University in St. Louis in 1949, a position he held until 1960. Investments he had made over the years enabled him to retire at that time. A gun enthusiast, he was a champion shooter with rifle, pistol, and shotgun.

PUBLISHED WORK:

ASF: 1939 (3, 6, 7)
UK: 1939 (4, 8, 11)

GLEESON, TONY (?) American artist. Gleeson learned to read from comic books, which explains, he believes, his love of the science fiction field. He moved to Los Angeles in 1977 and has been involved in numerous projects there, including all types of illustration, graphic design, and painting. Much of his science fiction work has been published by the Science Fiction Book Club. He is married with two children.

PUBLISHED WORK:

HC: *The Golden Helix, Mission of Gravity, Tales from the "White Hart"*
AMZ: 1974 (12); 1975 (5, 7, 9, 11); 1976 (1, 3, 6, 9, 12); 1977 (3)
FTC: 1975 (4, 6, 8, 10, 12); 1976 (5, 8, 11); 1977 (2, 6, 9, 12)

GOBLE, WARWICK WATERMAN (Nov. 22, 1862-Jan. 22, 1943) British artist. Goble was one of the three finest artists specializing in science fiction, along with Fred Jane★ and Henri Lanos★, who worked for British magazines at the turn of the century. Unfortunately, in common with the other two men, very little is known of his personal life. This book is the first time the year of his birth has ever been listed in any reference book.

Goble was born in Dalton (north London), the son of a commercial traveler, Brukitt Goble, and his wife, Mary (nee Waterman). Goble studied at Westminster School of Art and spent several years with a printing firm, where he learned chromolithography and commercial design. He became a careful and accomplished illustrator, working mainly for reproduction by the halftone process.

A prolific contributor to the quality monthly magazines, Goble is now best remembered for sixty-six of his illustrations that accompanied the first appearance in print of *The War of the Worlds* by H. G. Wells in 1897. For some unexplained reason, the 1898 London first-book edition omitted all of his fine artwork. Goble's vision of the war machines of the Martian invaders are among the most famous of all science fiction illustrations. He was a master of realistic detail, and there is no question that his illustrations added immeasurably to the popularity of this major work of science fiction.

Goble abandoned science fiction illustration in 1903. Meanwhile, his reputation as a color illustrator soared, and he became famous for his work, including Kingsley's *Water Babies*, Grace James's *Green Willow and Other Japanese Fairy Tales*, and other major children's books. Many of these editions became major collectors' items. Goble used his new-found fortune to travel extensively in Europe and the Orient. He died in Surrey in January 1943.

PUBLISHED WORK: 138 (All British).

HC: *The Oracle of Baal* (1896), *The War of the Worlds* (1898, first U.S. edition)

PEARSON'S MAGAZINE: "The Dust of Death" (Mar. 1903), "Four Days' Night" (Feb. 1903), "Four White Days" (Jan. 1903), "In the Abyss" (Aug. 1896), "Invisible Force" (June 1903), "London's Danger" (Feb. 1896), "The Raid of Le Vengeur" (Feb. 1901), "The War of the Worlds" (six parts, Apr. through Dec. 1897)

Richard Dalby

GOODFELLOW, PETER (b. 1950) British artist. Goodfellow studied at the Central School of Art, London, from 1967 to 1971. A freelance illustrator since 1972, he shows in his work a strong interest in symbolist and surrealist art—most notably in *Flying Saucer Vision, Phantasms and Magics*, and *The Illustrated Man*. Seven of his paintings are included in *The Flights of Icarus* (1977).

Richard Dalby

GOULD, JOHN FLEMING (b. 1906) American artist. Born in Worcester, Massachusetts, Gould studied at the Tiffany Foundation and graduated from Pratt, where he then taught for twenty-two years. He also taught at the Newark School of Fine and Industrial Art, as well as in classes at the Bethlehem Art Gallery.

Gould worked for the pulp magazines and was one of the most prolific artists ever to do art for those publications. Primarily an interior artist, he produced nearly twelve thousand illustrations, mostly for adventure and detective pulps of the 1920s and 1930s. He was one of the leading illustrators for Popular Publications and its many single-character pulps like *The Spider* and *Operator 5*. In 1930 he did most of the illustrations for *Astounding Science Fiction*, continuing from its first issue for nearly two years until other artists began working for the pulp.

After leaving the pulps, Gould began illustrating for *The Saturday Evening Post*. He later did artwork for many other major magazines and prepared numerous national advertisements. His watercolors are well known and held in many private collections and museums.

PUBLISHED WORK:

ASF: 1930 (1, 2, 3, 4, 5, 6, 7, 8, 9, 10, 11); 1931 (1, 2, 4)

GOULD, ROBERT (?) American artist. Noted for his delicate line work and detailed illustrations, Gould has become increasingly prolific in the 1980s. Among his most noteworthy paintings are a series of fine covers done for reissues of the Michael Moorcock heroic fantasy novels, including the famed Elric series. Gould's work closely resembles that of Thomas Canty*.

PUBLISHED WORK:

HC: *Gods of the Greataway* (84)

PB: *Bane of the Black Sword* (84), *The Bull and the Spear* (86), *Elric* (84), *The King of Swords* (85), *The Knight of Swords* (85), *The Oak and the Ram* (86), *The Queen of Swords* (85), *The Sailor on the Seas of Fate* (84), *Stormbringer* (84), *The Sword and the Stallion* (86), *The Vanishing Tower* (84), *Weird of the White Wolf* (84)

GRAEF, ROBERT A. (?- May 15, 1951) American artist. Born and brought up in Brooklyn, Graef always wanted to be an artist, and his first published art appeared in the pages of a Brooklyn newspaper at the age of ten. Like many other artists who grew up in New York, he attended Pratt Institute and received a degree from the School of Art and Design in 1896. On graduation, the art director at the school got Graef a job working for a prominent stained-glass-window operation. But after three days on the job, Graef resigned and became a freelance artist. He concentrated on il-lustrating magazine and book covers, working in Chicago, Buffalo, Boston, Texas, and New York. For a number of years, he did the drawings for the children's page of the *Delineator* magazine.

Graef began working for the Munsey chain in the 1920s. He was one of the first artists that the editors of *Argosy* specifically mentioned as being their specialist in portraying beings and beasts that inhabit other planets. Graef was an exceptional artist working for one of the best-paying maga-zines of the period, and his work was far superior to anything being pub-lished by the science fiction magazines. He was a fine painter of people and could also handle alien monsters without resorting to cartoon-style illus-tration. His covers featured action and drama and a fine feel for color. Graef shared cover assignments in the late 1920s and early 1930s with Paul Stahr*, and between the two men, both graduates of Pratt, *Argosy* featured the most dynamic fantastic adventure covers in the pulp field.

Some of the novels and short stories in *Argosy* that Graef illustrated included "A Brand New World" (1928), "Burn Witch Burn" (1932), "Caves of Ocean" (1931), "Flood" (1933), "The Jungle Rebellion" (1931), "Maza of the Moon" (1929), "The Planet of Peril" (1929), "The Prince of Peril" (1930), "Princess of the Atom" (1929), "The Radio Flyers" (1931), "The Radio Gun Runners" (1930), "The Radio Menace" (1930), "The Radio War" (1932), "The Sea Girl" (1929), "The Shadow Girl" (1929), "Tama of the Light Country" (1932), and "The War of the Purple Gas" (1932).

Several hardcover publishers during the same period used the cover paintings from *Argosy* for novels that they reprinted from that magazine. Thus a number of Graef paintings for science fiction novels later appeared as dustjacket art on hardcover editions of those same novels.

PUBLISHED WORK:

HC: *Planet of Peril* (29), *Prince of Peril* (30), *The Sea Girl* (30)

PS: 1942 (winter)

GRANDVILLE (Sept. 30, 1803–Mar. 17, 1847) French artist. Jean Ignace Isidore Gerard was the celebrated French caricaturist generally known by the pseudonym "Grandville."

Born at Nancy, France, Grandville received his first instruction in drawing from his father (a painter of miniatures). At the age of twenty-one he moved to Paris, where he soon published a collection of lithographs entitled *Les tribulations de la petite propriete.* His first success came in 1828 with *Methamorphoses du jour*, a series of seventy-three scenes in which creatures with the bodies of men and faces of animals play the human comedy.

For nearly twenty years Grandville contributed drawings to many periodicals and illustrated several classic works, including Swift's *Gulliver's Travels*. His greatest masterpiece, an extravaganza of satire and fantasy, was *Un autre monde*, a superb volume published in 1844. It contained 164 bizarre and humorous Grandville illustrations. The accompanying text was also by Grandville using another pseudonym, "Taxile Delord."

Among the memorable flights of fancy in this book are the solar eclipse depicted as a kiss, watched by an army of telescopes on earth, and the Bridge of Infinities spanning the Solar System. There are numerous echoes of his influence in the later work of Gustave Dore, Albert Robida*, Max Ernst, and the film maker Georges Melies.

Although Grandville died in March 1847, his collections of drawings and lithographs are still eagerly collected.

Richard Dalby

GRANT, MELVYN (b. 1944) British artist. Grant, who signs his work as "Melvyn," studied at the Brassey Institute, Hastings, Sussex, from 1960 to 1964. He is a prolific artist who does a great deal of work in the science fiction, fantasy, and historical fields. He is an expert at portraying prehistoric animals and imaginary leviathans. A selection of his best work was published in *The Flights of Icarus* (1977) and *The Fantastic Planet* (1980).

Richard Dalby

GURNEY, JAMES (b. June 14, 1958) American artist. Born in Glendale, California, Gurney knew that he wanted to be an artist from the time he was thirteen. In 1980 he received his undergraduate degree from the University of California, Berkeley, in anthropology with Phi Beta Kappa honors. While in school, Gurney studied paleontology, astronomy, European history, and geology. He continued his education for two semesters at the Art Center College of Design in Pasadena, California.

As a child Gurney went camping with his family in the Pacific Northwest and went sailing in the Pacific Ocean. In 1980 and 1981 he and another artist, Tom Kinkade, traveled across America on freight trains, earning their way by doing two–dollar portraits in local bars of the towns they visited. The two made numerous sketches during their adventure, and these pieces eventually formed the basis of *The Artist's Guide to Sketching*, published by Watson-Guptill in 1982, which has sold more than eighteen thousand copies.

The year 1983 was important for Gurney. He married another illustrator, Jeanette Lendino, who has since served as chief critic of his work as well as model, costume designer, and manuscript note taker. He also became involved in the science fiction field that year through the animated feature film *Fire and Ice*.

A project of Frank Frazetta* and Ralph Bakshi, *Fire and Ice* was a swords-and-sorcery feature in the heroic-fantasy tradition. Gurney worked as a background painter and designer for the film. He was required to do eleven paintings a week, and he did some five hundred in all. Gurney's work on the background design generated a great deal of interest in the SF art field since it was the first attempt to apply a realistic Hudson River School approach to animation art.

During this same period, Gurney began working as a freelance paperback cover artist, receiving his first commission from *The Magazine of Fantasy & SF* in 1982. Since that time he has prepared art for most of the major paperback houses. Like many artists, he submits several sketches (in oil) showing different ideas based on reading the story. The finished painting is oil on canvas. Gurney also works as an artist outside the science fiction field, most notably in the historical and mythological field for *National Geographic*.

Influenced by Rockwell, Cornwell, Gruger, and members of the Howard Pyle School, Gurney considers paperback cover work as one of the last remnants of the golden age of illustration, when illustrators were considered artists and given a great deal of editorial freedom.

PUBLISHED WORK:

PB: *The Alejandra Variations, Alpine Princess, The Annals of Klepsis, Armor, Atlan* (85), *Aubade for Gamelon, The City, City of Sorcery* (84), *The Digging Leviathan, The Dragon, Forty Thousand in Gehenna, Homecoming, Imaro 2 Quest for Cush* (84), *Imaro 3 Trail of Boku* (85), *Jagged Orbit, The Man Who Never Missed, Out of the Sun, The Pandora Stone, Procurator, Salvage and Destroy, Serpent, Song of Homana, Starrigger, The Steps of the Sun, The Tarturus Incident, The Yingling, Witches of Kregan* (84)

GUTIERREZ, ALAN (b. July 11, 1958) American artist. Born in Kansas City, Gutierrez moved to California in 1962. He attended Orange Coast Community College in Costa Mesa, California, as a civil engineer major beginning in 1976. In 1978 he became an art major. In 1979 he entered the Art Center College of Design in Pasadena, California, and graduated in September 1982.

Gutierrez entered the science fiction field as a result of reading SF magazines in his college library. He did not rise through fandom as many modern artists do but instead attended his first convention in 1980, several years after deciding to become a science fiction artist. Some artistic influences include Rick Sternbach★, David Hardy★, Dean Ellis★, and Paul Alexander★.

Guiterrez works in opaque watercolor as well as in oil. He has strong feelings about how to construct a cover painting, based on his art education. Rather than illustrating a specific scene in a story, Guiterrez prefers to go for the mood of the story. He believes that "a painting can be described in one sentence or paragraph. In story illustration, that should also describe an abstract of the story. Words translate into shapes on a cover, without regard to preconceived notions of the subject matter."

PUBLISHED WORK:

PB: *Ambassador of Progress, The Biofab War, Captive Universe, Chaos in Lagrangia, Cross the Stars, Damnation Alley, Earthblood, The Forlorn Hope, The Game Beyond, The Golden People, The Helix and the Sword, The Lagrangists, Man of War #2, Midas World, Orbit Unlimited, Survival*

FANTASY BOOK: 1983 (5, 8)

RIGEL: 1982 (1, 6, 9); 1983 (4)

HAMANN, BRAD (?) American artist. Born and brought up in New York City, Hamann has been reading science fiction since age nine. He attended Stuyvesant High School and then started studying fine arts at New Paltz State College. He transferred to Parsons School of Design and received a BFA with honors. He has since studied with a number of noted illustrators. His first science fiction illustrations appeared in 1978, and he has also done illustrations for *The New York Times, Science Digest, Scholastic, U.S. Air*, and *Business Week*. He has done advertising art as well. Although he began with science fiction interior art, he has since branched out into book-cover art.

In 1982 Hamann wrote and illustrated *The Science Fiction Design Coloring Book*. He hopes to become a science fiction writer as well as an illustrator.

PUBLISHED WORK:

ASF: 1979 (1, 3, 5, 6, 9, 11, 12); 1960 (3, 4, 9); 1981 (3, 5, 9, 11); 1982 (1, 3/1, 3/29,5)

GXY: 1978 (9, 11)

IASFM: 1982 (12, 12/15)

TZ: 1981 (9, 11); 1982 (1, 4, 5, 12)

HAMPSON, FRANK (Dec. 22, 1918–July 8, 1985) British artist. Creator of Dan Dare, the Mekon, and the dreams of a generation of British school-boys (among them the majority of today's finest British science fiction illustrators), Hampson was the artist who brought space-age adventure to postwar youth in the magazine *Eagle*. It was the battles of Dan Dare and his sidekick Digby against the green-headed, evil Mekon that made the comic the most successful such publication in British science fiction history.

Born in Audenshaw, Manchester, England, Hampson left school at age fourteen to become a telegraph boy for the post office. In the same year, he had his first cartoon published in *Meccano Magazine*. In 1938 he resigned from the Civil Service to become a full-time art student. On the outbreak of the Second World War, he joined the Royal Army Service Corps, serving as a driver and taking a commission in 1943.

After the war, Hampson freelanced as an illustrator for various magazines, including a religious monthly, *The Anvil*, edited by the Reverend Marcus Morris. Morris had ambitions to produce a weekly comic for boys founded on strong Christian principles to combat the flood of American crime and horror comics that were entering England at the time. The first *Eagle* went on sale on April 14, 1950. The name was supplied by Hampson's wife, Dorothy, inspired by the design of their church lectern. Hampson designed the striking layout and new look of the comic. He both wrote and drew the principal strips. His *Dan Dare—Pilot of the Future* was the front-page serial that became immediately inseparable from the *Eagle*. Colonel Daniel MacGregor Dare, chief pilot of the Interplanet Space Fleet and holder of the Order of the United Nations for his leadership of the Venusian Expedition of 1996, was a perfect hero for the space age. Hampson said that his creation was a projection of all of the things he had ever wanted to be, and Sir Hubert Gascoine Guest (marshal of space and Dan Dare's mentor) was modeled on Hampson's own father.

Hampson supervised the building of scale models of spaceships, including Dare's famous Anastasia space stations and interplanetary cities, so that his drawings of them would be correctly proportioned and accurately detailed from any angle. This desire for perfection was an important factor in leading to the mass merchandising of Dan Dare, taking in everything from toy ray-guns to play-suit uniform.

Together with a team of artists, scriptwriters, and scientific advisors, Hampson controlled the 1950s cult-figure spaceman and his interplanetary adventures until 1959, when he released control of the character to Frank Bellamy*. In the 1960s *Dan Dare* was shifted from the front page of the *Eagle*, and rearranged reprints began in black and white. The comic was amalgamated with its major rival, *Lion*, in 1967. It was revived fifteen years later.

Hampson contracted cancer of the trachea in 1970 but recovered after treatment. He took up a post as graphics technician at Ewell Technical College. In 1975 he was rediscovered by fans and was invited as a guest to the International Festival of Comics in Lucca, Italy. He was honored there with the Yellow Kid Award for a lifetime devoted to comic art. After his return home, Hampson was presented with the Ally Sloper Award as the best British strip artist at the first British Comics Convention. He died in Epson, England, in July 1985.

Hampson's passing received greater press and medium coverage and more tributes than that of any other British science fiction artist. His influence in the science fiction field in England is incalculable. A posthumous assessment of his life and work was done by Alastair Crompton in *The Man Who Drew Tomorrow*.

PUBLISHED WORK:

PB: *The Man Who Drew Tomorrow* (85)

Richard Dalby

HARDY, DAVID A. (b. April 1936) British artist. Hardy studied at the Margaret Street College of Art, Birmingham, England. Before joining the Royal Air Force for his national service in 1954, he was painting for an exhibition of the British Interplanetary Society, and he was asked to illustrate an early book by astronomer Patrick Moore entitled *Sun, Myths, and Men*. He quickly completed eight drawings, which introduced him to the world of book illustration and was the beginning of his long friendship with Moore.

One of Hardy's most important commissions was for *Challenge of the Stars* in 1972, which he cowrote with Moore. Hardy's thirty-six speculative paintings for this book, showing his ideas of the terrains of distant planets, were commended by NASA for their technical accuracy. He traveled to the United States in 1971 for the launch of the Apollo 15, and contacts at NASA keep him informed about the latest progress in their work.

Hardy's one-man exhibition at the London Planetarium led to the publication of *Stellar Radiance* as a fine-art print in 1969. This painting of an imaginary planet of a red star quickly became a best-seller. Some of Hardy's paintings are in the collections of the Manned Space Flight Center in Huntsville, Alabama, and in the Smithsonian Institute.

PUBLISHED WORK:

AMZ: 1974 (6)

F&SF: 1971 (6); 1972 (5, 10); 1973 (1, 5, 7); 1974 (1); 1975 (2, 4, 8, 11); 1976 (1, 5, 6, 9); 1977 (5, 11); 1978 (1, 4, 6, 10, 12); 1979 (4, 5, 8, 12); 1980 (5, 6); 1981 (4, 10); 1982 (2, 7, 10); 1983 (5, 11, 12); 1984 (5)

GXY: 1974 (9)

IF: 1973 (2, 8, 10)

HARDY, PAUL (1862–194?) British artist. Born near Bath, England, Hardy was the son of artist David Hardy and brother of Evelyn Stuart Hardy, a writer and illustrator of children's books. Educated in Clifton, Hardy settled in 1886 in Chelsea, London, where he remained an amazingly prolific book and magazine illustrator for more than fifty years. Virtually every early issue of the *Strand Magazine* contained artwork by him, and he also contributed to *Chums* from 1896 through 1940. Hardy contributed to many other magazines, and some of his earliest work was done for the *English Illustrated Magazine*, for which, in 1887, he illustrated a superb fantasy showing flotillas of Martian ships approaching a spaceship from Earth. This was later followed by plates for John Munro's "Is the End of the World Near?" a very graphic work that was recently reprinted in *New Worlds*. Hardy was very attentive to detail, especially the riggings of ships and period costumes. To maintain this authenticity, he gathered a large collection of old costumes specifically to be worn by his models. He also achieved recognition for his metal models of antique ships. Hardy's death was not recorded, but it is believed he died in the early 1940s.

PUBLISHED WORK: 144 (All British magazines).

CASELLS: "The Purple Death" (Feb. 1895), "The Wheels of Dr. Ginochio Gyves" (Nov. 1899)

STRAND: "Dr Trifulgas" (July 1892), "The Fire Bugs" (Jan. 1900), "The Purple Terror" (Sept. 1899), "The Spider of Guyana" (Jan. 1899), "The Stolen Body" (Nov. 1898)

Richard Dalby

HARRISON, HARRY (b. Mar. 12, 1925) American artist. Known primarily as a science fiction writer, Harrison started his career as a comic-book and science fiction artist. Born in Stamford, Connecticut, he was a science fiction fan and knew many SF writers through his membership in the Hydra Club in New York. Damon Knight, editor of *Worlds Beyond*, belonged to the club and bought art from Harrison and, later, his first short story. Along with writing and illustrating, Harrison also edited a number of science fiction magazines. Continued writing success convinced him that his future was in science fiction text, not art. He now lives in Ireland and is one of the most popular writers in the SF field.

PUBLISHED WORK:

HC: *Fairy Chessmen* (51)

GXY: 1951 (5)

IF: 1959 (11); 1960 (3)

MSS: 1951 (5, 8, 11); 1952 (5)

SpSF: 1952 (5)

WB: 1951 (1, 2)

HAY, COLIN (b. 1947) Scottish artist. Colin Hay attended Edinburgh College of Art in Scotland from 1965 to 1970. He works in many fields of illustration and has done some fine work in the science fiction field. He specializes in fantastic architecture, and many of his early pieces in the style appeared in *Science Fiction Monthly* in 1975–1976.

Richard Dalby

HERRING, MICHAEL (b. 1947) American artist. Born in Cherry Point, North Carolina, Herring was an "Army brat" who moved continually and had attended a dozen schools by the time he was a high school senior. Interested in fine art, he went to school in England, where he attended the Byam Shaw School of Drawing and Painting and the Royal College of Art in London. After completing his education Herring married and settled in California to begin his fine-art career. Major influences in painting included John Singer Sargent, Waterhouse, Maxfield Parrish, and obscure nineteenth-century painters such as Alma-Tadema.

In 1975 Herring moved to New York, divorced and broke, with no prospects and no portfolio. He tried for one night to be a waiter but discovered that this was not what he wanted from life. The next day he went to the office of Joe Mendola and talked to Lars Tegenborg. Herring showed the agent some photos of his recent painting of African scenes done in superrealistic style. The agent first thought the photos were scenes of Herring's vacation and, upon learning that they were of paintings, immediately agreed to represent him. Since then Herring has worked as an illustrator.

Herring never studied science fiction art, "toiling away in seclusion." His style derives from his training and his background in fine arts. Important influences now in SF are John Berkey* and Boris Vallejo*.

Herring's first published piece and one of his personal favorites was painted for *The Blue Hawk* published by Del Rey Books. Most of his art in science fiction has been for Del Rey, although he has also done artwork for Warner Books and Berkley as well. He swiftly branched out from science fiction after discovering the low pay scale, and fantasy now represents only about 15 percent of his total work. He paints mostly romance and adventure covers, with fantasy assignments serving primarily as relaxation. Remarried, he has gained fame during the past few years for his work on a series of reissues of the Oz books published by Del Rey Books. In 1985 he was featured in a major study in the *Oz* fan magazine.

Herring works in oil on canvas. He views SF cover art as a sort of puzzle. The artist has to do a painting that is accurate to the book because fans are picky about detail, but at the same time, the artist walks a fine line so as not to give away any major plot twists. Herring reads a manuscript while running a visual film of it in his head. He then picks two to three choices of scenes he would like to paint and goes on from there. For Del Rey Books, he is given the book with full freedom to come up with whatever he believes would suit the story.

PUBLISHED WORK:

PB: *Bane of Lord Caladon* (82), *Best of Fritz Leiber* (74), *The Changing Land* (81), *Dancers in the Afterglow* (78), *Deadly Silents* (81), *Diloisk the Damned* (82), *Dorothy and the Wizard in Oz*, *Elves and the Otterskin*, *Emerald City of Oz*, *Glinda of Oz*, *Land of Oz*, *Lost Princess of Oz*, *Magic of Oz*, *Ozma of Oz*, *Patchwork Girl of Oz*, *Rinkitinkin in Oz*, *Road to Oz*, *Scarecrow of Oz*, *She and Allan* (78), *Tik-Tok of Oz*, *Tin Woodman of Oz*, *When the World Shook* (78), *Wisdom's Daughter* (78), *Wizard of Oz*, *World's Desire* (77)

HESCOX, RICHARD (b. Oct. 8, 1949) American artist. Born in Pasadena, California, Hescox attended the College of Design at the Art Center in Los Angeles. He was always interested in both science fiction and art and studied art throughout school with the intention of becoming an artist and illustrator. An Edgar Rice Burroughs fan, he was influenced by N. C. Wyeth and J. W. Waterhouse in the art field. His first sale was to the Marvel Comics *Monsters Unleashed* magazine. His first SF cover was painted for *Walkers on the Sky* by David Lake.

Married, Hescox does most of his science fiction paintings for DAW books. He has recently done a great deal of "production illustration" for the movies, including work for *The Philadelphia Experiment* and *The Howling.*

In deciding what to illustrate, Hescox reads the manuscript and then picks scenes in which he likes the action and setup of figures. He likes adventure-based scenes and works primarily in acrylics, although originally, he did most of his work in oils.

Hescox enjoys science fiction illustration because he believes it is "one of the few areas that harken back to the days of academic art."

PUBLISHED WORK:

PB: *Crown of the Storm God* (80), *Fighting Slave of Gor* (80), *Fires of Scorpio* (82), *Forbidden Tower* (77), *Free Amazons of Darkover* (85), *Maeve* (79), *Magic of Camelot* (81), *Masks of Scorpion, Rogue of Gor* (81), *Shai's Destiny* (84), *Spell Sword* (74), *Walkers on the Sky* (76), *Werewolves of Kregan* (84)

HICKMAN, STEVE (b. Apr. 9, 1949) American artist. Born in Washington, D.C., Stephen Forrest Hickman was the son of Jon F. and Mary Lee Hickman. His father worked for the Department of State and later for the International Development. For years, Hickman and his brother John spent each school year in a different state or country. In the eighth grade, his family settled in Alexandria, Virginia, where he attended high school.

At Hammond High School, Hickman received what he thought was his most influential art training from Sydney F. Proctor, whose instruction was the artist's formal training in art. He attended the art school of the Richmond Professional Institute/Virginia Commonwealth University for two years, but this instruction consisted of classes in fine art. Hickman later taught himself anatomy, comic art, and painting. During this time he was strongly influenced by Frank Frazetta★ and Roy Krenkel, Jr.★, whom he met at the New York Comic Art Convention in 1967.

Hickman began working for comic-art fanzines at this time. He was soon contacted by Fred Fillah of the *Shirt Explosion* and spent the next few years doing designs for T-shirts. Also during that time he worked on sample paintings with hopes of breaking into the paperback field. When Hickman showed his portfolio to Charles Volpe, the art director at Ace Books, Volpe bought one of the pieces, which was used as the cover for *Lady of the Bees* by Thomas Burnett Swann. This was the beginning of his career as a full-time book and poster artist. At present, Hickman resides in Alexandria, Virginia, with his wife, Victoria (also an artist), and his daughter, Aurora.

Hickman believes that people who affected his way of looking at things are the ones most responsible for his art. Some of these influences thus include Dashiell Hammett and Raymond Chandler, P. G. Wodehouse, Harpo Marx, Alphonse Mucha, George Bridgeman, Charles Vess, Franklin Booth, Arthur Rackham, Robert Heinlein, H. P. Lovecraft, Clark Ashton

Smith, Da Dannan, Sir John Everett Millais, Sir Arthur Conan Doyle, J. W. Waterhouse, and many others, as well as his parents.

Hickman has strong feelings about translating a book into art. The artist states that "what sounds good in print does not always look good in a picture. Any work of art is based on real life... but each work of art, whatever the medium, is a *separate reality* unto itself, not to be confused with the reality from which it is derived." Thus Hickman believes that composition should be mostly a subconscious process, with rules brought in only when a problem arises. He also thinks that technique is secondary to imagination and good drawing. Hickman normally works in oils but has also used acrylics and watercolors.

PUBLISHED WORK:

PB: *Alien Way, Basilisk, The Brain Stealers, Brother to Demons—Brother to Gods, Delusion World, Destination Universe, Doctor to the Stars, Dominant Species, The Dragon Hoard, Dream Palace, Dreamrider, Escape Velocity* (83), *Fireship, The Glory That Was, Green Millenium, The Harem of Aman Akbar, High Sorcery, Hot Sleep, In Iron Years, Jhereg* (84), *Jirel of Joiry, Journel to Aprilioth, Khil to Freedom, King Kobold Revived* (84), *The King in Yellow, Knights Move, Lady of the Bees, Lords of the Triple Moon, Magus Rex, The Martian Inca, Moondust, Necromancer, The Phoenix and the Mirror, Princess of the Chamelyn, Purple Pterodactyls* (80), *The Reign in Hell, Runes of the Lyre, Seed of Earth, Seven from the Stars, The Ship That Sailed the Time Stream, Spacial Delivery, Stolen Faces, The Stone God Awakens, The Tactics of Mistake, The Warlock Enraged* (85), *The Warlock in Spite of Himself, The Warlock Unlocked* (82), *The Weirwoods, Weird Heroes #1, Weird Heroes #2, Yendl* (83)

AMZ: 1977 (3)

FTC: 1976 (5)

HILDEBRANDT, GREG (b. Jan. 23, 1939) American artist. Gregory and Timothy Hildebrandt* were identical twins, born to George and Germaine Hildebrandt in Detroit, Michigan. The twins both developed an interest in art very early in life and spent much of their time copying favorite cartoon and comic-book characters. They also made puppets and costumes from cloth and odds and ends around the house. Very close, the identical twins did most things together, and their interests were similar in most respects. They both read Edgar Rice Burroughs, including all of the Tarzan and Pellucidar and Mars novels. They both enjoyed science fiction films, and they both continued to draw, learning more through experience and persistence than through any formal early training.

A copy of *The Art of Animation* had a strong effect on the brothers during their high school years. Both were fascinated by animation and wanted to produce their own animated film. The gift of an 8mm camera was the final inspiration. The brothers worked many hours constructing models and doing storyboard work for numerous 8mm science fiction films for their own amusement.

Shortly after graduating from Avondale High School in June 1957, the twins joined the army to fulfill their military obligation. They spent six months in the army reserve program at Fort Leonard Wood, Missouri, and Fort Riley, Kansas.

After leaving the army, the twins attended the Meinzinger School of Art in Detroit. They studied eight months and then quit, feeling that the school did not have anything more to offer. While at Meinzinger, the twins studied basic drawing, perspective, color and design, anatomy, and life drawing. This brief period in school was their only formal art training.

The Hildebrandts joined the Jam Handy Studios immediately after leaving Meinzinger. Handy was the largest film-production house in the country, doing work for General Motors, Campbell Soup, and many other clients. The brothers worked for several years in the animation department, where they designed live-action and animated films for numerous firms.

In 1963 the twins were invited by Bishop Fulton Sheen of New York to make a film for the Catholic church. They continued to work for the church for the next six years. Soon after moving to the East Coast, Greg married Diana Stankowksi and moved to Jersey City, New Jersey. Tim, who lived across the street, married in 1965. Later, both families moved to Northern New Jersey. Greg and Diana have had three children, Gregory, Mary, and Laura.

In 1969 the church sent the brothers to Africa to film a documentary on church missionary work. However, the finished piece, which clearly showed the poverty and unrest throughout the continent, was not what the church expected, and the Hildebrandts were dismissed from their film-making jobs.

Needing work, the Hildebrandts showed a hastily assembled portfolio of work to various children's book publishers. Soon they were doing art for Holt, Rinehart and Winston. From there, they continued doing art for numerous other children's book publishers, as well as doing advertising art and editorial illustrations.

In 1975 a copy of the J.R.R. Tolkien Calendar with art by Tim Kirk crossed the brothers' hands. On the back was an invitation to artists to submit work for the next calendar. The Hildebrandts brought in samples to Ballantine Books, and a contract was quickly produced. Their style was perfectly suited to Tolkien's work, and the brothers worked fast. So similar was their technique and style that one could take over from where another had stopped working on a painting. They could thus work nonstop on a piece for days. Tight deadlines, problems for most artists, were not a major annoyance for the Hildebrandt brothers.

The 1976 Tolkien Calendar, with art by the "Brothers Hildebrandt" (as they were dubbed by Judy Lynn Del Rey) was a tremendous success. The art was praised everywhere as being a perfect match for Tolkien's work, and the Hildebrandts were quickly signed for the 1977 calendar.

The second calendar, with a much greater print run, sold out even faster than the first effort. The Hildebrandts were the rage of the science fiction and fantasy field, and they were besieged with offers of work. They soon were painting numerous paperback covers along with preparing art for a third Tolkien calendar.

Del Rey also matched the Hildebrandts with a new novel, very much in the style of Tolkien, *The Sword of Shannara* by Terry Brooks. The book had numerous similarities to *The Lord of the Rings*, and the Hildebrandts were able to do a number of paintings and black-and-white illustrations very much in the Tolkien vein. *Sword* received mixed reviews, but the Hildebrandt art helped propel it onto the best-seller list.

A third Tolkien calendar, for 1978, sold more than a million copies and had the Hildebrandts thinking of a movie version of *The Lord of the Rings*, using their art as preproduction material. Unfortuantely, Ralph Bakshi had already begun production on his version of the Tolkien epic, and the Hildebrandts were not part of his plans.

Disappointed, the brothers decided to base a film on a fantasy story of their own. Conceived first as a movie, *Urshurak* was sold to Bantam Books as a novel, with art by the Hildebrandts. The brothers worked almost exclusively on this project for more than a year. Their only break was to do the original movie poster for *Star Wars*, a project they completed in two days of continuous painting.

Urshurak in book form generated little excitement. The art was the usual fine work, but the story was nothing exceptional. It was in the Tolkien tradition but definitely was not Tolkien. The movie project, which was the actual reason for the book and the art, never sold. The book was to serve as the brothers' swan song.

It was during the project that the brothers decided to pursue separate careers. They had been working together most of their lives and finally felt the need for independent work. Their last work together was the poster art for *Clash of the Titans*. Both continued in art, but each went in a different direction.

Greg worked closely with his agent, Jean Scrocco, in finding new assignments. His first work was doing reproduction art for *Krull*, a movie by Peter Yates. He produced 160 pieces of art based on the script, none of which, in typical Hollywood fashion, was ever used.

Soon Scrocco sold Simon and Schuster the idea of doing a series of heavily illustrated, deluxe editions of classic novels and story collections. The first book in the series was Dickens' *Christmas Carol*. Since then Greg Hildebrandt has done the art for illustrated editions of *Dracula*, *The Wiz. of Oz*, and several children's books. At the same time, he also did art for a calendar based on Mary Stewart's Merlin trilogy and advertising art using fairy-tale characters as the central theme.

Today Greg Hildebrandt remains active in fantasy art, but his focus has shifted from modern fantasy art to the classics. Inspired in part by children's books, he has become one of the most popular and collected of artists doing new editions of these enduring works.

The importance of the brothers in the history of modern fantasy illustration cannot be overstated. For many people, their work on the Tolkien novels captured the very essence of the stories. Since Tolkien is probably the most popular fantasy author of the twentieth century, the close association of art and story emphasizes the enduring popularity of the brothers' work. Their art serves as a constant source of inspiration to a new generation of fantasy artists. Along with Michael Whelan★, Boris Vallejo★, and Rowena Morrill★, the Hildebrandts helped fuel the return of romantic fantastic imagery to science fiction illustrations.

PUBLISHED WORK:

HC: *A Christmas Carol* (83), *The Art of the Brothers Hildebrandt* (79), *Dracula* (85), *From Tolkien to Oz* (85), *Greg Hildebrandt's Favorite Fairy Tales* (84), *The Sword of Shannara* (77), *The Wizard of Oz* (85)

PB: *Apache Devil* (75), *The Best of C. L. Moore* (74), *The Early Del Rey Volume 1* (75), *The Early Del Rey Volume 2* (75), *My Name Is Legion* (76), *Run Come See Jerusalem* (76), *The Ship Who Sang* (76), *Stellar # 2* (76)

MISC: The 1976 J.R.R. Tolkien Calendar, the 1977 J.R.R. Tolkien Calendar, the 1978 J.R.R. Tolkien Calendar, "Clash of the Titans Movie Poster" (81), Gods & Goddesses Portfolio (81), Mary Stewart's Merlin Calendar (83), "Star Wars Poster" (77)

HILDEBRANDT, TIM (b. Jan. 23, 1939) American artist. Born in Detroit, Michigan, Hildebrandt was one of identical twins born to George and Germaine Hildebrandt. Much of his early life parallels that of his twin, Greg Hildebrandt★, since the two seemed to follow in identical footsteps. They were both interested in art, science fiction, comic books, and movies. Both attended Avondale High School, served for a short time in the army reserve, and then attended Meinzingers School of Art in Detroit for eight months. Tim thought that his major artistic influences were the classic animated Disney features of the period—Snow White, Pinnochio, Fantasia, and others. Later, he was also influenced by Hal Foster's Prince Valiant comic strips, as well as by the SF movies by George Pal.

The twins' first job was with the Jam Handy organization in Detroit, a company that produced industrial films, television, and theatrical productions. The brothers worked in the animation department, where Tim started as an *opaquer* (one who paints cells). He worked his way up to background painting, storyboard artist, production designer, and animator. After four years at Handy's, during which time the brothers designed several films that won various awards, they moved to New York to make documentary films for a religous company headed by Bishop Fulton J. Sheen and worked for this company for seven years, traveling around the world, directing and shooting numerous productions.

In 1965, while living in New Jersey, Tim met Rita Murray at choir practice, and they were married four months later. Since then they have moved to an old Victorian house in northern New Jersey and are the parents of one son.

While making the films, Tim Hildebrandt neglected his drawing. When a conflict with the church brought an end to the brothers' relationship to the film company, they assembled a portfolio and presented it to a number of children's book publishers. Soon they were swamped with assignments from Doubleday, Winston, Western Publishing, and other publishers. The brothers quit making documentary films and went into illustrating full time. They won several awards from the Society of Illustrators for their work on children's book illustrations. They also expanded into advertising art, magazine art, and paperback cover art.

In 1975 the brothers noticed an invitation to artists on the back of the Tolkien Calendar, featuring art by Tim Kirk*, published by Ballantine Books, asking for submissions from artists for future calendars. The twins had been fans of Tolkien and his *Lord of the Rings* for years and decided to submit art to Ballantine. Their submission resulted in the immediate offer of a contract. The 1976 J.R.R. Tolkien Calendar was a huge success and established the Hildebrandt brothers as important fantasy artists. Del Rey Books, which had already used some Hildebrandt art for paperback covers, immediately signed the brothers for another Tolkien calendar. The 1977 and 1978 Tolkien calendars, the best-selling *Sword of Shannara*, and numerous other projects followed. In two hectic days, the brothers did the art for the *Star Wars* movie poster.

After working together for nearly forty years, frictions that had built up over a long period caused the artists to break up, each pursuing his own career. Although most of their early fame in the fantasy field came from the Tolkien illustrations, which they did as the "Hildebrandt Brothers," each artist has been very successful on his own.

In the past few years, Tim Hildebrandt has illustrated work by his wife, Rita, including a cookbook and a novel, *Merlin and the Dragons of Atlantis*. He also has done the art for some calendars and has returned to illustrating children's books. Tim usually works in acrylics but also has worked with watercolor and pen and ink. On rare occasions, he has used oils.

PUBLISHED WORK:

PB: *Apache Devil* (75), *The Best of C. L. Moore* (74), *The Early Del Rey #1* (75), *The Early Del Rey #2* (75), *My Name is Legion* (76), *Restoree, Run Come See Jerusalem* (76), *The Ship Who Sang* (76), *Stellar #2* (76), *The Sword of Shannara* (77)

MISC: The 1976 J.R.R. Tolkien Calendar, the 1977 J.R.R. Tolkien Calendar, the 1978 J.R.R. Tolkien Calendar, "Clash of the Titans Movie Poster" (81), "Star Wars Movie Poster" (78)

HINGE, MIKE (?) American artist. Coming from a varied background, Hinge was born in Polynesia, his father in England, and his mother in Africa. He studied at the Seddon Memorial Polytechnic, where he learned everything from still life to drawing from plaster casts to woodworking to architectural drawing. He then worked for the largest ad agency in New Zealand.

Thereafter, Hinge moved to Los Angeles, where he studied at the Art Center of the College of Design. He then worked as an artist for J. C. Penny, May Co., and other advertising clients. He moved to New York in 1966 and worked as art director for several ad agencies. Since that time he has worked with computer technology, has designed alphabets, and has worked on numerous other projects combining high tech and art. He is a member of Engineers, Artists and Technology and has helped design *2001: A Space Odyssey*. Among his non-SF credits are the *Time* magazine covers of Hirohito and Richard Nixon. Much of his science fiction work has been done for the Science Fiction Book Club.

PUBLISHED WORK:

HC: *Choice of Gods* (72), *Masters of Everon*

PB: *Assignment in Tomorrow* (72), *Leaves of Time* (71), *Shaggy Planet* (73)

AMZ: 1969 (11); 1970 (3, 5, 7, 9, 11); 1971 (1, 7, 11); 1972 (5, 7); 1973 (1, 3, 8, 10); 1974 (12); 1975 (9)

ASF: 1973 (7, 8); 1974 (2); 1975 (9); 1976 (4, 7, 9, 10, 11); 1977 (1, 2, 4, 5, 7, 8, 9, 19, 12); 1978 (1, 2, 3, 6, 7, 8, 9, 10, 12, yearbook); 1979 (3, 4, 5, 6)

FTC: 1969 (10); 1970 (2, 4, 6, 8); 1971 (2, 6, 8); 1972 (4, 10)

HOLLAND, BRAD (b. 1943) American artist. Born in Fremont, Ohio, Holland was always interested in art. At age seven he found *Classic Illustrated* versions of *The Odyssey* and *The Iliad*. Not liking the ending of *The Iliad*, he rewrote it and then illustrated the work himself. In high school Holland took one art class in the ninth grade but had no other formal training. He settled on doing pen-and-ink drawings since this was the first medium he found that he could work in without instruction.

When Holland was seventeen, he left home and moved to Chicago. His unusual pen-and-ink pieces were not an immediate hit, and for a short time Holland worked in a tattoo parlor. He then began working for John Dioszegi as a "short-order artist." In 1964 he moved to Kansas City and worked as an artist for a short time for Hallmark cards. At the same time, he formed Asylum Press "to print eccentric projects with friends."

In 1967 Holland moved to New York City. He soon was being published in underground newspapers including *Screw*, *The Rat*, and *New York Ace*, as well as major publications such as *Playboy*, *Avante-Garde*, and *Evergreen Review*. His ink drawings in the counterculture press brought him to the attention of the editors of the *New York Times*, for which, in 1971, he became one of the founding artists of the Op-Ed page. His art in *Playboy* led to paintings that have appeared in nearly every U.S. publication, including work for *Time*, *Newsweek*, *The Atlantic Monthly*, *The New York Times Magazine*.

In 1977 T. Y. Crowell published a book of Holland's drawings entitled *Human Scandals*. His drawings and paintings have been exhibited in museums around the world, including the Louvre in 1974 and the U.S. Library of Congress in 1979. He has designed a postage stamp of Indian chief Crazy Horse and has produced a ten-by-thirty-foot mural for the United Nations Building in New York.

Holland is one of the most highly regarded pen-and-ink artists living today. His work has come into much critical acclaim, with one writer declaring that "Brad Holland's drawing is the foremost example of compassionate yet critical art. . . . His images are richly resonant with humor, concern and intellect." Holland has been awarded gold medals from the Art Director's Club of New York, the Society of Illustrators, and the Society of Publication Designers. He twice received the Playboy Editorial Award.

Much of Holland's work is fantastic. His pen-and-ink illustrations reflect a strong feeling for the bizarre and the unusual and have made his editorial illustrations so unique. In many ways, his work resembles that of a modern-day Heinrich Kley but remains uniquely his own. Holland also contributed, among many other works, a number of cover paintings to books published by the Science Fiction Book Club.

PUBLISHED WORK:

HC: *Alph* (72), *Beyond the Beyond* (69), *Time of Changes* (71)

HORNE, DAN (b. June 3, 1960) American artist. Born in Pittsburgh, Pennsylvania, Horne attended the York Academy of Design. Influences include the Howard Pyle School of Artists, Tom Lovell, and Sir Lawrence Alma-Tadema. He works in oil on masonite, canvas, or board. He has said of his art that "I try to bring characters to life while portraying them honestly. I'm really a very straight-forward illustrator. If I have a goal with these pictures, it's to uphold and revitalize the tradition of great illustration."

Horne has been working in the science fiction field since 1982, illustrating for *The Dragon* magazine and other role-playing games for TSR and Iron Cross Publishers. He has done artwork for *Heavy Metal* and well as for the Science Fiction Book Club and a number of the major paperback publishers. He is a member of Buckhorn Studios.

PUBLISHED WORK:

HC: *The Belgariad, Her Majesty's Wizard, The Incorporated Knight* (87), *The King's Justice, Orphan of Creation, Robots of Dawn*

PB: *Blood River Down* (86), *Web of Defeat* (87)

HOWITT, JOHN NEWTON (1885–1958) American artist. A well-known landscape artist, portrait painter, and illustrator, Howitt turned to the pulp magazines for work during the Depression. Although not truly a science fiction illustrator, he did numerous cover paintings for magazines such as *Operator #5* and *The Spider* that featured novels bordering on science fiction. Howitt did more death rays, incredible scenes of attacks on the United States, and future war battles than most science fiction illustrators of the time. For *Horror Stories* and *Terror Tales*, he did a series of astonishing covers that remain unmatched as perfect examples of the pulp vision of madness unleashed. A typical Howitt cover of the period featured a solitary heroine fleeing down an abandoned subway tunnel with a horde of madmen with knives and spears in pursuit. All around her are rats and corpses, while in front, around a turn in the passage, lurks another fiend armed with a glistening axe. The men are wearing the remnants of clothing and have wild and insane expressions, while the girl's face is a model of horrified innocence.

Howitt thought little of his work for the pulps and wanted to be remembered for his landscapes, which are now all but forgotten. His horror paintings if published now would perfectly complement the finest horror fiction of today. His work was the stuff of modern nightmares—with madmen in the sewers, lunatics running wild in asylums, fiends hunting for innocents in deserted night streets. Men and women hang from meathooks in the aptly entitled "City That Dared Not Eat." While virtually unknown outside a small group of pulp-magazine collectors of the 1930s, Howitt ranks as one of the premier illustrators of modern horrors.

HUNTER, ALAN (?) British artist. A British technical illustrator, Hunter first had his fantasy drawings published in the August 1950 issue of *New Worlds*. Soon his illustrations were appearing in most of the leading British science fiction magazines. In 1958, when the British science fiction market went through an extended slump, Hunter started his own business as a news agent. Ten years later he sold his shop and began freelancing again as an illustrator. A portfolio of his new work was published in *Stardock 3* in January 1970. Since that time he has been a prolific contributor to fanzines and small-press publications in England, especially for the British Fantasy Society and the *Ghost and Scholars* series.

PUBLISHED WORK:

NEB: (1, 2, 3, 4, 5, 6, 7, 8, 9, 10, 11, 12, 16, 17)

NW: 1951 (spring, summer, fall, winter); 1952 (1, 3, 5); (16, 17, 18, 19, 20, 21, 23, 24, 27, 28, 30, 31, 32, 33, 34, 36, 37, 38, 40, 41, 44, 45, 47)

ScF: 1951 (winter); 1952 (spring, fall); 1953 (spring); (7, 8, 10, 11, 12, 13, 16)

Richard Dalby

HUNTER, MEL (b. 1929) American artist. Hunter, who had no formal art training, had a background in advertising copy writing and production engineering. He entered the SF field in the early 1950s and quickly made a name for himself with his detailed, accurate astronomical paintings using bright, bold colors. In addition to preparing illustrations, he served as art director of *IF* magazine from December 1955 through December 1957. Hunter was famous for a series of paintings he did featuring a distinctive robot in a variety of unusual settings, each painting complete in itself.

PUBLISHED WORK:

HC: *Best from F&SF #4* (55), *Born of Man and Woman* (54), *Deep Space* (54), *Door into Summer* (57), *Double Star* (56), *Dragon in the Sea* (56), *Fittest* (55), *Man of Many Minds* (53), *Mind Partner* (61), *Not This August* (55), *One in Three Hundred* (54), *Reprieve from Paradise* (55), *Space Tug* (53), *Star Bridge* (55), *Star Conquerors* (59), *Time Is the Simplest Thing* (61), *Year after Tomorrow* (54)

AMZ: 1953 (12); 1954 (5)

F&SF: 1953 (11); 1954 (8); 1955 (10); 1957 (7); 1958 (1, 3, 6); 1959 (9, 12); 1960 (3, 5, 7, 12); 1961 (3, 6, 8); 1962 (1, 3, 7); 1964 (3, 9); 1965 (1, 5); 1966 (5); 1970 (1, 5, 9, 12); 1971 (3, 10, 12)

FU: 1955 (5, 7, 9, 11, 12); 1956 (3, 9)

GXY: 1953 (2, 4, 5, 6, 8, 11); 1954 (1, 7, 10, 12); 1955 (1, 2, 3, 4, 5, 7, 9); 1956 (1); 1960 (10); 1961 (4)

IF: 1953 (11); 1955 (2, 3, 12); 1956 (2, 4, 6, 8, 10, 12); 1957 (2, 4, 6, 8, 10, 12); 1958 (2, 4, 6, 8, 10, 12); 1959 (2); 1960 (11)

SAT: 1957 (8); 1958 (4, 8)

SFA: 1954 (2)

SPWY: 1953 (12); 1954 (2, 4)

UNI: 1953 (3)

INGELS, GRAHAM (b. June 7, 1915) American artist. A staff instructor for the Famous Artists School, Ingels produced magazine art for the Fiction House pulp chain.

Born in Cincinnati, Ohio, he moved with his family first to Georgia and then to New York when he was twelve. He went to school in Yonkers and later on Long Island. The death of Ingels's father when he was fourteen forced him to start working. By the time he was sixteen, he was doing display art for theaters. He married when he was twenty and began working as a freelance artist.

Ingels served in the navy during the Second World War but was stationed on Long Island. He worked whenever possible for Fiction House Publications, for its *Planet Stories* comics and other comic publications. It was then only a short step to providing artwork for its *Planet Stories* pulp magazine and other, nonscience fiction pulps. Ingels did a number of excellent black-and-white illustrations for *Planet Stories*, as well as one cover.

When he left Fiction House after the war, Ingels worked for a number of other comic publishers before landing a job with EC Comics. It was there, doing artwork for the EC horror line, that Ingels gained fame for his particularly gruesome comic horror art and was dubbed "Ghastly" Graham Ingels. After the EC Comics were killed by the Comics Code, Ingels did some more comic artwork and then turned to teaching painting. He then became affiliated with the Famous Artist School for which he served as a full-time staff instructor. He later moved to Florida, where he now works with a graphic arts studio.

PUBLISHED WORK:

PS: 1944 (spring); 1945 (fall)

ISIP, PAGSILANG REY and M. (?) American artists. Brothers who worked in the science fiction field, primarily doing artwork for the Street & Smith pulps, in the late 1930s and early 1940s. Pagsilang also worked on many of the comic books during that period as an artist. He was a member of the Bert Whitman comic strip shop and later the Iger Studios in the early 1940s. He also did work for Street & Smith's comic line as well as the Pines, Fiction House, Nita, and Great Comic companies. The Isip brothers often signed their work separately but sometimes together. All of their artwork, however produced, is listed below.

PUBLISHED WORK:

ASF: 1939 (8, 9, 11, 12); 1940 (1, 2, 3, 5, 6, 7, 8, 9); 1941 (2, 3, 4, 6, 8); 1942 (4, 10, 12); 1943 (1, 3, 4)

SSS: 1941 (8)

UK: 1939 (3, 4, 8, 9, 11, 12); 1940 (1, 2, 3, 5, 6, 7, 9, 11, 12); 1941 (2, 4, 6); 1942 (2, 4, 6, 8, 10, 12); 1943 (2, 6)

JACKSON, JAY (Sept. 11, 1907–1950) American artist. One of the staff artists for the Ziff-Davis magazine line of the early 1940s, Jackson had the distinction of being perhaps the first black artist to work in the science fiction field. Since so little is known about many of the people who worked for the pulp field, it is possible that Jackson was the first black artist working for the pulp magazines.

Jackson was born in Oberlin, Ohio, when few blacks went to college, much less became illustrators. As a young boy he worked hammering spikes near Columbus, Ohio, and later in a steel mill in Pittsburgh. He attended Ohio Wesleyan University in Delaware, Ohio, while driving a mail truck at night. He majored in art.

At nineteen, Jackson started a sign-painting business and married "the girl of his dreams." His business was successful until he developed a severe case of lead poisoning. After he recovered, Jackson traveled to Chicago, where he became a poster artist and then shop foreman for a chain of theaters. It was soon after this that tragedy struck—with his father, his wife, and his first child all dying. At twenty-two he found himself with an infant daughter to care for and bitter at the world.

For the next four years, Jackson continued to paint murals and posters for movie houses as well as speakeasies. But finally, even the Depression hit that business, and he was out of work in 1933. Jackson gave up his apartment and moved into a fine hotel to keep up his morale. He soon got a job working on murals for the Century of Progress. He also submitted a series of illustrated verses he had done while in college to a Pittsburgh newspaper, and they were immediately accepted. Soon he was working for a Chicago magazine as well as a national weekly newspaper, and he had a contract from a New York newspaper publisher to do work for the weekly magazine section.

It was in the Chicago office of this publisher that Jackson met his second wife. Successful once again, he began freelancing along with his other duties and sold art to most of the pulps in the Chicago area.

Later in life Jackson became involved in civic affairs and became a well-known figure in Chicago's black community. Highly regarded by all who knew him, he died in 1950.

PUBLISHED WORK:

AMZ: 1938 (6, 8, 10); 1940 (6, 7); 1941 (1, 2, 3, 4, 5, 6, 7, 8, 9, 10, 11, 12); 1942 (1, 2, 5, 6, 7, 8, 10, 12); 1943 (3)

FA: 1939 (7, 9); 1940 (1, 3, 5, 6, 8); 1941 (1, 3, 5, 7, 10, 11, 12); 1942 (1, 2, 4, 5, 6, 11, 12); 1943 (1, 3); 1945 (1)

FTC: 1966 (1); 1967 (11); 1968 (8); 1971 (6)

WT: 1938 (10)

JAMPEL, JUDITH (b. 1944) American artist. Jampel was born during the Blitz in London, England. Her parents had escaped Hitler by moving to England before the war, and her family later moved to the United States when she was four years old. She studied at Hunter College from 1961 through 1963 and was interested in archaeology. She also started sculpting. In 1965–1966 she worked for a half year in a commercial art studio, and that work convinced her to do more studying in visual arts in 1966.

Jampel's first book cover was for *The Sentinel* and was a demon-type figure; this was also one of the first die-cut covers. In the mid–1970s she did a number of excellent fantasy covers for Del Rey Books. Along with this work, she also produced some covers for *National Lampoon*.

From preparing a stationary type of sculpture, she moved into animating her work, and she also became interested in the performing genre. In her thirties she began doing the type of sculpture she is best known for, using cloth. She prefers using a stocking type of nylon fabric and human or artificial hair, depending on the figure.

Most of her work now is for private exhibitions and trade magazines for the pharmaceutical companies. She began working on a government grant in 1984 (A National Endowment—Craftsman Grant in Fiber). During this time she also did a tableau on the homeless for Abbott Pharmaceuticals.

No longer working in illustration, Jampel does not view herself as belonging to the science fiction art field.

JANE, JOHN FREDERICK THOMAS (Aug. 6, 1865-March 8, 1916) British artist. Born in Richmond, Surrey, Jane was the eldest son of the Reverend John Jane, vicar of Upottery (Devon, in southwest England).

Known professionally as Fred T. Jane, the artist was one of the leading British science fiction writers and illustrators for a short period in the 1890s. His own novels were *Blake of the "Rattlesnake"*, 1895 (a future naval war story); *The Incubated Girl*, 1896 (artificial creation by chemical means); *To Venus in Five Seconds*, 1897 (with intelligent giant insects four years before *The First Men in the Moon* by Wells); and *The Violet Flame*, 1899 (a mad scientist and a disintegration ray). He illustrated three of his own novels and also wrote a number of nonfantasy novels during this same period.

Jane illustrated George Griffith's famous epic SF novels, *The Angel of the Revolution* and *Olga Romanoff*. He also did the artwork for E. Douglas Fawcett's *Hartmann the Anarchist*. Warfare and weapons were very dominant in these illustrations. On a somewhat more peaceful level, his imaginative series *Guesses at Futurity* appeared monthly in the *Pall Mall Magazine* from October 1894 to May 1895.

Apart from weaponry, Jane's greatest love was the sea. He became naval correspondent for *The Engineer* and *The Standard* and wrote several books on naval subjects. He invented the Jane Naval War Game in 1903. He launched the first edition of *Jane's All the World's Fighting Ships* in 1898 and *Jane's All the World's Aircraft* in 1909. These important annual reference works have survived into the present, making their creator's name world famous.

Fred T. Jane died suddenly in Southsea, Hampshire, in March 1916.

PUBLISHED WORK: (Illustrated work only).

HC: *The Angel of the Revolution* (1893), *Blake of the "Rattlesnake"* (1895), *Hartmann the Anarchist* (1893), *How the Jubilee Fleet Escaped Destruction* (1899), *Olga Romanoff* (1895), *The Violet Flame* (1899), *To Venus in Five Seconds* (1897)

MISC: *"Guesses at Futurity"* in the *Pall Mall Magazine* (Oct. 1894–May 1895), "War on the Water," *Pearsons Magazine* (Feb. 1896)

Richard Dalby

JOHNSON, KEVIN EUGENE (b. Nov. 17, 1954) American artist. Born in Vancouver, Washington, Johnson attended Centralia Community College and then Western Washington University from which he graduated in 1977 with a BA in art. His first encounter with the science fantasy field was in fourth grade when he saw an issue of *Creepy* magazine. His first professional contact with the field was through sending out a slide portfolio to publishers when he was a senior in college. He received a cover assignment as a result of this in 1978 from DAW books, for *Perilous Dreams* by Andre Norton. Major influences include Frederick Leighton, William Holman Hunt, John Everett Millais, David, Girodet, John Marton, and Frederick Church.

Johnson bases his paintings on a reading of the manuscript. He works in oil on masonite or linen canvas. Personal favorites among his paintings include unpublished paintings for "Lohengrin" and "Ride of the Valkyries."

Johnson has a flair for the dramatic in his paintings and, using bright, bold colors and beautiful women, is one of the rising stars in the modern SF art field.

PUBLISHED WORK:

HC: *Cugel's Saga, Dark Valley Destiny, Eros Ascending, Eros at Zenith, Gods of Riverworld, The Saga of Cuckoo, Spellsinger, The Stars in a Shroud, Under the Andes, The Undying Land, Witchwood* (83), *Wonders Child* (84)

PB: *The Adventures of Alyx, An X-T Called Stanley, The Aqualiad, The Colors of Space, Conflict, The Fire in His Hands, I-The Sun, Nightchild, Passing of the Gods, Queen of the Legion* (83), *Rumour of Angels, The Seekers and the Sword* (85), *The Selkie, Time Patrol, Winter's Shadow*

JONES, EDDIE (b. Jan. 18, 1935) British artist. One of the world's most popular and prolific science fiction artists, Jones has done more than a thousand covers and illustrations in the SF field.

Born Edward John Jones, he was educated at Bootle Grammar School, where he was an avid reader of *Fantastic Adventures* and *Planet Stories*. His first jobs were as a print buyer and production manager of an advertising agency in Liverpool. He taught himself how to illustrate in his spare time, and his first accepted artwork was published by *New Worlds* and *Nebula* in 1958. He continued producing art part time until 1969, when he was offered the position of art editor for *Visions of Tomorrow*.

Jones's many covers show the amazing versatile range of his imagination and his wide use of different techniques. Although he works mainly in gouache, he also uses watercolors, acrylics, and sometimes the air brush. Most of his British commissions have been for Sphere Books. Among his best paintings are the covers for *The Hugo Winners, 1963–1967*; Larry Niven's *Neutron Star*; Roger Zelazny's *Damnation Alley*; Piers Anthony's *Macroscope*; and Anne McCaffrey's *Dragonquest*.

Jones's art has been in great demand by many German publishers, especially Fischer, Bastei Verlag, Williams (Star Trek titles), *Terra Astra* (a weekly magazine), and Pabel who created a science-fiction series as a vehicle for his illustrations.

On many of these commissions, Jones used a pen name, including S. Fantoni. He averages nearly a dozen paintings a month for various publishers. He is also an enthusiastic collector of original art by other science fiction artists, one of the few such collectors interviewed for this book.

Richard Dalby

JONES, JEFFREY (b. Jan. 10, 1944) American artist. Born in Atlanta, Georgia, Jones was interested in drawing as a child but after a short time developed an interest in science. When he was seventeen years old, he became friends with B. B. Sams, and for the next two years the two young men tried to impress each other with their art. At the same time, Jones remained interested in science and began college at George State college as a geology major. After two years, he switched to fine arts in 1964. Artists whose work influenced him the most included Mort Drucker, Frank Frazetta*, Howard Pyle, Hal Foster, and Gustav Klimt. Later Jones took half of the Famous Artists Correspondence course. He was primarily a self-taught artist, learning his anatomy from George Bridgemann's anatomy books. His first published art was in *Georgia Golf*, with his first fantasy illustration appearing in *Creepy* magazine in 1967.

Jones moved to New York with his wife in 1967 and lived there for more than a year in a one-room basement apartment. He worked as an illustrator for the Warren illustrated magazines and also became known for his heroic fantasy paperback covers. He worked with large sizes and in oils, taking about a week or longer for a painting. He often used himself or his friend comic artist Bernie Wrightson for a model. He also experimented with making plaster statuettes, which were very well received. During this period, he did nearly one-hundred paperback covers.

In 1971 Jones created a comic strip, *Idyl*, for *National Lampoon* magazine, an experience that helped him clarify his goals. Little by little, he slowed his work in the science fiction and fantasy field and soon even dropped out of the comic-art field. Except for a few collections of his art and several books for Donald Grant, Jones has done very little illustration, concentrating instead on gallery art.

PUBLISHED WORK:

HC: *The Book of Kane* (85), *Red Shadows* (78)

PB: *Across Time, All about Venus* (68), *Almuric, Bedlam Planet* (68), *Beyond the Gates of Dreams* (69), *Big Ball of Wax*, *The Big Jump*, *Black Is the Color* (69), *Book of Ptath*

(69), *Book of Robert E. Howard* (76), *Bring the Jubilee* (72), *The Burning Court* (69), *The City* (68), *City of the Chasch, The Cleft* (69), *Conjure Wife* (70), *Curse of Rathlaw* (68), *The Curse of the Undead* (70)), *The Dark Planet* (71), *Dark of the Woods* (70), *Dark Ways to Death* (69), *Darker Than You Think* (69), *Day of the Beasts* (71), *Devil Soul* (70), *Diabolus* (72), *The Dirdir* (69), *Doors of His Face-Lamps of His Mouth and Other Stories* (74), *Dragon's Teeth* (73), *Earth Unaware* (68), *Eathrmen and Strangers* (68), *Emphyrio* (70), *The Expedition* (71), *Far Out Worlds of A. E. van Vogt, Five to Twelve* (69), *Flamewinds* (69), *Gent from Bear Creek* (75), *Giant of World's End* (69), *The Goblin Tower* (68), *Goddess of Ganymede* (67), *Hand of Kane* (70), *Haunting of Alan Mais* (69), *Haunting of Drumroe* (71), *The Incomplete Enchanter* (68), *Incredible Adventures of Dennis Dorgan* (75), *Iron Man* (76), *Jewels of Aptor* (68), *Kandar* (69), *The Killing Bone* (69), *Kothar Barbarian Swordsman* (69, 73), *Kothar and the Conjurer's Curse* (70), *Kothar and the Demon Queen* (69), *Kothar and the Magic Sword* (69), *Kothar and the Wizard Slayer* (70), *Legion from the Shadows* (76), *Lost Valley of Iskander* (76), *Master of the Etrax* (70), *Messenger of Zhuvastou* (73), *The Moon of Gomrath, Moondust* (68), *The New Adam* (69), *Nine Princes in Amber* (72), *Pathless Trail* (69), *Pigeons from Hell* (76), *Planet Wizard* (69), *The Pnume* (70), *Postmarked the Stars* (69), *Purple Pirate* (70), *Queen Cleopatra* (69), *Quest of the Dark Lady* (69), *The Quest of Kadji* (71), *Quest beyond the Stars, Sargasso of Space* (69), *Satan's Child* (68), *Sea Siege, Second Book of Robert E. Howard* (76), *Seetee Ship* (68), *Seetee Shock* (68), *Servants of Wankh* (69), *Shadow People* (69), *The Solarians* (73), *Solomon Kane* (70), *Sons of the Bear God* (69), *The Sorcerers* (71), *Sorcerer's Amulet* (68), *Sorceress of the Witch World* (68), *Sowers of the Thunder* (75), *Spawn of the Death Machine* (68), *Star Barbarian* (69), *Star Hunter, Star Hunter and Voodoo Planet, Stealer of Souls* (73), *Strangers in Paradise* (69), *Sword of Gael* (75), *Sword of Morning Star* (69), *Swords against Death* (70), *Swords and Deviltry* (70), *Swords of Lankhmar* (68), *Swords in the Mist* (68), *Swords against Wizardry* (68), *Thongor and the Dragon City* (70), *Thongar at the End of Time* (68), *Thongor Fights the Pirates of Tarakus* (70), *Thongar and the Wizard of Lemuria* (69), *Three Hearts and Three Lions* (70), *Tiger River* (71), *Tigers of the Sea* (75), *Tower of Medusa, Twilight of the Serpent* (77), *Uncharted Stars* (69), *Undying Wizard* (76), *Unending Night, Vampire Women* (73), *Vampires of Finstere* (70), *Vultures of Whapeton* (75), *The Wednesday Visitors* (69), *What's It Like Out There* (74), *Whom the Gods Would Slay* (68), *Witches Omen* (71), *Wolfling* (69), *Worms of the Earth* (75), *The Yngling* (71), *Zanthar of the Many Worlds* (67), *Zanthar at Moon's Madness* (68), *Zanthar at Trip's End* (69), *Zero Stone* (68)

AMZ: 1966 (4); 1967 (12); 1968 (2, 6, 9, 11); 1969 (1); 1970 (1, 5, 7, 9, 11); 1971 (1, 3, 5, 11); 1973 (8, 10, 12); 1974 (2, 4, 8, 10, 12); 1975 (3); 1976 (3)

ASF: 1976 (12); 1977 (5)

FTC: 1967 (11); 1968 (1, 3, 5, 8, 10); 1969 (12); 1970 (2, 4, 6, 8, 10, 12); 1971 (2, 4, 6, 8, 10); 1972 (2, 8); 1973 (4, 7, 9, 11); 1974 (1, 3, 5, 7, 9, 11); 1975 (2); 1976 (5)

IF: 1968 (5, 6)

JONES, PETER (b. 1951) British artist. Jones studied at St. Martin's School of Art, London, from 1971 to 1974. While in his second year of studying graphics, he became interested in the novels of Isaac Asimov and

Larry Niven. He subsequently turned to science fiction imagery for his designs and spent hours in bookstores studying the composition of paperback covers. A store manager showed some of his work to art directors, and a commission for Granada Publishers soon followed. His first cover, painted for *King Kobold* in 1974, featured a futuristic long ship ploughing through turbulent seas.

Jones progressed from a series of Chris Foss★ look-alike paintings (*The Night Watch*, *Stranglers Moon*, and so on) to the genres of romance and oriental gothic, sword and sorcery, and robots and monsters. He was strongly influenced by the pulp tradition in science fiction, especially the art and colors of Frank R. Paul.★ Among other influences, Jones lists Norman Rockwell and David Hockney.

In 1975 Jones codesigned the television title sequence with BM Animation for BBC's coverage of the Apollo/Soyuz rendezvous in Earth's orbit. In the late 1970s, he began began expanding his markets by doing artwork for numerous European paperback and magazine publishers. As a result of this activity, in 1977 he was asked by BORN bv., an independent Dutch publisher, to style covers for its SF/fantasy line and redesign the whole image of its series. Jones's treatment of the design, typographic, logo, and overall look of the books boosted the company's sales figures after a long slump. Subsequently, another Dutch company, Elsevier bv., requested the same service after buying the previous company.

In 1979 a collection of Jones's early cover art, *Solar Wind*, was published by Dragon's World. At the same time, Jones formed Solar Wind Ltd. to market his work, branching out into film, television, and video production. He also began producing some rock album covers.

In 1982 TV Francaise 1, Paris, did a documentary on Jones's work. In 1982–1983 Jones worked on the BBC's "Captain Zep Space Detective" show. He formed Smart Moves with designer and animator Peter Goring and Peter Western to design work for the program. This enterprise led to the formation of Airwave, a division of Solar Wind Ltd., doing design and illustration for film, television, and video. Airwave produces work for numerous clients, including many film companies, major advertisers, and, most importantly, the BBC. In 1983 Jones worked on the *Fighting Fantasy* games books for Puffin. His work on this series led to other commissions for other publishers in this fast-growing field.

At present, Jones continues to market his work via his company in the areas of product design, motion pictures, and merchandising. His most recent project is a series of fantasy cartoon characters, which he hopes will be marketed for various important projects. Recently, he also completed work on the BBC's major show "Origins" about the evolution of life in our solar system and began the long task of redesigning the Arrow science fiction book list. Meanwhile, he is continuing to work with major foreign clients and advertisers in the field of design and television production.

Jones's work is noteworthy for his exceptional use of vivid color. In college he was encouraged to grind his own pigments, work with white objects, and perform numerous color–chart experiments. He learned how to use tempera and glazes of oil paint before he ever started art school. He uses acrylic–oil paint along with mixes of other material and often uses acrylic paints for background and landscapes, while highlighting the main characters in oil. He sometimes uses mixtures of oil- and water-based pigment to produce an interesting effect. He usually works on hardboard but has used other material to achieve the desired effect for a specific need.

PUBLISHED WORK:

PB: *All My Sins Remembered* (78), *Apparitions* (74), *Berserker* (74), *The Best of Robert Silverberg* (75), *Beyond the Barrier* (78), *The Birth Grave* (77), *The Black Beast* (75), *The Book of Frank Herbert* (76), *Buy Jupiter* (75), *By the Pricking of My Thumb* (77), *A Canticle for Liebowitz* (79), *A Castle of Iron* (79), *Chalk Giants* (74), *The Chalk Giants* (77), *The Chase* (77), *Clans of the Alphane Moon* (74), *Claws of Death* (76), *Colony Ship* (79), *The Complete Enchanter* (79), *Dark Twin* (74), *Death of the Sea King* (77), *Deep Space* (76), *The Enchanter Completed* (79), *Escape to Venus* (75), *The Fabulous Riverboat* (74), *The Female Man* (76), *Firestorm* (77), *A Gift from Earth* (77), *The Godmakers* (77), *The Imperial Stars* (75), *In the Ocean of Night* (78), *Inferno* (76), *Infinite Dreams* (78), *Interface, Volteface, Multiface* (77), *Jumbee* (76), *The Killer Mice* (77), *King Kobold* (74), *Lord Tedric* (77), *Lucid Dreams* (74), *The Man Who Awoke* (77), *Mercenary* (79), *Midworld* (78), *Mutants* (76), *Nebula Award Stories 7* (74), *Neural Atrocity* (76), *Neutron Star* (77), *New Eden* (79), *The Night Watch* (76), *Nightland* (78), *Omnivore* (76), *Orn* (76), *Orphans of the Sky* (74), *Out of the Body Experiences* (74), *Ox* (76), *Phoenix without Ashes* (76), *Phssthpok* (80), *The Primitive* (77), *Protector* (78), *Ring around the Sun* (75), *Robert "E" Howard Omnibus "Kidnapped"* (76), *The Quest of the D.N.A. Cowboys* (75), *Rogue Ship* (75), *Scenaptic Manhunt* (76), *The Second Experiment* (75), *Shadowfire* (78), *The Silent Invaders* (78), *The Space Merchants* (77), *Space Pirates* (78), *Star Dance* (79), *The Storm Lord* (77), *Stranglers Moon* (76), *Strike Carrier* (78), *Sun Glilders* (79), *Telempath* (78), *Three Bladed Doom* (76), *Timesnake & Superclown* (75), *Titan* (79), *To Ride Pegasus* (77), *Today We Choose Faces* (75), *Tyranopolis* (77), *UFO Trek* (77), *The Undercover Aliens* (75), *The Unholy City* (75), *The Venus Trap* (76), *Warlock in Spite of Himself* (74), *Weird Legacies* (76), *The Wizard of Anharitte* (74), *A World Out of Time* (78), *The World of Ptavvs* (77), *The Zap Gun* (74)

Richard Dalby and Robert Weinberg

JONES, RICHARD GLYN (b. 1946) British artist. After studying at Sheffield University, Jones progressed to postgraduate work in experimental psychology. In spite of having no formal art training, he became one of the most important illustrators for *New Worlds* magazine in the late 1960s, and he helped design the last few issues. In 1980 he contributed art to the first two issues of *Something Else* (a late descendent of *New Worlds*). His inventive artwork is among the most interesting in modern black-and-white science fiction illustration.

Richard Dalby

JONES, ROBERT GIBSON (?) (American artist. A staff artist for the Ziff-Davis chain, Jones provided cover art for all of its pulp magazines in the early 1940s. Discovering a flair for science fiction, he became the mainstay of their two SF pulps, *Amazing Stories* and *Fantastic Adventures*. Like most of the artists working for Ziff-Davis (located in Chicago), Jones lived in Chicago. When the magazine moved its editorial offices to New York, he found himself without work. He then did a number of cover paintings for Ray Palmer, who had been editor for *Amazing* for much of the 1940s and who was publishing *Other Worlds* in a Chicago suburb. Eventually, Jones dropped out of the science fiction field as the Palmer magazines declined.

According to Jones, his art education consisted of "a grand total of forty-two hours. Not the student type definitely." In the same interview, run in *Amazing Stories* in September 1951, he mentioned that he shared a residence studio in Chicago with J. Allen St. John★.

Jones worked almost exclusively with acrylics. He was an excellent painter, adept at portraying people and aliens, and he had a vivid imagination. Many of his paintings were done entirely on his own, and afterwards a story was written around the scene depicted. Along with Earle Bergey★, Jones was the artist who most strongly defined the "pulp" style of science fiction art in the 1940s.

PUBLISHED WORK:

AMZ: 1942 (10, 11); 1943 (5, 9, 11); 1945 (3, 6, 9, 12); 1946 (9, 10); 1947 (2, 3, 6, 10, 11, 12); 1948 (3, 4, 5, 6, 8, 9, 11); 1949 (2, 7, 12); 1950 (2, 3, 4, 6, 7, 8, 9, 10, 11); 1951 (1, 2, 3, 4, 5, 6, 8, 9, 10, 12)

FA: 1942 (8, 11, 12); 1943 (1, 2, 3, 4, 6, 7, 8, 10, 12); 1944 (1, 2); 1945 (1); 1947 (1, 3, 5, 9, 10, 11, 12); 1948 (1, 2, 3, 4, 5, 6, 9, 10); 1949 (1, 5, 9, 11); 1950 (2, 3, 4, 6, 7, 8, 9, 10, 12); 1951 (1, 2, 3, 4, 5, 6, 7, 8, 9, 10, 12); 1952 (11, 12)

OW: 1952 (8, 10, 11, 12), 1953 (4, 5, 6, 7); 1955 (7, 9, 11)

ScS: 1954 (4)

UNI: 1953 (2); 1954 (4, 5, 6)

JORDAN, SYDNEY (b. May 28, 1928) British artist. Born in Dundee, Scotland, Jordan studied at Miles Aircraft Technical College in Reading from 1945 through 1947. His first artwork was comic strips for a Scottish daily newspaper. This work was inspired by Alex Raymond's★ *Rip Kirby* and Milton Caniff's *Steve Canyon*. Later, another major influence on his work was the space art of Chesley Bonestell★.

It was not until he moved to London in 1952 that Jordan began seriously to work on a science fiction strip that was sold to the *Daily Express* in 1954. *Jeff Hawke, Spacerider* ran daily for twenty years, during which time it moved through a series of stories that kept pace with the real world of space flight. Jordan's early aeronautical training helped make *Jeff Hawke* exceptionally popular. One of the early strips, published in 1959, forecast man's first step on the Moon as taking place on August 9, 1969.

A policy change removed *Jeff Hawke* from the *Daily Express* in 1974, but the strip is still done by Jordan (modified from his feature *Lance McLane*, done in color for the *Scottish Daily Record*) for syndication in Europe, Scandinavia, the Near and Far East, and Australia. Recent strip adventures include *Sails in the Red Sunset*, an encounter between the Mars base personnel and mysterious winged machines, leading to a modern confrontation with Cthulhu, Nyarlathotep, and others in the Lovecraft mythos (including H. P. Lovecraft himself) in a series of strips entitled *Even Death May Die*.

Although the more-than nine thousand *Jeff Hawke* strips can be regarded as Jordan's life work during the past thirty years, he also found time to do occasional magazine covers in the SF field, including three for *New Worlds*. His most notable painting was the August 1961 issue of that magazine featuring a robot "with a tear for mankind."

Jordan uses black ink on a smooth card, with color overlays, for the Scottish newspaper. He uses zipatone for his syndication work. Jordan is now working on two new features, science fiction and fantasy, with Rich Theyen*.

PUBLISHED WORK:

NW: 1961 (1, 4, 8)

KALUTA, MICHAEL W. (b. 1947) American artist. Kaluta received his professional art training at the Richmond Professional Art Institute. A comic book fan, he was strongly influenced by the art of Al Williamson, Roy Krenkel*, and Frank Frazetta*, as well as the work of Maxfield Parrish. Kaluta worked for a number of major comic fanzines before entering the field in 1970 with interior work for *Amazing Stories* and *Fantastic*. His detailed, fine-lined art made him a fan favorite in the comics, and he became well known for his comic-book version of the pulp character The Shadow. Kaluta works infrequently for the science fiction hardcover market, but all of his art in that vein has been of high quality.

PUBLISHED WORK:

HC: *The Grand Adventure* (85), *The Legacy of Lehr* (86), *The Lost Valley of Iskander* (74), *Swords of Shahrazar* (76)

FTC: 1970 (4, 6, 8, 12); 1971 (2, 4, 6, 8, 10, 12); 1972 (2, 4, 6, 8, 10, 12); 1973 (2, 4, 9, 11); 1974 (1, 3, 5); 1975 (2); 1977 (12)

KATZ, LES (?) American artist. Strongly influenced by the work of Frank Frazetta★ as well as the Marvel Comics line, Katz knew, as a teenager, that he wanted to be an artist. He entered the University of Bridgeport in 1972, where he studied industrial design. Afterwards, he studied basic painting, design, and different techniques of illustration at the School of Visual Arts in New York. Katz then turned to freelance illustration to make a living. Serving many clients, he has done a number of assignments for the Science Fiction Book Club.

Like most science fiction artists, Katz first reads the manuscript of any story he is illustrating. He searches for a central theme or image to convey the essential points of the book and then does several sketches based on his ideas. After one of the sketches is approved, he does a tight pencil drawing of the picture and then finishes the work in acrylics. He also has worked in pastels, crayons, and inks.

PUBLISHED WORK:

HC: *Circus World*

KELLY, KEN (b. 1946) American artist. Born in Connecticut, Kelly studied with Frank Frazetta★ and sold his first painting in 1969. He is best known for his violent, graphic paintings done for Robert E. Howard novels.

PUBLISHED WORK:

HC: *The Hour of the Dragon, People of the Black Circle, Red Nails*

PB: *Almuric* (77), *Angado* (83), *Banners of Sc'yen* (81), *Banners of the Sa'Yeri* (81), *Bili the Axe* (83), *Birthgrave* (75), *Black Canaan* (78), *Black Vulmea's Vengeance* (79), *Book of Dreams* (81), *Book of Ptath* (84), *Book of Robert E. Howard* (78), *Book of Shai, Castaways in Time* (82), *Cat of Silvery Hue* (79), *Champion of the Last Battle* (83), *Color Out of Time* (84), *Comic of the Horseclans* (82), *Crystal Crown* (84), *Cyrion* (82), *Day Star and Shadow, Death of a Legend* (81), *Delusion's Master* (81), *Diamond Contessa* (84), *Down to a Sunless Sea* (84), *Dragonrouge* (84), *Forest of Peldain* (85), *Ghosthunt* (82, 83), *Horseclans Odyssey* (81), *Horses of the North* (85), *Hour of the Dragon* (77), *Imaro* (81), *Jandar of Callisto* (77), *Kelly Country* (84), *Last Ride* (78), *Lost Valley of Iskander* (79), *Marchers of Valhalla* (78), *Matilda's Stepchildren* (79), *Mind Guest* (84), *Moongather* (82), *Moonscatter* (83), *Parallel Man* (83), *Patrimony* (80), *People of the Black Circle* (77), *Players of Gor, Rebel of Antares, Red Blades of Black Cathay, Ren Nails* (77), *Renegade of Callisto* (78), *Revenge of the Horseclans* (82), *Ring of Truth* (83), *Savage Mountains* (80), *Seg the Bowman* (84), *The Seven Magical Jewels of Ireland* (85), *Skullface* (78), *Son of the White Wolf* (78), *Survival World* (71), *Sword Woman* (79), *Swords of the Horseclans* (81), *Swords of Shahrazar* (78), *Under the Canopy* (80), *Vazkor, Son of Vazkor* (78), *Vultures of Whapeton* (80), *Warrior Rearmed, Wild Ones, Will of the Gods* (84), *Witch Goddess* (82), *Woman of the Horseclan* (83)

AMZ: 1975 (11)

FTC: 1975 (6)

KIDD, TOM (b. Aug. 10, 1955) American artist. Born in Tampa, Florida, Kidd attended college but found that he learned mostly from observation, which he believes "is the best training." Kidd read science fiction as a child and was always attracted by the covers. Art influences were the Impressionists and the Brandywine School of Illustrators. When he decided to enter the art field, science fiction art seemed the best choice. He moved from Tampa to New York to break into the market and painted his first cover for Berkley Books, although he primarily works for TOR Books at present and lives in New York with his wife, Andrea.

Kidd reads each book to help him decide what to illustrate for the cover. He tries to capture the feel of the book but prefers storytelling illustration to surrealism. He prefers realism in all of his paintings and works in oils. His favorite work was prepared for *Sherlock Holmes through Time and Space* for Bluejay Books. His work has grown increasingly popular with science fiction fans, and in 1985 he was nominated for the Hugo Award.

PUBLISHED WORK:

HC: *Infinity Link* (84), *Sherlock Holmes through Time and Space* (84)

PB: *Earth Descended* (81), *Oron #3 Mosutha's Magic* (82), *Oron # Valley of Agrum* (82), *Sorcerer's Shadow* (78), *Spacepaw* (82), *Zanthodon* (80)

F&SF: 1984 (1, 9)

KIEMLE, H. W. (?) American artist. Pulp artist who did interiors for a number of the science fiction magazines of the late 1940s and early 1950s. Kiemle first began working for the Fiction House Chain in 1944 and branched out into the other pulps in the early 1950s.

PUBLISHED WORK:

AMZ: 1951 (11)
DYN: 1952 (12); 1953 (3)
FA: 1952 (2)
FUT: 1951 (7, 9, 11); 1952 (1, 3)
PS: 1944 (fall, winter); 1945 (spring, summer, winter); 1946 (spring, summer, fall, winter); 1947 (spring, summer, fall); 1948 (winter)
SF: 1957 (3)
SFQ: 1951 (8, 11); 1952 (8, 11); 1955 (8); 1956 (5)
SS: 1947 (7, 9, 11)
TSF: 1951 (spring)

KIRBY, JOSH (b. 1928) British artist. Born in Waterloo, Liverpool, England, Kirby studied at the Liverpool City School of Art for six years. In 1950 he was the youngest painter ever to be commissioned by the city of Liverpool for the presentation portrait of the lord mayor.

Moving to London, Kirby became a freelance illustrator and started a long career as a paperback cover artist. He obtained commissions from various publishers, including the publisher of *Authentic Science Fiction* magazine in 1956. A short story by Brian Aldiss, "Out of Reach," was the starting point of Kirby's career as a professional science fiction illustrator. He also worked in other genres as well, from romance fiction to westerns to war stories.

Ian Fleming's James Bond novel, *Moonraker*, published by Pan in 1956, carried Kirby's first science fiction book cover. During the past thirty years, Kirby has illustrated numerous covers in the genre (chiefly for Panther, Corgi, Mayflower, New English Library, and Four Square in Britain; Ace and DAW in the United States). He also has produced artwork for German and French books.

Usually, Kirby paints actual book-cover sizes, prepared meticulously. He uses gouache, acrylic, oil, or watercolor and often combines two methods. His alien creatures, notably in Fritz Leiber's *Swords of Lankhmar*, are among the most imaginative and grotesque in modern science fiction illustration, and he was voted best professional artist at the World Science Fiction Convention in Brighton in 1979. Afterwards, he did a portfolio of illustration for Schanes and Schanes, Publishers, entitled *Voyage of the Ayeguy*.

In recent years, Kirby has been providing interior artwork for Corgi, illustrating a series of role-playing books under the general title *Tunnels and Trolls*. Important covers include his work for Ray Bradbury's *Illustrated Man* and *Farenheit 451* as well as Silverberg's *Lord Valentine's Castle* and Terry Pratchett's *Color of Magic*. He also worked on numerous film posters for English releases of major science fiction films including *Krull*, *Starflight One*, *The Beastmaster*, and *Return of the Jedi*.

Kirby's work has been exhibited at many science fiction conventions internationally and at several fine-art galleries throughout Britain. He now lives in a four-hundred-year-old house near Diss in Norfolk.

PUBLISHED WORK:

PB: *8th Armada Ghost Book* (83), *11th Armada Ghost Book* (83), *13th Pan Book of Horror Stories* (73), *50 Years of Science Fiction Magazines* (75), *Ahead of Time*, *Aldair in Albion* (75), *Alfred Hitchcock's Deathbag* (73), *Alice's World* (69), *Alien Planet*, *The Aliens amongst Us* (70), *Angels and Spaceships* (62), *Anyone for Murder* (67), *Aries Rising* (82), *Bar the Doors* (71), *Benighted* (63), *The Best of Henry Kutter*, *Beyond Infinity* (64), *Beyond the Locked Door* (66), *Big Bang* (82), *The Big Death* (77), *The Biological Time Bomb* (68), *Black Tales* (64), *Blue Moon* (69), *Book of Philip Jose Farmer* (75), *Book of the Werewolf* (72), *Breakdown* (67), *Bumsider* (72), *Calling Dr. Patchwork* (80), *Captive Scorpio* (78), *Carson of Venus* (66), *Case of the Friendly Corpse*, *Caves of Steel* (58), *Cee Tee Man* (57), *A Century of Great Short SF Novels* (69), *A Century of SF Novels* (69), *Chain Reaction* (66), *The City and the Stars* (69), *Close of Critical* (67), *The Colour of Magic* (84), *Coming of the Strangers* (62), *The Communipaths* (70), *The Craft of Terror* (66), *Count Down* (64), *Currents of Space* (58), *The Dark Mind* (64), *A Darkness in*

My Soul (76), *Darya of the Bronze Age* (81), *The Day before Tomorrow* (72), *Dimension of Miracles* (70), *The Dreamers* (64), *The Elephant Man* (72), *The Elixer of Life* (65), *Eloise* (79), *Ensign Flandry* (72), *Eric of Zanthodon* (81), *Escape on Venus* (66), *Escape to Venus* (58), *Eye of the Zodiac* (79), *Farenheit 451* (63), *Far Out* (63), *A Fighting Man of Maars* (66), *Flight of the Plactic Bee* (67), *For Fear of Little Men* (74), *Games Killers Play* (73), *The Gates of Time* (70), *Get Me to the Wake on Time* (69, 73), *The Girl with a Symphony in Her Fingers* (74), *God of the Labyrinth* (81), *Golden Apples of the Sun* (64), *Golden Scorpio* (78), *The Grey Ones* (62), *Half in Shadow* (64), *Haunted Houseful* (65), *Haven of Darkness* (79), *Heil Hibbler* (80), *Hello Lemuria Hello* (81), *Hero of Downways* (73, 81), *History of the SF Magazines* (81), *Horror* (65), *The Hour of the Phoenix* (64), *Hurok of the Stone Age* (79), *I Can't Sleep at Night* (66), *I Sing the Body Electric*, *Illustrated Man* (63), *Interpreter*, *The Island Snatchers* (77), *Jack of Shadows* (79, 81), *The Jagged Orbit* (72), *John Carter of Mars* (66), *Journey beyond Tomorrow* (65), *Journey to the Underground World* (79), *The Kraken Wakes* (76), *Krozair of Kregan* (76), *The Last Leap* (64), *The Late Unlamented* (67), *The Left Hand of Darkness* (72), *Light Fantastic* (85), *The Light That Never Was* (74), *Llana of Gathol* (66), *Lord Valentine's Castle* (81), *The Lord's Pink Ocean* (73), *The Lost Perception* (67), *Majipoor Chronicles* (83), *A Man Called Poe* (72), *Marooned* (65), *Meet Death at Night* (66), *Melmoth the Wanderer* (66), *The Menace from Earth* (67), *Midsummer Century* (73), *The Mind Behind the Eye* (71), *Mindbridge* (77), *The Monitors* (70), *A Month of Mystery* (72), *Moonraker* (56), *Morlock Night* (78), *A Mote in Time's Eye* (74), *Murders I Fell in Love With* (69, 73), *My Bones and My Flute* (65), *Nelson Algrin's Book of Lonely Monsters* (65), *The New Minds* (66), *Newfoundland* (83), *Night Side* (66), *Night Spiders* (64), *Nightmare* (64), *Nightshades and Damnations* (68), *No Time for Heros* (69), *The Novel of the Black Seal* (65), *The Novel of the White Powder* (65), *Occam's Razor*, *Ole Doc Methuselah* (72), *One against Time*, *Ossians Ride* (60), *The Other Foot* (68), *The Other Side of the Sky* (66), *The Panchronicon Plot* (76), *Patron of the Arts* (75), *Pitman's Progress* (74), *Planet of the Dreamers* (61), *Planet of Exile* (70), *The Plastic Magicians*, *Polymath*, *Prince of Scorpio* (76), *Propellor Island* (64), *Rax* (77), *Reproductive System*, *Return to Tomorrow* (57), *The Robot in the Closet* (80), *Rolling Gravestones* (73), *Saturn over the Water* (63), *Secret Scorpio* (75), *Seed of Light* (60), *Sentinel Stars* (63), *Seven Days in New Crete* (73), *SF 12* (67), *SF 13* (68), *SF 14* (68), *SF the Best of the Best 2* (69), *The Shape of Things to Come* (67), *The Shark Hunters* (70), *Shock* (62), *Shock II* (65), *Shock One* (77), *Shock Two* (77), *The Shores of Space* (65), *The Silver Locusts* (64), *The Sleep Eaters* (64), *Something Wicked This Way Comes* (64), *The Son of the Tree* (71), *Spectrum of a Forgotten Sun* (79), *Split Image* (57), *The Stone God Awakes* (70), *Stories They Wouldn't Let Me Do on TV* (74), *Storm over Warlock* (72), *Stress Pattern* (74), *Sundog* (65), *Suns of Scorpio* (75), *Swampworld West* (73), *The Swords of Lakhmar* (70), *Swords of Mars* (66), *Swordships of Scorpio* (75), *Syzygy* (73), *Tales of Horror and the Supernatural* (64), *Tales of Supernatural Terror* (73), *Tarzan and the Ant Men* (67), *Tarzan of the Apes* (67), *Tarzan and the Castaway* (67), *Tarzan and the City of Gold* (67), *Tarzan at the Earth's Core* (67), *Tarzan and the Forbidden City* (67), *Tarzan the Invincible* (67), *Tarzan and the Jewels of Opar* (67), *Tarzan's Jungle Tales* (67), *Tarzan and the Leopard Men* (67), *Tarzan and the Madman* (67), *Tarzan the Magnificent* (67), *Tarzan's Quest* (67), *Time Story* (72), *Timeliner* (64), *Times without Number* (74), *Tomorrow Lies in Ambush* (72), *The Town and the City* (69, 73), *Transit to Scorpio* (69, 74), *Twenty Second Century* (60), *A Twilight of Briareus* (75), *Undersea*

City, Undersea Fleet, Undersea Quest, The Unquiet Grave (68), *Untouched by Human Hands* (66), *Upside Downside* (81), *Valentine Pontifax* (84), *Vanity of Duluoz* (72), *Vathek* (65), *Victory on Janus* (72), *Warlocks and Warriors* (70), *Warrior of Scorpio* (75), *Weird Shadows from Beyond* (65), *What's Become of Screwloose* (73), *The Weird Ones* (66), *A Whiff of Madness* (81), *The Wicked Cyborg* (77), *The Whitchraft Reader* (72), *Wizards Warriors and You Books 3, 4, 5, 6* (84), *Wooden Centauri* (75), *The World Menders* (73), *Worlds Best SF* (74, 75), *Worlds of the Imperium* (70), *Years Best Fantasy Stories #3* (80), *Years Best Fantasy Stories #6* (80)

AUTH: 1956 (80, 81, 82, 83, 48)

FILM POSTERS: "Krull" (83), "Return of the Jedi" (83), "Seven Cities of Atlantis" (80), "The Beastmaster" (83), "Starflight One" (83)

PORTFOLIO: Voyage of the Ayeguy (81)

Richard Dalby

KIRK, TIM (b. Oct. 30, 1947) American artist. Born in Long Beach, California, Kirk went through the Long Beach Unified Schoool District. He had wanted to be an artist since he was four years old, and after high school, he became an art major at California State University in Long Beach, from which he received a master's degree, using for his thesis twenty-six paintings done for *The Lord of the Rings*. Afterwards, thirteen of these paintings were used in the 1975 Tolkien Calendar published by Ballantine Books. He had worked at a number of jobs, including school librarian and gardener, before taking a job with Hallmark Cards in 1973.

Kirk has been an active member of science fiction fandom for a number of years and has won Hugo Awards in 1970, 1972, 1973, 1974, and 1976 as Best Fan Artist. His strongest influence was that of Donald Duck comic artist Carl Barks. Other influences include Sydney Sime, Andrew Wyeth, Arthur Rackham, and many science fiction artists including George Barr★, Virgil Finlay★, Jack Gaughan★, and Robert Pepper★.

As to his feelings about his art, Kirk stated that "my primary goal in illustration has always been to express my reaction to a subject in a way that is pleasing to both the viewer and myself. I think that the human race is a lot funnier than it realizes, and I've tried to deal with this in my humorous work as unoffensively as possible."

PUBLISHED WORK:

HC: *Approaching Oblivion* (74), *The Art of the Fantastic* (79), *An Atlas of Fantasy* (73), *The Complete Tales from Gavagan's Bar* (78), *The Conan Grimoire* (72), *Dreams from R'Lyeh* (75), *Directory of Dealers in SF and Fantasy* (75), *A Dreamers Tale* (79), *Faster Than Light* (76), *A Gent from Bear Creek* (75), *A Guide to Middle Earth* (71), *Half in Shadow* (78), *Heroes and Horrors* (79), *Literary Swordsmen and Sorcerors* (76), *The Pride of Bear Creek* (77), *The Purple Dragon and Other Fantasies* (76), *Rime Isle* (77), *Science Fiction Handbook* (75), *Star Trek Concordance* (76), *Tales of Three Hemispheres* (76),

Tigers of the Sea (74), *The Tolkien Scrapbook* (79), *Whispers* (77), *Whispers 2* (79), *Whispers 3* (81)

PB: *Bernhard the Conqueror* (73), *Burrowers Beneath* (74), *Changling Earth* (73), *The Complete Feghoot* (75), *Conan the Liberator* (79), *Conan: The Sword of Skelos* (79), *Conan the Swordsman* (78), *A Gent from Bear Creed* (75), *A Guide to Middle Earth* (74), *The Hills of the Dead* (79), *King Chondo's Ride* (82), *Road of Kings* (79), *Skulls in the Stars* (79), *Stormtrack* (74), *The Suns of Scorpio* (73), *The Tolkien Quizbook* (79), *Transit to Scorpio* (72), *The Trouble with Tribbles* (73), *Under the Green Star* (72), *Warrior of Scorpio* (73)

FgF: 1971 (4)

IASFM: 1977 (summer, fall); 1978 (3); 1979 (spring, 6); 1980 (4, 7, 9, 10, 12); 1981 (2, 3, 5, 6, 7, 8, 9, 12); 1982 (2/15, 4, 5, 12/15)

IF: 1970 (7)

VORTEX: 1973 (4, 6, 8, 10, 12); 1974 (4, 6, 8, 10); 1975 (2)

WC&S: 1971 (1, 5)

KOLLIKER, W. A. (?) American artist. An interior artist who contributed numerous interiors to *Astounding* from late 1939 through the early 1940s, Kolliker first signed his work "W. A. Koll, " but in 1940 he began using his full name, "Kolliker." Either way, the art was not very good. It featured thick line work and cartoonlike characters; the aliens were stiff and unbelievable. In the opinion of most readers of the magazine, Kolliker's art did little more than take up space.

PUBLISHED WORK:

ASF: 1939 (8, 9, 12); 1940 (1, 2, 3, 4, 6, 8); 1941 (7, 8, 9, 10, 11); 1942 (1, 2, 4, 6, 7, 8, 9, 10, 11, 12); 1943 (1, 2, 6, 8, 9)

SS: 1941 (1, 7, 9)

StrS: 1940 (2, 4, 6, 8, 10); 1941 (2)

TWS: 1941 (3)

UK: 1940 (6); 1942 (4, 6, 8, 10, 12); 1943 (2, 6, 8, 10)

KRAMER, FRANK (?) American artist. An interior artist who worked primarily for *Astounding SF* in the 1940s, Kramer was a prolific contributor and a very good artist who was capable of strong line work and could use a grease pencil effectively. His people looked like people, and his aliens were reasonbly well done. Although Charles Schneeman★ usually was given the best stories to illustrate during the same period, Kramer was his equal in both presentation and style.

PUBLISHED WORK:

ASF: 1939 (6, 7, 10); 1940 (2, 3, 4, 5, 8, 9, 10, 11); 1941 (1, 4, 5, 7, 8, 9, 10, 11, 12); 1942 (1, 2, 3, 5, 6, 7, 9, 11, 12); 1943 (1, 2, 3, 4, 5, 6, 7, 8, 9, 10, 12); 1944 (1, 4, 8, 9, 10, 11, 12); 1945 (3, 4, 5, 7, 8, 9, 11); 1946 (1, 2, 3)

FA: 1941 (11)

FFM: 1944 (9)

SSS: 1949 (1, 7)

UK: 1939 (8, 9, 11, 12); 1940 (3, 4, 6, 7, 9, 10, 11); 1941 (2, 6, 8, 10); 1942 (2, 4, 6, 8, 10, 12); 1943 (2, 4, 6, 8, 10)

KRAMER, VERNON (?) American artist. Kramer did a few paintings in the early 1950s for science fiction magazines and then left the field. When Cele Goldsmith modernized *Amazing Stories* and *Fantastic* in 1960, Kramer returned as one of the artists she used to upgrade the cover art. Unfortunately, he did only a few paintings and then again left the science fiction field.

PUBLISHED WORK:

AMZ: 1963 (2)

FTC: 1953 (11); 1954 (1); 1961 (5, 7); 1962 (8); 1963 (1, 5, 8)

KRENKEL, ROY GERALD, JR. (1918–1983) American artist. Born in the Bronx, Krenkel lived in New York .except for a short period in the Philippine Islands during the Second World War. When he was still a young boy, he discovered the Tarzan stories by Edgar Rice Burroughs and the art of illustrator J. Allen St. John*. A fascination with the fiction and art led him into the fantasy field. Krenkel loved the pulps and collected all of the science fiction and weird-fiction pulps, as well as many adventure and detective magazines. Meticulous, he kept all of his magazines in mint condition.

Krenkel attended Hogarth's School of Visual Arts, Cooper Union, and later took courses at the Art Students League. He lived with his parents in their home in Queens and worked on the fringes of the comic-book field. He began producing art for the comics in the early 1950s, but being a slow worker, believing in perfection in every detail, he was not able to satisfy the more demanding pace of comic art. His best-known art during this period consisted of several pieces he did for EC Comics. It was through EC that Krenkel became friends with Frank Frazetta*.

Constantly doodling and drawing, Krenkel contributed many of his sketches to *Amra*, a Robert E. Howard-oriented fanzine. Early in 1962 Donald Wollheim, editor of Ace Books, was preparing to reprint works of Edgar Rice Burroughs in paperback, and the *Amra* illustrations, very much in the J. Allen St. John tradition, convinced him to approach Krenkel with some art assignments, both for the Burroughs novels and other novels in the Burroughs tradition.

Although Krenkel had never tried painting, having worked exclusively in pen and ink, he took the assignment. His first painting was for *Planet of Peril* by Otis Adelbert Kline. He continued to do paintings for Ace, but after working on a few others, Krenkel asked Frazetta for help in completing several compositions. At the same time, Krenkel continually suggested Frazetta to Wollheim as an artist for the same series. Wollheim finally used Frazetta, and that artist became so popular that Krenkel was eventually replaced on the Burroughs covers. However, his artwork for Ace did bring him a Hugo Award in 1963 as Best Artist of the Year from science fiction fandom.

Krenkel continued to work in the science fiction field, primarily doing cover paintings for paperbacks. When Donald Wollheim left Ace Books and founded his own company, Krenkel did many of the heroic adventure covers for DAW in the same manner that he had done them for Wollheim at Ace.

Krenkel's constant sketching and pen-and-ink work won him a small but enthusiastic following. One of these fans was publisher Donald Grant, who saw Krenkel as an artist very much in the tradition of J. Clement Coll★. Grant published several collections of Robert E. Howard stories lavishly illustrated with pen-and-ink illustrations by Krenkel. One book, *The Sowers of the Thunder*, was praised in reviews more for the fine art than for the Howard fiction.

A lifelong bachelor, Krenkel lived alone in a small home on Long Island. Somewhat eccentric, he worked hard enough to support himself and collect the things he liked. But he was not ambitious. He was a familiar sight at New York comic-book conventions, walking around with a portfolio of sketches for sale. He died from cancer in 1983, soon after being given a special award for his art from the 1982 World Fantasy Convention.

Krenkel was one of the finest pen-and-ink artists to work in the fantasy field in the past fifty years. Unfortunately, since most of his work was published in fanzines or a few limited-edition books, he never achieved the recognition that the quality of his work should have brought him.

PUBLISHED WORK:

HC: *The Cave Girl, Land of Terror* (63), *Road to Azrael, The Sowers of the Thunder* (68), *Tales of Three Planets* (64), *Tarzan and the Tarzan Twins* (63)

PB: *As the Green Star Rises* (75), *At the Earth's Core* (62), *Back to the Stone Age* (63), *By the Light of the Green Star* (74), *Cave Girl* (63), *Chessmen of Mars* (62), *Eternal Savage* (63), *Escape on Venus, Fighting Man of Mars* (62), *Flight of Opar* (76), *Hadon of Ancient Opar* (74), *Highways in Hiding* (67), *Ironcastle* (76), *King Kull* (67), *Land of Hidden Men* (63), *Land That Time Forgot* (63), *Mastermind of Mars* (62), *Moon Maid* (62), *Out of Time's Abyss* (63), *Pellucidar* (62), *People That Time Forgot* (63), *Pirates of Venus* (62), *Planet of Peril* (61), *Port of Peril, Prince of Peril* (62), *Road to Azrea, Tanar of Pellucidar* (62), *Tarzan at the Earth's Core* (62), *Tarzan Triumphant* (63), *Thuvia, Maid of Mars* (62)

ASF: 1961 (5, 11, 12); 1962 (3, 5)

FF: 1953 (11)

MSS: 1952 (5)

SFA: 1954 (2, 5)

SpSF: 1953 (9)

KRESEK, LARRY (?) American artist. Kresek studied painting at the Art Center College of Design in Los Angeles, at the University of Delaware, and in Europe. He works as a freelance illustrator and has done a great deal of advertising art. Other major projects include a series of pharmaceutical illustrations, medically related art, and movie illustrations. His paintings are included in private collections throughout the United States. Much of his science fiction art has been done for the Science Fiction Book Club.

PUBLISHED WORK:

HC: *The Best of Fritz Leiber, The Best of Henry Kuttner, Case and the Dreamer* (74), *The Seven Deadly Sins of Science Fiction, Time Masters* (71), *The Winter of the World* (75)

PB: *Final Circle of Paradise* (76), *Fury* (72)

KRUPA, JULIAN S. (Jan. 7, 1913–?) American artist. Born in Poland, Krupa immigrated with his family to the United States while still a baby. Always interested in art, he took a correspondence course in illustration in 1933. Concluding that learning by mail was not working, he attended art school and then became a freelance artist. In the middle 1930s he secured a job with a Polish newspaper, doing rotogravure layouts, lettering, and graphic design. During this time, he wrote and illustrated a science fiction adventure comic strip in Polish, *The Adventures of Richard Arnold.* Krupa was also an accomplished musician, playing with several orchestras and conducting his own band. Like many artists working for the Ziff-Davis publications, he illustrated for all of the magazines published by the chain including *Radio News, Pets, Flying,* and *Popular Aviation.* He did all of his interior black-and-white illustrations with a brush, working primarily in stipple.

PUBLISHED WORK:

AMZ: 1938 (10, 11, 12); 1939 (1, 2, 3, 4, 5, 6, 7, 8, 9, 10, 11); 1940 (1, 2, 3, 4, 5, 6, 7, 9, 10, 11, 12); 1941 (1, 2, 3, 4, 5, 6, 7, 8, 9, 10, 11); 1942 (5, 6); 1943 (5, 6, 7, 8, 9); 1944 (1, 5, 9, 12); 1945 (3, 9, 12); 1946 (2, 5, 6, 7, 9, 10, 12); 1947 (1, 4, 6, 7, 8, 10, 12); 1948 (1, 2, 4, 6, 7, 8, 12); 1949 (1, 2, 3, 4, 5, 6, 7, 10, 11, 12); 1950 (1, 2, 3, 4, 6, 7, 8, 9, 10, 11); 1951 (1, 2, 3, 5, 8, 11); 1952 (1); 1966 (4); 1968 (2); 1969 (9); 1971 (3)

FA: 1939 (5, 7, 9, 11); 1940 (1, 2, 3, 4, 5, 6, 10); 1941 (1, 3, 5, 6, 7, 8, 9, 11); 1942 (4, 10); 1943 (5, 6, 7, 12); 1944 (2, 6, 10); 1946 (9); 1947 (1, 7); 1948 (6, 9, 10, 12); 1949 (1, 2, 3, 4, 5, 7, 8, 11); 1950 (3, 4, 5, 6, 10, 11); 1951 (3)

FTC: 1966 (7); 1968 (3); 1972 (2)

OW: 1957 (9)

LADD, ERIC (b. July 23, 1949) American artist. The third of ten children, Ladd was born in Putney, Vermont, but his family moved to North Kingston, Rhode Island, when he was five or six years old. Many members of his family are artists, including two sisters, Maria and Beth; his brother Thomas is a potter.

Eric attended parochial schools and Seminary High School. After graduation, he entered Boston College, planning to become a priest, but a year later, in 1969, he changed his mind and enrolled in Boston's School of the Museum of Fine Arts. There he met Steven Lisberger, and the two of them formed Lisberger-Ladd, Inc., in 1971, a studio specializing in full-cell airbrush animation. Their most outstanding work was *Cosmic Cartoon*, a ten-minute film that was nominated for a student academy award. During this period, Ladd married but was divorced a few years later.

Ladd then left the partnership and did freelance artwork, primarily industrial projects and magazine illustrations. He entered the Rhode Island School of Design in 1975. That same year, he attended the Boston Science Fiction convention, Boskone, where his art attracted the attention of David Hartwell (then editor of Timescape Books) and Donald A. Wollheim (of DAW Books). These contacts drew Ladd into the SF art field. At the same convention he also met Carl Lundgren★ and Michele Lundgren, who gave him a great deal of useful advice. Ladd later collaborated with Carl Lundgren on several paintings.

Ladd has done work for several of the major SF publishers. He has been commissioned for many projects but prefers to paint on speculation. One painting, titled *Archeress*, was shown to Berkley Books and was liked so much that the publisher decided to use it for the third book of Elizabeth Lynn's Watchtower trilogy and commissioned Ladd to do paintings for the first two books. Lynn liked those paintings so much that she wrote the scene they depicted into her novel.

Ladd began working in acrylics and then moved into oils. This occurred when he did the cover for *Space Lords* for Jove Books. Unfortunately, the "frisket" stencil covering the foreground was put on too early to allow adequate drying, and half of the painting was pulled off the masonite with the stencil. The painting was redone, with a spare completed just as a precaution. Ladd dried this one, and most of his oil paintings since that first disaster, using a hair dryer pointed at the painting and going full force, for a night and a day of quick drying, in addition to the drying that took place during the long car trip from Rhode Island to New York.

In 1982 Ladd enrolled in the University of Rhode Island at Kingston, in the engineering school, specializing in computer graphics. After a one-year stay, he signed on at Omnibus Computer Graphics in New York. With the computer, he believes he has found the ultimate paint brush.

Ladd has done a number of paintings that have never been published in the United States but have appeared as covers of European and Japanese books. Unfortunately, those works are beyond the scope of the bibliography below.

PUBLISHED WORK:

HC: *The Dancers of Arun* (78), *A Different Light* (79), *The Northern Girl* (79), *A Private Cosmos* (82), *The Watchtower* (78), *The Woman Who Loved the Moon* (80)

PB: *The Best of E. E. "Doc" Smith* (79), *Beyond the Imperium* (80), *The Cache* (80), *Convergent Series* (79), *The Falling Torch* (78), *Irsud* (78), *The Pleasure Tube* (78), *Space Lords* (78), *Starfall* (79, in collaboration with Carl Lundgren), *Tongues of the Moon* (78, in collaboration with Carl Lundgren), *Wyst* (78)

LAKEY, VAL (b. Sept. 6, 1951) American artist. One of the increasing number of women science fiction illustrators, Val Lakey Lindahn was born in West Virginia. She started Artifact Studio with two other illustrators living and working in Otto, North Carolina. Much of her published art is signed "Val Lakey/Artifact."

Lakey attended Miami-Dade Community College in 1969–1970 and then went to work for Screen Gems and Columbia Music Publishers while also working as a freelance artist in Miami, Florida. She found that she hated working from nine to five and dropped out, becoming a housewife for a year and deciding what direction she wanted to follow in the art field.

Assembling a group of slides of her work as a portfolio, Lakey used these illustrations to get work from Warren Publishing (*Creepy* and *Eerie* magazines) and *Cavalier*. She sent a group of slides to George Scithers, editor of *Isaac Asimov's Magazine*, and he commissioned her first true science fiction artwork. She continued to work for *Asimov's Magazine* from 1979 to 1981, and when Scithers moved to *Amazing*, she went with him.

She has been twice nominated for the Hugo Award for her art. Along with continuing her science fiction art, she has been doing video packaging for movie posters for Vestron Video.

Married to artist Ron Lindahn, Lakey is the mother of a son. She works very closely with her husband on many assignments. They discuss their projects in great detail, and he does much of the air brushing used on her art.

Together they often build models of clay, plaster, liquid rubber, and plasticene for use in visualizing her paintings. She photographs these models with appropriate directional light, convinced that the lighting on many pieces is illogical since it comes from all directions instead of from one source. She often uses friends for models and will make costumes and even use makeup to get the proper feel for the illustration.

Like most artists, she first reads a manuscript to be illustrated and then tries to take the most exciting sequence for her inspiration. She prefers scenes with aliens and hardware and works in acrylics on her color work and gouache on her black and whites.

Lakey holds Bernard Fuchs as well as N. C. and Andrew Wyeth in high regard and wants to bring to science fiction a highly detailed, photo-realistic style. She is happy with her work and is thrilled when her concepts and the concepts of an author match. In the future, she and her husband hope to build and design aliens for the movies.

PUBLISHED WORK:

ASF: 1980 (6, 9, 11); 1981 (1, 5, 8, 9, 10, 11, 12); 1982 (1, 2, 3, 3/29, 5, 10, 11)

IASFA: 1979 (spring, summer)

IASFM: 1978 (11); 1979 (3, 10, 11); 1980 (1, 7, 11); 1981 (1, 4, 6, 8, 8/31, 9, 10, 11, 12); 1982 (1, 4, 5, 6, 8, 9, 10, 12, 12/15)

LANOS, HENRI (?) French artist. An important French painter and illustrator who worked in Paris and London from 1886 to 1916, Lanos was born in Paris. He first contributed to *L'Illustration* and *La Caricature* and then illustrated several works by Daudet, Gaboriau, Maupassant, and Zola, as well as children's books, including *Alphabet de la guerre*.

At the turn of the century, he was one of the three most important science fiction artists based in London (along with Fred T. Jane★ and Warwick Goble★). Today, he is best remembered for his eighteen fine, intricate illustrations that accompanied H. G. Wells's *When the Sleeper Wakes* in *Graphic Magazine*. These plates have often been reprinted, usually without crediting the artist.

Of equal interest were his commissions for the *London Magazine*. His illustrations for Santos Dumont's "Future of Aerial Navigation" (June 1905) show the advent of the aerial yacht and railway stations in the air, reached by means of elevators from the streets. "The Call of Another World" in May 1907 speculated on life on Mars and especially whether the Martians were trying to signal us.

Lanos gave full rein to his imagination with the remarkable picture "The Chief Diversion of the Martians," which showed a group of Martians as distant spectators of one of our street scenes, the representation of which is shown in Mars reflected upon a screen by an enormously powerful optical instrument. Another fine Lanos illustration, "How We Might Signal across the Limitless Interstellar Space," portrayed the three luminous points seen in the telescope and the three mysterious signals recorded by the wireless telegraph instruments. Lanos was described during this time as "one of the most imaginative of living artists."

It is believed that Lanos was killed while working as a war artist during the later stages of the First World War.

PUBLISHED WORK:

GRAPHIC MAGAZINE: "When the Sleeper Wakes" (1898–1899, eighteen illustrations)

LONDON MAGAZINE: "The Call of Another World" (May 1907, four illustrations); "The Future of Aerial Navigation" (June 1905, four illustrations)
STRAND: "A Hole through the Middle of the Earth" (Sept. 1909, four illustrations)
Richard Dalby

LARKIN, ROBERT (b. 1950). American Artist. Larkin was retained by Bantam Books to do the covers of the popular Doc Savage series. James Bama★ had effectively sold the series for Bantam, and when he departed for more lucrative endeavors, Frank Pfeiffer★ and then Boris Vallejo★ were tried on the covers. Neither man seemed to capture the Doc Savage mystique, and Larkin was given the assignment. His work for the series has proven to be popular, and he has been handling covers for eight years and more than thirty books. Larkin has also done some science fiction covers and cover art for a number of Marvel Comics' black-and-white magazines.
PUBLISHED WORK:

PB: *Awful Egg* (78), *Conan the Liberator* (79), *Devils of the Deep & The Headless Men* (84), *The Dragon Lensman* (80), *The Flying Goblin* (77), *Goblins & Secret of the Su* (85), *Golden Man & Peril in the North*, *Golden Sword* (77), *Hate Genius* (79), *Hills of the Dead* (79), *Laugh of Death & King of Terror*, *One Eyed Mystic & Man Who Fell Up*, *Ost* (77), *Pirate Isle & Speaking Stone*, *Purple Dragon* (78), *The Red Spider* (79), *Talking Devil & Ten Ton Snakes*, *Three Wild Men & Fiery Menace*, *Tunnel Terror*, (79), *Z-Lensman* (83)

LAYZELL, BOB (b. 1940). British artist. Born in Brighton, England, Layzell is a self-taught artist who began painting in a mystical and flowery art–nouveau style under the influence of William Morris and Salvador Dali. His first published artwork appeared in *Science Fiction Monthly* in 1975, and this led to paperback cover assignments, including *Farthest Star* by Jack Williamson and Fred Pohl, published by Pan in 1976.
Richard Dalby

LEHR, PAUL (b. 1930) American artist. Born in White Plains, New York, Lehr studied at Wittenberg University in Springfield, Ohio, from which he received the BFA in 1951. He then attended Pratt Institute from 1953 to 1956 and was awarded a certificate of illustration in 1956. He studied with Philip Guston, Richard Lindner, Calvin Albert, and Stanely Meltzoff★.

In 1958 Lehr sold his first science fiction painting to Bantam Books, for *Satellite E-One* by Jeffrey Lloyd Castle. The story was about the first manned space station, and Lehr produced the cover with the help of a model made from a ping-pong ball, a toilet-paper cardboard roll, and some wire.

Lehr has sold work to most major magazines in the United States, including *The Saturday Evening Post*, *Time*, *Life*, *Fortune*, *Business Week*, *Playboy*, *Omni*, and *Analog*. Since painting his first SF cover in 1958, he has produced hundreds more for both hardcovers and paperbacks, including many for novels by Robert A. Heinlein and Arthur C. Clarke. In 1980 he won the Merit Award from the Society of Illustrators, New York, for artwork done for Paramount Pictures. His work is in many major art collections throughout the world, including The National Air and Space Museum. Lehr works in a variety of mediums including oils, acrylics, and Winsor-Newton designers gouache.

Paul and his wife, Paula, are parents of four grown children. Two, Diana and Jennifer, are artists. A son, Seth, is in the music business in California, and their other son, Michael, attends college. Paul and Paula live on a farm in Pennsylvania, where, in addition to painting, the artist indulges in his other artistic passion, sculpture.

Having been involved in science fiction art for more than twenty-five years, Lehr has a unique perspective on the changing nature of cover illustration in the field. "In the old days at Berkley Publishing, they let me do pretty much what I wanted, and as result, the covers were very personal, and I loved to do them. The paperback business has changed dramatically from those days, and I think that the work tends to look more standardized—almost like the advertising business—slick."

PUBLISHED WORK:

HC: *Enchanted Pilgrimage* (75), *Last Starship from Earth* (68), *Orbit 5* (69), *Orbit 10* (72), *Orbit 11 (72), Orbit 12 (73), The Overman Culture* (72), *Pollinators of Eden* (69), *Sea Horse in the Sky* (69), *Slaves of Heaven* (74), *Sturgeon Is Alive and Well* (71)

PB: *A Choice of Gods, Adventures in Time and Space* (66), *Aliens among Us* (69), *Anome* (73), *Asutra* (74), *The Best SF Stories from New Worlds 6, Brave Free Men* (73), *Conquerors from the Darkness* (68), *The Deep Range* (58), *The Door into Summer, Dorsai* (76), *Four from Planet 5* (59), *Life for the Stars* (62), *Methuselah's Children* (60), *Miners in the Sky* (67), *Moon Children* (73), *Nine Tomorrows, No Place on Earth, Players of Null-A* (74), *Power of Blackness* (76), *Quicksand, Satellite E-One* (58), *Scourge of Screamers* (68), *Soldier, Ask Not* (67), *Space Gypsies* (67), *Starship Trooper*

ASF: 1978 (3, 4); 1979 (1, 2, 3, 4, 5, 9)

SAT: 1959 (5)

LEWIS, BRIAN MONCRIEFF (June 3, 1929–Dec. 4, 1978) British artist. Lewis, along with Gerard Quinn★, was one of the two major cover artists working for the British science fiction magazines of the 1950s. He was educated at a technical school and first started reading science fiction during his seven years in the Royal Air Force. He subsequently became a technical artist with Decca Radar, where he stayed until 1960. Lewis first appeared in the SF magazines in *New Worlds* and *Science Fantasy* as an interior artist. By 1957 he had graduated to the covers and soon became the most prolific magazine cover artist at that time, with more than eighty paintings to his credit. His surrealistic style was reminiscent of Richard Powers★, and it added a rare distinction to the magazines he illustrated, raising them high above the level of most other British science fiction publications.

John Carnell, editor of *New Worlds*, encouraged Lewis to strive constantly for more unusual work. The artist himself stated in *New Worlds* in 1958 that "there is no limit to the color combinations and abstract symbolisms that can be used, and I feel that we are setting a new standard of cover illustration specifically suited to the science fiction field."

In 1960 Lewis took a new job drawing picture strips for Beaverbrook Newspapers. He continued to provide covers for Carnell's magazines until outside illustrations were phased out in 1962. Lewis then became involved in stop-motion animation and puppet films. He died of a heart attack when he was only fifty.

PUBLISHED WORK:

NW: 1954 (26, 29, 30); 1955 (34, 42); 1956 (47, 54); 1957 (55, 56, 57, 58, 59, 61, 64, 65, 66); 1958 (69, 70, 71, 72, 73, 74, 75, 76, 77, 78); 1959 (79, 81, 82, 83, 84, 85, 86, 87, 88, 89); 1960 (90, 91, 92, 96, 98, 100, 101); 1961 (103, 104, 106, 107, 108, 111, 113); 1962 (115, 117, 119)

NWUS: 1960 (4, 5, 6, 7)

ScF: 1954 (11); 1955 (12); 1957 (26); 1958 (27, 28, 29, 30, 31, 32); 1959 (33, 34, 35, 36, 37, 38); 1960 (40, 41, 42, 43); 1961 (45, 46, 47, 48)

SFA(BR): 1958 (3); 1959 (6, 7, 8, 9, 10, 11, 12); 1960 (13, 14, 15, 16); 1961 (18, 19, 20, 21, 22, 23); 1962 (24, 25, 26, 27)

Mike Ashley

LEYDENFROST, ALEXANDER (1889-June 16, 1961) American artist. One of the most famous commercial artists of the 1920s and 1930s, Leydenfrost did science fiction illustrations for the pulps for several years. Born in Debrecen, Hungary, he studied at the Royal Academy of Fine Arts in Budapest. By age twenty-four he was serving as a professor of perspective and applied art at the academy. He immigrated to the United States in 1923 and worked with Willy Pogany on murals and interior designs. In 1929 he joined the staff of Norman Bel Geddes, the stage and industrial designer. Among the many projects he worked on was the General Motors exhibit at the New York Worlds Fair in 1939. However, with the outbreak of World War II in Europe, constuction work in the United States slowed down. Leydenfrost could not find a great deal of architectural or interior design work, so magazine art provided an alternative source of income.

Malcolm Reiss, editor of *Planet Stories*, signed Leydenfrost for a series of covers and interiors for his magazine. But Reiss knew that he would not be able to keep Leydenfrost for long. He was right, and soon Leydenfrost was doing work for *Life*. Although he did only a few illustrations for *Planet Stories*, they were among the best to appear in that magazine. When the artist returned to the slicks, his two sons began working for *Planet Stories*.

Bob Leydenfrost did illustrations for two issues of the pulp, May 1943 and fall 1943. His brother Harry did art for the May 1943, summer 1946, and winter 1946 issues. Although both used a style similar to that of their father, neither was as accomplished an artist, and they were not popular with the fans.

Leydenfrost continued to work for the science fiction pulps for a number of years, but the art represented only a small part of his illustrating duties. A series of illustrations of American planes in action done for *Esquire* furthered his reputation. He later did numerous illustrations for rockets and missiles for major magazine publications in the 1940s and 1950s.

Leydenfrost was primarily a black-and-white illustrator for the science fiction magazines. He did two interesting covers, but neither was as good as his interiors. He worked well with shadows and produced strong illustrations employing unusual contrasts to create unusual effects. He was capable of drawing effective aliens, and many of his creatures were memorably grotesque. Although not as prolific as many of the artists working in the field in the 1940s, Leydenfrost was near the top in terms of quality and style. He died in June 1961 in New Rochelle, New York.

PUBLISHED WORK:

ASH: 1942 (10)

FFM: 1948 (8); 1949 (2, 6, 12)

FN: 1950 (3)

PS: 1942 (spring, summer, fall, winter)

SSS: 1942 (8); 1949 (7, 9); 1950 (3, 5)

LITTLE, MIKE (b. 1952) British artist. Born in Northumberland, England, Little studied at Teesside College of Art from 1970 to 1973. His main interests were science fiction and rock music. Little was an early contributor to *Science Fiction Monthly*, and many science fiction paperback covers followed. He also designed numerous record album covers as well as some children's books.

PUBLISHED WORK:

PB: *Is Anyone Out There? New Worlds 9, New Worlds 10, Strange Powers*
                                                                  Richard Dalby

LoGRIPPO, ROBERT (b. Sept. 19, 1947) American artist. Born in Manhattan, New York, LoGrippo always wanted to be an artist, so he aimed toward the art field from the beginning of his schooling. He attended the High School of Music and Art in New York, graduating in 1965; he then went to the School of Visual Arts in New York. One of his teachers there introduced him to the work of Hieronymous Bosch, which fired his imagination and started him on the road to SF illustration. Along with the work of Bosch, Bruegel's work also served as a major influence.

LoGrippo's first published piece was an ABC record, "Rare Bird," illustrated in early 1970. Most of his science fiction artwork was done for the Adult Fantasy Series published by Ballantine Books in the early 1970s. LoGrippo's distinctive art, very much in the style of Bosch, was among the most unusual art ever to appear as book covers in the fantasy genre.

In recent years LoGrippo has painted some textbook covers, has produced art for The Franklin Library's editions of *The Deerslayer* and works of Hans Christian Anderson, and has done book illustrations for Random House, Macmillan, and many other publishers. He has had artwork in *Redbook*, *Playboy*, *Seventeen*, *Forbes*, *Readers Digest*, and many other magazines. LoGrippo also has prepared art for American Artists Greeting Cards and has produced record-cover illustrations and a great deal of advertising art. Among his best-known work is the ABC Olympic Poster for the 1984 Summer Games.

LoGrippo taught at both Parsons School of Design and Pratt Institute. He had one-man shows in major galleries in the New York area, and his work is included in a number of important collections.

Working in acrylics, LoGrippo reads the material to be illustrated and comes up with a concept. The job itself determines what the piece will look like in the end. He has received two Gold Medals and many awards of merit for his work from the Society of Illustrators.

PUBLISHED WORK:

PB: *Boats of Glen Carrig* (71), *Night Land 1* (72), *Night Land 2* (72), *Three Imposters* (72)

LUNDGREN, CARL (b. 1947) American artist. Born in Detroit, Lundgren was strongly influenced by the mood of the times. During his senior year in high school, he was a professional folksinger in the Detroit area. He also worked on underground films, writing, directing, producing, and editing. He was a reader and collector of comics and science fiction and was impressed by the work of Frank Frazetta★, Jeff Jones★, and Norman Rockwell. At the same time, Lundgren saw many other covers that he thought he could do better.

After graduating from high school, Lundgren was accepted at the University of Southern California. However, when he admitted that he wanted to be an illustrator, he was referred to the Hollywood Art Center. He attended that school for one semester until he ran out of funds. Then he returned to Detroit and enrolled in the Famous Artist Correspondence School. He gave up after the eighth lesson and considers himself self-taught.

Lundgren soon found himself involved in the counterculture wave of the late 1960s. He founded *Tales from the Ozone* comics and produced many comics and posters for alternative press publishers. He still wanted to be a professional illustrator and thus, encouraged by his wife, Michele, moved to New York.

Success was not immediate, but through persistence, Lundgren sold several covers to Pinnacle Books. He sold his first SF cover, for *To Die in Italbar*, to DAW Books in 1974. Soon he was placing covers with DAW, Dell, and Ballantine Books. Like many other science fiction artists, once established, he found that his work was in constant demand. He won numerous awards for best artist and best of show at many of the major science fiction conventions.

Lundgren works in oils but with no single technique. "My work is my own and I strive to perfect it every waking hour of the day" is the artist's personal philosophy. He tries to communicate with his paintings as well as to illustrate and believes his best works are ones that create a response in their own right. A personal favorite is "Pigs in Thought," used as the cover for *The Best of Damon Knight*.

Lundgren is married to writer–agent Michele Lunden and is the father of a daughter, Cara Lunden.

PUBLISHED WORK:

PB: *The Best of Damon Knight, The Black Beast, To Die in Italbar, Earthwind* (78), *Earthwind* (78), *The Face in the Frost, Fires of Paratime* (82), *Green Odyssey* (83), *Hunters of the Red Moon* (78), *I Will Fear No Evil, The Last Defender of Camelot, Luck of Brink's Five* (79), *The Man in the Tree, Masters of Space* (79), *The Nearest Fire* (82), *One Million Centuries* (81), *The Red Magician* (82), *The Sable Moon, Sword of the Horseclans* (72), *Stranger in a Strange Land, Starship Troopers, Where the Time Winds Blow* (82)

F&SF: 1982 (4)

LUROS, MILTON (?) American artist. A prolific pulp artist, Luros started working for the science fiction pulps at the end of the first major magazine publishing boom in the early 1940s. He returned to the field in the early 1950s, working again for the smaller chains publishing science fiction. He was a capable cover artist who produced reasonably good interior art as well. Luros served as art director for *Future, Science Fiction Quarterly*, and *Science Fiction* from 1955 through 1956.

PUBLISHED WORK:

ASH: 1943 (2, 4)

DYN: 1952 (12); 1953 (3, 6, 8, 10); 1954 (1)

FUT: 1943 (2); 1950 (11); 1951 (1, 3, 5, 7, 9); 1952 (1, 3, 5, 7, 9, 11); 1953 (1, 3, 5, 7, 9, 11); 1954 (1, 3)

SF: 1943 (4, 7)

SFQ: 1942 (winter); 1943 (spring); 1951 (5, 8, 11); 1952 (2, 5, 8, 11); 1953 (2, 5, 8, 11); 1954 (2, 5, 8); 1955 (2)

MAGARIAN, ALBERT and FLORENCE (?) American artists. A husband and wife team, the Magarians illustrated for the Ziff-Davis chain, contributing numerous excellent black-and-white illustrations to *Amazing Stories* and *Fantastic Adventures* in the 1940s. Art was done in a stipple style much like Virgil Finlay★ but without the photographic clarity that Finlay achieved. Although most of their work was listed as being done in collaboration, many of the pieces were signed by Florence alone.

PUBLISHED WORK:

AMZ: 1941 (6, 7, 8, 9, 12); 1942 (1, 7, 10, 11, 12); 1943 (2, 4, 6, 7); 1944 (1, 3, 9); 1946 (8)

FA: 1941 (5, 6, 7, 8, 9, 10); 1942 (1, 5, 6, 7, 9, 10, 11, 12); 1943 (2, 3, 4, 5, 6, 7, 8, 10); 1944 (2, 6, 10); 1945 (1, 7); 1947 (5)

FTC: 1971 (2)

MAGEE, ALAN (b. 1947) American artist. Born in Newtown, Pennsylvania, Magee attended the Tyler School of Art and the Philadelphia College of Art. His art was first published in *Scholastic* magazine in 1969. Since then he has done artwork for *McCalls*, *Good Housekeeping*, and *Penthouse* in the magazine field. He has produced numerous paperback covers as well. In 1976 he was awarded the New York Book Publishers Award for his art.

MAITZ, DON (b. June 10, 1953) American artist. Born in Bristol, Connecticut, Maitz's interest in art began with copying comic-book heroes. Later he was strongly influenced by Frank Frazetta★. Maitz first attended the University of Hartford Art School in 1970. Afterwards he studied at the Paier School of Art, from which he graduated in 1975 receiving the Top of the Class Award. His first published artwork, an inside magazine illustration published in 1974, was done in response to a contest held for students at the school. After graduation Maitz attended school for an additional half year of courses in life drawing and portfolio critique.

Since 1975 Maitz has worked as a freelance fantasy and science fiction artist. He is one of the most versatile of the new group of artists including Rowena Morrill★, Carl Lundgren★, and Michael Whelan★, who have dominated the paperback scene for the past ten years. His figures have a unique grace and style that set his paintings apart from those of most of his contemporaries. Maitz's covers for the highly acclaimed series Book of the New Sun by Gene Wolfe were so closely identified with the books that Timescape Books, the publisher of the novels, issued a special poster featuring one of the Maitz paintings as an advertisement for the series.

Maitz is single and works from a third-floor studio in a Connecticut suburb. In preparing a painting, he first reads a book and prepares three sketches for the art director. He then prepares the finished piece, incorporating any suggestions that he might have been given. Work is usually in oil or acrylic on masonite.

Along with doing science fiction and fantasy art, Maitz has produced a number of advertising pieces. His illustration "Captain Henry Morgan" for Seagram & Son in 1983 was used as the trademark for a rum product and in a national advertising campaign. Some of his other advertising clients include NBC, *TV Guide*, Bell Telephone, and various New York ad agencies. Maitz has also done portrait and landscape art for commissions.

Maitz's artwork has been included in numerous exhibitions, and he won a Silver Medal from the twenty-second Society of Illustrators Exhibit in 1980. He won a World Fantasy Award for Best Artist at the sixth Annual World Fantasy Convention and was Artist Guest of Honor at the eighth World Fantasy Convention in Connecticut. In 1979 he was nominated for an American Book Award for his work.

Personal favorites among his work include *The Wizard*, a piece from the artist's portfolio done only as a print, and *The Second Drowning*, which was used for the cover for Richard Cowper's novel *The Road to Corlay*.

PUBLISHED WORK:

HC: *Best of Edmond Hamilton* (77); *Best of Fredric Brown* (76); *Book of Skaith* (76); *Citadel of the Autarch* (82); *Claw of the Conciliator* (80); *Hounds of Skaith* (76); *Man, Time, and Space* (76); *Shadow of the Torturer* (80); *Sometimes after Sunset* (80); *Sword of the Lictor* (81); *Talisman* (84)

PB: *Ariel #4, Ariosto* (79), *Assault on the Gods* (81), *Balance of Power* (78), *Bard* (81), *Beneath an Opal Moon* (81), *Beyond Apollo* (79), *Black Cauldron* (76), *Book of the Beast* (81), *Book of Three* (76), *Borribles Go for Broke* (81), *Bright Companion* (79), *Camelot in Orbit* (78), *Captive* (80), *Castle of Llyre* (70), *Citadel of Autarch* (83), *City of the Sun* (77), *Claw of the Conciliator* (80), *Cosmic Rape* (79), *Dai-San* (80), *Day by Night* (80), *Divine Queen* (81), *Douglas Convolution* (79), *Dragons of Darkness* (81), *Drinking Sapphire Wine* (76), *Electric Forest* (78), *Fane* (80), *Fantasy Almanac* (79), *Far Traveler* (78), *Flashing Swords #3: Warriors and Wizards* (76), *Flashing Swords #4* (76), *Former King* (81), *Gods of Xuma* (77), *Grand Wheel* (77), *Green Gods* (79), *Haven of Darkness* (77), *Hestia* (79), *High King* (76), *Invisible Death* (78), *Island of Dr. Death* (80), *Keeper's Price* (79), *Kill the Dead* (80), *Light on the Sound* (82), *Lion of Ireland* (80), *Lucky Starr & the Big Sun of Mercury* (77), *Lucky Starr & the Oceans of Venus* (77), *Lucky Starr & the Rings of Saturn* (77), *Lucky Starr Space Ranger* (77), *Mirror of Helen* (83), *Nemesis of Evil* (78), *None but Man* (77), *Orphan* (79), *Out There Where the Big Ships Go* (80), *A Plague of Butterflies* (81), *Prison of Night* (77), *Profundis* (80), *Purgatory Zone* (80), *Road to Corlay* (79), *Rose for Armagedon* (82), *Second Ring of Power* (79), *Shadow of the Torturer* (80), *Shallows of Night* (80), *Silver Metal Lover* (81), *Song of the Kingdom* (80), *Space Opera* (79), *Sunset Warrior* (80), *Tamastara* (84), *Time Out of Mind* (80), *Virgin and the Wheel* (76), *Volcano Ogre* (78), *Warlord of Ghandor* (77), *Wave without a Shore* (80), *Web of Sand* (79)

F&SF: 1983 (1)

MALONEY, TERRY (b. 1917) British artist. Francis Joseph Terence Maloney was the mainstay cover artist for *New Worlds* between the lull in appearances of Gerard Quinn★ and the supremacy of Brian Lewis★. Most of his work is signed simply "Terry," although he also did six paintings published under the name "Jose Rubios."

A scientist and astronomer (F.R.A.S.), Maloney worked primarily as a general artist for newspapers and magazines. He turned to science fiction when a national newspaper wanted a futuristic illustration of Trafalgar Square in A.D. 2137. His illustrations subsequently appeared in *Everybody's Weekly* and *New Scientist*. His first cover for *New Worlds* was for issue 45 (in March 1956), and he painted fourteen covers for that magazine.

Generally, Maloney's covers lacked the impact of Quinn's or Lewis's. They were often flat and uninspired, but occasionally they had a deeper sense of wonder, as in his illustration for John Brunner's "Threshold of Eternity" (*New Worlds* 68, February 1958).

Maloney was one of the early artists to both write and illustrate his own book on space. *Other Worlds in Space*, published in London by the Acorn Press in 1957, detailed the solar system according to the knowledge of the day along with some scientific speculation. Maloney illustrated the text profusely with both black-and-white drawings and colored planetary vistas. He has written a number of other technical nonfiction books that lack the speculative nature of his first work.

PUBLISHED WORK (As "Terry" and "Jose Rubios").

NW: (45, 48, 50, 52, 53, 55, 56, 57, 58, 60, 62, 63, 67, 68)

ScF: (18, 22, 23, 24, 25)

SFA(BR): (1, 2)

Richard Dalby

MARCHIONI, MARK (b. 1910) American artist. Born in New York City, Marchioni studied art at the Art Student's League and the Grand Central Art School. His first science fiction sale was to *Wonder Stories*, but he soon branched out to sell art to all of the pulps of the 1930s. Along with his science fiction illustrations, Marchioni did commercial illustration for various advertising agencies.

PUBLISHED WORK:

ASF: 1932 (6, 11); 1933 (3); 1934 (1, 2, 3, 4, 5, 6, 7, 9, 11, 12); 1935 (1, 4, 5, 6, 7, 8, 9, 10, 11, 12); 1936 (1, 2, 3, 4, 5, 6, 7, 8, 10, 11); 1937 (7, 9, 11)

CF: 1940 (summer); 1942 (spring, summer); 1943 (winter, summer); 1944 (spring)

DYN: 1939 (2)

SS: 1939 (3, 7); 1940 (3, 9); 1941 (3, 5, 9); 1942 (1, 11); 1943 (1, 3, 6, fall); 1944 (fall); 1945 (winter, summer, fall); 1946 (3, spring, summer, fall); 1947 (3, 5, 7)

StrS: 1939 (2, 6); 1940 (4, 6, 8)

TWS: 1936 (8, 10, 12); 1937 (2, 4, 6, 8, 10, 12); 1938 (10); 1939 (2, 6, 10, 12); 1940 (6, 9, 11, 12); 1941 (1, 2, 4, 6, 8, 10, 12); 1942 (4, 12); 1943 (6, 8, fall); 1944 (winter, spring, fall); 1945 (fall); 1946 (summer, fall, 12); 1947 (2, 4, 6, 10, 12); 1948 (4, 6)

MAROTO, ESTABAN (b. 1942) Spanish artist. Born in Madrid, Maroto began his art career as an assistant to Manuel Lopez Blanco on an adventure comic strip in the early 1960s. Along with Carlos Gimenez, he began work on his own doing a number of comics published in Spain. In 1963 he started working in the Garcia Pizarro studio, helping produce comic features for the English market. Soon he joined Selecciones Illustradas in Barcelona, where he contributed several strips. The strength and imagination of his work brought him to the attention of a number of U.S. publishers, and Maroto began illustrating stories for Warren Publications' *Creepy* and *Eerie* magazines. This work led to commissions for Ace Books and the Science Fiction Book Club. A fine draftsman, Maroto is known primarily for his black-and-white interiors, although he also does paintings.

PUBLISHED WORK:

HC: *Cachalot*

PB: *Changeling* (81), *Pigeons from Hell* (79), *Sowers of the Thunder, Year's Best Fantasy Stories #4* (78)

MARTIN, DON (b. May 18, 1931) American artist. Born in Paterson, New Jersey, Don Edward Martin was brought up in nearby Brookside, New Jersey. His father, Wilbur Martin, was a school supply salesman, so there always were pencils, crayons, and paper around the house. Encouraged by his mother and his older brother, Martin began drawing. Fascinated by the art in *Colliers* and *The Saturday Evening Post*, he decided to become an illustrator and attended the Newark School of Fine and Industrial Art. Afterwards, he took classes at the Pennsylvania Academy of the Fine Arts in Philadelphia, finishing his training in 1952.

For the next few years Martin held a variety of jobs including working as a bellhop, creating window displays, and working in a framing store. He then moved to New York, where he worked as a pasteup artist and sold freelance illustrations on the side.

In 1955 Martin sold some record-album covers in the jazz field and did some art for *Metronome* magazine. Soon he submitted some artwork to *Mad* magazine. His bizarre, humorous style immediately caught the eye of editor Al Feldstein, and Martin soon became a regular contributor. He also began doing illustrations for the science fiction magazines, most notably a series of offbeat pieces for *Galaxy*. Although he was never a prolific science fiction illustrator, his work was well suited for some of the zany stories that appeared in the late 1950s and early 1960s. As he became more popular as a result of his art in *Mad*, his work on other, outside assignments fell off. In the past few years, Martin has become known throughout the country from the numerous paperback collections of his work in *Mad*. Thirteen such collections have appeared through 1983.

Martin married Rosemary Troetschel in December 1957, and at the urgings of his wife, they moved to Florida in the early 1960s. A son, Max, resulted from the marriage, which ended in divorce in 1977. In 1979 Martin married Norma Haimes, whom he met during his student days in Philadelphia. He remains one of the most popular and distinctive artists working in the American humor scene today.

PUBLISHED WORK:

GXY: 1956 (10); 1957 (2, 6, 7, 9); 1958 (1, 2); 1959 (6, 8); 1960 (12); 1961 (6, 8)

MATANIA, FORTUNINO (1881-Feb. 8, 1963). British artist. An Italian portrait painter, Matania later specialized in historical paintings. Born in Naples, Italy, he joined the staff of the *Sphere* in London at the age of twenty-four and spent the rest of his life in England. He drew for all of the principal magazines and quality newspapers in Europe and America, concentrating mainly on pictures of Roman life and pageantry, with occasional forays into science fiction and fantasy. He illustrated Edgar Rice Burroughs's *Pirates of Venus* in 1933 and *Lost on Venus* in 1933–1934 for the British magazine *Passing Show*. These twenty-nine plates were reprinted by Dover Books in 1963. The reprinted artwork caused a minor sensation in the Burroughs field since Matania was an unknown Burroughs illustrator whose work compared favorably to the best in the field. In 1935 Matania did artwork for *The Secret People*, a nine-part serial by John Beynon running in *Passing Show* from July through September.

Matania died in London in February 1963, leaving a daughter, Celia Matania, a character actress who has appeared in a number of movies including *Don't Look Now* with Julie Christie.

PUBLISHED WORK:

PB: *Pirates of Venus & Lost on Venus* (63)

Richard Dalby

MATTINGLY, DAVID B. (b. June 29, 1956) American artist. Born in Fort Collins, Colorado, Mattingly first encountered science fiction as a small child through comics and later through works of Clarke, Asimov and Heinlein when he learned to read. He started to draw and paint at the age of eight and seriously decided to become an illustrator in his early teens. After high school he attended the Colorado Institute of Art in Denver and later transferred to the Art Center College of Design in Pasadena, California. After graduation he worked for Howard Ziehm, the producer of the movie *Flesh Gordon*. Mattingly did production design on the sequel to the film, which has never been produced. He was then hired by the Walt Disney Studios as a matte artist.

In May 1978 Mattingly married his wife, Barbara. During the next three years, he assisted Harrison Ellenshaw and worked as a matte artist on a number of Disney films including *The Black Hole*. At twenty-two he became the youngest full union matte artist in the history of the motion picture industry. At twenty-four he became the youngest department head in Walt Disney Studio's history. As head of the matte department, he supervised matte work on a number of Disney films including *The Devil and Max Devlin* and *The Watcher in the Woods*.

While at Disney Studios Mattingly began doing freelance art and his first published piece was the album cover for "The Commodores Greatest Hits." His first sale of art for a book was for *A Wizard in Bedlam* to DAW books. Freelance work soon was Mattingly's major interest, so he resigned from Disney Studios to devote full time to his painting. In May 1983 David and his wife moved to New York City.

One of the new group of young artists who dominate the science fiction paperback cover scene, Mattingly has produced artwork for Ace, Berkley, Ballantine, Del Rey, DAW Books, Playboy Press, TOR Books, and Signet Books, among the paperback publishers. He has had artwork appear in all of the major science fiction magazines and has also done some movie poster work, as well as some toy design and art. Recently, he did interior and cover art for some Find-Your-Own-Fate paperbacks.

In doing a paperback cover, Mattingly first reads the book he has been assigned. If he finds good scenes, he usually illustrates one of them. If no scene stands out and concepts seem more important, he does a collage of several important elements. Although art directors sometimes make suggestions, they usually leave it up to him what to illustrate. Mattingly works in acrylic and on illustration board. His favorite illustration is the cover for *Orion* by Ben Bova, published by TOR paperbacks.

PUBLISHED WORK:

HC: *Code of the Life Maker* (83), *Starburst* (82)

PB: *4 Lords of the Diamond—Cerberas* (82), *4 Lords of the Diamond—Charon* (82), *4 Lords of the Diamond—Lilith* (81), *4 Lords of the Diamond—Medusa* (83), *The Anarch Lords*, *Armies of Daylight* (83), *Cenotaph Rload* (82), *Children of the Lens*, *Downbelow Station*, *First Lensman*, *Galactic Patrol*, *Gray Lensman*, *The Ivanhoe Gambit* (84), *King of Argent*, *Lilith: A Snake in the Grass* (81), *The Nautilus Sanction* (85), *Orion* (84), *The Pimpernel Plot* (84), *Prelude to Chaos* (83), *Second Stage Lensman*, *Serpent's Reach* (80), *Showboat World*, *Time of the Dark* (82), *The Timekeeper Conspiracy* (84), *Triplanetary*, *Trullion Alastor 2262*, *Undersea City* (83), *Undersea Quest* (82), *Wall Around a Star* (83), *Walls of Air* (83), *Wizard in Bedlam*, *The Zenda Vendetta* (85)

McCALL, ROBERT THEODORE (b. 1919) American artist. Born in Columbus, Ohio, McCall has been interested in space and art all of his life. He attended Columbus College of Art and Design on an art scholarship and also attended the Art Institute of Chicago. During the Second World War, he served as a U.S. Army Air Corps bombadier instructor, flying B–17s, B–21s and B–24s. Since that time, he has done a great deal of art for the air force art collection.

After serving in the army McCall worked with Bielefelt Studios in Chicago for three years and then went to the Charles Cooper studio in New York. He worked on a great variety of advertising and industrial and story illustration, specializing in aviation and space art. When the space program began in the 1950s, McCall worked with *Life*, covering early space efforts. His work in that publication led to his doing the advertising art for *2001: A Space Odyssey*, which propelled him into the forefront of science fiction movie artists.

Since then McCall has served as consultant on a number of other science fiction films, including *Star Trek—The Movie* and *The Black Hole*, for which he was credited as art director.

McCall also did a huge six-story-high mural for the National Air and Space Museum in Washington, D.C., in 1976 and an equally large mural for EPCOT Center in Florida in 1983. Many of his pieces are in the Collection of the National Air and Space Museum. Among other accomplishments, McCall has designed fourteen U.S. postage stamps. He has also worked with NASA documenting the manned space program for the NASA fine-arts program.

Although not primarily a science fiction artist, McCall has remained in the forefront of the field because of his science fiction movie work and his many published paintings of future space exploration in numerous national magazines.

PUBLISHED WORK:

HC: *A Vision of the Future* (82), *Our World in Space* (73)

PB: *Space Art* (78)

McCAULEY, HAROLD W. (July 11, 1913–1983) American artist. A Chicago native, McCauley began his education in aviation but switched to art instead, studying at the Art Institute of Chicago for four years. Also attending the Art Institute with McCauley was Rod Ruth★, who later also worked for the Ziff-Davis magazine chain when McCauley was with that publisher. Afterwards, he worked for a year for an engraving house and next studied for a year at the American Academy of Art. McCauley then studied with J. Allen St. John★, whose work for the Edgar Rice Burroughs books had introduced McCauley to science fiction in 1927 and had made him a lifelong fan of the genre.

McCauley became a staff artist for the Ziff-Davis publishing chain in Chicago, which published *Amazing* and *Fantastic Adventures*, doing covers and interiors for them. He was noted for his attractive women on covers—

dubbed "The Mac Girl." McCauley also did advertising art for Coca Cola, Pepsi, Orange Kist, and Schlitz beer, as well as some calendar art. When Ray Palmer, the editor of *Amazing* in the 1940s, began several new magazines including *Imagination* and *Imaginative Tales*, McCauley brought his Mac girl covers to those magazines. In 1951 he married a former model. McCauley died in retirement in Florida.

PUBLISHED WORK:

HC: *Empire of the Atom* (57)

AMZ: 1938 (1, 6, 7, 8, 12); 1939 (1, 3, 4, 11); 1940 (3); 1941 (2, 9); 1942 (2, 5, 8, 9); 1943 (1, 4, 5, 6, 7, 8, 9); 1946 (8); 1947 (1, 5); 1948 (3, 6, 10, 12); 1949 (5, 10)

FA: 1939 (9); 1940 (1, 8); 1941 (1, 6, 7, 10); 1942 (1, 2, 9, 11, 12); 1943 (1, 5, 6, 8, 12); 1944 (2, 4); 1945 (1, 12); 1946 (2, 5); 1947 (1, 7); 1950 (2, 4, 5, 8)

FTC: 1968 (12)

IMG: 1951 (11); 1952 (1, 3, 5, 7, 9, 10, 12); 1953 (1, 2, 4, 5, 6, 7, 8, 9, 10, 11, 12); 1954 (1, 2, 3, 4, 5, 6, 7, 8, 9, 10, 12); 1955 (1, 3, 4, 5, 6, 7); 1956 (4)

IMGT: 1954 (9, 11); 1955 (1, 3, 5, 7, 9, 11); 1956 (1, 5)

OW: 1951 (1, 3, 5, 6, 10); 1952 (1, 3, 11, 12); 1953 (1, 3, 4, 5); 1956 (2, 4, 9, 11)

ScS: 1954 (2)

UNI: 1953 (1, 2); 1954 (6, 7, 8)

McKIE, ANGUS (b. 1951) British artist. McKie studied at Newcastle-Upon-Tyne College of Art from 1969 to 1973. He is one of the leading British artists specializing in space hardware and planetary landscapes. Among his major influences are Chris Foss★, Frank Hampson★, and Frank Bellamy★. A selection of his best work was published in *The Flights of Icarus* (1977).

Richard Dalby

McLEAN, WILSON (b. 1937) American artist. Born in Glasgow, Scotland, McLean moved to London when he was ten. He had no art training, but his first job was doing magazine layouts. He decided to try freelancing in Copenhagen but found that he liked London better and returned and freelanced there until deciding to move to the United States in 1966.

McLean's carefully designed and tightly done compositions were popular in the United States and were highly influential in the art field. He has done illustrations for numerous advertising clients as well as artwork for nearly all of the major magazines, including *Sports Illustrated*, *Time*, *Redbook*, *New York*, *Playboy*, and *Penthouse*.

McLean taught at the School of Visual Arts and Syracuse University, exhibited at the Society of Illustrators Show, and won a number of awards.

McQUARRIE, RALPH (?) American artist. McQuarrie is perhaps one of the most influential artists in the science fiction field even though he has done relatively few assignments in the book industry. Instead, McQuarrie, who was originally a commercial artist, had his impact through his visualization of the tremendously popular and extremely influential *Star Wars* films.

McQuarrie was raised in a small town in Montana during the Depression. His grandfather was a small publisher, and both he and Ralph's mother were active artists. McQuarrie began art classes at the age of ten, and his talent showed immediately. He graduated from high school in 1948 and immediately began technical art classes. He started work in 1950 for Boeing Company in Seattle, the youngest of a group of nearly fifty artists. However, the Korean conflict cut this job short, and McQuarrie was drafted and sent to Korea.

After numerous close calls with death, McQuarrie returned to the United States and his job with Boeing. He later freelanced and did some technical paintings for NASA. He became an expert in depicting spacecraft and hardware in realistic detail.

When George Lucas proposed the first *Star Wars* film to Twentieth Century Fox, response was less than enthusiastic. Studio executives could not visualize the film. McQuarrie was brought in by two of Lucas's friends, and after the artist read the working script, he prepared a number of rough sketches for several of the main characters. McQuarrie captured the essence of Lucas's ideas. With five paintings by McQuarrie in hand, Lucas was able to convince studio executives to provide seed money. Later, after seeing more of McQuarrie's work, full funding was provided.

McQuarrie did many of the concept paintings for *Star Wars*. When the movie was successful, he did work on its sequel, *The Empire Strikes Back*. By then, the demands and pressure of the film work began affecting the quality of his work, so he decided to move on to other films. He worked on the enormously popular *E.T.*, designing the alien spacecraft, and in 1985 served as production designer for the film *Cocoon*.

At present, McQuarrie continues to work on film concepts and to do paintings for the science fiction book market. One of the finest photorealist painters in the motion picture field as well as a highly respected storyboard artist, McQuarrie is recognized as one of the men who helped make the *Star Wars* films such huge successes.

PUBLISHED WORK:

HC: *Industrial Light and Magic* (86)
PB: *Best of Jack Williamson* (78), *Star Wars* (76)

MEAD, SYD (b. July 18, 1933) American artist. Born in St. Paul, Minnesota, Sydney Jay Mead was a child prodigy. He worked on illustration throughout high school and began his first professional work as a cartoon animator for a Colorado Springs film company. He served a brief term in the U.S. Army, where he rose to the rank of sergeant. During this time Mead designed three-dimensional training progress charts and continued to experiment with different design motifs.

Upon completing his military service, Mead enrolled in the Art Center School of Los Angeles. He graduated with great distinction in industrial design and was hired by Ford Motor Company to design experimental body shells, including a two-wheeled, gyroscopically stabilized show car. After working for Ford for two years, he went on to do several books for U.S. Steel on the potential of steel as a design material. The success of these books gave Mead international attention, which brought him invitations from multinational corporations to help with design problems. He began exhibiting his work in major shows throughout Europe and Japan.

As a consultant, Mead helped design economy cars for American Motors, produced consultant designs for Volvo, Chrysler, BMW, and Jeep. He conceived a high-speed yacht for Halter Marine of New Orleans and designed the entire exterior and interior of the Norwegian Caribbean Line's proposed cruise liner for Ring Design of Spain. For NASA he provided the illustrations for the interior of Skylab and conceived a foldup chair system to accommodate different-sized crew members. He has done many architectural renderings for major firms throughout the United States and has done illustrations for many major buildings.

In the fantasy field, Mead designed "V'ger" for *Star Trek—The Motion Picture* and did the conceptual work for the fantasy settings and landscapes of Walt Disney's *Tron*. This work brought him an invitation to work on *Blade Runner*. Originally retained to design futuristic cars for the film, Mead's work was so impressive that his job was expanded to include the conceptual "look" of the entire film. Each of these films was nominated for an Academy Award for its visual effects.

Mead's work has been featured in *Omni*, and in 1979 his book *Sentinel*, containing an overview of his futuristic illustration, was published in England.

MELTZOFF, STANLEY (b. Mar. 27, 1917) American artist. Born in New York City, Meltzoff was one of the first paperback cover artists to be noted for his work in the science fiction field. He attended Townsend Harris, City College of New York (CCNY), and the New York University Institute of Fine Arts. He was a member of the Art Students League. Meltzoff served in World War II, in Africa and Italy, working for *Stars and Stripes*. Before and after the war he taught art history and practice at CCNY. In the late 1940s he began also teaching at Pratt and started a career as an illustrator. Along with paperback cover paintings, Meltzoff did work for numerous magazines, including *Scientific American*, *Life*, *Fortune*, and the *Saturday Evening Post*.

The winner of twenty-five Society of Illustrator Awards, the artist collected and constructed the Meltzoff Reliquarium, a private museum reflecting his long interest in aquatic art. He was the first, and probably the most preeminent, fish painter. His underwater paintings are a regular feature in *National Geographic,* and he continues to write articles on art history.

Meltzoff painted a number of early science fiction covers for Signet Books that succeeded as being both good science fiction and good paintings. He was probably the first paperback artist who specialized in science fiction covers. Influenced by the highly acclaimed James Avati, Meltzoff painted dramatic works that escaped the pulp influence evident with most other paperback SF until then. His work, along with those paintings by other Signet artists of the time, helped establish the notion that not all science fiction was cheap pulp literature. The artist's personal favorite of his science fiction art was his cover for *The Puppet Masters* by Robert A. Heinlein.

Equally important to the science fiction art field was Meltzoff's influence as a teacher. Working at Pratt, he taught both Paul Lehr★ and John Schoenherr★, and their early work shows his influence. Meltzoff was one of the most important artists of the 1950s who changed the direction of science fiction paperback art away from the emphasis on action and violence.

PUBLISHED WORK:

PB: *Assignment in Eternity* (54), *Beyond the Moon* (50), *Currents of Space* (53), *Day after Tomorrow* (51), *Demolished Man* (54), *Destination: Universe* (53), *Green Hills of Earth* (52), *I Am Legend* (54), *Man Who Sold the Moon* (51), *Mission Interplanetary* (52), *Puppet Masters* (52), *Revolt in 2100* (55), *Tomorrow, the Stars* (53)

MILLER, IAN (b. Nov. 11, 1946). British artist. Born in London, Miller studied at Northwich College of Art from 1963 to 1967. He continued his studies for three more years at St. Martin's College in London. He then was invited to teach art at Sir John Cass College. He began his career as a book and magazine illustrator in 1972.

An enthusiastic admirer of fantasy authors ranging from J. R. R. Tolkien to Algernon Blackwood, Miller mixes medieval figures with mechanical fantasy and peculiar machines. He is a specialist in outré and bizarre covers such as the work he did for Clifford Simak's *Werewolf Principle* published by Pan Books. An exhibition of his work was held in the Greenwich Theatre Gallery of London in June 1973.

Richard Dalby

MILLER, RON (b. 1947) American artist. Born in Minneapolis, Minnesota, Miller was brought up in Columbus, Ohio, and graduated from the Columbus College of Art and Design with a BFA in illustration. He worked for several commercial-art studios before joining the Smithsonian's National Air and Space Museum as art director for the Albert Einstein Planetarium. He was a member of the NASA Fine Arts Program.

Since leaving the museum, Miller has freelanced under the name Black Cat Studio, producing mainly astronomical and science fiction artwork. He is a founding member of the International Association of Astronomical Artists and is an honorary member of the Planetary Society. He is presently living with his wife, Judith, in Virginia.

Miller has had illustrations in numerous magazines including *Space World, Science Digest, Omni, Sky and Telescope, The Washington Post Magazine,* and *Space 86.* He has produced book jackets and interior art for publishers such as Macmillan, TOR, Ace, Berkley, Starblaze, and Doubleday and has worked as production illustrator for Dino DeLaurentis productions of *Dune* and *Total Recall.* He also contributed to the National Commission on Space and NASA's Solar System Exploration Committee.

Miller has written extensively about science fiction art and was nominated for a Hugo Award. Among his books are *The Grand Tour,* which has appeared in five languages since its publication in 1981. He also has written *Worlds Beyond: The Art of Chesley Bonestell* and *Space Art.* At present, Miller is illustrating several art books, including *Amazing Space, Deep Space, Firebrands, Extraordinary Voyages,* and *Spaceships.*

PUBLISHED WORK:

HC: *Out of the Cradle* (84), *The Grand Tour* (81), *Worlds Beyond: The Art of Chesley Bonestell* (83)

PB: *Space Art* (79)

AMZ: 1974 (4, 12)

FTC: 1974 (7)

MINNS, B. E. (?) Australian artist. Minns was very busy contributing illustrations to London magazines (especially *Strand* and *Pearsons*) from 1896 through 1910. In 1905 he illustrated a number of stories by H. G. Wells for *Pearsons* magazine.

PUBLISHED WORK:

PEARSONS: "Aepyornis Island" (Feb. 1905), "The Diamond Maker" (Mar. 1905), "The Flowering of the Strange Orchid" (Apr. 1905), "Story of a Bacillus" (June 1905)

Richard Dalby

MOLL, CHARLES (?) American artist. Moll is a decorative surrealist illustrator who began working in the paperback field in the 1960s. He did a great deal of science fiction during the early years of his career and now does primarily romance and horror cover paintings.

PUBLISHED WORK:

PB: *Deep Gods* (73), *Dreaming City* (72), *Return of Kavin* (72), *Sleeping Sorceress* (72), *Space Vampires* (77), *Star Wolf* (71), *Starblood* (72)

MONAHAN, P. J. (?) American artist. One of a number of cover artists who did work for the Munsey chain of pulp magazines during the teens and twenties, Monahan illustrated a number of important science fiction and fantastic adventure serials, including several major Edgar Rice Burroughs novels. As was often the case at that time, some of Monahan's paintings were later used as jacket art for the same novels. Some of the magazine serials that featured covers by Monahan included *Chessmen of Mars* (22); *A Man without a Soul* (13); *The Moon Maid* (23); *The Mucker* (14); *The Return of the Mucker* (16); *The Son of Tarzan* (15); *Sweetheart Primeval* (15); *Tarzan and the Golden Lion* (22); *Tarzan and the Jewels of Opar* (16); *Tarzan the Terrible* (21); *Tarzan and the Valley of Luna* (20); and *Thuvia, Maid of Mars* (16).

PUBLISHED WORK:

HC: *Darkness and Dawn* (14), *The Flying Legion* (15), *Thuvia Maid of Mars* (20)

MOORE, CHRIS (1947) British artist. One of a number of modern British paperback artists whose art is very much in the style of Chris Foss★, Moore studied at the Doncaster School of Art from 1965 through 1966, at Maidstone College of Art from 1966 to 1969, and at the Royal College of Art from 1969 through 1972. He is a specialist in space hardware, and many of his paintings feature the usual huge spaceships and futuristic machines that populate Foss's worlds. A number of his best paintings were reproduced in *Parallel Lines*, published by Dragon's Dream in 1981, which collected art by him and Peter Elson★.

PUBLISHED WORK (All British publications).

PB: *Capitol, Cemetary World, Choice of Gods, Clash by Night, Colony, The Crack in Space, Decade the Sixties, Doctor Futurity, Far Out, The Fountains of Paradise, Heritage of Stars, High Justice, Hot Sleep, Journey, My Name Is Legion, The Naked Sun, On a Darkling Plain, Our Spaceship Moon, The Proud Robot, So Bright the Vision, Space Colony, Starbridge, Starcrossed, Three Tomorrows, Time and Place, Time Is the Simplest Thing, Tomorrow's Children, Trips around the Black Hole, The Unteleported Man*
Richard Dalby

MOREY, LEO (?–1965) American artist. Morey had the difficult task of replacing the first popular artist in science fiction magazine art. Although he was a competent artist, he never succeeded in making the readers of *Amazing Stories* forget Frank R. Paul★. In early 1929, through a series of complex financial moves, Hugo Gernsback lost control of *Amazing Stories*, the only science fiction magazine being published. Gernsback immediately started two new science fiction magazines, *Science Wonder Stories* and *Air Wonder Stories*. Paul, who had been the primary illustrator and cover artist for all of the Gernsback issues of *Amazing*, left with Gernsback and worked on the new magazines. *Amazing* was left without a regular cover artist, and from July 1929 through January 1930, covers were done by Harry MacCay and Hans Wesso*. With the February 1930 issue, Morey took over cover duties for *Amazing* and painted nearly all of the covers for the magazine until 1938.

Born in Peru of a wealthy family, Morey attended Louisiana State University as an engineering major. He worked as chief illustrator for his college yearbook. After graduation, he did commercial illustration for a newspaper in Buenos Aires. Then he moved back to the United States, where he worked for a while in New Orleans as an artist. In 1929 he began illustrating interior features for *Science and Invention* magazine. Morey's work was so good that he was asked to do a cover and soon was the magazine's regular cover artist. Since the company that owned *Science and Invention* also owned *Amazing Stories*, Morey soon found himself illustrating stories for that magazine as well. His first cover for *Amazing* was for the February 1930 issue.

At first, Morey was given specific scenes to illustrate for his covers. However, as he grew to know the field better, he was given greater editorial freedom. Unlike many pulp artists, Morey did not work from a studio in his home. Instead, he had an office at the headquarters of Teck Publications, the publisher who owned *Amazing Stories*. Morey later branched out into western and detective covers for other Teck magazines and was soon their leading cover artist. Like most of the science fiction artists of the time, he tried to read everything he illustrated and worked hard at making his illustrations and paintings reflect the authors' descriptions of their creations.

When *Amazing Stories* was bought by Ziff-Davis in 1938, Morey was replaced by staff artists from that chain. He continued to work in the SF field producing covers and interiors for a number of other smaller chains, but when the war cut into the science fiction market, he moved to the comic-book field. However, he continued to do work in science fiction throughout the 1950s and early 1960s.

Morey's work was always well executed but did not have the excitement or originality of that of many other illustrators of the time.

PUBLISHED WORK:

AMZ: 1930 (2, 3, 4, 5, 6, 7, 8, 9, 10, 11, 12); 1931 (1, 2, 3, 4, 5, 6, 7, 8, 9, 10, 11, 12); 1932 (1, 2, 3, 4, 5, 6, 7, 8, 9, 10, 11, 12); 1933 (8, 10, 11, 12); 1934 (1, 2, 3, 4, 5, 6, 7, 8, 9, 10, 11, 12); 1935 (1, 2, 3, 4, 5, 6, 7, 8, 10, 12); 1936 (2, 4, 6, 8, 10, 12); 1937 (2, 4, 6, 8, 10, 12); 1938 (2, 4); 1939 (7, 8); 1940 (3, 4, 6, 8, 10, 12); 1941 (2, 3); 1960 (12); 1961 (1, 2, 3, 4, 6, 12); 1962 (4, 6, 11); 1963 (1); 1965 (10); 1966 (2, 4, 6, 8); 1967 (2, 6, 8); 1968 (6, 9, 11)

AQ: 1930 (spring, summer, fall, winter); 1931 (spring, summer, fall); 1932 (winter, spring-summer, fall-winter); 1933 (spring-summer, winter); 1934 (fall)

ASF: 1962 (1, 3)

ASH: 1940 (8, 10, 12); 1941 (2, 4, 9, 11); 1942 (3, 6, 10, 12); 1943 (2, 4)

COM: 1940 (12); 1941 (3, 7)

COS: 1941 (3, 5, 7)

CF: 1940 (winter, fall); 1941 (winter, fall); 1942 (fall); 1944 (spring)

FA: 1939 (7); 1940 (3, 4, 5)

FTC: 1967 (1, 3, 5, 7, 9, 11); 1968 (1, 5, 12)

FUT: 1950 (9); 1951 (5)

PS: 1940 (spring, summer, fall, winter); 1941 (spring, summer, fall, winter); 1942 (spring, summer, fall)

SAT: 1957 (8, 10, 12); 1958 (2, 4, 8, 10, 12); 1959 (2, 3, 4, 5)

SFQ: 1951 (8)

SS: 1940 (11); 1941 (11); 1942 (1, 3, 7, 11); 1943 (1); 1944 (fall); 1945 (spring, fall); 1946 (spring); 1947 (1, 3, 5); 1948 (5, 7); 1950 (9)

SSS: 1940 (9, 11); 1941 (1, 3, 5, 8, 11); 1942 (2, 5, 11); 1943 (2, 5); 1950 (9); 1951 (8)

STI: 1941 (2)

StrS: 1939 (2, 6, 10); 1940 (2, 6)

TSF: 1951 (spring)

TWS: 1938 (4, 8, 10, 12); 1939 (12); 1940 (3, 9); 1941 (3, 4, 8, 10); 1942 (2, 4, 6, 8, 12); 1943 (2, 4, 6, fall); 1944 (spring, summer); 1945 (spring, summer); 1946 (spring); 1947 (2, 4, 8, 12); 1948 (4); 1949 (4)

MORRILL, ROWENA (b. Sept. 14, 1944) American artist. One of the most popular artists now working in the SF-fantasy field, Morrill was born into a military family and thus traveled extensively as a child. After one year of college as a piano major, she dropped out of school and married a lieutenant in the air force. After several years of extensive travel, she grew restless and took an art course. She quickly became fascinated with art and devoted herself completely to learning how to be an artist. This obsession broke up her marriage and alienated her from her family for several years. She received a BA from the University of Delaware in 1971, although she thought much of her formal art training was useless. Influences include Rubens, Van Eyck, Vermeer, and Ingres, as well as Bosch and Brueghel.

After graduating from the University of Delaware she moved to Philadelphia to attend the Tyler School of Arts and enrolled in its Master of Fine Arts Program. She did not produce work fast enough for the Tyler program and was dropped from the school, a decision that she believes actually helped her career. Forced out of the formal school environment, she spent several years teaching herself how to paint.

Morrill got into paperback illustration by quitting her job at an advertising agency in New York, consulting the Yellow Pages for publishers, and showing her portfolio to the first one listed—Ace Books. Charles Volpe at Ace gave her an assignment for a romance cover, and her paperback-cover career was launched. Her first artwork in the SF-fantasy field was for *Isobel*, a horror novel by Jane Parkhurst, from Jove.

Working with oil on illustration board, Morrill uses an unusual technique of coating her paintings with a high-gloss glaze that gives the work an almost unnatural brightness. Her goal is always to depict any subject using as few coats of paint as possible, applied as thinly as possible. The few coats are for speed, the thin application for translucency and brilliant color.

Morrill starts by transferring an accurate line drawing to a smooth, gessoed ground. Over this she puts a thin wash of raw umber and burnt sienna acrylic paint mixed with an acrylic matte medium and water. This fixes the pencil drawing so that it does not smear. Over that, she does a rendering of all values in burnt umber oil paint and lets it dry. Afterwards, she mixes her paint and paints all of the figures and forms. Finally, she does the background and finishes the foreground so that the things in front overlap the things in back. Afterwards, she usually applies an additional coat of paint to the figures to enhance the colors to create a glaze. She detailed this step-by-step technique of doing a painting in a collection of some of her best artwork, *The Fantastic Art of Rowena*, published by Timescape Books in 1983.

In a field traditionally dominated by men, Morrill was one of the first women artists to have an impact on paperback cover illustration. Her strong, bold artwork was the foot in the door that helped other women break into the science fiction art marketplace. Yet she was accused of sexism at a science fiction convention because her painting for *King Dragon* featured a chained woman being attacked by a winged dragon. One of the female organizers of the art exhibit thought that the painting should be removed from the show because it was degrading to women. The painting remained, however, and the controversy soon died when it became apparent that banning one such painting would mean banning many more.

PUBLISHED WORK:

HC: *Blue Adept, Circumpolar, Courtship Rite, The Divine Invasion, Dream Park, Golem 100, Madwand, Project Pope, The Return of Retief, The Shattered World, Split Infinity, The Sword Is Forged, The Sword of Winter, The Warhound and the World's Pain*

PB: *Abode of Life, Alchemy and Academe, Basilisk, The Best of Randall Garrett, Blace Fire, Blue Adept, Burning, The City of the Singing Flame, The Color out of Space, Courtship Rite, The Dark Dimensions, Darker Than You Think, The Devil Wives of Li Fong, Dimensions of Miracles, Diplomat at Arms, The Divine Invasion, Dracula Book of Great Vampire Stories, The Dreaming Jewels, Dunwich Horror, Dying of the Light, The Eyes of Sarsis, Faith of Tarot, The Fall of Worlds, The Fantastic Art of Rowena, Firebird, God of Tarot, The Golden Swan, Golem 100, Hounds of Tindalos, In the Hands of Glory, Into the Alternate Universe, The Iron Dream, The Iron Lords, Isoabel, King Dragon, The Last Incantation, The Malacia Tapestry, Master of the Five Magics, Meanwhile, Neveryona, Nightwalk, No Earthly Shore, Project Pope, Prometheus Design, Retief of the CDT, Retief to the Rescue, Retief's War, Rite of Passage, Sandkings, Shadows Out of Hell, The Shape Changer, The Shattered World, Split Infinity, The Star Dwellers, The Stars Are the Styx, A Swiftly Tilting Planet, The Sword Is Forged, The Sword of Winter, The Synthetic Man, Tales of Neveryon, This Immortal, Three from the Legion, Thrice upon a Time, The Time Bender, Titan's Daughter, The Unknown Five, Unless She Burn, Vision of Tarot, The Warhound and the World's Pain, Web of the Spider, Whispers, Who Fears the Devil? The World Shuffler, Yearwood*

MORROW, GRAY (b. 1934) American artist. Dwight Graydon Morrow attended the Chicago Academy of Fine Arts and took the Famous Artist Correspondence Course. He was influenced by Joseph Coll★, Mitchell Hooks, Virgil Finlay★, Austin Briggs, and other fine line artists.

Morrow's first work was done for the Atlas and AG Comics group. He soon moved on to science fiction magazines, producing a great deal of artwork for *Galaxy* and *IF*. By the late 1960s he was one of the most popular science fiction magazine cover artists. He also began working for Ace Books and produced more than a hundred covers for the Perry Rhodan series done by Ace.

Morrow has done artwork for comic books, men's magazines, posters, educational filmstrips, children's books, and advertising art and has done television animation art as well as science fiction illustration. He contributed to *National Lampoon* and *Heavy Metal* magazines and worked on the comic strip *Big Ben Bolt*.

PUBLISHED WORK:

HC: *Claimed* (66), *Explorers into Infinity* (65), *The Forgotten Planet* (65), *The Hothouse World* (65), *The Illustrated Roger Zelazny* (78), *Jason Son of Jason* (66), *The Mouthpiece of Zitu* (65), *Palos of the Dog Star Pack* (65), *The Planet of Fear* (68), *When the Red King Woke* (66)

PB: *2nd Avon Fantasy Reader* (69), *Altar of Asconol* (65), *Avon Fantasy Reader* (68), *Barbarians of Mars* (66), *Behind the Walls of Terra* (70), *Blades of Mars* (66), *Dark World, Day of the Minotaur* (66), *Dolphin and the Deep* (68), *Endless Shadow* (64), *A Harvest of Hoodwinks* (70), *High Sorcery* (70), *Hunter Out of Time* (65), *The Illustrated Roger Zelazny* (78), *Jewel in the Skull* (67), *Key to Irunium* (67), *Languages of Pao, Lord Tedric* (78), *Mad Gobin/Lord of the Trees* (70), *Mask of Circe, Masters of the Lamp* (70), *Planet of the Double Sun* (67), *Quest of the Three Worlds* (66), *Space Pirates* (77), *Sunless World* (67), *Thief of Llarn* (66), *Thongor of Lemuria* (65), *Warriors of Mars* (66), *Wierwoods* (67)

AMZ: 1965 (3, 5, 6, 8); 1966 (6, 8, 10); 1967 (2, 4, 6, 8, 10, 12); 1968 (2, 7); 1970 (3, 5); 1973 (12); 1974 (4, 6)

ASF: 1965 (12)

F&SF: 1965 (11); 1966 (3, 8); 1967 (1, 4, 11); 1968 (11); 1969 (6)

FTC: 1965 (3, 4, 5, 6, 9, 11); 1966 (1, 3, 5, 7, 9, 11); 1967 (1, 3, 5, 7, 9); 1968 (5); 1970 (6, 8, 10); 1971 (4); 1973 (11); 1974 (1)

GXY: 1959 (10, 12); 1964 (2, 4, 6, 8, 10, 12); 1965 (2, 4, 6, 8, 10, 12); 1966 (1, 2, 3, 4, 7, 8, 9, 10, 11, 12); 1967 (1, 2, 3, 4, 5, 6, 8, 9, 11, 12); 1968 (1, 2, 4, 7)

IF: 1959 (7, 9, 11); 1960 (1, 3, 7); 1964 (1, 5, 7, 8, 12); 1965 (1, 2, 3, 4, 5, 6, 7, 8, 9, 10, 11, 12); 1966 (2, 6, 8, 10, 12); 1967 (2, 4, 6, 10, 12); 1968 (2, 4, 6, 11, 12); 1969 (1, 10)

MOH: 1965 (winter)

WOT: 1963 (8); 1964 (2, 4, 6, 8, 11); 1965 (1, 3, 5, 7, 9, 11)

MORTIMER, JOHN (?) British artist. Mortimer first appeared in the science fiction field with a black-and-white (with a red overprint) comic strip in Hamilton's *Authentic Book of Space* in 1954, based on the popular *Old Growler* series by Jon J. Deegan. He soon became a regular black-and-white contributor to the magazine *Authentic Science Fiction* until shortly before its demise in 1957. He left the field and later worked in the British comic-book industry.

Mortimer's illustrations were highly stylized, with gaunt, stark figures that were very unattractive. However, they evidently imparted an "arty" appearance that the publisher wanted. The artist's color covers for the magazine were much better. His paintings were beautifully colored, presenting accurate astronomical scenes in the best tradition of Chesley Bonestell★. They were among the best covers featured in British magazines during the period. Of particular interest was the March 1956 (no. 67) cover, which showed a self-portrait of the artist against a spacial background.

His covers and artwork alternated with those of "E. L Blandford." However, since the Blandford paintings were of the same style and appearance and several of them were actually signed "Mortimer," it seems certain that Blandford was a Mortimer pseudonym.

PUBLISHED WORK:

AUTH: (52, 53, 54, 55, 56, 57, 58, 59, 60, 61, 62, 63, 64, 65, 66, 67, 68, 69, 70, 71, 72, 73, 74, 75, 76, 77, 79)

Philip Harbottle

MUGNAINI, JOSEPH (?) American artist. Born in Viareggio, Italy, Mugnaini soon moved with his family to the United States. He was educated in Los Angeles and attended the Otis Art Institute from 1940 to 1942. He then served in the army and returned to Otis as an instructor. He retired as head of the drawing department in 1976.

One of the best-known interior artists in the United States, Mugnaini has worked in many fields. He is best known for his illustrations of the stories of Ray Bradbury. In addition, he designed sets for the Seattle Opera Company; produced a short film, *Icarus*, based on a Bradbury story, which was nominated for an Academy Award; and wrote a number of textbooks on drawing. His art is in many of the major collections throughout the country, including the Smithsonian and the Library of Congress. Mugnaini is a favorite artist of the Limited Editions Club and has done a number of his finest interiors for that publisher.

A true expert in the field of interior illustration, Mugnaini uses great care to capture the feel of each story he illustrates through a combination of technique and style and is a strong believer that the graphic elements of each story must be matched by the "physical potentials of the medium and the instrument through which a concept is materialized." Mugnaini works with pen and ink and brush drawing on much of his work, often using a textured gesso surface to help support and enhance his design.

PUBLISHED WORK:

HC: *Fahrenheit* 451, *Mission of Gravity* (54), *No Place on Earth* (58), *The Golden Apples of the Sun* (53), *The Halloween Tree*, *The Martian Chronicles* (74), *The October Country* (55), *The War of the Worlds and the Time Machine* (64)

MUSGRAVE, REAL (b. June 7, 1949) American artist. Born in Odessa, Texas, where his father was working as a geophysicist, Musgrave and his family soon returned to Colorado but, after much traveling, permanently settled in Dallas, Texas, by the time he was five. Always interested in art, Musgrave attended Texas Technological University to get an engineering degree in art. He later switched to the School of Fine Arts when it offered a bachelors degree in art.

While in college, Musgrave met and married his wife, Muff, a nutrition major. He began providing art for Dunlap's, a chain of Texas department stores. After graduating in 1972 with a degree in drawing and painting, he became art director for Dunlap's. In 1973 he and Muff spent four months traveling in Europe, where he studied art and architecture. After returning to Dallas, Muff took a full-time job, and he opened a studio, producing advertising art. He also did staff and editorial illustrations for local and regional magazines and newspapers.

Late in 1974 Musgrave began doing a series of fantasy fine-art prints, many of them featuring small, whimsical green dragons he called "Pocket Dragons." In 1976 his work was collected in book form for the first time as *Real Fantasies*, which is now in a second printing of the fifth edition. By 1978 he had moved to a larger studio, and his wife was working full time as his business manager. In 1979 he joined the Texas Renaissance Festival as an exhibitor. Soon he became the official artist, producing all posters, graphics, and advertising. In 1980 he received the Award of Excellence from the Texas Arts and Crafts Foundation, the highest honor given by that organization. In addition, his work was placed in a national touring show from the foundation.

In 1981 Musgrave signed with Otters & Others, San Diego, California, who brought out a signature line of greeting cards, "Real Magic," featuring Musgrave's Pocket Dragons and other whimsical fantasy creations. During the past few years, his work has continued to grow in popularity as he has exhibited at numerous science fiction conventions and one-man shows in art galleries throughout the country. He has won a number of Best in Show awards from the major SF and fantasy conventions. At present he is working on a series of children's books with his wife, using the characters featured in his art.

As can be seen from much of his art, Musgrave has been strongly influenced by the children's book artists from the late nineteenth century, including Arthur Rackham and Kay Neilsson. However, his work is distinctively his own. As to his own personal thoughts on what he illustrates, he stated: "Perhaps the greatest thing about fantasy art is its narrative aspect. We as artists are allowed to tell whole stories within a single picture. Of course, most illustrators try to make their stories consistent with those of the writer. But still, the art must stand on its own, tell its own story, to be effective. I find myself willing to illustrate only those stories that are consistent with my particular vision, and I tackle advertising or commercial illustration as if a story were being told. Then I select drawings that will mean something to me and to others when 'disconnected' from their origin."

Musgrave is one of a small but increasing number of science fiction and fantasy artists who is succeeding through his art without working as a magazine or book illustrator. In many ways, he is probably one of the most influential artists in the fantasy field today, demonstrating that an artist can be successful in fantasy without painting covers or doing interior illustrations for magazines. His success has provided motivation for many other fantasy artists with hopes of attaining the same success he now enjoys.

PUBLISHED WORK:

HC: *Real Fantasies* (76)

NAPOLI, VINCENT (?) American artist. A prolific interior illustrator, James Vincent Napoli worked for both the weird-fiction and science fiction pulps and magazines. Originally from Ohio, he was strongly influenced by the work of Harry Clarke★, and many of his early pieces are very derivative of Clarke's Poe illustrations. In 1931 Napoli began selling artwork to *Weird Tales*. His earliest efforts were fairly simple line-work illustrations, but within a short time, he had developed a strong style of his own with a form of "feathering" (using numerous pen strokes to create a feeling of depth), which worked well on inexpensive pulp paper.

Napoli left *Weird Tales* in the middle 1930s and moved on to other magazine illustration. He later reappeared in the science fiction field in the 1940s, doing art for most of the major magazines of the time. Going full circle, he returned as a regular *Weird Tales* illustrator during the waning years of that publication.

PUBLISHED WORK:

HC: *Far Boundaries* (51), *Whispers 3* (81)

AMF: 1950 (2)

ASF&FR: 1953 (1)

FFM: 1947 (10)

FSQ: 1950 (fall); 1951 (winter, summer, fall); 1952 (winter, spring, fall)

MSS: 1951 (2, 5, 8, 11)

PS: 1947 (summer, fall); 1948 (summer); 1951 (9)

SS: 1947 (11); 1948 (1, 9, 11); 1949 (1, 3, 5, 7, 11); 1950 (1, 3, 7); 1951 (5, 11); 1952 (1, 2, 5, 6, 8)

TSF: 1951 (spring)

TRE: 1964 (1); 1965 (2)

TWS: 1947 (6, 10, 12); 1948 (2, 4, 6, 8, 10, 12); 1949 (2, 6, 10, 12); 1950 (2, 4, 6, 8, 10, 12); 1951 (2, 4, 8, 12); 1952 (2, 8)

WB: 1951 (1, 2)

WSA: 1951, 1952, 1963R

WT: 1932 (4); 1935 (1, 2, 5, 8, 9, 10, 11, 12); 1936 (1, 2, 3, 5, 6, 8); 1937 (6); 1948 (1, 7, 9, 11); 1949 (1, 3, 5, 7, 9, 11); 1950 (1, 3, 5, 7, 9, 11); 1951 (1, 3, 5, 7, 9, 11); 1952 (1, 3, 5, 7, 11); 1953 (1, 7, 9, 22); 1954 (3)

NODELL, NORMAN J. (?) American artist. A prolific interior artist, Nodell primarily worked for *Galaxy* and its companion magazines in the 1960s. Usually signing his name with only one *l*, he began his career as a comic-book artist in the early 1950s. Among the many series he worked on, Nodell illustrated a number of Classics Illustrated comics. After his science fiction career, he returned to the comic field and did some black-and-white comic stories for the Warren magazines. He experimented with various styles, ranging from tightly drawn line-work illustrations to grease-pencil sketches. Unfortunately, none of his work was of much note.

PUBLISHED WORK:

AMZ: 1965 (8, 10, 12); 1966 (2)

ASF&FR: 1953 (4)

GXY: 1963 (6, 8, 10, 12); 1964 (4, 6, 8); 1965 (4, 6); 1966 (8)

IF: 1963 (5, 7, 9, 11); 1964 (1, 3, 5, 7, 8, 12); 1965 (1, 2, 4, 5, 6, 8); 1966 (2, 3, 6); 1967 (1)

WOT: 1963 (6, 8, 10, 12); 1964 (2, 4, 6, 8, 11); 1965 (1, 5, 7, 9, 11)

NUETZELL, ALBERT A. (Jan. 18, 1901–1969) American artist. Born in New Albany, Indiana, Nuetzell as a young boy played in the Louisville Orchestra, but in high school he grew interested in art after working as art editor on the school yearbook. His family moved to California, and he attended art school at night, learning the fundamentals of his trade. He worked in architecture, cartooning, and fine art before settling down to a career in commercial art. He worked for Fox West Coast Theaters for many years, doing oil paintings to be used in theatre lobbies as advertising for current features.

In 1931 Nuetzell married Betty Jane Stockberger. Several years later, living in San Francisco, they had twin sons, the oldest dying soon after birth. The other son, Charles, grew up to be a science fiction fan, author, and editor. Later Nuetzell taught at the California Institute of Art in Los Angeles. He went to work for Pacific Title and Arts Studio, the company that does most major motion-picture titles. An excellent artist, Nuetzell has had work displayed in several galleries and has won a number of awards. He enjoyed doing silk-screen prints and did thousands of them as a hobby.

Nuetzell entered the SF art field at the urgings of his son Charles. The artist submitted his first cover illustration, a painting of a crashed spaceship, to *Science Stories* because his son wanted to own some original artwork without having to pay for it. Between handling other art projects, Nuetzell continued to do covers for the rest of his life. His work was somewhat surrealistic, with graceful spaceships usually the main image of the painting. Nuetzell, who retired in the early 1960s, was never a science fiction fan, but he enjoyed the challenge and the imagery that the fiction presented.

PUBLISHED WORK:

AMZ: 1959 (3, 7, 9); 1960 (3, 4, 9); 1961 (7)

F&SF: 1957 (4)

FTC: 1960 (1, 8)

ScS: 1954 (2)

VORTEX: 1973 (4)

OCHAGAVIA, CARLOS (?) American artist. Born in Spain and educated in Argentina, Ochagavia came to New York when he was awarded a scholarship to study with Morris Kantor at the Art Students League. When he returned to Argentina, he specialized in etchings, serigraphics, and paintings. He received a number of awards for his work during this period.

Ochagavia's interest in film led him to create several short subjects and animated films, one of which won a mention in the French film festivals of Annecy and Tours. He also participated in the Venice festival of film in advertising in 1964.

In 1974 Ochagavia left Argentina and moved to the United States. His work is still on exhibit at the Museo Nacional del Grabado in Buenos Aires as well as in the Museo Nacional de Bellas Artes. Much of his science fiction art has been done for the Science Fiction Book Club.

PUBLISHED WORK:

HC: *Dream Park*

ORBAN, PAUL (?) American artist. At fourteen, Orban was paid five dollars for two weeks' work on a watercolor and decided that such "easy" money was for him. He attended the Chicago Academy of Fine Arts and then started working for the Chicago *Tribune* for which he illustrated several Fu Manchu novels. Later he became an art director for an advertising agency. He then moved to New York and became a freelance artist, his work appearing in *The New York Times*, *Reader's Digest*, and many other nongenre magazines as well as in many pulps.

Although Orban did some cover art, he mostly worked as an interior artist for the SF magazines. He used an attractive cross-hatched style that worked well on the inexpensive paper used for most pulp publications. Although Orban is remembered primarily as an artist who did a great deal of excellent work for *Astounding SF*, he also contributed to many other science fiction magazines. He illustrated "Deadline" by Cleve Cartmill, a story that appeared in *Astounding* in 1944, and found himself quizzed by military intelligence agents about the story. It was not until after the war that he discovered that the story described the atomic bomb over a year before it was ever used.

PUBLISHED WORK:

HC: *Marooned on Mars* (52), *Sons of the Ocean Deeps* (52), *Vault of the Ages* (52)

PB: *Universe Maker* (53)

2CSAB: 1951 (spring)

AMZ: 1955 (1, 3, 12); 1956 (2)

ASF: 1933 (10, 12); 1934 (1, 3, 5); 1938 (8, 9, 10, 11); 1939 (2, 3, 4, 5, 6, 7, 9, 10, 12); 1940 (1, 5, 7, 8, 10, 12); 1941 (1, 8, 10, 11); 1942 (1, 2, 3, 5, 6, 7, 8, 9, 10, 12); 1943 (1, 3, 4, 5, 6, 7, 9, 10, 11, 12); 1944 (1, 2, 3, 4, 5, 6, 7, 8, 9, 10, 11, 12); 1945 (1, 2, 3, 4, 5, 6, 7, 8, 9, 10, 11, 12); 1946 (1, 2, 4, 5); 1947 (1, 2, 3, 4, 5, 6, 7, 10, 12); 1948 (2, 5, 6, 7, 8, 9, 10, 11, 12); 1949 (1, 2, 3, 4, 5, 6, 7, 8, 9, 10, 11, 12); 1950 (1, 3, 4, 6, 10, 12); 1951 (1, 2, 3, 4, 5, 6, 7, 8, 9, 10, 11); 1952 (2, 3, 4, 6, 7, 8, 9, 11, 12); 1953 (1, 2, 3, 5, 7, 8); 1954 (1, 2, 7, 8)

CF: 1942 (spring); 1944 (winter)

DYN: 1952 (12); 1953 (3, 8, 10); 1954 (1)

FF: 1953 (2, 6)

FSQ: 1950 (summer, fall); 1951 (winter, spring, summer, fall); 1952 (winter, spring, summer, fall); 1953 (1, 3, 5, 7); 1954 (spring, summer, fall); 1955 (winter, spring)

FTC: 1954 (12)

FUT: 1959; 1952 (11); 1953 (1, 3, 5, 7, 9, 11); 1954 (1, 3, 6, 8, 10); 1955 (28); 1956 (30); 1957 (31, 32); 1958 (36, 37, 8, 10, 12); 1959 (2, 4); 1960 (4)

IF: 1953 (5, 7, 9, 11); 1954 (1, 3, 4, 5, 6, 7, 8, 9, 10, 11, 12); 1955 (1, 2, 3, 4, 5, 6, 8, 20, 23); 1956 (2, 4, 6, 8, 10, 12); 1957 (2, 4, 6, 8, 10, 12); 1958 (2, 4, 6, 8, 10); 1959 (2)

INF: 1956 (8, 10); 1957 (2, 4, 6, 7, 9, 10); 1958 (4)

PS: 1951 (1, 3)

RS: 1953 (4, 7)

SF: 1953 (1); 1954 (2); 1955 (1, 3, 5, 7, 9, 11); 1956 (1, 3, 7, 9); 1957 (1, 3, 5, 7, 9, 11); 1958 (8); 1959 (2, 3); 1960 (1)

SFA: 1952 (11); 1953 (2, 3, 5, 7, 9)

SFQ: 1952 (11); 1953 (2, 5, 8, 11); 1954 (2, 11); 1955 (8, 11); 1956 (5, 8, 11)

SpS: 1952 (12); 1953 (2, 4)

SpSF: 1952 (5, 9, 11); 1953 (2, 3, 5, 7, 9)

SS: 1941 (5); 1942 (9); 1943 (3); 1946 (winter); 1950 (5, 9, 11); 1951 (1, 3, 5, 7, 9); 1952 (1, 2, 4, 6, 10, 11, 12); 1953 (1, 4, 5, 10); 1954 (1, spring); 1955 (winter, spring, summer)

SSF: 1956 (12); 1957 (2, 4, 6, 8, 10, 12); 1958 (2, 4, 6, 8, 10, 12); 1959 (2, 10)

StrS: 1939 (2, 4, 6, 12); 1940 (6)

TRE: 1964 (1); 1965 (2)

TWS: 1940 (6); 1943 (2); 1950 (4, 6, 8, 10, 12); 1951 (2, 4, 6, 8, 10, 12); 1952 (2, 4, 6, 8, 10, 12); 1953 (2, 8); 1954 (spring, summer)

UK: 1939 (3, 4, 5, 6, 7, 9, 11, 12); 1940 (1, 3, 8); 1941 (8, 10, 12); 1942 (2, 4, 6, 8, 10, 12); 1943 (2, 4, 6, 8)

WSA: 1952, 1953

PAPE, FRANK CHEYNE (1878–1972) British artist. A British artist of French ancestry, Pape illustrated many books from 1900 to the late 1930s, ranging from *Siegfried and Kriemhild* in 1912 to *The Complete Works of Rabelais* in 1927 to *Tales from the Arabian Nights* in 1934. His best works were the series of illustrations for books by Anatole France and James Branch Cabell done in the 1920s. Pape was extremely popular and had numerous fans during this time. His name was closely linked with that of Cabell, and he was considered by many critics to be the artist best suited to illustrate that author's work. Pape matched Sidney Sime★ and Harry Clarke★ as a master of the fantastic and the grotesque. His burst of imaginative creativity lasted well into the 1930s. He did superb macabre drawings, including "The Midas Touch" for *Nash's Pall Mall Magazine*.

Increasingly bad sight led to blindness, cutting short Pape's career at age sixty. He spent the last thirty-four years of his life in relative obscurity after being hailed as one of the great fantasy illustrators of the 1920s.

PUBLISHED WORK (Dates are for British first editions).

HC: *At the Sign of the Reine Pedauque* (22), *The Cream of the Jest* (27), *Domnei* (30), *Figures of Earth* (25), *The High Place* (23), *Jurgen* (21), *Mother of Pearl* (29), *Penguin*

Island (25), *The Revolt of the Angels* (24), *The Silver Stallion* (28), *Something about Eve* (29), *Thais* (25), *The Way of Ecben* (29), *The Well of St. Clare* (28)

Richard Dalby

PARKHURST, H. L. (?–1950) American artist. Parkhurst studied at the Art Institute of Chicago, where he completed a four-year course in two and a half years of intensive work on anatomy. The artist credited this background for the naturalness and solidity of his illustration work.

After graduation Parkhurst went to work for the *World* and the *Journal* as a newspaper illustrator. Afterwards, he spent fifteen years in the advertising field as art director and visualizer of national accounts. He became well known for his work for Colgate, American Tobacco, and Eastman Kodak. During this time he began doing freelance illustration, and his work soon was appearing on most major magazine covers.

Like many other magazine illustrators, Parkhurst found that the Depression put him in a position in which any work was better than none. Beginning in the early 1930s he did illustrations for the pulps and soon became established with the Fiction House Publishing Chain for which he worked most of his later life. He also did numerous covers for the Spicy pulp magazines, published by Trojan Magazine Company.

Although Parkhurst did science fiction magazine covers, he was much better known for his covers in the detective and weird-menace vein. He worked primarily in oils and painted large sizes: his cover paintings were usually twenty-four by thirty-two inches, often even larger. His anatomy background served him well for these paintings, and he was an expert at depicting beautiful women in peril. Like many artists of the time, his science fiction paintings featured excellent humans but poorly done monsters.

Parkhurst lived in Garden City, New York, where he helped to establish an Art Center for that city. He was prominent in many clubs and art organizations in the New York area and served four consecutive years as chairman of the Graphic Art Group of the Advertising Club of New York.

PUBLISHED WORK:

PS: 1944 (fall, winter); 1945 (spring, summer, fall, winter); 1946 (spring)

SS: 1942 (7); 1947 (9)

StrS: 1939 (2, 6)

TWS: 1943 (2); 1946 (fall)

PAUL, FRANK R. (1884–June 29, 1963) American artist. Frank Rudolph Paul was the first of the great science fiction pulp illustrators. Although perhaps not as accomplished an artist as many who followed, Paul effectively captured the feel of the science fiction published in the pulps during the 1920s and 1930s. More than any other illustrator, he epitomized the "sense of wonder" that was a prominent feature of early science fiction.

Born in Austria, Paul studied architecture there and later studied art in Austria, Paris, and New York. He originally worked for a rural newspaper in New Jersey, where he was discovered by Hugo Gernsback in 1914. The artist was given an assignment for Gernsback's magazine *Electrical Experimenter*, and the results proved so positive that he soon was doing numerous illustrations for that magazine. Paul contributed many of the interior illustrations as well as the covers to the magazine, which changed its title to *Science and Invention*.

In 1926 Gernsback started publishing the first all-science fiction magazine, *Amazing Stories*. Paul not only provided the cover painting for the magazine but also did the black-and-white interiors. He continued to paint the covers and do the interiors for *Amazing* from 1926 through 1929 while also working on other Gernsback magazines including *Science and Invention*. He additionally worked at his regular job, illustrating textbooks, and considered science fiction illustrating a sideline. Paul lived in suburban New Jersey for most of his adult life with his wife, three daughters, and a son. He played the violin and the mandolin for a hobby.

In 1929 Gernsback lost control of *Amazing Stories* through a complex bankruptcy proceeding. Gernsback immediately began several new magazines, including *Science Wonder*, *Air Wonder*, and *Wonder Quarterly*. Paul remained with Gernsback and provided all of the covers and most of the interior illustrations. In 1930 Clayton magazines started publishing *Astounding Stories*, and within a short time, he began illustrating for it as well.

Paul was extremely popular with the fans of the early 1930s. His art was bright and garish; his people were stiff and simplistic, but his cities and spaceships were imaginatively done with great detail. He relied on his architectural training, and his paintings and interiors betrayed a fondness for huge panoramas and titanic structures. His art was also influenced by the cheapness of his publishers—Gernsback was notoriously stringent in his expenses, so red and yellow backgrounds often dominated Paul paintings because of the lesser expenses involved in using a three-color instead of a four-color press.

In 1936 Gernsback sold his science fiction magazines, and for several years, Paul did very little work in the field. During this period, however, he was featured in *The Family Circle* magazine, which had a circulation of more than 1.4 million. The article "Bogeyman," August 26, 1938, concentrated much more on Paul's art than on the artist but still was probably the most exposure any science fiction artist had received in a national publication. It was heavily illustrated with many of Paul's best covers. In the piece, Paul mentioned that his own personal favorite of his paintings was done for the December 1926 *Amazing Stories*. The unusual painting of a huge ocean liner being taken to an alien world by two glowing globes was not based on any story. Instead, it was an original illustration done by Paul for which readers were invited to write a story around the art for a cash prize.

With the boom in science fiction magazines in the early 1940s, Paul returned to the pulps as an old favorite. He contributed a large number of interior illustrations to many of the magazines of the time. *Amazing Stories* and *Fantastic Adventures* had both begun a series of back-cover paintings, unrelated to the stories in the issue but based instead on some common theme month after month. Paul was a frequent back-cover artist for these magazines, contributing a series of paintings: *Life on Other Worlds*, *Cities on Other Worlds*, *Mythology*, and *Stories of the Stars*.

Paul contributed very little to the science fiction magazines during the war years. Afterwards, he again resumed illustrating, working primarily for the Popular Publications reprint magazines. His old-fashioned art, still popular with the older fans, was perfectly suited for reprints of stories from *All-Story* and *Argosy* from the 1920s and earlier.

In 1953 Gernsback published his last science fiction magazine, *Science Fiction +*. Not surprisingly, Paul was a frequent contributor to the publication. When it died after less than a year, Paul stopped working in the science fiction field. However, he continued to do some fantastic illustrations even then. Hugo Gernsback each year published a professional little booklet, *Forecast*, which he sent as a Christmas card to hundreds of people. Filled with articles on advances in science as well as Gernsback's own predictions for future advances, these attractive publications usually featured a number of excellent Paul illustrations.

In 1961 when *Amazing Stories* published a special reprint issue for its twenty-fifth anniversary issue, special consultant Sam Moskowitz was able to convince the publisher to have Paul paint a new back-cover illustration. The attractive painting featuring a fantastic scene on a distant planet showed that Paul had lost none of his skills even after years of retirement from science fiction art.

The importance of Frank R. Paul to the history of science fiction cannot be denied. Recently, he has become the focus of some criticism from scholars and fans unhappy with the early history of science fiction. His work has been downgraded and called unimportant, usually with the same breath that attacks Hugo Gernsback and his early publications.

Technically, Paul could not match many of the artists who followed him. However, his art perfectly matched the early exuberance of the stories it illustrated. Science fiction fans who grew up with Paul remain his most vocal defenders. For example, Donald Tuck, in his *Encyclopedia of Science Fiction and Fantasy*, said of Paul that "he was a master of science fiction art, and his work most appropriately portrayed the ideals and wonder of the field in its magazine infancy."

Although Paul never won a Hugo Award (the awards began after he stopped illustrating), he was guest of honor at the first World Science Fiction Convention in 1939.

PUBLISHED WORK:

HC: *Complete Book of Outer Space* (53), *Immortal Storm* (54), *Skylark of Space* (50)

AA: 1927

AMZ: 1926 (4, 5, 6, 7, 8, 9, 10, 11, 12); 1927 (1, 2, 3, 4, 5, 6, 7, 8, 9, 10, 11, 12); 1928 (1, 2, 3, 4, 5, 6, 7, 8, 9, 10, 11, 12); 1929 (1, 2, 3, 4, 5, 6); 1939 (4, 5, 6, 7, 8, 9, 10, 11, 12); 1941 (1, 2, 3, 4, 5, 6, 7, 8, 9, 10, 11, 12); 1942 (1, 2, 3, 4); 1943 (2, 3, 4, 5, 6, 8); 1944 (9); 1945 (3); 1946 (8); 1948 (1); 1961 (4); 1962 (2R, 5R); 1963 (10R); 1965 (10R, 12R); 1966 (2, 4, 10); 1967 (4); 1968 (6, 7, 9); 1972 (7)

AQ: 1928 (winter, spring, summer, fall); 1929 (winter, spring, summer); 1930 (summer); 1931 (spring)

ASF: 1931 (6, 9, 10, 11); 1932 (2); 1933 (1)

ASH: 1942 (12); 1943 (2)

AW: 1929 (7, 8, 9, 10, 11, 12); 1930 (1, 2, 3, 4, 5)

CF: 1940 (winter, spring, summer, fall); 1941 (winter, spring, summer, fall); 1942 (winter)

COM: 1941 (1, 5)

DYN: 1939 (2, 4)

FA: 1939 (5, 7, 9, 11); 1940 (1, 2, 3, 4, 5, 10); 1942 (7, 8, 9, 10, 11, 12); 1943 (1, 2, 3, 4, 7, 10); 1944 (4, 6); 1945 (7, 10); 1946 (2, 5, 7)

FFM: 1939 (12); 1940 (1, 2, 3, 8, 10); 1941 (4, 6, 10, 12); 1942 (4, 6, 7, 8, 9, 10)

FN: 1940 (9); 1941 (1); 1948 (5); 1949 (11); 1950 (5, 9)

FTC: 1965 (9R); 1966 (3, 5, 7, 9, 11); 1967 (1, 3, 9); 1968 (3, 10); 1969 (4); 1972 (12)

FUT: 1939 (11); 1940 (3, 11); 1941 (4, 8)

MSS: 1938 (11); 1951 (5, 8, 11)

PS: 1940 (summer, fall, winter); 1941 (spring, summer, fall, winter); 1942 (spring, summer, fall, winter); 1943 (3, 5); 1945 (spring)

SAT: 1957 (12); 1958 (2, 6)

SF: 1939 (3, 6, 8, 10, 12); 1940 (3, 6, 10); 1941 (1, 3, 6, 9)

SF+: 1953 (3, 4, 5, 6, 8, 10, 12)

SFD: 1930 (4)

SFQ: 1941 (winter, spring, summer)

SS: 1939 (1, 7); 1940 (3, 5, 7, 9, 11); 1941 (1, 5, 11); 1942 (1); 1943 (6); 1944 (1, summer)

SSS: 1943 (2); 1949 (1, 4, 7, 9); 1950 (7, 9, 11); 1951 (1)

StrS: 1939 (2, 4, 8, 10, 12); 1940 (12)

SW: 1929 (6, 7, 8, 9, 10, 11, 12); 1930 (1, 2, 3, 4, 5)

SWQ: 1929 (fall); 1930 (winter, spring)

TWS: 1939 (2, 4, 10); 1940 (1, 2, 3, 4, 5, 7, 8, 9, 10); 1941 (3, 6, 10)

WS: 1930 (7, 8, 9, 10, 11, 12); 1931 (1, 2, 3, 4, 5, 6, 7, 8, 9, 10, 11, 12); 1932 (1, 2, 3, 4, 5, 6, 7, 8, 9, 12); 1933 (1, 2, 3, 4, 5, 6, 8, 10, 11, 12); 1934 (1, 2, 3, 4, 5, 6, 7, 8, 9, 10, 11, 12); 1935 (1, 2, 3, 4, 5, 6, 7, 8, 9, 10, 11); 1936 (1, 3)

WQ: 1930 (summer, fall); 1931 (winter, spring, summer, fall); 1932 (winter, spring, summer, fall); 1933 (winter)

PEAKE, MERVYN LAWRENCE (July 9, 1911-Nov. 17, 1968) British artist. Born in Kuling, China, Peake was the son of a medical missionary. He returned to England at the age of twelve and was educated at Eltham College and later studied at Croydon School of Art and the Royal Academy Schools. He taught life drawing at Westminster School of Art from 1935 until 1938 and began his unique career as writer, illustrator, and painter in 1939 with the publication of his first book, *Captain Slaughterboard Drops Anchor.*

His main influences were Goya, Rowlandson, Cruikshank, Dore, and, most importantly, Stanley L. Wood★. "This man was my secret god. His very signature was magic" stated Peake in 1947.

Peake was at his best interpreting fantasy, both his own work and that of other writers. The lively humor present in his early work was matched by a strong feeling for the grotesque and the macabre, and these qualities combined in the monstrous facial caricatures that recurred in his artwork.

Peake became a cult figure for his remarkable novels (inaccurately known as the "Gormenghast trilogy"): *Titus Groan, Gormenghast,* and *Titus Alone.* At Peake's request, these three novels were first published without illustrations, but the manuscripts were accompanied by numerous sketches, and some of them appeared as illustrations in later editions.

After 1955 Peake became gradually incapacitated by Parkinson's disease. He spent his last four years in the hospital, where he died in November, 1968.

PUBLISHED WORK (Illustrations only).

HC: *Drawings of Mervyn Peake* (49), *Figures of Speech* (54), *Gormenghast* (50), *Mr. Pye* (53), *Poems and Drawings* (65), *Titus Alone* (59), *Titus Groan (new edition)* 68)

Richard Dalby

PEARSE, ALFRED (1856-Apr. 29, 1933) British artist. Born in St. Pancras, London, Pearse was one of the most prolific black-and-white illustrators of his generation. His family comprised six generations of artists dating from 1700. Educated privately, he studied wood engraving from 1872 to 1875 and began illustrating professionally at the age of nineteen. His output was huge and varied for more than half a century. His busiest markets were *Pictorial World*, for which he served as "special" artist from 1879 until 1886, *Strand*; *Wide World*; and *Boys Own Paper*, for which he illustrated seventy-six serials and many short stories from 1878 to 1923. He illustrated several fantasy stories, including lost race novels by William Le Queux and George Griffith. These drawings were usually signed "A. P."

Pearse was specially commissioned to sketch the coronation of King George and Queen Mary in 1911. He later designed royal costumes for various investitures and royal ceremonies. Other works by him include 160 Victoria Cross pictures for the British government and two paintings (each two inches square) for Queen Mary's Doll House. He died in April 1933.

PUBLISHED WORK:

HC: *The Adventurs of Louis de Rougemont as Told by Himself* (1899), *The Eye of Istar* (1897), *The Great White Queen* (1896), *The Romanace of Golden Star* (1897), *The Veiled Man* (1899)

STRAND: "The Great White Moth" 1904 (1), "The New Accelerator" 1901 (12), "The Thames Valley Catastrophe" 1887 (12)

Richard Dalby

PEDERSON, JOHN, JR. (?) American artist. An excellent artist, Pederson worked for the SF magazines in the late 1950s into the 1960s. He specialized in astronomical scenes and produced a number of attractive covers for the *Galaxy* chain as well as *The Magazine of Fantasy & SF.*

PUBLISHED WORK:

AMZ: 1970 (5, 7); 1971 (3); 1972 (1)

F&SF: 1957 (6); 1958 (11); 1963 (2)

FTC: 1972 (6)

GXY: 1957 (5, 11); 1958 (2, 5, 6); 1963 (8); 1964 (8); 1965 (10, 12); 1968 (12); 1969 (2, 8)

IF: 1959 (7, 9, 11); 1960 (7, 9); 1962 (3); 1963 (5); 1964 (5, with Dember*); 1965 (6); 1966 (2); 1968 (1, 5)

WOT: 1963 (4); 1965 (7)

PELHAM, DAVID (b. May 12, 1938) British artist. Pelham studied at St. Martin's School of Art. From book and magazine illustration, he went on to become art director of *Harper's Bazaar*. He later became art director of Penguin Books, and he was responsible for the change of style and new look of Penguin covers in the early 1970s.

Pelham's interest in science fiction was inspired by the novels of J. G. Ballard. His most famous covers in the genre were those he did for the Penguin editions of Ballard's *The Drought*, *The Drowned World*, *The Terminal Beach*, and *The Wind from Nowhere*. Using an air-brush technique, his symbolic machines, representing the debris of our society, are instantly recognizable. Modern artists like Richard Lindner and Eduardo Paolozzi were important influences on his work.

Richard Dalby

PENNINGTON, BRUCE (b. May 10, 1944) British artist. Pennington, who studied at Beckenham School of Art from 1960 to 1964, began illustrating covers in the historical and western genres. He entered the science fiction field with the cover painting for Heinlein's *Stranger in a Strange Land* published by New English Library in 1967. During the next two years, he produced distinctive covers for a series of Ray Bradbury paperbacks including *The Illustrated Man, Dandelion Wine*, and *Something Wicked This Way Comes*, all for Corgi Books. He also did artwork for a series of Brian Aldiss paperbacks for New English Library as well as numerous covers for Frank Herbert reprints.

Pennington's strong use of color and surrealistic landscapes are among the best in the genre. The impression of vastness, depth, and luminosity in his work is achieved by incorporating a variety of inks and varnishes to the gouache colors. Two fine examples of covers done in this manner were the works he completed for M. John Harrison's *Pastel City* and Poul Anderson's *Satan's World*.

Blake, Goya, and Bosch are among the early painters Pennington admires most. Many of his vivid illustrations were reproduced in *Science Fiction Monthly*, and he was the first artist interviewed in that magazine. A portfolio of some of his best work, *Eschatus*, was published in 1977.

Richard Dalby

PEPPER, ROBERT (b. Oct. 23, 1938) American artist. Born in Portsmouth, New Hampshire, Pepper grew up in Los Angeles and studied at the Los Angeles City College, Chouinard Art Institute, and Los Angeles County Art Institute. He received a scholarship to the Art Center School in Los Angeles from which he graduated with distinction in 1962. Pepper believes that the greatest influence on his work was James Hill, an illustrator in the 1960s, and Gustav Klimt. Walt Disney was also an influence.

Pepper settled in Brooklyn Heights, New York, and began working as an art director for the J. Walter Thompson Advertising Agency. While there, he also freelanced for magazines, and his first big job was for *The Saturday Evening Post*; it encouraged him to strike out on his own as a freelance illustrator. Since then his work has appeared in numerous national magazines, including *McCalls, Modern Bride, Newsweek, Vista, Cue, Ms., American Home*, and *Sports Illustrated*.

Pepper's next big break came with Nonesuch Records. He had total color freedom and illustrated fifty-six album covers for that company. By the time he contacted Ballantine Books, he had a large portfolio of his work. His first fantasy art assignment was for the *Gormenghast* series by Mervyn

Peake, which Ballantine was reprinting in paperback. Pepper was impressed with the series "because the writing was far more visual than any piece of art could hope to be." He was pleased with his surrealistic answer to the problem, but Ballantine insisted that the paintings be more realistic. "The answer to the problem is alright but I prefer my approach," Pepper recently stated.

In the late 1960s psychedelic art was popular, and the Ballantine adult fantasy series was particularly popular. Pepper had always loved fantasy, and his decorative, designed, colorful approach fit in with what Ballantine wanted. He soon was doing art for all of the major paperback and hardcover publishers; clients included Harper and Row, Dell, Avon, Macmillan, Doubleday, Pocket Books, Ballantine, Belmont, DAW, Ace, and Pyramid. In the period from 1968 to 1973 he was one of the best-known and highly regarded science fiction artists.

In 1972 Pepper was chosen to do the National Book Week Poster and was included along with several other top illustrators in a collection of art for the International Advertising Council on the picturing of moral values.

His art has won many awards including the Award of Merit from the Society of Publication Designers (1976), the Award of Excellence from the Society of Illustrators (1968), twenty-seven Awards of Merit from that society (1963–1981), as well as many other honors. His paintings have been exhibited in numerous shows and galleries, and he has had a number of showings in major group shows including ones sponsored by the Society of Illustrators, the Brooklyn Museum, and Kent State University. One of his pieces, *The Wild Bull*, is in the Permanent Museum Collection of the Society of Illustrators.

As paperback publishing grew more conservative, Pepper found himself less interested in the science fiction and fantasy field. His style did not fit in with the trend toward "mechanical renderings of spaceships and unicorns." He still did some work in the genre, however, and his most enjoyable job was in 1981 when he produced thirty-eight cards for the Dragonmasters Game for Milton Bradley. Just recently, he created six covers for DAW books illustrating the Philip K. Dick novels.

Pepper originally worked only in gouache but now works in gouache and dyes. His earlier work was much rougher in execution than the work he does now. Originally, he let his natural impulses have free reign over his work, but now he is in control of every detail.

In doing a painting, Pepper will always read the book and take notes about descriptions of places, people, and symbols and thoughts about the meaning of the book. Then he will "mull it over for a while and finally come up with what I feel the author is saying and what symbols will best convey that in a limited space. I begin to look through anything which will fit my theme, collecting, symbols, layouts, color combinations, etc. Finally, I begin in thumbnail size, to put it all together in a design. (I prefer a design rather than a scene.) When the design begins to take shape, I juggle, move about, exaggerate, etc. in a larger size to make things work. This period takes me the longest; the actual painting takes very little time." Pepper prepares the work two to three times the printed size in a more detailed work than his initial sketch.

Some of Pepper's personal favorites of his fantasy illustrations include *Clarion III*, *Dark Side of Earth*, *Deus Irae*, *Do Androids Dream of Electric Sheep*, *Ellison Wonderland*, *The King of Elfland's Daughter*, *Legends from the End of Time*, *New Lands*, *Passing for Human*, *Saga of Hrolf Kraki*, *Shores of Another Sea*, *The Silver Stallion*, and *We Can Build You*. He was always interested in fantasy much more than science fiction and thought that because of this his worst work in the field was the Lucky Starr covers he did for the Isaac Asimov series.

The father of two children, Morgan and Danyael, Pepper lives in Brooklyn. He taught illustration at Pratt in 1983 and presently is giving serious thought to new directions for his art. Gallery shows and poster work are both in his future plans. His career in the science fiction field is a perfect reflection of the changes that have taken place in the past twenty years. During the boom years of the late 1960s and early 1970s, new ideas in both books and art made great inroads in the fairly conservative science fiction market. Then as the boom died, conservative values in both art and fiction again took hold, forcing out many of the newer, more innovative workers. Although the field in 1985 is again going through a boom period, there seems to be little room for innovation or experimentation. It is ironic that a genre of unusual ideas and far-out concepts has no place for anything but conservative illustration.

PUBLISHED WORK:

PB: *Ashes and Stars* (77), *Book of the Damned* (72), *Caviar* (69), *Clarion III* (73), *Continent Makers* (71), *Dark Side of Earth* (70), *David Starr Space Ranger* (71), *Day of Their Return* (74), *Demolished Man* (70), *Deryni Checkmate* (71), *Deryni Rising* (70), *Deus Irae* (83), *Do Androids Dream of Electric Sheep* (71), *Don Rodriguez* (70), *Driftglass* (72), *E Pluribus Unicorn* (69), *Ellison Wonderland* (74), *Fahrenheit 451* (69), *Figures of Earth* (69), *Flesh* (72), *Gormenghast* (67), *Idyll of White Lotus* (74), *Island of the Mighty* (70), *Islands in the Sky* (71), *The Islar* (71), *Jack of Shadows* (72), *Journey to Arcturus* (68), *King of Elfland's Daughter* (69), *League of Grey Eyed Women* (71), *Legends from the End of Time* (76), *The Living Demons* (67), *Lord Tyger* (72), *Lucky Starr and the Big Sun of Mercury* (71), *Lucky Starr and the Moons of Jupiter* (71), *Lucky Starr and the Oceans of Venus* (71), *Lucky Starr and the Pirates of the Asteroids*, *Lucky Starr and the Rings of Saturn* (71), *Mask of Circe* (71), *A Maze of Death* (83), *Messiah at the End of Time* (77), *Monday Begins on Saturday* (77), *More Than Human* (69), *New Lands* (73), *New Lands (Islandia)* (70), *The October Country* (68), *The Omega Point* (71), *Passing for Human* (77), *Saga of Hrolf Kraki* (73), *A Scanner Darkly* (83), *Shores of Another Sea* (70), *The Silver Stallion* (69), *Starburst* (70), *Tales of Sake* (65), *Three Stigmata of*

Palmer Eldridge (83), *Titus Alone* (67), *Titus Groan* (67), *Ubik* (83), *Voyage to a Forgotten Sun* (74), *We Can Build You* (82), *Wild Talents* (73)

MISC: Dark Tower Computer Game (81), Dragonmaster Card Game (81)

PETTEE, CLINTON (?) American artist. Staff cover artist for the Munsey Publications chain, Pettee achieved immortality in the science fiction field as the result of one cover. In 1912 he painted the cover illustration for *Tarzan of the Apes* by Edgar Rice Burroughs, which appeared complete in the October 1912 issue of *All-Story Magazine*. The cover, which showed Tarzan, armed only with a knife, battling a lion, became one of the most famous illustrations in the history of the fantasy genre and has been reprinted innumerable times.

PFEIFFER, FRANK (?) American artist. Pfeiffer took over the *Doc Savage* series after the departure of James Bama★. His work did not attract readers, and first Boris Vallejo★ and then Robert Larkin★ were brought in. Pfeiffer has done science fiction paperback art as well.

PUBLISHED WORK:

PB: *Crimson Serpent* (74), *Derrick Devil* (73), *Golden Peril* (73), *King Maker* (75), *Land of Fear* (73), *Metal Master* (73), *Murder Mirage* (72), *Mystery on the Snow* (72), *Quest of the Spider* (72), *Seven Agate Devils* (73), *South Pole Terror* (74), *Spook Hole* (72), *Stone Man* (75)

PITTS, JIM (?) British artist. A British fantasy artist, Pitts specializes in black-and-white illustrations for fanzines. He has had artwork appear in *Ghosts and Scholars*, *Fantasy Tales*, and *Balthus* as well as in publications of the British Fantasy Society. Some of his early color drawings were published as covers for *Fantasy Tales*. He also illustrated the Michel Parry paperbacks *Savage Heroes* (1977) and *Spaced Out* (1977). *Savage Heroes* was reprinted in hardcover in 1980 in the United States with additional drawings. Sidney Sime★ and Frank Hampson★ are among Pitt's major influences.

Richard Dalby

PODWIL, JEROME (b. 1938) American artist. Born in New York City, Podwil attended Pratt Institute and the Art Students League from 1955 through 1960. He graduated from the Pratt School of Art and Design in 1960. Along with providing art for various science fiction magazines, he also sold art to *Playboy* and other magazines. He won a Gold Medal from the Society of Illustrators and won Awards for Excellence from Chicago shows in 1974 and 1976.

PUBLISHED WORK:

PB: *And Others Shall Be Born* (68), *Bell from Infinity* (68), *Bloodhype* (73), *Crisis on Cheiron* (67), *Demolished Man* (78), *Tama of the Light Country* (65), *Tama Princess of*

Mercury (66), *Terror* (62), *Thief of Thoth* (68), *Universe Maker* (79), *Wandering Tellurian* (67)

POPP, WALTER (?) American artist. Popp was a prolific paperback and magazine artist who worked in the science fiction field for a short time during the boom years of the early 1950s. His covers were uniformly excellent. He kept away from alien monsters and instead concentrated on people. His women were attractive and his men, heroic. Popp moved on to the paperback field and left science fiction when the big boom went bust in 1954.

PUBLISHED WORK:

AMZ: 1952 (6, 8, 9, 10, 11)

FA: 1952 (6, 7, 8, 9, 10)

FSQ: 1953 (7); 1954 (summer)

SpS: 1953 (4)

SS: 1952 (9, 11); 1953 (3, 5, 8); 1954 (1)

TWS: 1952 (12); 1953 (6, 11); 1954 (spring)

POTTER, JEFFREY KNIGHT (b. July 10, 1956) American artist. Born in Riverside, California, Potter spent most of his life in the southern states. At present, he and his wife, Catherine, live in Louisiana.

A self-taught artist, Potter was strongly influenced by the work of Clarence John Laughlin, creator of the first American surrealist photographs. Laughlin and his work, especially his photographic book *Ghosts along the Mississippi*, convinced Potter that he could make a career of doing photographic illustrations in the fantasy field.

Potter worked in the production department for Warren Publications for a summer after high school. Afterwards, he returned to Louisiana, where he worked for ten years as an air-brush artist/retoucher for various photo labs.

Potter entered the horror-fantasy illustration field through fandom, gaining immediate recognition for his unusual art in the pages of the leading Lovecraft fanzine *Nyctalops* as well as in *Xenophile* and *Weirdbook*. He quickly crossed over into hardcovers and is most noted for his artwork in books published by Scream Press.

Potter works with photographic images as well as textured pen-and-ink illustrations to produce a combination piece that is more than either medium alone can provide. Being trained as a photographer as well as an air-brush artist, he has always had a strong interest in cinematic effects, and this has influenced his art. He is fascinated by movie stills and thinks of his own work as "movie stills without a movie." As such, his illustrations have a photographic realism along with a menacing horror image that is totally unique. He always reads all of the material that he illustrates and rarely works from suggestions from an art director.

PUBLISHED WORK:

HC: *Books of Blood* (85), *The Dark Country* (1982), *The Face That Must Die* (83), *Red Dreams* (84), *Skeleton Crew* (85), *Tales of the Werewolf Clan 1* (1979), *Tales of the Werewolf Clan 2* (1980), *Things beyond Midnight* (84), *Who Made Stevie Crye?* (84)

POULTON, PETER (?) American artist. One of the many artists to enter the science fiction field during the boom years of the early 1950s, Poulton was one of the best. He used a sharp pen-and-ink style as opposed to the many artists who worked in grease pencil or wash during the period. For shading he used detailed cross-hatching and stipple work to produce the desired effect. In many ways, his work was very much in the style of Virgil Finlay★. Although Poulton did not have the near photographic realism of Finlay, his art often expressed a lighter, more humorous touch. Poulton handled human figures well but also was not afraid to depict unusual aliens or strange machinery in his art. Although he was primarily an interior artist, he also painted several attractive covers for *Future Science Fiction*.

PUBLISHED WORK:

HC: *Earthbound* (53)

ASF: 1955 (9)

FSQ: 1951 (winter); 1952 (9, 11); 1953 (1, 3, 5, 7, 9); 1954 (winter)

FUT: 1951 (1, 3, 5, 7, 9, 11); 1952 (1, 3, 5, 9)

SF: 1956 (1); 1958 (5); 1959 (11)

SF+: 1953 (10, 12)

SFQ: 1951 (5, 8, 11); 1952 (2, 5, 8); 1955 (5); 1957 (11)

SpS: 1952 (10, 12); 1953 (4, 6)

SpSF: 1952 (9)

SS: 1950 (11); 1951 (3, 5, 9); 1952 (1, 3, 8, 10, 11); 1953 (1, 3, 4, 8); 1954 (1, spring, summer); 1955 (summer)

TRE: 1965 (2)

TWS: 1950 (12); 1951 (2, 4, 8, 10); 1952 (4, 6, 8, 10, 12); 1953 (2, 6, 11); 1954 (winter)

WSA: 1952, 1953

POWERS, RICHARD M. (b. 1921) American artist. One of the most prolific science fiction artists ever, Powers ranks as one of the most influential, rivaled only by Virgil Finlay★ and Frank Frazetta★ for lasting and important influence in the science fiction field. More than any other artist, Powers changed the perception of science fiction from space opera to real literature. He ranks as the most influential in terms of setting a standard and style continued by many other artists such as Vincent Di Fate*, Paul Lehr*, and Jack Gaughan*. Although never honored by science fiction fandom with awards, Powers did change the face of science fiction art in the 1950s, and his influence is still felt today.

Powers was born in Chicago, and early on he was impressed by the work of an uncle who was a painter and by trips to the Art Institute of Chicago. After attending Jesuit schools, he went to the Art Institute for a year. During the summer, he attended a commercial art academy. Not caring for either place, he then attended the University of Illinois Fine Arts School. When the war came, Powers was drafted, and he served in the Signal Corps film studios working out of Queens, New York. After the war, he was living in New York, married, and the father of the first of his four children.

Deciding to become a commercial artist, he used the GI Bill to attend the School for Illustrators, run by Dan Content. Afterwards, he attended the New School, where he studied painting, and then worked with artist Jake Conoway in New England, studying landscape and marine painting. He also took his portfolio to all of the New York publishers but landed only a few small jobs. However, while working with Conoway in Maine, Powers received his first book assignment, *Gulliver's Travels* for World Publishing. After that first assignment, things fell into place. Doubleday gave him a number of jacket assignments, ranging from westerns to mysteries to science fiction. Since Doubleday was just starting to publish science fiction, Powers's work soon got him known as a science fiction artist. Horace Gold, editor of *Galaxy* magazine, contacted Powers, and magazine work followed.

While this was happening, Powers's art was featured in a four-man show at the Museum of Modern Art in 1952. About then he became affiliated with the Rehn Gallery. This gallery helped provide a showcase for his impressionistic paintings not in the science fiction vein and placed a number of his pieces in important collections of modern American art.

When Powers began working, there was a vacuum in the science fiction illustration field that he helped fill. Science fiction had been published in pulps for twenty-five years but had rarely been in book form. The small-press science fiction publishers went to artists like Hannes Bok* and Edd Cartier*, who were popular in the pulps, when they looked for illustrators. However, Doubleday and Simon and Schuster were not looking for typical science fiction pulp art, and most of their books were aimed at libraries, not collectors. They wanted more respectable covers, and Powers's art was much more commercial and practical. He soon became one of the most widely used artists in the fast-growing science fiction book field.

Powers had not grown up as a science fiction fan, nor was he a product of magazine illustration. His influences were classical painters as well as Matta, Miro, Tanguy, and other European surrealists. He was not influenced in any way by pulp art, nor was he familiar with the popular science fiction artists of the period. Thus his work was entirely his own. It was surrealistic and symbolic, done in one or two colors due to the demands of the publishers. Often he was not even given the manuscript to read but was just given a title and the author's name. Art had little to do with the story other than trying to catch the essence of the mood of science fiction. Powers's work was totally different from the usual straightforward illustrations that had been appearing up to that time. It was a new and different look in science fiction, a look much different from anything else that was appearing on books or paperbacks of the time. It set off science fiction from other works and yet did not give the books a garish, pulp appearance.

When Ian Ballantine began Ballantine Books, Powers was approached by an agent who promised that he could get the artist a great deal of work if he let the agent represent him. Powers agreed and soon was handling all of the covers for the important Ballantine series. Again, Powers got the assignment because there were very few artists working in the paperback field who wanted to do science fiction covers all the time. Powers himself stated in an interview published in *Algol* magazine (1979): "If the number of good artists who are painting good SF now were working in the early 50's when Ballantine approached me to do the work, he might not have approached me, he might have approached somebody else and the competition would have been a hell of a lot stronger than it was."

Powers's earliest pieces for Ballantine featured spacemen and spaceships but were done in the style of Chesley Bonestell★, although without the near photographic clarity of that artist's work. Instead, Powers combined his own surrealistic use of colors with the stock images of space travel. The covers were popular, and Ian Ballantine permitted Powers to experiment with more abstract pieces. His work for *Childhood's End* was much more symbolic, much more abstract, and still was popular. After a while, Powers was left on his own to create covers in his own style. Ballantine science fiction and Powers covers became an accepted standard in science fiction.

The combination was extremely important. Ballantine's line stressed important, innovative works of science fiction. The emphasis was on modern, thoughtful literature instead of pulp action stories. While Ace Books was reprinting novels from the pulps, Ballantine was publishing stories from the current digest magazines and reprinting novels from England. The books were aimed at a more adult reading audience, and the Powers covers were an integral part of that package. More important, it set science fiction off from other pulp-type literature as the realm of imagination. Although Powers covers rarely bespoke the actual contents of the books they covered, they made it clear that they were works of the imagination and mind. It is impossible to conceive of a surrealist paperback western cover, whereas, through Powers's influence, surrealism and science fiction seem a natural combination.

Ace, the only other major publisher with a monthly science fiction line, featured pulp-style fantasy with pulp-style covers. Ballantine featured adult science fiction with adult covers. Powers's covers challenged the reader. They packaged science fiction in respectable fashion. It was a change from the pulps and even the digest magazines of the time. It was a style that soon many other publishers followed.

Powers never found himself lacking for work. Although science fiction grew in popularity in the 1950s and 1960s, there was no tremendous boom in publishing until years later. Although he could not do all of the covers of science fiction paperbacks published, since most of the companies rarely did more than one book a month, he was able to do many of them. His covers dominated the paperback and hardcover science fiction field for two decades. He did nearly a hundred covers for Ballantine Books and eighty-eight covers for Dell Publishers. He also worked for Pocket Books, Berkley, Belmont, and McFadden paperbacks.

When the boom finally came, Powers's influence on artists was evident. His style had brought science fiction paperback illustration away from the pulps and into the modern era. Not surprisingly, a number of new artists followed his lead. Publishers, looking to emulate the popularity and respectability of the Ballantine series, packaged books in the same style as that earlier group. Even if they did not use Powers for the covers, they used artists who worked very much in the Powers style.

More important, Powers had demonstrated that science fiction did not have to be packaged to aim at juveniles or young adults to sell. He showed that books could feature challenging, unusual covers that did more than illustrate a scene from a story and still could sell well.

Today Powers lives and works in Connecticut with his wife, Tina. He still combines a career as a successful illustrator along with that of a well-known American surrealist. Along with his science fiction art, Powers has done a great deal of children's book art, cover designs for classic poetry and literature books from Dell, and a series of art for "Major Cultures of the World" for World Publishing Co. His magazine assignments outside of science fiction include work for *Esquire*, *The Saturday Evening Post*, *Redbook*, *Life*, and *Natural History*. In 1983 Doubleday published a portfolio of sixteen of his surrealist paintings, *Space Time Warp*.

Although trained to work in oils and watercolors, Powers switched to acrylics because of their quick drying time. He has experimented with many other types of media as well and often uses layers of glaze to give his paintings a viscous, glistening, wet-skin-type effect.

PUBLISHED WORK:

HC: *Ahead of Time* (55), *Another Kind* (55), *Beyond Eden* (54), *Born Leader* (54), *Childhood's Light* (53), *Computer Connection* (75), *Dark Dominion* (54), *Deathstar Voyage* (69), *Double in Space* (51), *The Eternal Frontiers* (73), *Frozen Year* (57), *Girls from*

Planet 5 (55), *Gladiator at Law* (55), *Hero's Walk* (54), *The House in November* (70), *Infinite Cage* (72), *Lord of Thunder* (62), *Midwich Cuckoos* (57), *Night of Delusions* (72), *Of All Possible Worlds* (55), *Pebble in the Sky* (50), *Re-birth* (55), *Rogue Queen* (51), *Ruins of Earth* (71), *Sea Siege* (57), *Secret Masters* (53), *SF Showcase* (59), *Solution T– 25* (51), *Space Merchants* (53), *Star Gate* (58), *Star Rangers* (53), *Star SF Stories* (53), *Tomorrow the Stars* (52), *Treasury of SF Classics* (54), *Tunnel through the Depths* (72), *Undying Fire* (53), *Unwise Child* (62), *Werewolf Principle* (67), *World out of Mind* (53)

PB: *2nd Foundation*, *13 Great Stories of SF* (60), *A for Andromeda*, *Against the Fall of Night* (54), *Ahead of Time* (53), *Aliens* (60), *Alone by Night* (61), *Alternating Currents* (55), *Another Kind* (55), *ASF SF Anthology*, *Assignment in Eternity* (54), *Away and Beyond* (63), *Beasts of Tarzan* (63), *Beyond* (63), *Beyond Eden* (55), *Brain Wave* (54), *Bright Phoenix* (55), *Bring the Jubilee* (53), *Broken Lands* (68), *Brother Assassin* (69), *Burning World* (64), *Bypass to Otherness* (61), *A Case of Conscience* (58), *Caviar* (55), *Checkpoint Lambia* (66), *Childhood's End* (53), *Citizen in Space* (55), *City* (53), *City at Worlds End* (57), *Climacticon* (60), *Clock Strikes 12* (61), *Costigans Needle* (54), *Creatures of the Abyss* (61), *Crossroads in Time* (53), *Cycle of Fire* (56), *Dark Dominion* (54), *Deals with the Devil* (58), *Destination Universe* (64), *Double Star* (57), *E Pluribus Unicorn* (56), *Earthlight* (54), *Emperor Fu Manchu* (59), *End of Eternity* (58), *Expedition to Earth* (53), *Explorers* (54), *Fahrenheit 451* (53), *Far and Away* (55), *Fourth Galaxy Reader* (60), *Future Tense* (64), *Get Off of My World* (66), *Ghost That Was* (71), *Girls from Planet 5* (55), *Gladiator at Law* (55), *Glory That Was* (71), *Graveyard Reader* (58), *Green Odyssey* (56), *Greeks Bearing Gifts* (64), *Hell's Pavement* (55), *Hero's Walk* (54), *High Vacuum* (56), *Human Angle* (55), *Incomplete Enchanter* (60), *Infinite Cage* (74), *Invisible Men* (60), *Jungle Tales of Tarzan* (63), *Killing Machine* (64), *Lost World* (54), *Lovers* (61), *Man of Earth* (58), *Messiah* (54), *Mindwarpers* (65), *Mirror for Observors* (58), *Monster from Earth's End* (59), *More Than Human* (53), *Mortals and Monsters* (65), *Natives of Space* (65), *Needle in a Timestack* (66), *Nerves* (55), *New Maps of Hell* (61), *Night's Black Agents* (61), *Nine Horrors*, *No Boundaries* (55), *No Time Like the Future* (54), *Not Long for This World* (61), *Occam's Razor* (56), *October Country* (55), *Of All Possible Worlds* (55), *Operation Terror* (62), *Other Passenger* (61), *Other Side of Nowhere* (64), *Out of the Deeps* (53), *Outsiders* (54), *Palace of Love* (67), *Paradox Men*, *Pebble in the Sky* (57), *People Maker* (59), *Planet of the Bling* (68), *Planet Explorer* (57), *Prelude to Space* (54), *Pstalmate* (71), *Reach for Tomorrow* (55), *Rebirth* (55), *The Rest Must Die* (59), *Return of Tarzan* (63), *Robots and Changelings* (58), *Sardonicus* (51), *Search the Sky* (54), *Secret Masters* (53), *Shadow of Tomorrow* (53), *Shadows with Eyes* (62), *Shadows in the Sun* (54), *Shield* (63), *Silver Eggheads* (61), *Sirens of Tiltan* (59), *Six Fingers of Time* (65), *Slan* (61), *Slave Ship* (56), *So Close to Home* (61), *Son of Tarzan* (63), *Space Merchants* (53), *Spectrum*, *Star Bridge* (77), *Star King* (64), *Star of Life* (59), *Star SF 2* (54), *Star SF 3* (54), *Star SF Stories* (53), *Star Short Novels* (54), *Star Surgeon* (63), *Starmaker* (61), *Strangers from Earth* (61), *Survivor and Others* (62), *Tales to Be Told in the Dark* (60), *Tales of Gooseflesh and Laughter* (56), *Tales of Love and Horror* (61), *Tales from the White Hart* (56), *Tarzan and the Ant Men* (63), *Tarzan of the Apes* (63), *Tarzan and the City of Gold* (64), *Tarzan at the Earth's Core* (64), *Tarzan and the Forbidden City* (64), *Tarzan and the Foreign Legion* (64), *Tarzan and Golden Lion* (63), *Tarzan the Invincible* (64), *Tarzan and the Leopard Men* (64), *Tarzan and the Lion Man* (64), *Tarzan Lord of the Jungle* (63), *Tarzan and the Lost Empire* (63), *Tarzan the Magnificent* (64), *Tarzan the Terrible* (63), *Tarzan Triumphant* (64), *Tarzan the Untamed*

(63), *Tarzan's Quest* (64), *Things with Claws* (61), *Three Times Infinity* (58), *Tide Went Out* (58), *To Live Forever* (56), *Tomorrows Gift* (58), *Trace of Memory* (63), *Twists of Time* (60), *Undying Fire* (53), *Untouched by Human Hands* (54), *A View from the Stars* (65), *Wailing Asteroid* (60), *War with the Gizmos* (58), *Wolfbane* (59), *Zacherly's Midnight Snaces* (60), *Zacherly's Vulture Stew* (59)

ASF: 1978 (5, 9, 10, 11)

BEY: 1953 (7, 9)

FTC: 1953 (3)

GXY: 1951 (12); 1952 (2, 4)

STAR: 1958 (1)

WSA: 1957, 1963

MISC: Space Time Warp portfolio (83)

POYSER, VICTORIA (b. Nov. 26, 1949) American artist. Born in Columbia, South Carolina, Poyser attended North Texas State University, Central Washington University, and the University of Washington, receiving a BA in 1980 from the Evergreen State College in Olympia, Washington. Classical influences on her art include David, Rubens, Ingres, Jan Van Eyck, Delacroix, John William Waterhouse, Hunt, Millais, Doré, and Howard Pyle.

Poyser first came into contact with science fiction art through books, comics, and magazines. Her first real experience with the field was at Westercon 30, in July 1977, in Vancouver, British Columbia. She first displayed and sold her art at Norwescon I, in Seattle, Washington, in March 1978. Two years later she was nominated for a Hugo Award as Best Fan Artist. In 1981 she was nominated and won the Hugo Award at the World SF Convention in Denver, Colorado. She was nominated and won the award again in Chicago in 1982. She then withdrew her name from further consideration in the fan category due to her changing status as she entered the professional field.

Poyser married Kennedy Poyser in December 1967. They have two children, Astra, born in 1974, and Bryan, born in 1975.

Poyser's first professional art was a Showcase spot in *Galaxy SF* in 1978. Her first book jacket art was for the *Prisoner of Zhamanak* published by Phantasia Press in 1982. Since then she has done artwork for a number of major publishers as well as the small presses. She has won numerous awards for her work and has had her art displayed at the Canton Art Institute in Ohio. She was artist guest of honor at the 1985 World Fantasy Convention in Tucson, Arizona.

Poyser reads the manuscripts of the books she illustrates and bases her illustrations on her reading. She works in oil on masonite or linen canvas. Her favorite artwork was for *Sung in Shadow* published by DAW Books in 1982 and *Ralestone Luck* published by TOR in 1983. Poyser believes that she has improved technically a great deal, but she does not always get her favorite subject matter to illustrate. She has hopes of doing some serious painting on her own but wonders when she will find time.

Adding to Poyser's popularity with art fans and collectors is the fact that much of her art has been made available in a series of fine-quality, limited-edition prints. These prints, produced by Matrix, a company run by her husband, have become a major new medium at science fiction art shows. Done by a photographic process that captures the full quality of the painting, they make it possible for fans to own inexpensive reproductions of major works of science fiction art. A number of other artists have also formed companies to produce and sell such prints. Such prints have made the art of Poyser accessible to nearly everyone and have made her one of the most popular artists among fans of the 1980s.

PUBLISHED WORK:

HC: *Bones of Zora, Dicing with Dragons, Fire Sanctuary, Juxtaposition, Moonsingers Friends* (85), *Planet of Whispers, Red as Blood, The Prisoner of Zhamanak* (82), *The Silver Horse*

PB: *The Bones of Zora, Castle Crespin, A Century of Progress, City of Cain, Emperor of Eridanus, Fifth Grade Magic, First Book of Swords, Goorgon and Other Beastly Tales* (85), *Greyhaven, Hoka, Mail Order Wings, Moon Called, The Pig Plantagenet, Power of Three, Ralestone Luck* (83), *Ralestone Trick* (84), *Second Book of Swords, Stardance, Sung in Shadow* (82), *Sword and Sorcerers* (84), *Swords and Sorceress, Vision of Beasts 2, Vision of Beasts 3, Web of Darkness*

PUNCHATZ, DON IVAN (b. Sept. 8, 1936) American artist. Born in Hillside, New Jersey, Punchatz attended the School of Visual Arts in New York on a full-tuition scholarship and later attended Cooper Union School of Fine Arts. In college he studied under Burne Hogarth, Bob Gill, and Francis Criss. While still attending college in the early 1950s, Punchatz worked for Warwick and Legler Advertising as assistant television art director, finishing his classwork in night school. He later worked as art director for Animatic, Inc., producing filmstrips and animated clips. In 1959 he was drafted by the army and, while in the service, served as a medical illustrator and produced training films.

After his discharge, Punchatz worked as art director with Ketchum MacLeod and Grove Advertising. It was during this period that he began working on the side as a freelance illustrator. In 1966 he became a full-time freelance artist. In 1970 he formed his own studio, The Sketch Pad, in Arlington, Texas.

At first, Punchatz was known primarily as a paperback artist and produced science fiction and fantasy covers for Ace, Berkley, Dell, and Avon. However, as his work became better known, he soon was doing artwork for most major magazines including *Time, Omni, National Lampoon,* and *Playboy.* He has been awarded many professional honors from various art directors clubs as well as the Society of Illustrators. Along with his illustrations, his fine art has been exhibited at numerous one-man shows and in many major museums. In addition to painting, Punchatz also teaches at Texas Christian University and East Texas State University.

PUBLISHED WORK:

HC: *Neanderthal Planet* (69)

PB: *Foundation, Foundation and Empire, Man in the Maze* (69), *Second Foundation, Time Hoppers* (68)

QUINN, GERARD A. (b. 1927) British artist. With Brian Lewis★, Quinn was one of the major SF artists for the British SF magazines of the 1950s, working predominantly for John Carnell's magazines. A self-taught artist, Quinn, who was born and still lives in Northern Ireland, found early work drawing strip cartoon pages for British reprints of American comics (most of them being extra adventures of *Sheena, Queen of the Jungle*). His special passion for science fiction and fantasy led him to submit drawings to Carnell at the beginning of 1951, and his first drawings appeared in the spring of 1951 in *New Worlds*; his first cover followed in January 1952. This exposure brought him assignments for interior illustrations and jacket paintings from Sidgewick and Jackson.

Quinn's interior art required intricate line work, taking eight to twelve hours for a single illustration. Economic pressures caused him to seek other, less demanding work, and even his SF art became less complex, although, in an interview in *Science Fantasy*, he was quick to assure fans that the "simpler method [was] not synonymous with poor work." Self-portraits of Quinn are contained in his covers for *Science Fantasy* numbers 14 and 15.

His work became less evident in the late 1950s, with no covers by him appearing between 1958 and 1961. During that period he changed his techniques considerably, switching to colored inks to produce an oil-painting effect.

Although the Carnell magazines folded in 1964 (their subsequent revival having a totally different artistic slant), Quinn did not disappear from the scene. He painted a number of covers and interiors in black and white for *Vision of Tomorrow* and, more recently, for the short-lived *Extro*, which was published in his native Belfast.

PUBLISHED WORK:

HC: *Alien Dust* (55), *Earthlight* (55), *Gateway to Tomorrow* (54), *Green Hills of Earth* (54), *Islands in the Sky* (54), *Mysteries of Space and Time* (55), *Prelude to Space* (53), *True Book about Space Travel* (54), *True Book about the Stars* (54)

PB: *Prelude to Space* (54), *Spaceways* (54)

EXT: 1982 (5, 8)

NEB: (3, 25, 27, 28, 29, 34, 35, 37, 41)

NW: 1951 (spring, summer, fall, winter); 1952 (1, 3, 5, 16, 17, 18, 19, 20, 21, 22, 23, 24, 25, 26, 27, 28, 29, 30, 31, 32, 33, 34, 35, 36, 37, 38, 39, 40, 41, 42, 43, 44, 45, 46, 47, 48, 49, 50, 51, 52, 53, 54, 55, 110, 112, 114, 116); 1963 (8, 9, 10, 11, 12)

ScF: 1951 (winter); 1952 (spring, fall); 1953 (spring); (7, 8, 9, 10, 11, 12, 13, 14, 15, 16, 17, 18, 19, 20, 31, 49, 50, 51, 52, 53, 54, 57, 59, 60)

SFA(BR): (28, 31, 32)

VofT: 1969 (12); 1970 (2)

Richard Dalby/Mike Ashsley

RANKIN, HUGH (1879–1957) American artist. Rankin was a newspaper illustrator who began working for *Weird Tales* in 1927, when he was in his late forties and semiretired. He was one of the first artists who worked for that magazine who was reasonably competent, and his art was a sharp departure from the illustrations of C. C. Senf★ and Andrew Brosnatch★, whose work dominated *Weird Tales* before Rankin started illustrating. Rankin soon was doing a vast majority of the interiors for *Weird Tales* in the late 1920s while sharing the cover duties with Senf.

Rankin lived in Chicago when he first began illustrating for the pulps, but he moved to the West Coast after several years. His association with the pulps ended when it became too complicated to work entirely through the mail.

Rankin's paintings were done in pastel watercolors and had a shadowy, indistinct style that produced an eerie effect. His interiors were done in charcoal and grease pencil and again had that same indistinct feeling. Rankin was one of the earliest weird-fiction illustrators who was not afraid to attempt an otherworldly creature, and he effectively captured the feeling of many fantasy stories. His monsters were those of the borderline, hidden in shadows or in indistinct outlines.

Rankin also did artwork for *Weird Tales* using regular illustration pencil and ink. These works were done in an uncluttered, distinct style and were signed "DOAK." Some illustrations in this style were signed "P.E.N."

PUBLISHED WORK:

HC: *The Purple Sea* (29)

FTC: 1967 (1)

WT: 1927 (7, 8, 9, 10, 11, 12); 1928 (1, 2, 3, 4, 5, 6, 7, 8, 9, 10, 11, 12); 1929 (1, 2, 3, 4, 5, 6, 7, 8, 9, 10, 11, 12); 1930 (1, 2, 3, 4, 5, 6, 7, 8, 9, 10, 11, 12); 1931 (1, 2, 4); 1932 (5); 1933 (12); 1934 (2, 4, 5, 7, 8, 9, 10, 11, 12); 1935 (1, 4, 5, 6, 7, 11); 1936 (2, 4, 5, 6)

RAYMOND, ALEX (Oct. 2, 1909–Sept. 6, 1956) American artist. One of the most famous science fiction artists of all time, Alexander Gillespie Raymond never contributed an illustration to the science fiction magazines or did a piece of art for a science fiction book. He created the most famous and influential science fiction newspaper comic strip of all time, *Flash Gordon*.

Raymond was born in New Rochelle, New York, in 1909. He attended the Iona Preparatory School in New Rochelle and then the Grand Central School of Art in New York. He first worked on the comic strip *Tillie the Toiler* for Russ Westover and then with Lyman Young on *Tim Tyler's Luck* from 1930 to 1933. During 1932 and 1933 he ghosted the strip for Young.

In 1933 Raymond was asked by King features to create several features for the Sunday comics. He came up with *Flash Gordon*, a space adventure, and *Jungle Jim*, a jungle adventure strip. In addition, he did daily art for *Secret Agent X–9*, which was scripted by Dashiell Hammett. He later left *X–9* when the work load became too great.

Raymond was one of the greatest of all comic-strip artists. His clear, crisp style was widely imitated, and he influenced a generation of comic-strip readers. He was a master of "feathering," a technique using fine pen strokes to create contours and depth in his strip. *Flash Gordon* was the ultimate science fiction fantasy featuring beautiful women, heroic and manly heroes, and terribly evil villains. Raymond took the standard elements of space opera and raised it to new heights.

In 1944 Raymond left the comics and joined the U.S. Marine Corps. He served in the Pacific theater. After leaving the service, he created another comic strip, *Rip Kirby*, featuring a smart detective hero. The strip soon rivaled his early works in popularity.

Raymond died while at the top of his career in an auto accident near Westport, Connecticut, in 1956.

REINERT, KIRK (b. Aug. 31, 1955) American artist. Born in Cleveland, Ohio, Reinert received a great deal of informal training before ever attending art school. His grandfather Fred Reinert was the sports cartoonist for the *Cleveland Plain Dealer* for thirty-five years, and his uncle Rick Reinert worked on cartoon animation for the major television networks. Although Reinert received a great deal of encouragement, his interest in monsters and imaginative pieces was not highly regarded by his relatives. A fan of the Warren magazines (*Creepy*, *Eerie*, and *Famous Monsters*) as well as Vincent Price movies, Reinert always wanted to work for Warren.

Reinert attended Cooper School of Art in Cleveland and received a degree in commercial design and production. Influences range from Norman Rockwell to Salvador Dali, Bosch, Maxfield Parrish, Frank Frazetta★, and Richard Corben★.

After graduating from art school, Reinert went to Warren magazines in New York for an interview. Even without much being published in the field, he was able to sell Warren several pieces. Then it was just a matter of time and hard work for him to develop a regular clientele.

At present, along with continuing to do paperback cover art, Reinert has also been doing production work as a conceptual designer for motion pictures and has been doing calendar and poster art as well. He has also produced the covers for a number of video games.

PUBLISHED WORK:

HC: *Day of Dissonance*

PB: *The Alchemists, Angles, The Bloody Sun, The Blue Sword, The Broken Citadel, Camp, Castledown, Conan the Defender, Conan the Invincible, Conan the Triumphant, Conan the Unconquered, The End of the Empire, Hide and Seek, King Chondos Ride, Lamplighter, The Last Warrior Queen, The Lost Prince, Mahogany Trinrose, Marrakesh Nights, Mindspell, Mystery Walk, The Planet Savers, The Shapes of Midnight, Slate, Star of Danger, Sword of Aldones, Token to Terror, Treasure Hunters, The World Wreckers*

RICHARDS, JOHN (?) British artist. Richards was the art editor and mainstay cover artist for *Authentic Science Fiction Monthly* between 1953 and 1955. In the early 1950s *Authentic* featured some of the most drab and uninteresting covers on any science fiction magazine. There was a sudden marked improvement with the debut of Richards on the February 1953 (number 30) issue of the magazine. Most readers approved of the art, although many thought it was better suited for a weird-fantasy magazine than for a science fiction publication. After two covers, however, Richards's name disappeared from the cover, although from issue 41 (January 1954) he was listed as art editor, succeeding John Deericks. The main artist attributed to cover art at this time was "Davis." This was the name of the interior artist who did mediocre black-and-white illustrations for *Authentic*. The answer seems to be provided by the October 1954 (number 50) issue of the magazine, in which the cover is clearly signed "Richards" but is internally listed as by "Davis." Although it may have been a publishing error, it seems likely that Davis was the real name of the artist who did not want it known that he was acting as both art editor and main illustrator for the same magazine (although this was common practice for many magazines in both Britain and the United States). Adding to the mystery is the similarity to the interior illustrations done by "Roger Davis"★ in the magazine *Weird World* (in 1955–1956). Davis signed his art in two manners, with a formal signature and a printed name. The printed inscription is identical to the printed inscription used by Richards. Thus it seems possible that Davis and Richards were the same person.

Authentic's covers between July 1953 and February 1955 fell into two annotated series. "From the Earth to the Stars" followed man's exploration of space from the depiction of a three-stage orbital rocket to a starship's destination at a distant planet. "Tour of the Solar System" (issues 49 to 54) depicted scenes on each of the planets. Both series brought favorable comments from the readers, including SF historian Donald H. Tuck, who in the *Tuck Encyclopedia of Science Fiction*, remarked "they are . . . amongst the best of any on the prozines today." The art also attracted the attention of aspiring artist David Hardy★, who submitted his early work to *Authentic* although without success.

Richards ceased to work as art editor after issue 53 (January 1955), although he provided covers for issues 55 and 57. Thereafter, both Richards and Davis vanished from the science fiction magazine scene. *Authentic* was published by Hamilton & Co., of London, who also published the Panther series of SF paperbacks, and it seems likely that Richards also painted the covers for many of these books during this period.

PUBLISHED WORK:

AUTH: (29, 30, 31, 32, 33, 34, 35, 36, 37, 38, 39, 40, 41, 42, 43, 44, 45, 46, 47, 48, 49, 51, 52, 53, 54, 55, 57)

Mike Ashley

RIGO, MARTIN (b. 1949) Spanish artist. Born in Barcelona, Spain, Rigo attended the School of Art in that city. His father was a painter, and Rigo wanted to follow in his footsteps. By the age of seventeen, he was working for a scientific publishing house, where he was employed for five years illustrating books on human anatomy, biology, astronomy, physics, and other sciences. This work gave Rigo invaluable experience in doing detailed, highly developed illustration.

While doing scientific illustration, Rigo also spent time doing nonscientific paintings, exhibiting in galleries throughout Spain and in other major European cities as well. He entered a number of national art contests, winning numerous awards.

Since the early 1970s his work has appeared in magazines as well as on book jackets on both sides of the Atlantic. Much of his science fiction work has been done for the Science Fiction Book Club.

PUBLISHED WORK:

HC: *Downbelow Station*

RIOU, EDOUARD (Dec. 2, 1833–Jan. 27, 1900) French artist. Born in St. Servan, France, Riou was a highly regarded French artist. He specialized for many years in landscape painting and commemorative tableaux, and he executed the impressive series *a Venetie rendue a L'Italie* for *Le Monde Illustre* in 1866. During the next four years he was employed by the French publisher Hetzel to illustrate some of Jules Verne's greatest works, most notably *Voyage au centre de la terre* and *Vingt mille lieues sous les mers*. Just after Verne completed writing the latter book in December 1869, he was requested by Hetzel to pay a special visit to Paris to sit for Riou. Verne posed for the role of Professor Pierre Aronnax in Riou's fine illustrations for this book. Soon Riou was summoned to Egypt to work with Ferdinand de Lesseps for the next four years, and the remainder of the 111 illustrations for *Vingt mille lieues* were completed by Alphonse de Neuville★.

Riou completed several fine paintings for the Khedive Ismail I to commemorate the inauguration of the Suez Canal. Among his later commissions was a trip to Russia in 1874 to portray the marriage of the tsar's daughter. Riou received the *Legion d'honneur* in celebration of his distinguished career. He died in Paris in January 1900.

PUBLISHED WORK: (All done for Jules Verne's *Voyages Extraordinaires*. The French edition by Hetzel is given first and then the English title and publication date.)

HC: *Cinq semaines en ballon* (1867), 80 illustrations: *Five Weeks in a Balloon* (1870); *Le chancellor* (1877), 58 illustrations, in collaboration with Jules Ferat★: *Survivors of the Chancellor* (1877); *Les aventures du Capitaine Hattaeras* (1867), 261 illustrations: *The English at the North Pole* (1874) and *Field of Ice* (1876); *Les enfants du Capitaine Grant* (1868), 177 illustrations: *Voyage Round the World (1876–1877)*; *Vingt mille lieues sous les mers* (1870), 111 illustrations in collaboration with de Neuville: *Twenty Thousand Leagues under the Seas* (1873); *Voyage au centre de la terre* (1867), 56 illustrations: *Journey to the Center of the Earth* (1872)

Richard Dalby

ROBERTS, KEITH (JOHN KINGSTON) (b. Sept. 20, 1935). British artist. One of Britain's most notable science fiction writers, Roberts was born in Kettering in Northamptonshire. He studied at the Northampton School of Art and spent some years as a background artist in an animation studio before entering the advertising business.

Roberts's debut in the science fiction art field occurred as his earliest stories began appearing in the science fiction magazines. His first cover painting illustrated his own short novel, *The Furies*, which appeared in the July 1965 issue of *Science Fantasy*. He designed all but seven of the covers for this magazine from January 1965 through February 1967. He also did artwork for *New Worlds* in 1966.

Roberts's striking expressionist covers were influential in changing the appearance of British science fiction magazines twenty years ago. He also designed covers for a number of Michael Moorcock novels.

PUBLISHED WORK (All British publications).

Imp: 1966 (4, 5, 6, 7, 8, 9, 10, 11, 12); 1967 (1)
ScF: 1964 (9); 1965 (1, 5, 6, 7, 8, 11); 1966 (1, 2)

Richard Dalby

ROBERTS, TONY (b. 1950) British artist. A specialist in hardware color illustration, Roberts studied art for two years at Wolverhampton College, followed by three years at Ravensbourne College of Art. He has done many paperback covers in the Chris Foss★ style.

PUBLISHED WORK (All British).

PB: *The Best of A. E. Van Vogt, The Best of Fritz Leiber, Dorsai, Double Star, Necromancer, Soldier Ask Not*

Richard Dalby

ROBIDA, ALBERT (May 14, 1848–Oct. 11, 1926) French artist. Robida was one of the most prolific and important science fiction fantasy illustrators in France during the late nineteenth century. He anticipated the later predictive elements of science fiction art in his many drawings of weapons and inventions of the future.

Robida joined the humorous periodical *La Caricature* in 1879. At the same time, he began writing and illustrating a long saga describing the fate of several families in midtwentieth-century France: *Voyages tres extraordinaires de Saturnin Farandoul.* All of his work appeared first in long periodical series, most of which were reprinted in book form, all published in Paris. Some were affectionate pastiches of Jules Verne (for example, *Round the World in More Than 80 Days*). Unlike the works of some of his contemporaries (Georges Roux★, Edouard Riou★, Jules Ferat★, Leon Benett★, and Henri de Montaut★), his *Le vingtieme siecle* series was not published outside France. Robida also illustrated editions of Rabelais, Villon, and Swift's *Gullivar's Travels.* All of these works were very popular in their handsome Paris editions.

Robida had a strong influence on the future-war genre, and he predicted bacteriological warfare. Working with crayon and lithographic pencil, he brought great vigor to his imaginative and witty drawings of airships, aeronautical taxicabs, rejuvenating incubators, and *telephonoscopique* kiosks. He died in October 1926 in Neuilly-sur-Seine.

PUBLISHED WORK:

La vie electrique (*The Electric Life*) (1883), a periodical series, book form in 1892; *Le vingtieme siecle* (*The Twentieth Century*) (1882–1887), a periodical series, book editions in 1883, 1887, 1892, 1895; *Voyage de Fiancailles au vingtieme siecle* (1892); *Voyages tres extraordinaires de Saturnin Farandoul* (1879), a periodical series in one hundred parts, reprinted as five books: *Le Roi des singes, Le tour du monde en plus de 80 jours, Les quatre reines, A la recherche de l'elephant blanc, S.Exc.M.le Gouverneur du Pole Nord* (1882–1883)

Richard Dalby

ROGERS, HUBERT (Dec. 21, 1898–1982) Canadian artist. Rogers was the most important Canadian SF artist who worked in the science fiction art field during the 1940s. His covers added a touch of class to *Astounding Science Fiction* that helped distinguish it as a cut above the other magazines being published then.

Rogers was born in Alberton, Prince Edward Island. He attended Acadia University in Nova Scotia and later studied art at the Toronto Technical

School in Toronto. He worked as a map draftsman and later as a gunner in World War I. When he returned from the war, he used the Soldiers Civil Re-establishment Plan to resume his art training at the New Toronto Central Technical School. After graduation, he worked for a while as a designer at a department store on Prince Edward Island. However, when it became apparent that job opportunities were limited, he moved to Boston. He studied at the Massachusetts Normal Art School and the School of the Museum of Fine Arts, while working as a commercial artist.

In 1925 Rogers moved to New York, where he began his career as an illustrator. He worked for a number of hardcover publishing houses and also did a number of pulp cover paintings, including many covers for *Adventure* magazine, one of the best-selling pulps of the time. He also contributed paintings to *Argosy*, the best-selling weekly pulp, which featured numerous science fiction and fantastic adventure novels. Among his covers was that for *Tarzan and the Magic Men* (1936).

After serving as a contributing artist to the *New York Herald Tribune* for several years and as an art lecturer for the CCC in the West, Rogers began providing artwork for *Astounding Science Fiction* beginning with the cover art for the February 1939 issue of that magazine. He contributed fifty-eight cover paintings for *Astounding* from 1939 through 1952. During the war years he worked in Canada illustrating war posters and did not contribute any science fiction art from 1942 through 1947. After the war he continued his science fiction work and painted dust jackets for several small-press publishers as well as preparing artwork for *Astounding*.

As Rogers grew older, he did less science fiction art and instead switched to portrait painting. He became well known as a Canadian portraitist and did a number of well-known paintings of important Canadian political figures.

Rogers brought style and class to the science fiction pulp field. His paintings and interior illustrations rarely featured action but were pictures of people in dramatic poses. There was no violence in his paintings and rarely any bug-eyed monsters. Instead, his art was muted, subdued, and often symbolic of the content of the stories. He was technically skilled, and much of his art resembled that of J. C. Leyendecker in both form and composition. It was Rogers's cover illustration for *Gray Lensman* by E. E. Smith that defined that character for most readers. His cover art for *Fury* by Henry Kuttner was often identified as one of the finest science fiction paintings ever done for *Astounding*. Rogers frequently did portraits of the leading characters of the story as interior illustrations, a practice that had been used for years in other Street & Smith magazines but one that he introduced to the sicence fiction genre. In an era when garish covers were the norm, Rogers brought the first touch of class to science fiction. He was one of the most important and influential artists of the 1940s. Rogers died in 1982, survived by a wife, Helen, and three children.

PUBLISHED WORK:

HC: *Gray Lensman* (51, 62), *Green Hills of Earth* (51), *Man Who Sold the Moon* (50), *Revolt in 2100* (53)

ASF: 1939 (2, 9, 10, 11); 1940 (2, 4, 5, 6, 7, 8, 9, 10, 11, 12); 1941 (1, 2, 3, 4, 5, 6, 7, 8, 9, 10, 11, 12); 1942 (1, 2, 3, 4, 5, 6, 7, 8); 1947 (3, 5, 8, 9, 10, 11, 12); 1948 (1, 2, 3, 4, 5, 10, 11, 12); 1949 (1, 2, 7, 8, 9, 11, 12); 1950 (1, 2, 3, 4, 5, 6); 1951 (1, 4, 5, 6, 7, 8, 9, 11, 12); 1952 (1, 2, 4); 1953 (9); 1954 (1, 4, 6); 1955 (8, 10, 11); 1956 (1)

SSS: 1942 (8)

UK: 1939 (4, 5)

ROGNAN, LLOYD (?) American artist. A Chicago artist who worked for William Hamling's *Imagination* and *Imaginative Tales* in the 1950s, Rognan produced black-and-white illustrations that were average. But he was a capable cover artist and painted a number of attractive pulp-style covers.

PUBLISHED WORK:

IMG: 1955 (12); 1956 (2, 4, 6, 8, 10, 12); 1957 (2, 4, 6, 10)

IMGT: 1955 (9, 11); 1956 (1, 5, 7, 9, 11); 1957 (5, 9, 11); 1958 (1, 3)

ROUNTREE, HARRY (1878–Sept. 26, 1950) British artist. Born in Auchland, New Zealand, the son of a banker, Rountree worked as a lithographer in a commercial studio before immigrating to London in 1901. He soon became well known for his humorous drawings of animals and was a prolific contributor to *Little Folks*, *The Humorist*, *The Jolly Book*, *Playtime*, *Punch*, and many other magazines. He also illustrated more than sixty books (mainly animal stories and fairy tales), including several written by himself. Among his own works are *Birds, Beasts, and Fishes* in 1929 and *Rabbit Rhymes* in 1934.

In the science fiction field, Rountree illustrated two Professor Challenger novels for the *Strand* magazine. They were *The Lost World* in 1912 and *The Poison Belt* in 1913. Only a small fraction of these memorable illustrations were reproduced in the later book editions. The author of the novels, Arthur Conan Doyle, himself, posed for Rountree as Professor Challenger, complete with fake eyebrows, wig, and a large black beard.

After more than forty years as one of the busiest artists in London, Rountree retired to the Piazza Studios in St. Ives, Cornwall, where he died in September 1950 in relative poverty. He is commemorated with a plaque on the harbor jetty.

PUBLISHED WORK:

HC: *The Lost World* (12), *The Poison Belt* (13)

STRAND: "The Lost World" 1912 (4–11); "The Poison Belt" 1913 (3–7); "The Terror of Blue John Gap" 1910 (8)

ROUX, GEORGES (1850?–1929) French artist. A French painter and illustrator, Roux is now remembered primarily for his artwork commissioned by Hetzel Publishers to accompany the work of Jules Verne and Andre Laurie. For Laurie, his illustrations for *Les exiles de la terre* (*The Conquest of the Moon*), especially "*Le collecteur d'energie solaire*," are particularly memorable and have often been reprinted. Among the other Laurie novels that Roux illustrated are *Tito le florentin*, *Axel Ebersen*, and *Memories d'un collegien russe*.

Roux alternated with Leon Benett★ as the busiest illustrator of Verne's books during the last two decades of the great novelist's career, and he continued the role for fifteen years after the death of Verne. Notable among the works he illustrated are *La chasse au meteore* (1908), the prophetic novel published when a giant meteor hit Siberia (Roux's illustrations of Judge Proth's house were based on Verne's own home); *Le secret de Wilhelm Storitz* (1910), a novel about an invisible man; and *Hier et demain* (1910), which includes some SF shorts. Roux's superb illustrations for *L'Etonnante aventure de la mission Barsac* (1919) proved a brilliant swan song for his forty-year career in illustration.

Peter Costello, writing in his 1978 biography of Jules Verne, noted: "The vision of the secret city and the illustrations of it are quite magnificent. In designing the city, Roux seems to have been directly inspired by the latest advances in architecture, for his fortress and factories owe something to the designs of the model factory at the Werkbund exhibition at Cologne in 1914 by Walter Gropius, with the same flat roofs, small windows and open stairs. Verne was well served by his designers to the very end." Roux illustrations for this book foreshadowed the classic Fritz Lang picture *Metropolis* by seven years.

PUBLISHED WORK:

BOOKS BY ANDRE LAURIE: *Tito le florentin* (1885), *Les exiles de la terre* (1888); *The Conquest of the Moon* (1889), *Memories d'un collegien russe* (1890), *Axel Ebersen* (1892), *L'Ecolier d'Athenes* (1897)

VOYAGES EXTRAORDINAIRES BY JULES VERNE (French 1st edition listed first, followed by the number of illustrations and the English edition).

Cesar Cascabel (1890), eighty-five illustrations: *Cesar Cascabel* (1891); *Hier et demain* (10), illustrated in collaboration with Myrbach and Benett; *La chasse au meteore* (08), twenty-four illustrations: *The Chase of the Golden Meteor* (09); *Le chemin de France* (1889), forty-two illustrations including six color plates: *Flight to France* (1889); *Le phare du bout du monde* (05), thirty-three illustrations: *The Lighthouse at the End of the World* (23); *Le pilote du Danube* (08); *Le secret de Wilhelm Storitz* (10); *Le serpent de mer* (01), thirty-two illustrations; *Le sphinx des glaces* (1897), sixty-eight illustrations: *An Antarctic Mystery* (1898); *Le superbe orenoque* (1898), seventy-two illustrations; *Le testament d'un excentrique* (1899), sixty-one engravings: *The Will of an Eccentric* (1900); *Le village aerien* (01), thirty-eight illustrations; *Le volcan d'or* (06), sixty-three illustrations; *Les freres Kip* (02), sixty-one illustrations; *Les naufrages du Jonathan* (08);

L'Etonnante aventure de la mission Barsac (19); *Maitre du monde* (04), thirty-six illustrations: *Master of the World* (14); *Mirifiques aventures de Maitre Antifer* (1894), seventy-seven illustrations: *Captain Antifer* (1895); *Sans dessus dessous* (1889), thirty-six illustrations including seven color plates: *Purchase of the North Pole* (1891); *Seconde patrie* (1900), sixty-eight engravings; *Un billet de loterie* (1886), forty-two illustrations including three color plates: *The Lottery Ticket* (1887)

Richard Dalby

ROWENA. See MORRILL, ROWENA.

RUTH, ROD (b. 1912) American artist. Born in Benton Harbor, Michigan, Ruth grew up close to the shores of Lake Michigan and developed a love of nature during this period. Later in life he traveled throughout North America, hunting, fishing, and camping, and he even spent several months in a fur-trading post as a caribou hunter and dog-team driver. This love of nature served him well later in his artistic career.

Ruth attended the Chicago Academy of Fine Arts, graduating in 1932, and then studied at the Frederick Mizen School of Art as well as the Institute of Design, both in Chicago. During this period he became friends with Harold McCauley★. After graduating from the Institute of Design, Ruth became a freelance artist and worked for various art studios. He even tried selling art to Farnsworth Wright, the editor of *Weird Tales* magazine in Chicago, but had little luck. He later became one of the staff illustrators for the Ziff-Davis magazine chain, also being published in Chicago.

Ruth primarily worked as an interior artist, painting only a few covers for the publisher. At that time, the house paid $7.50 for a full-page illustration, $15.00 for a double-page spread. He worked with grease crayon on board to get an interesting halftone effect that would reproduce well on pulp paper. He also illustrated a series of Greyhound Bus travel posters and produced some national advertising art. In 1941 he began working on the syndicated comic strip *The Toodles*, which he continued to illustrate for the next sixteen years.

When Ziff-Davis moved to New York in 1950, Ruth found that continued work for the chain was impossible due to the distance involved. He left the science fiction illustration field and moved into wildlife illustration, becoming well known for the book illustrations he did for most major publishers. He also did a number of species charts for the National Marine Fisheries. As a watercolorist, Ruth exhibited at the Artists Guild of Chicago fine-arts shows. His work has won numerous awards from the Society of Illustrators, the Printing Industry of America, and the Artists Guild.

Ruth lives with his wife, Mary Spencer, in the suburban Chicago area. He is the father of three sons and is a grandfather as well. A life member of the Art Institute and the Field Museum of Chicago, his interest in nature is still as great as when he was a young boy.

PUBLISHED WORK:

HC: *More Science Fiction Tales* (74), *Science Fiction Tales* (73)

AMZ: 1940 (2); 1941 (11); 1942 (1, 2, 3, 4); 1943 (1, 2, 6); 1945 (6, 9, 12); 1946 (5, 11, 12); 1947 (2, 9, 10); 1948 (4, 5, 6, 7, 9, 11); 1949 (5, 6, 7, 10); 1950 (1, 3, 4, 9, 12); 1951 (3, 5, 9); 1967 (10)

FA: 1940 (1, 4, 5, 6, 8, 10); 1941 (3, 5, 6, 7, 8, 10, 11, 12); 1942 (1, 2, 3, 4, 5, 6, 7, 8, 9, 10, 11, 12); 1943 (1, 2, 3, 4, 5, 6, 7, 8, 10, 12); 1944 (2, 6); 1945 (4, 10, 12); 1946 (5, 7, 9, 11); 1947 (1, 3, 7, 9, 10, 11, 12); 1948 (2, 4, 5, 7, 11, 12); 1949 (2, 7, 8); 1950 (3, 4, 5, 7); 1951 (1, 3)

FTC: 1966 (7); 1968 (10); 1969 (4)

OW: 1950 (1)

SALTER, GEORGE (1897–1967) American artist. Born in Bremen, West Germany, Salter moved to Berlin with his family as a child. He studied at the Municipal School of Arts and Crafts in Charlottenburg from 1919 through 1921. From 1921 through 1927 he worked in stage and costume design, beginning work as a graphic designer in 1927. From 1931 through 1934 he served as the director of the commercial art division of the Graphic Arts Academy of Berlin.

In 1934 Salter moved from Germany to the United States and, almost immediately, was hired by Simon and Schuster to design jackets for several of its books. During the rest of his career, he designed more than six hundred covers for all of the major hardcover publishers.

In 1938 Salter began a long association with Mercury Publications. He served as art director there and designed the covers, lettering, logos, and typography for all magazines published by Mercury. In this capacity, he entered the science fiction field in 1949, when Mercury began publishing *Fantasy & SF* (originally *The Magazine of Fantasy* but with a quick title change after the first issue). At first, Salter did some cover illustration as well as cover design. His covers were unusual, stylistic pieces that resembled nothing else published before in the science fiction field. They gave F&SF a distinctive and much more dignified look than any magazine ever done. Soon other artists took over the cover assignments, but Salter remained as art editor until 1958. He also served as art director for *Venture Science Fiction*.

Salter was known primarily in the art field as a great calligrapher. He taught at Cooper Union in New York from 1937 through 1967 and was extremely influential in the book and magazine design field. He died in New York in 1967.

PUBLISHED WORK:

HC: *Adventures in Time & Space* (46)

F&SF: 1950 (winter, spring, summer, fall); 1951 (4, 10, 12); 1952 (4); 1955 (5); 1966 (2)

SANJULIAN, MANUEL (b. June 24, 1941) Spanish artist. Born in Barcelona, Spain, Sanjulian sold his first professional artwork in 1964 and has done more than one thousand paintings since then. Much of his early art was for Warren Publications, including covers for the horror magazines *Creepy*, *Eerie*, and *Vampirella*. He quickly moved on to the swords-and-sorcery field, where his full-bodied women and heroic men were in the Frazetta* style but not slavish imitations. Sanjulian did a great deal of work for nearly all of the U.S. paperback publishers including Ace Books, Berkley, Dell, and Jove. Much of his work has been in the historical adventure field and perhaps his most heralded artwork was the paperback cover for the best-selling *Name of the Rose*, which, although not fantasy, gave the artist free rein with its Middle Ages setting and theme to paint a fantasy-oriented mural of stunning originality.

PUBLISHED WORK:

PB: *Children of the Dragon, Conan, Conan and the Sorceror, Three Bladed Doom, Treasure of Tranicos, Worms of the Earth, Year's Best Fantasy Stories #9* (83), *Zarsthor's Bane* (78)

SAUNDERS, NORMAN (b. Jan. 1, 1907) American artist. Born in Minneapolis, Minnesota, Saunders and his family soon moved to a homestead in northern Minnesota and later to Roseau County, Minnesota. After high school, he took a mail-order art-study program. In 1928 he began working in Minneapolis for Fawcett publications. In 1934 he moved to New York and studied under Harvey Dunn at the Grand Central School of Art. At the same time he began painting covers for the pulp magazines as a freelance artist. Saunders produced art for nearly all of the pulp chains and was noted for his attractive women and fast action scenes. Although not noted as a science fiction artist, he did many science fiction and fantasy covers for pulps that featured occasional SF stories. Among his finest paintings were several done for the 1930s pulp, *Mystery Adventures*, for the science fiction adventure series featuring Zenith Rand, space adventurer, by Richard Tooker. Saunders also did some horror covers for the Ace Magazine pulp chain. Like many of the pulp artists, he worked incredibly fast and did nearly one hundred paintings a year. He produced an average of two paintings a week from 1935 through 1942.

Saunders served in the army during the Second World War. Afterwards, he returned to civilian life and continued to do pulp work. In 1948 he branched out into the paperback field and painted numerous paperback covers for all of the major houses, including Ace, Ballantine, Bantam, Dell, Lion, and Popular Library. Saunders was known for his western covers as well as his science fiction work. When the pulps died, he moved to the men's action field, doing work for *Male*, *Adventure*, *Argosy*, and many others. In 1965 he started working for the Topps Card company. Saunders was already a veteran of the nonsports card-illustration scene, having done the art for the famous *Mars Attacks* series of gum cards published in the 1950s. He did Civil War cards, Batman and Robin cards, World War II cards, and "Wacky Packs," a series of humor gum cards.

PUBLISHED WORK:

AMF: 1950 (2, 4, 7, 10)

AMZ: 1952 (1)

DYN: 1939 (4)

FFM: 1950 (6, 8); 1952 (8); 1953 (2)

FN: 1950 (3, 5, 9)

MSS: 1938 (8); 1939 (4); 1950 (11); 1951 (2, 5)

PS: 1942 (summer)

SSS: 1950 (3)

SAVAGE, STEELE (?-Dec. 5, 1970) American artist. Trained as a book illustrator, Savage illustrated classic textbooks and art volumes for many years. He first started doing science fiction artwork in the early 1950s, providing pulp art for Popular Publications. After an absence of many years from the field, he returned to paint a number of brightly colored paperback covers in the late 1960s. Savage died of a heart attack in his sixties.

PUBLISHED WORK:

PB: *Barrier World* (70), *Citadel of Fear* (70), *Golden Blood* (67), *Report on Probability A* (70), *Sorcerer's Skull* (70), *Well of the Unicorn* (67)

FFM: 1951 (1, 3)

SSS: 1951 (4, 6)

SCHELLING, GEORGE LUTHER (b. 1938) American artist. Schelling was a prolific black-and-white artist who did both interior work and cover paintings for most of the major SF magazines starting in the early 1960s.

PUBLISHED WORK:

AMZ: 1962 (5, 10, 11, 12); 1963 (1, 2, 3, 5, 6, 10, 12); 1964 (2, 3, 4, 5, 6, 7, 8, 9, 10, 11, 12); 1965 (1, 2, 3, 4, 5, 6, 8)

ASF: 1962 (5, 6, 7, 8, 9, 10, 11, 12); 1963 (1, 2, 3, 4, 5, 6, 7, 8, 9, 10, 11, 12); 1964 (1, 2, 3, 4, 5, 6, 7, 8, 9, 10, 11, 12); 1965 (1, 2, 3, 4, 5, 6, 7, 8, 9, 10); 1976 (5, 6, 9, 11); 1977 (3, 6, 7, 8, 9, 10, 11); 1978 (6, 11); 1979 (1, 2, 7)

FTC: 1961 (9, 10); 1962 (5, 7, 8, 9, 10); 1963 (2, 5, 6, 7, 8, 9, 10); 1964 (3, 4, 5, 6, 7, 8, 9, 10, 11, 12); 1965 (1, 2, 4, 5)

GXY: 1961 (10); 1962 (8, 10); 1963 (6); 1964 (10); 1965 (4, 6)

IF: 1962 (7); 1963 (1); 1965 (5); 1966 (5)

WOT: 1964 (8, 11); 1965 (1, 3, 5, 9)

SCHLEINKOFER, DAVID J. (b. 1951) American artist. Born in Philadelphia, Schleinkofer attended Bucks County Community College and then the Philadelphia College of Art. He sold his first illustration in 1974 and has been painting paperback covers ever since. He also has done editorial art for *Cue* and *Cosmopolitan* magazines.

SCHNEEMAN, CHARLES, JR. (Nov. 24, 1912-Jan. 1, 1972) American artist. Born on Staten Island, Schneeman studied at Pratt and other schools, graduating from the Pratt School of Art and Design in 1933. He had a solid art education and was well versed in drawing figures. His first science fiction illustrations were done for *Wonder Stories* in 1934, and he began working for *Astounding Stories* in 1935. When John W. Campbell, Jr., became editor of that magazine in late 1937, Schneeman became the chief interior artist for the pulp. He painted several covers but was noted primarily for his black-and-white interiors. His cover for the April 1939 issue of *Astounding* was the first of the astronomical covers for that magazine and set the tone for the use of such illustrations in years to come by artists such as Chesley Bonestell★ and Rick Sternbach★.

Working in the early 1940s for *Astounding* gave Schneeman the opportunity to illustrate many of the major stories for the first golden age of science fiction, and his art was closely associated with many of those works, including the Lensman novels by E. E. Smith, *Final Blackout* by L. Ron Hubbard, and many of Heinlein's short stories and novels. Schneeman's art was not the detailed stipple work of Virgil Finlay★ or the imaginative work of Hannes Bok★. Instead, there were flowing lines and a nice feel for background. Schneeman was excellent at drawing scenes with people instead of gadgetry, and his drawings were smooth and uncluttered. They blended well with the typical story being published in *Astounding* during the period.

Schneeman left the magazine in 1942 when he joined the armed forces. After the war he turned to full-time newspaper work, starting with the *New York Daily News* and then moving to *The Denver Post* and finally to the *Los Angeles Herald Examiner*. He moved with each newspaper job and thus ended up living on the West Coast. He did try to continue some science fiction work, but the problems of working across a continent were too much. His last art for *Astounding* was an astronomical cover done for the November 1952 issue. Schneeman, who was married and the father of three children, died after a long illness.

PUBLISHED WORK:

AMZ: 1947 (8)

ASF: 1935 (7); 1936 (1, 2, 5, 6, 7, 9); 1937 (8); 1938 (2, 3, 4, 5, 6, 7, 9, 11, 12); 1939 (1, 2, 3, 4, 6, 7, 9, 10, 11, 12); 1940 (1, 2, 4, 5, 6, 7, 8, 9, 10, 11, 12); 1941 (1, 2, 3, 4, 5, 6, 7, 8, 9, 11); 1942 (3, 4, 5, 6, 8, 9, 12); 1947 (6); 1950 (9); 1951 (9); 1952 (11)

StrS: 1940 (4)

UK: 1939 (9); 1940 (1, 5, 8, 10); 1941 (2, 4, 6, 8, 10)

SCHOENHERR, JOHN (b. 1935) American artist. Although he rarely works any more in the science fiction field, Schoenherr remains one of the most highly regarded and popular of all science fiction artists. His work for *Dune* by Frank Herbert helped define and visualize that important novel for millions of readers.

Born in New York City, Schoenherr started reading science fiction with the Jules Verne classics in the 1940s. The Verne novels led him to magazine science fiction, and he became a regular *Astounding* reader by the time he was in high school. In school Schoenherr planned to be a biologist until his senior year, when he decided that "I enjoyed doing drawings of dissections and experiments more than doing the dissecting and experimenting" (*Algol* 1978). Like many New York area artists, he attended Pratt Institute in Brooklyn, where he was a classmate of Paul Lehr★.

At Pratt Schoenherr studied art with Stanley Meltzoff★, Fred Castilano, and Richard Bove. Major influences from the science fiction art field were Richard Powers★ and Edd Cartier★, both of whom Schoenherr felt often did work that outshone the books or stories they illustrated. Other influences included Degas, Hokusai, Vermeer, Tanguy, Roger Vanderwiden, and Andrew Wyeth. While at Pratt Schoenherr did a great deal of wildlife art as class assignments, and later his work doing such illustrations would serve him well.

After graduation Schoenherr worked for a brief time in a studio and then struck out on his own as a freelance artist. Having been a science fiction reader and fan for most of his life, he illustrated science fiction, selling his first piece of art to *Amazing* for twenty dollars late in 1956. During the next twelve years, he did a large volume of quality artwork for several paperback houses. Much of his early paperback art was in the surrealistic school and showed a strong influence of Richard Powers. After a while the Powers influence faded as Schoenherr developed his own style, using much more recognizable images although in a dramatic, often surrealistic setting. In the magazine field, he primarily worked for *Astounding*, which published many of his best interiors and paintings.

Schoenherr's excellent interior work was done primarily on scratchboard using dry brush, with fine details added by pen. He preferred using Ross scratchboard from Philadelphia until the brand was discontinued with the death of the maker. Schoenherr was an excellent draftsman who used a variety of texture to achieve a feeling of depth that is noteworthy in many of his paintings as well as his interiors. According to SF artist and critic Vincent Di Fate★, "Using large, looming shapes, dramatic back lighting and set against middle-value skies, Schoenherr's subject matter, organic or otherwise, often takes on the characteristics of animal life." Di Fate also described Schoenherr as having a knack for depicting scale, a talent that often added a great deal of drama to his best pieces, especially those done for *Dune*.

The animal images in Schoenherr's art reflected a lifelong interest in the outdoors and wildlife. While still working in the science fiction field, Schoenherr was approached about doing the illustrations for a children's wildlife novel, *Rascal*. This was the first of a long series of such books including the classic *Gentle Ben*, which eventually led Schoenherr out of science fiction. The better paying wildlife art market and a growing sense of dissatisfaction with science fiction art prompted the move. As the artist himself put it in an interview in *Algol* in 1971, "I got out of science fiction painting because I can't stand mediocrity and for the most part . . . there's no space for anything really good. There's no budget for anything really good." After leaving science fiction art for several years, Schoenherr returned in the early 1970s and continued to work again in the genre for several years until he again departed for more profitable areas of work.

Schoenherr and his wife, Judy, live on a twenty-acre farm in New Jersey. They are parents of two children, Jennifer and Ian. Even now, with only a few rare pieces appearing in the science fiction field from time to time, Schoenherr remains one of the most highly regarded artists to have worked in the genre in the past twenty-five years. He was nominated eleven times for a Hugo Award and won the honor once, in 1965.

PUBLISHED WORK:

PB: *4 for the Future* (62), *Anything Tree* (70), *Battle of Forever*, *Best from F&SF 5*, *The Bird of Time*, *Black Mountains* (71), *Bogey Men* (63), *Bow Down to Nul*, *Catch a Falling Star* (65), *Catseye*, *Children of Tomorrow* (70), *Dune* (65), *Earth War* (63), *Encounter* (62), *Flying Eyes* (62), *Galactic Patrol* (64), *Ghoul Keepers* (61), *Green Millenium* (69), *Green Planet* (61), *Herod Men*, *Kar Kaballa* (69), *Man Who Wanted Stars* (65), *More Macabre*, *Night Monsters* (69), *Orbit Unlimited* (61), *Our Friends from Frolix 8*, *Planet Strappers* (61), *Radio Planet*, *Space Barbarians* (64), *Space Opera* (65), *Supermind* (63), *The Unexpected* (61), *Unknown* (63), *Unknown Five* (64), *We the Venusians*, *Weapon Shops of Isher*, *Where Is the Bird of Fire* (70)

AMZ: 1957 (2, 5, 6, 8, 9); 1958 (6, 7); 1959 (2); 1963 (8)

ASF: 1958 (6, 7, 10, 11); 1959 (1, 2, 4, 7); 1960 (4, 5, 6, 7, 8, 9, 10, 11, 12); 1961 (1, 2, 3, 4, 5, 6, 7, 8, 9, 10, 11, 12); 1962 (1, 2, 3, 4, 5, 6, 7, 8, 9, 10, 11, 12); 1963 (1, 2, 3, 4, 5, 6, 7, 8, 10, 11, 12); 1964 (1, 2, 3, 4, 5, 6, 7, 8, 9, 10, 11); 1965 (1, 2, 3, 4, 5, 6, 7, 8, 9, 10, 11); 1966 (2, 3, 4, 5, 6, 7, 8, 9, 10, 11); 1967 (3, 4, 5, 6, 7, 8, 10, 12); 1968 (1, 9, 10); 1971 (9, 10, 11); 1972 (1, 2, 3, 4, 6, 7, 8, 9, 10, 11); 1973 (1, 2, 3, 5, 6, 8, 9, 10, 12); 1974 (2, 4, 7, 8, 9, 11); 1975 (1, 2, 3, 4, 5, 6, 7, 8, 9, 12); 1976 (1, 2, 3, 4, 5, 8, 9, 10, annual); 1977 (2, 3, 6)

F&SF: 1959 (4, 5)

FTC: 1957 (3, 4, 5, 6, 7); 1958 (11)

INF: 1957 (6, 7, 9, 10, 11); 1958 (1, 4, 8)

SAT: 1957 (6)

SFA: 1958 (1, 3)

VEN: 1957 (9, 11); 1958 (3, 5)

SCHOMBURG, ALEX (b. May 10, 1905) American artist. Schomburg is not only the oldest active science fiction artist but also is the only science fiction artist whose career spans six decades. His first published science fiction art appeared in 1925, and he is still active today.

Schomburg, the youngest of four brothers, was born in Puerto Rico in 1905 of a German father and Spanish mother. His entire family moved to the United States in 1912. He attended school in New York City, where it was noticed that he had artistic talent; he then received private art instruction from a German artist and teacher.

In 1923, along with his three older brothers, Schomburg opened an art studio in midtown Manhattan. Their agency was successful, having for clients General Electric, Westinghouse, Sanka Coffee, Great Northern Railroad, and many others. They also did window displays featured on Fifth Avenue and in Grand Central Station.

In 1925 Schomburg was introduced to the world of science fiction by Hugo Gernsback, for whom he worked for a period of more than forty years. His earliest artwork for Gernsback included covers for *Science and Invention* and *Electrical Experimenter*. He also painted more than fifty covers for *Radio Craft*, also published by Gernsback. These magazines, published before the birth of *Amazing Stories*, featured science fiction stories and articles on future science possibilities illustrated by Schomburg.

In 1928 Schomburg married and had two children, Richard and Diana. In 1930 he and his brothers dissolved their art studio, and all went freelance. Schomberg then took a job with a film company in New York but still continued to do magazine illustration as well as general magazine art. Both he and his brother August were well-known pulp illustrators, doing many works of war and aviation art as well as science fiction. Schomburg did a great deal of art for Standard magazines, and he remains good friends with Monroe Ettinger, who edited many of the Standard pulps. He did artwork for many astrology magazines of the period and also worked a great deal in the comic field, painting many covers for Marvel Comics in the early 1940s, works that since have become collectors items. Among comic collectors, Schomburg is considered one of the finest of the artists from the golden age of comics.

The 1950s were Schomburg's most prolific period as a science fiction illustrator. He did a great deal of work using an air brush and was noted for his many paintings involving spaceships. He provided the endpaper illustrations for the Winston Juvenile hardcover series as well as many of the dust jackets for the books.

In 1954 Schomburg moved from the East to West Coast. Illustrating became much more difficult because of the long distances involved. Eventually, most of the magazines publishing SF died, and Schomburg found that there was just not that much work other than paperback covers, so in 1967 he semiretired from the science fiction field.

Some years later, Schomburg returned to science fiction when he was assigned the production design of Stanley Kubrick's film *2001*. As art directors ralized that a longtime professional was still available to do artwork, more assignments began to come in, and Schomburg's art was suddenly appearing again on magazine covers.

All of Schomburg's paintings are done in watercolor and tempera with the air brush, and he makes highly detailed roughs before preparing the finished piece. He works on heavy-weight illustration board, and interiors are done in pen and ink.

In 1962 Schomburg was nominated for the Hugo Award as Best Science Fiction Artist. In 1978 he received the Doc Smith Lensman Award, and in 1984 he was awarded the Frank R. Paul Award for his work in the field.

His personal favorite among all of his art is the January 1978 cover for *Analog*, showing a space station with a space shuttle arriving. This was done well before the time of the first NASA shuttle.

A grandfather, Schomburg is still active in science fiction at age eighty in a career that began before there was a magazine solely devoted to the genre. A modest man, he remarked that "I feel very fortunate to be still around to do science fiction art since most of the small group that dominated that field in the 1950s are now gone. Friends like Frank R. Paul★, Earle Bergey★, Virgil Finlay★, and Hugo Gernsback. Guess I am one of the last."

PUBLISHED WORK:

HC: *Danger, Dinosaurs* (53), *Islands in the Sky* (52), *The Lost Planet* (56), *Missing Men of Saturn* (53), *Mission to the Moon* (56), *Mists of Dawn* (52), *The Mysterious Planet* (53), *Planet of Light* (53), *Rocket Jockey* (52), *Rocket to Luna* (53), *Rockets to Nowhere* (54), *Secret of the Martian Moons* (55), *Secret of Saturn's Rings* (54), *Son of the Stars* (52), *Step to the Stars* (54), *Trouble on Titan* (54), *Vandals of the Void* (53), *The World at Bay* (54)

PB: *Best of Astounding* (78), *Earth's Last Citadel, Exile of Time* (64), *Judgment on Janus, Lord of Thunder, Time Axis, Well of the Worlds*

AMZ: 1960 (10, 12); 1961 (2, 5, 9, 10, 11); 1962 (2, 6, 8, 12); 1963 (11); 1964 (1, 2, 4, 6, 11); 1965 (8)

ASF: 1978 (1)

COS: 1977 (9)

DYN: 1953 (8, 11)

F&SF: 1953 (1); 1977 (3); 1978 (8); 1979 (6); 1980 (4); 1981 (1)

FTC: 1960 (11); 1961 (1, 3, 6, 9, 10); 1963 (11)

FSQ: 1951 (summer, fall); 1952 (spring, summer, Sept., Nov.); 1953 (1, 3, 5, 7, 9); 1954 (spring); 1955 (winter, spring)

FU: 1953 (6, 10); 1954 (7, 9, 11, 12); 1955 (1, 2, 3)

FUT: 1953 (11); 1954 (1, 3)

GXY: 1953 (4)

IASFA: 1978 (fall)

IASFM: 1977 (fall, winter); 1978 (3, 5, 7, 9, 11); 1979 (1, 3, 5, 6, 7, 8, 11, 12); 1980 (1, 2, 4, 6, 7, 9, 10); 1981 (1, 2, 4, 6, 8, 10, 12); 1982 (1)

RS: 1953 (7)

SAT: 1957 (2, 6, 10); 1958 (2, 10); 1959 (2)

SF: 1953 (1)

SF+: 1953 (3, 4, 6)

SFA: 1953 (7, 12)

SFQ: 1954 (5)

SpS: 1952 (10); 1953 (2, 4, 6)

SS: 1939 (5); 1940 (3, 9); 1943 (1); 1951 (7, 11); 1952 (4, 5, 6, 7, 8, 9, 10, 11, 12); 1953 (1, 2, 3, 4, 5, 10); 1954 (1, spring, fall); 1955 (summer, fall)

StrS: 1939 (2, 4, 6); 1940 (4, 8)

TWS: 1938 (4, 8, 10, 12); 1939 (2, 6, 8); 1940 (2, 4, 5, 11); 1941 (2); 1942 (4); 1944 (fall); 1951 (6, 8, 10); 1952 (4, 6, 8, 10, 12); 1953 (2, 4, 6, 8); 1954 (spring, summer, fall); 1955 (winter)

UNC: 1941 (4)

WSA: 1951, 1952, 1953

SCHULZ, ROBERT (1928–1978) American artist. Schulz was one of the early paperback artists whose work on the science fiction paperbacks of the 1950s was extremely influential on the changing nature of science fiction as well as the science fiction art field. Along with Stanley Meltzoff* and Richard Powers*, Schulz's work helped gain acceptance of science fiction through art as something more than pulp literature. Unfortunately, as is the case with many science fiction artists, Schulz received no recognition in the science fiction community when he was alive and is forgotten today.

Born in Cliffside Park, New Jersey, Schulz was confined to bed for several years because of a serious childhood illness. His parents encouraged him to draw and paint, and he devoted himself to an artistic career. he earned a degree in architecture at Princeton University, where he studied under Joe Brown and Alden Wicks. He served as art editor of *The Princeton Tiger* while attending school. During the summer Schulz also attended the Art Students League, where he met Frank Reilly. He studied with Reilly from 1948 through 1952 and later helped teach with Reilly at the Art Students League. Also studying with this famous teacher was Jack Faragasso*, who illustrated several early science fiction paperback covers, as well as a number of other artists who made their mark in paperback illustration.

Schulz began his career as an illustrator in the early 1950s. He illustrated paperback covers and men's adventure magazine covers. During this period he met his wife, Evelyn, and moved to Stockholm, New Jersey; he became the father of three boys. Schulz continued to produce paperback covers for the next fifteen years, and he painted many western covers, including a series of Zane Grey illustrations, for a reissue of that author's works by Pocket Books, which received a great deal of attention. Gradually, Schulz's name became well known as a realistic artist of the Old West, and in time he began to achieve some measure of financial success, enabling him to concentrate more on commissions for historical paintings and portraits.

Finally, in 1977 Schulz decided to embark on a project that he hoped would win him recognition as a major American artist. This was a series of paintings called "Man's Place in Nature," which featured stunning, large paintings, each of which was a commentary on science and the importance of man in the universe. While working on this series, Schulz died suddenly only three days after his fiftieth birthday.

Schulz brought to science fiction a strong sense of style and an attention to detail that was often missing in most pulp-style art. His men and machinery looked futuristic but also believable. His paintings were well executed and not garish. While strictly science fiction, they seemed respectable, especially when compared to most science fiction art being published during the early 1950s. His work helped bring a feeling of maturity to the young science fiction paperback field.

PUBLISHED WORK:

PB: *Caves of Steel* (55), *A Martian Odyssey* (62), *Operation Future* (55), *Operation Outer Space* (57), *Sentinels from Space* (53), *Space Tug* (54), *Sword of Rhiannon* (53)

SCOTT, HAROLD WINFIELD (?-Nov. 16, 1977) American artist. A graduate of Pratt, Scott was a contemporary of Walter Baumhofer and Rudolph Belarski★. He did a great deal of magazine artwork and was noted for his western pulp covers done for Street & Smith. Like many Pratt graduates, he returned to teach at Pratt and steered a number of artists to the pulps as a source of income during the later years of the Depression. Edd Cartier★ was one of those students. Scott was friends with John Fleming Gould★, who also taught at Pratt during the same period. Scott's main importance to the science fiction art field was as a major influence on new artists, although he also produced several excellent fantasy paintings for Street & Smith's *Unknown*.

PUBLISHED WORK:

UK: 1939 (3, 5, 6, 7, 9); 1940 (1)

SENF, CURTIS C. (1879–1948) American artist. A successful commercial artist, Senf began illustrating for *Weird Tales* magazine in 1927. During the next five years, until early 1932, he contributed forty-five cover paintings and several hundred black-and-white illustrations to that publication. When he left the pulps, he returned to commercial illustration and was a highly regarded advertising artist until his death in 1948.

Senf was a competent craftsman and was technically able, thus a great improvement over Andrew Brosnatch* and other early illustrators for *Weird Tales*. However, he was much more comfortable painting normal people than degenerate humans or unmentionable horrors. Many of Senf's paintings featured characters in eighteenth- and nineteenth-century clothing, characteristic of a period that he believed highlighted his best work.

Senf's greatest problem as an illustrator for the pulp magazines was that he did not read the stories he illustrated. This was common practice for many magazine illustrators: the artist would just open to a page of the manuscript and pick a description or paragraph that sounded worthwhile. This method worked fine for detective or western stories but not so well for weird fiction. Senf was not a fantasy fiction fan, and his ignorance of the genre was often evident in his art. In 1931 he did the art for the serial *The Horror from the Hills* by Frank Belknap Long. In a passage near the beginning of the novel, Long stated that the hideous octopoid monster of the title had a "trunk like an elephant." Senf latched onto that one line, and his illustration for the novel featured a man dead at the base of a statue of an elephant.

Surprise endings never seemed to worry Senf either. In illustrating H. P. Lovecraft's "Whisperer in Darkness," Senf's art for the story revealed the surprise ending of the story in the illustration accompanying the title page of the work. Not surprisingly, among *Weird Tales* contributors, Senf was known as the "Master Assassin."

PUBLISHED WORK:

WT: 1927 (3, 4, 5, 6, 7, 9, 10, 11); 1928 (1, 2, 3, 4, 5, 6, 7, 8, 9, 10, 11); 1929 (1, 3, 4, 5, 7, 8, 9, 10, 11); 1930 (1, 3, 4, 5, 7, 8, 9, 10, 11); 1931 (1, 2, 4, 6, 8, 9, 10, 11, 12); 1932 (1, 2, 3, 4, 5, 6, 7)

SETTLES, JAMES B. (?) American artist. Settles was a Chicago artist who worked as a member of the Ziff-Davis art staff in the 1940s. Primarily a cover artist, he produced a number of back covers for both *Amazing* and *Fantastic Adventures*, and did a few interior black-and-white illustrations for Ziff-Davis, but those pieces were much inferior to his color work. Settles was an imaginative painter and was especially good at depicting unusual machinery.

PUBLISHED WORK:

AMZ: 1942 (5, 6, 7, 8, 9, 10, 11, 12); 1943 (1, 3, 7, 9, 11); 1944 (3, 5, 12); 1945 (6, 9, 12); 1946 (2, 5, 6, 7, 8); 1947 (11); 1948 (1, 2, 3, 4, 5, 7, 10); 1950 (12); 1951 (4); 1966 (6, 8)

FA: 1944 (2); 1945 (1, 4); 1946 (11); 1947 (11, 12); 1948 (2, 4, 5); 1949 (6, 7); 1950 (11)

FTC: 1966 (1)

OW: 1951 (1, 9)

SEWELL, AMOS (1901–1983) American artist. Along with John Newton Howitt*, Sewell dominated the pages of Popular Publications weird horror magazines of the 1930s. Whereas Howitt was master of cover art, Sewell controlled the interior illustrations, doing nearly all of the black-and-white art for publications such as *Horror Stories*, *Terror Tales*, and *Dime Mystery*.

Sewell was born in San Francisco and studied nights at the California School of Fine Arts while working days for a bank. After doing this for some time, he decided to try his luck as an illustrator on the East Coast. Having no funds, he shipped out as a sailor on a lumber boat going east by way of the Panama Canal.

In New York Sewell studied at the Art Students League and at the Grand Central School of Art. Going to school part time and at night, Sewell worked for the pulps doing black-and-white dry-brush illustrations primarily for Popular Publications. He had a fine touch for horror: his women looked properly innocent and terrified; his heroes were tall and heroic; and his monsters and deformed villains perfectly matched the horrors that Howitt depicted on the covers of the same magazines.

In 1937 Sewell landed an assignment with *Country Gentleman*, and soon he began getting work from *The Saturday Evening Post*. Sewell left the pulps for the better paying, more prestigious markets and soon became one of the *Post*'s most popular cover artists. In contrast to the impression he created with his early pulp horror art, Sewell became known for his talent for homespun, rural art, and his love of children. Winner of numerous awards from the Art Directors Club of New York, Sewell died in 1983.

SHAPERO, HANNAH (b. June 25, 1953) American artist. The daughter of well-known Boston fine artist Esther Geller, Shapero originally wanted to be a professor of the classics. She did her undergraduate work at Brandeis and graduate work at Harvard. She has an MA in the classics/Greek and Latin but found that the academic world was not what she wanted.

Shapero had no intention of being an artist and had an eclectic art education. She first attended the DeCordova Museum outside Boston and then the Boston Museum School and finally the Boston University Art School. Early influences on her work were the nineteenth-century illustrators H. J.

Ford and Arthur Rackham and the pre-Raphaelites. Now she believes her strongest influences are the work of Paul Alexander★ and Vincent Di Fate★.

The decision of what to illustrate is usually made by Shapero's clients. She has done commercial art, interior art for magazines, book-cover art, and advertising art. Private commissions make up a high percentage of her work as do miniatures (fantasy portraits of people in special garb or in fantasy backgrounds). She has done a number of pieces for the Darkover series and has become known as the unofficial Darkover artist. Shapero works in acrylics, although her first sale was a watercolor miniature.

Shapero sees her work moving from pure fantasy to art with architectural overtones, as with a spaceship. Even now, when possible, she likes to put buildings into whatever she draws. Eventually, she believes she might become an architect but knows that she will always be involved in fantasy art, which is still one of her prime interests.

PUBLISHED WORK:

PB: *Hawkmistress* (82), *Home Sweet Home 2010, The Monitors, Sharra's Exile, Sword of Chaos, Thendara House*

SHAW, BARCLAY (b. 1949) American artist. Born in Bronxville, New York, Shaw attended Trinity College in Hartford, Connecticut, graduating with a BA in philosophy of religion in 1972. He then worked for New York sculptor Joseph MacDonnell for two years. Shaw returned to Hartford in 1974 to do his own sculptures. In 1975 he moved to Aspen, Colorado, but in 1976 returned to Boston, where he worked as a woodworker with the Charles Webb Furniture company.

Shaw returned to school full time in 1977 as a student in the New England School of Art and Design. It was there that he worked with Bob Stewart, who pointed him toward the science fiction field. Shaw began doing science fiction illustrations while working part time for an ad agency and as a freelance photoretoucher. His earliest assignment included a number of illustrations for *Future Life* magazine as well as for several science fiction publishers.

In 1980 Shaw moved to New York looking for work. A week after his move, author Harlan Ellison took an interest in his work. Ellison was one author who made sure his work was illustrated the way he visualized it being done. Shaw was his choice for a major series of reprints done by Ace, a series that helped establish Shaw as one of the best of the new generation of SF artists of the late 1970s.

In late 1982 Shaw moved to Hastings-on-Hudson, New York, and he married Kathleen Lake in October 1983. As evidence of his popularity in the SF field, he was nominated for the Hugo Award in both 1983 and 1984. At present, he is working exclusively in the SF and fantasy field and "loving every minute of it."

For influences, Shaw lists H. R. Giger, the Vienna School of Fantastic Realism, and many others including van Eyck, Bosch, Rubens, Michelangelo, Durer, Waterhouse, Rodin, Parrish, and Rick Griffin, as well as styles such as photorealism, pop art, and surrealism.

As to method, Shaw stated, "I like to illustrate the feel of the story itself rather than a specific scene. Although I like a lot of action–oriented narrative illustrations, I am drawn to those covers that capture a mood or feeling in a strong simple way—without a lot of clutter. For something as small as a book jacket, a single strong element is often more effective than an involved scene and can capture the feeling of an entire book rather than a description of part of it."

PUBLISHED WORK:

HC: *Dr. Adder* (83), *Neuromancer* (86), *Night's Master* (84), *Robots of Dawn* (83)

PB: *Anvil of the Heart* (84), *Ariel* (83), *Ascendancy* (84), *Beast Who Shouted Love at the Center of the World, Cats Eyes* (82), *Clans of the Alphane Moon* (84), *Dark Fountain* (83), *Dawning Light* (81), *Dawning Light* (81), *Deadly Streets* (83), *Deathbird Stories* (83), *Dr. Adder* (83), *Dr. Bloodmoney* (84), *Ellison Wonderland* (84), *End of Eternity* (84), *First and Final Rites* (84), *Garden of Winter* (80), *Gentleman Junkie* (82), *The Glass Teat* (82), *The Gods Themselves* (84), *Healer* (83), *I Have No Mouth and I Must Scream* (83), *In a Lonely Place* (82), *Journey to the City of the Dead* (84), *The Long View* (84), *A Lost Tale* (84), *Love Ain't Nothing but Sex Misspelled* (82), *The Man Who Used the Universe* (82), *Memos from Purgatory* (83), *Merchanter's Luck* (82), *Nine Tomorrows* (84), *No Doors No Windows* (82), *Not a Stranger* (83), *Not This August* (81), *The Other Glass Teat* (82), *Paingod* (83), *Partners in Wonder* (82), *Picnic on the Near Side* (84), *Poenultimate Truth* (83), *Regiments of Night* (82), *Rissa and Tegare* (84), *Rooftops* (82), *Scapescope* (84), *The Seren Cenacles* (83), *Shadow of a Broken Man* (82), *Shadow Singer* (84), *The Shrouded Planet* (80), *Songs from the Drowned Lands* (83), *Souvenir* (83), *Spiderkiss* (81), *Streetlethal* (83), *Technicolor Time Macine* (80), *Time out of Joint* (84), *Toyman* (81), *Transmutations* (82), *Voyager in Night* (83), *Web of the City* (82), *Wheels within Wheels* (84), *Where the Songtrees Grow* (82), *Who Needs Enemies* (84), *Young Rissa* (84), *Zap Gun* (84)

F&SF: 1979 (3, 7); 1980 (1, 3, 9, 10); 1981 (6, 8); 1982 (9)

GXY: 1979 (6, 9); 1980 (7)

SHEPPERSON, CLAUDE ALLIN (Oct. 25, 1867–Dec. 30, 1921) British artist. Initially a law student, Shepperson, who was born in Beckenham, Kent, became one of the most respected and popular illustrators of the late nineteenth century. He was equally adept as a draftsman in pastel and black and white or as a lithographer, an etcher, or a painter in oil and watercolor. He worked for most of the popular magazines, especially *Punch*, which regularly featured the "Shepperson Girl," who embodied complete aristocratic refinement. He specialized in outdoor scenes, drawn in a hazy and slightly elongated manner, and always managed to capture a genuine feeling for light.

A prolific book illustrator, usually of whimsical light fiction, Shepperson was the surprise choice (made by the editor of the *Strand Magazine*) to illustrate *The First Man in the Moon* by H. G. Wells. Although several of his drawings for the novel were satisfying (recalling the work of Sidney Sime*), Shepperson's approach to the commission was firmly tongue in cheek, in the same vein as E. Nesbit and E. V. Lucas, whose stories he was illustrating at the same time. This attitude is not known to have pleased Wells. If the story had been offered to *Pearson's Magazine*, it would undoubtedly have been been illustrated by the much more imaginative Warwick Goble*. Only one-fifth of Shepperson's illustrations appeared in the first book edition of the novel when published in 1901. He later did eight drawings for "The Country of the Blind" in 1904.

Elected a member of the Royal Academy in 1919, Shepperson died in December 1921.

PUBLISHED WORK:

HC: "The Country of the Blind," in the *Strand Magazine*, April 1904, eight illustrations; *The First Men in the Moon* (1901); *The First Men in the Moon* in the *Strand Magazine*, December 1900-August 1901, sixty-five illustrations

Richard Dalby

SHUSTER, JOE (b. July 10, 1914) American artist. Although his name is not well known to most science fiction fans, Shuster helped create one of the most important characters in the history of science fiction—Superman.

Born in Toronto, Canada, Shuster moved with his family to Cleveland, Ohio, in 1923. There he met Jerry Siegel, who wanted to be a writer. Together, the two science fiction fans published several early science fiction fan publications, their first being a booklet, *The Metal Giants*, reprinting a story by Edmond Hamilton from *Weird Tales*. While working on their fanzine, *Science Fiction*, the two boys read *Gladiator* by Philip Wylie and came up with the concept of Superman. Since both teenagers were fans of the pulps, it seems likely that the name "Clark Kent" came from Clark Savage, Jr. (Doc Savage) and Kent Allard (The Shadow).

Shuster studied art at John Huntington Polytechnical Institute and the Cleveland School of Art. In 1936 he entered the comic field working for National Periodicals, on its New Fun Comics. He illustrated strips such as *Dr. Occult, Federal Man,* and *Radio Squad.*

In 1938, after several years spent developing the character, Siegel and Shuster sold their first Superman story to National for $130. The strip appeared in the first issue of *Action Comics* and was an immediate success. Superman soon became the most popular comic-book character of all time.

Shuster had a blocky, primitive style that seemed to suit the strip *Superman*. His art was nothing special but seemed to appeal to the fans. He continued to draw the comic stories and the syndicated comic strip until 1947 but later dropped out of the comics industry and resurfaced only briefly during an extended legal battle with DC Comics over the rights to *Superman*.

SIME, SIDNEY HERBERT (1867–May 22, 1941) British artist. Sime was an artist of great originality whose best work was comparable to and often excelled that of Harry Clarke★ and Aubrey Beardsley. His meteoric career—rising from pit-boy to artist within a few years—made him a household name in London at the turn of the century. His fantastic and mysterious illustrations were published in all well-known weekly and monthly magazines of the time including *The Idler, Pall Mall, Ludgate, Sketch, Butterfly, Pick-Me-Up*, and the *Illustrated London News*. The illustrations were considered sensational at the time, and many of them were published without any text, their mysterious imagery apparently inspired by some private mythological world of the artist.

Sime was born in Manchester, England, and as a child worked first in a coal mine and then for a draper, a baker, and a shoemaker; finally, he was apprenticed to a signmaker. During that period, he attended classes at the Liverpool School of Art and won several prizes and a medal for his work at school. After finishing his course work, Sime became a freelance artist. In 1892 he began illustrating for the *Illustrated London News*, and in 1896 he became well known to the public for a series of caricature drawings done for theater criticisms.

In 1898 Sime inherited a small fortune from an uncle. Along with the money came a large house in Perthshire, Scotland. Sime married in the same year and began living half of the year in London and the other half in Scotland. Meanwhile, his popularity continued to increase; among his most popular works during this time were a series of humorous drawings about the happenings in Heaven and Hell, and he also did some fine illustrations for Mother Goose rhymes.

In early 1905 Sime was well known enough for William Randolph Hearst to offer him a position in New York. Sime took the job but returned to England after only a few months. The artist missed England and thought his future as an artist was in that country. After his return to England, he sold his house in Scotland and moved to a cottage in Worplesdon, near Wimbledon.

Lord Dunsany, the famous Irish fantasy author, was a central figure in Sime's life as professional collaborator, patron, and friend. Their long and harmonious collaboration began in 1905, when Dunsany approached Sime with an offer to illustrate his first collection of stories, *The Gods of Pegana*. Sime accepted the invitation and thus began a collaboration of artist and author that was to last for fifteen years. His designs for *Time and the Gods* were among the outstanding imaginative achievements of graphic art of the time.

Sime's work for other authors consisted mainly of cover designs and/or frontispieces. Among his best were those for Arthur Machen's *House of Souls* in 1906 and *The Hill of Dreams* by the same author in 1907. Sime also did fine work for William Hope Hodgson's *Ghost Pirates* in 1909.

When England entered World War I in 1914, Sime was forty-seven years old. He joined the Army Service Corps and was sent to the east coast of Britain but was released in 1918 in bad health. He then returned to Worplesdon and concentrated on painting. Sime did a number of other illustrations for novels by Lord Dunsany; unfortunately, though, printing costs had risen, and most of these pieces were never used in the published books. He had several exhibitions in 1924 and 1927 and then dropped completely out of the public eye.

In the latter part of his life, Sime became a recluse in his country house in Worplesdon. He died in May 1941. It was an inconspicuous end for a man once dubbed by the *American-Journal-Examiner* as "the Greatest Living Imaginative Artist."

Sime worked in lampblack, using a brush with a sponge. He also used india ink and a pen to draw his figures. His vast output was undoubtedly an important influence on many later fantasy and science fiction artists. Works like "The Flight of the Gods to Vallhala" and "The Ship Comes Home," both in the *Illustrated London News*, have rarely been excelled in the fantasy field.

PUBLISHED WORK (All British editions).

HC: *Bogey Beasts* (23), *The Book of Wonder* (12), *A Dreamer's Tales* (10), *The Gods of Pegana* (05), *The Ghost Pirates* (09), *The Hill of Dreams* (07), *The House of Souls* (06), *Sidney H. Sime* (1978), *Sidney Sime: Master of the Mysterious* (1980), *The Sword of Welleran (08), Tales of Wonder* (16), *Time and the Gods* (06)

Richard Dalby and Robert Weinberg

SMITH, MALCOLM (1912–1966) American artist. Born in Memphis, Tennessee, Smith, like many artists, always wanted to be involved in art from his earliest childhood. He started reading science fiction in the early 1920s with the serial version of *Taranno the Conqueror* by Ray Cummings, serialized in *Science and Invention* magazine. Smith bought the first issue of *Amazing Stories* when they were published in 1926. "A long, tall southerner," as described by one of his friends, Smith was an expert archer and participated in archery tournaments as a young man.

In 1935 Smith attended the American Academy of Art in Chicago for two years. He originally worked at being a display artist but, when he discovered how poorly it paid, became an illustrator instead. In 1940 Smith submitted a number of paintings for *Amazing Stories*, published by Ziff-Davis in Chicago. The art was accepted, and Smith began doing freelance work for the chain. When the publisher expanded its line of magazines soon after, Smith was hired as a member of the art department. He soon worked up to art director of the Ziff–Davis pulp line.

In 1948 Smith left Ziff–Davis and started his own studio. Soon he joined Bendelow and Associates, a group of commercial artists who worked in a huge cooperative studio. In the 1950s Smith became art director of *Other Worlds* and *Fate* magazine, returning to work for Ray Palmer, who had been editor of *Amazing* in 1940 and bought his first work.

Smith, who was married and the father of two boys, often used live models for his paintings. Once he had his whole family dress up in red pajamas, with his wife wearing a collander and his two sons wearing football helmets, while the family dog wore a red jacket and knit cap with an antenna sticking out of the top. A photo of the group served as the basis for a science fiction magazine cover. In the early 1950s Smith developed an unusual technique of color-dyed photo prints for covers that gave some of his paintings an unusual mix of the real and the imaginary.

In the late 1950s Smith did several hundred illustrations for the nonfiction book *Life on Other Worlds*. The book was for a major publisher, which had accepted it when a change in editorial staff suddenly forced it from the schedule. The art has never been published.

Smith started a clipping file in 1935 for reference help and had hundreds of thousands of newspaper and magazine clippings on every possible subject. This file was donated to the University of Alabama when Smith died.

PUBLISHED WORK:

HC: *Cloak of Aesir* (52), *Space on My Hands* (51), *Who Goes There?* (51)

PB: *Time Trap* (49), *Worlds Within* (50)

AMZ: 1942 (1, 4, 8, 10, 12); 1943 (8, 9, 11); 1944 (3, 5); 1945 (3, 6, 9, 12); 1946 (2, 7, 9, 11, 12); 1947 (2, 5, 6, 7, 8, 9, 11); 1948 (2, 7, 10, 11, 12); 1949 (1, 2, 12)

FA: 1942 (4, 5, 6, 8, 12); 1943 (2, 4, 5, 6, 7, 8, 10, 12); 1944 (4, 6, 10); 1945 (4); 1946 (5); 1947 (3, 7, 12); 1948 (1, 3, 4); 1949 (1)

IMG: 1951 (2, 4, 11); 1952 (3, 5, 12); 1953 (6, 7, 9, 10, 12); 1954 (6); 1956 (4, 6); 1957 (8, 12); 1958 (2, 4, 6, 8, 10)

IMGT: 1956 (3); 1957 (1, 3, 7)

OW: 1949 (11); 1950 (1, 3, 5, 7, 9, 10, 11); 1951 (12); 1952 (3, 4, 6, 7, 8, 10, 12); 1953 (2, 3, 5); 1955 (9); 1956 (4); 1957 (7)

SpTr: 1958 (7)

UNI: 1953 (1, 2, 3); 1954 (7)

SMITH, WALLACE (1887–1937) American artist. Both author and illustrator, Smith was perhaps the only fantasy artist ever to be thrown in jail for his work in the field. A Chicago-born journalist, newspaper artist, and author, Smith spent several years in Mexico, part of the time fighting with the forces of Pancho Villa.

In 1922 Smith illustrated Ben Hecht's privately printed erotic horror novel *Fantazious Mallare*. The exceptional pen-and-ink drawings by Smith were masterpieces of style and fine line work, very much in the tradition of Beardsley and Clarke. Unfortunately, the U.S. government did not feel that way. The Hecht book was judged obscene and suppressed, and Smith was prosecuted for obscenity and jailed. After his short tenure in jail, Smith turned in disgust from art and became a full-time writer. He was a financially successful author and moved to Hollywood, where he worked on a number of screenplays. He died of a heart attack in 1937.

Although Smith's books are now forgotten, his artwork for *Fantazious mallare* is still considered among the finest ever done in the fantasy field. He was a major influence on Mahlon Blaine, among others. Ronald Clyne issued a portfolio of Smith's art in the 1940s.

PUBLISHED WORK:

HC: *Fantazious Mallare* (22)

ST. JOHN, JAMES ALLEN (1872–May 27, 1957) American artist. Born in Chicago, St. John was the grandson of Hilliard Hely, a well-known artist of the nineteenth century. Hely's daughter (St. John's mother) also wanted to be an artist and traveled to Paris when her son was only eight years old, taking the boy with her. The young child was allowed to wander at will through the Louvre and other major art museums of Europe, and he began to sketch and paint before he could read or write.

St. John returned to America and began his formal schooling. His father tried to make him a businessman and, when the artist was sixteen, bought him a partnership with an experienced businessman. St. John protested and finally was sent west to live on his uncle's ranch in California. On a trip to Los Angeles, he met Eugene Torrey, a western artist, and they became fast friends. St. John immediately decided to become an artist and spent time the next several years traveling throughout the West, drawing and painting.

St. John moved to the East Coast in the waning days of the nineteenth century, working as a portrait painter in the New York area and also doing landscapes and nature scenes. By then he was a well-regarded society artist.

St. John moved to Chicago in the early years of the twentieth century. The artist lived in his own private studio in his native city, in a three-story artist complex known as "The Tree Studio." The special building was designed specifically for artists and combined living quarters and studio space. Each residence had a large studio with a skylight. St. John's apartment was on the first floor and had a private garden with a fountain. He lived there with his wife, Ellen, until his death in 1957.

St. John worked as an illustrator for the numerous publishing companies in Chicago for nearly fifty years. The first book he illustrated, *The Face in the Pool*, was published in 1904. It was the first of many works he would illustrate for the A. C. McClurg company.

Along with a busy career as an illustrator, St. John worked as an instructor of painting and illustration at the Art Institute of Chicago for twenty years. He later joined the faculty of the American Academy of Art, where he served as professor of life drawing and illustration.

St. John's first artwork of importance in the science fiction field was done in 1916, when he illustrated the first hardcover edition of *The Beasts of Tarzan* by Edgar Rice Burroughs. The book featured more than thirty black-and-white illustrations by St. John and a color jacket. He even did the lettering for the book, a tradition he was to continue for all of the Burroughs books he illustrated. In 1917 he was given the assignment of illustrating *The Son of Tarzan*. Again, the artist turned out more than thirty pen-and-ink illustrations, along with a color jacket and the lettering for the title page. When the A. C. McClurg company prepared to publish Burrough's third Mars novel, the art assignment was given to St. John, who was becoming known as the Burroughs artist. For *The Warlord of Mars*, he did a stunning oil painting for the jacket. It was probably the finest illustration done for any Burrough's novel up to that time. When McClurg made plans to publish the next Mars novel, *Thuvis, Maid of Mars*, St. John was again given the cover assignment along with a commission for ten full-page illustrations. He had then become the accepted Burroughs artist.

Burroughs was not the only author for whom St. John did book illustrations, but he was definitely the most famous, and his name became closely linked with the Tarzan author. St. John continued doing work for Burroughs novels into the early 1930s, mostly for hardcover editions, although he did a cover for *Bluebook* magazine as well, illustrating one of the later Tarzan novels. St. John also did jacket art for a number of other McClurg hardcover editions, including several science fiction novels by Ray Cummings.

St. John was an accomplished artist and did excellent work in all mediums. Most of his paintings were done in oils, but he also was adept in watercolors. His interior work was done in both pen and ink and in gouache. He also did interior art in pencil and charcoal crayon. He worked with large sizes, and many of his full-page wash paintings that were used as black-and-white illustrations in book form were twenty-two by thirty-two inches or larger. When St. John did the jacket painting for *Jungle Tales of Tarzan*, A. C. McClurg asked him to do a large painting so that they could use it on a tour to sell the book. The painting, of an eagle carrying Tarzan away, was four by six feet.

In the early 1930s Edgar Rice Burroughs formed his own publishing company to print his novels. Feeling that St. John charged too much for his art, Burroughs began using other artists, including some of his own relatives such as Studley Burroughs and John Coleman Burroughs*. By

1936 the last of St. John's art for the Burroughs company appeared in hardcover. Losing his best client, St. John tried to get started in the comic-strip field, producing a Sunday page based on the John Carter series. Nothing came from this attempt.

Living in Chicago, St. John was well known as an artist and art teacher. Looking for other assignments to make up for the loss of the Burroughs work, St. John found *Weird Tales* magazine being published in the city. He soon began doing covers for that magazine along with its sister publication, *Magic Carpet*. In late 1932 *Weird Tales* serialized *Buccaneers of Venus* by Otis Adelbert Kline, a fantasy novel very much in the Burroughs style. St. John was the obvious choice to illustrate the novel, and he did four covers for the serial.

Unfortunately, the artist soon found himself without assignments from the pulp. Margaret Brundage★ also began doing work for the same magazine in late 1932. Although St. John's paintings were much more fantastic than Brundage's, magazine editor Farnsworth Wright thought that sex sold better than fantastic monsters. Brundage was retained, and St. John was dropped from the covers. He later did a few *Weird Tales* cover paintings, but the magazine never became a steady source of income. An interesting sidelight of St. John's work for *Weird Tales* was that in doing cover illustrations for the pulp, he did his own lettering for the logo of the magazine. Even after they stopped using the artist for the covers, *Weird Tales* retained the cover logo style, and it became closely identified with the magazine.

In late 1940 Ray Palmer, editor of the Ziff-Davis science fiction magazines *Amazing* and *Fantastic Adventures*, bought a series of novelettes from Edgar Rice Burroughs to run in those publications. Ziff-Davis was located in Chicago and the company tried to have local artists do the magazine illustrations. Palmer, a longtime science fiction collector, immediately contacted St. John, who illustrated the Burroughs novelettes and continued to work for the two science fiction magazines throughout the 1940s.

St. John also continued to teach in Chicago throughout the 1940s and early 1950s. He did a few more paintings for Chicago-based magazines, including *Fate* and *Other Worlds*, during this period, and he sold a number of his originals to collectors visiting his studios. He died in May 1957.

With the revival of interest in Burroughs's work in the 1960s, St. John's name once again became famous. His influence on the work of Roy Krenkel★ and Frank Frazetta★ was noted and appreciated by modern fantasy fans. A commemorative volume reproducing much of his art also helped boost his reputation. Among older collectors, St. John was already considered one of the greatest of all fantasy artists. With the new attention accorded him, he became equally well known among younger fans and artists. His originals, always scarce, became prime collectibles and have been sold for thousands of dollars, making his works among the most expensive of all fantasy illustrators.

PUBLISHED WORK:

HC: *At the Earth's Core* (22), *Beasts of Tarzan* (16), *Brigands of the Moon* (31), *The Cave Girl* (25), *The Chessmen of Mars* (22), *The Eternal Lover* (25), *Jungle Tales of Tarzan* (19), *The Land That Time Forgot* (24), *Lost on Venus* (35), *The Mad King* (26), *Man Who Mastered Time* (27), *The Mastermind of Mars* (28), *The Monster Men* (29), *The Moon Maid* (26), *The Mucker* (21), *The Outlaw of Torn* (27), *Pellucidar* (23), *Pirates of Venus* (34), *Port of Peril, Son of Tarzan* (17), *Swords of Mars* (36), *Tarzan and the Ant Men* (24), *Tarzan at the Earth's Core* (30), *Tarzan and the Golden Lion* (23), *Tarzan the Leopard Man* (35), *Tarzan Lord of the Jungle* (28), *Tarzan the Terrible* (21), *Tarzan the Untamed* (20), *Tarzan's Quest* (36), *Thuvia, Maid of Mars* (20), *Warlord of Mars* (19)

AMZ: 1941 (1, 3, 4, 5, 6, 8, 10); 1942 (2, 3, 4, 7, 10, 11, 12); 1943 (9); 1944 (3, 9, 12); 1945 (3); 1946 (2, 7); 1947 (12); 1948 (4, 5, 9, 10 11, 12); 1949 (1, 3, 9, 11, 12); 1950 (11); 1961 (4R); 1964 (1R)

FA: 1940 (10); 1941 (3, 7, 11); 1942 (3, 7, 11); 1943 (3, 5); 1944 (2, 4, 6, 10); 1945 (1, 7, 10, 12); 1946 (2, 5, 7, 11); 1947 (5); 1948 (1, 4); 1949 (4); 1950 (12)

FTC: 1968 (8); 1972 (4)

OW: 1951 (6); 1952 (11); 1953 (2, 3); 1955 (11); 1956 (2)

ScS: 1953 (10); 1954 (2)

WT: 1932 (6, 11, 12); 1933 (1, 2, 4, 5); 1936 (10, 12)

STAHR, PAUL (Aug. 8, 1883-Jan. 6, 1953) American artist. A New Yorker all his life, Stahr was born in New York City and attended school in Yorkville, where he went to Morris High School. He studied at the Art Academy of New York and the Art Student's League, where he worked with George Bridgeman. He later was a pupil of John Ward.

Stahr started off painting posters for new Broadway shows. He often was sent to other cities to see shows that were starting on the road so that he could make sketches and get ideas for posters before the show came to Broadway. Much of his art was done while riding on trains.

During the First World War, Stahr produced posters for the Red Cross, the Liberty Loans, and the national defense. Afterwards, he turned to magazine illustrations and worked for *Life, Colliers, Harper's Bazaar*, and most other major magazines. He did a famous portrait of John Phillip Sousa on his last major tour.

Stahr did several hundred cover paintings for *Argosy*, the best-selling of all pulp magazines. He shared much of the cover duties from the 1920s and 1930s with Robert Graef*. Both men specialized in action covers and painted numerous science fiction covers illustrating major novels and novelettes by the top names in the science fiction field. Among the many serials Stahr illustrated were the following novels by Edgar Rice Burroughs: *Apache Devil* (28), *Lost on Venus* (33), *The Pirates of Venus* (32), *Tarzan and the City of Gold* (32), and *The War Chief* (27). Other important science fiction novels with Stahr covers included *New Worlds* (32), *The Phantom of the Rainbow* (29, and *The Snake Mother* (30).

As was often the case during this period, serials that were reprinted in book form used the same cover art from the initial serial installment. A number of Stahr covers thus also served as hardcover jacket art.

PUBLISHED WORK:

HC: *The Phantom of the Rainbow* (29), *Tarrano the Conqueror* (30)

PB: *The Face in the Abyss*, *The Metal Monster*

STANLEY, ROBERT (?) American artist. A prolific paperback cover artist who worked primarily for several companies in the 1950s, Stanley did science fiction artwork for those publishers as part of his regular art assignments. Thus Stanley became the cover artist for Beacon Books when that adult-novel publishing house did a series of science fiction reprints for Galaxy Publishing. Although he did not produce many science fiction paintings, due to the risqué nature of most of them, the art became favorites among science fiction fans and collectors. His first published science fiction piece was for the rare Dell dime paperback edition of Heinlein's *Universe*.

Stanley began providing artwork in the paperback field for Bantam Books in 1949. He switched to Dell in 1950 and worked for that company for nine years, doing both paperback art as well as magazine covers. During that period he did a great deal of artwork for Lion books and Beacon Books. He was credited as being one of the artists who helped develop "the Dell look" for paperbacks.

The artist often used used himself and his wife, Rhoda Rozenzweig, as models for his cover paintings. Other relatives also made it into his art. He was a member of the Westport, Connecticut, artists group.

PUBLISHED WORK:

PB: *The Deviates* (59), *The Male Response* (61), *The Mating Cry* (60), *Odd John* (59), *Pagan Passions* (59), *The Sex War* (60), *Sin in Space* (61), *Space Prison* (60), *Universe* (51), *Virgin Planet* (60), *A Woman a Day* (60)

STARK, JAMES (?) Scottish artist. Stark was the best of a small group of Scottish artists championed by *Nebula Science Fiction*, which was published in Glasgow. He first did some black-and-white art for the magazine but soon graduated to cover paintings. Editor Peter Hamilton featured Stark on his covers for nine issues during 1956 through 1958.

The artist's compositions tended to match his name, but his work had a pleasing color sense. The paintings often depicted futuristic cities, space travel, and manmade bases on airless satellites. They had the look of authentic hardware about them and were the very antithesis of standard pulp scenes.

PUBLISHED WORK:

NEB: (7, 9, 15, 17, 18, 19, 21, 22, 23, 26, 32)

Philip Harbottle

STEADMAN, EVAN TENBROECK (?) American artist. "Brock" Steadman was born in Northhampton, Massachusetts, and was brought up in northern New Jersey. He was first attracted to science fiction after seeing *The Thing* at age seven. In the fourth grade he read H. G. Wells's *Time Machine* and was hooked on science fiction. He also was a devoted "Star Trek" viewer.

Originally planning to become a marine biologist, Steadman was more attracted to art. However, several years ago he became a certified scuba diver, enabling him to continue as a hobby what he originally thought would be his profession. He studied printmaking at the University of Denver and illustration at the Parsons School of Design. He began working as a full-time commercial artist doing children's magazine illustrations, artwork for *The Saturday Review*, and advertising art. He also did paperback work, including some science fiction titles. In late 1978 he sold his first illustration to *Analog* and became one of the regular artists for that magazine. Steadman is fascinated by spiders and keeps a number of them in his studio/apartment.

PUBLISHED WORK:

ASF: 1978 (5, 9, 10, 12, yearbook); 1979 (1, 2, 6, 7, 8, 10); 1980 (1, 2, 3, 5, 6, 7, 8, 9, 10, 11); 1981 (2, 3, 3/30, 5, 6, 7, 10, 11, 12); 1982 (2, 3, 6, 7, 8, 9, 11)

DEST: 1979 (1, 4, 10); 1980 (2, spring, summer, fall); (winter, vol. 3#2)

IASFM: 1981 (8, 12); 1982 (1, 7, 8)

TZ: 1981 (7, 8, 9, 10, 11, 12); 1982 (1, 2, 3, 5, 8)

STEIN, MODEST (1871–Feb. 26, 1958) American artist. Another newspaper artist who made the transition into magazine and book illustrations, Stein did courtroom art for *The New York Herald* and *The World*. He began working for *The Argosy* and *All-Story Magazine* early in their history and painted a number of covers for important science fiction and fantasy stories. Among the many famous fantasy stories that Stein illustrated were "The Girl in the Golden Atom" (19), "The Radio Beasts" (25), and "The Man Who Mastered Time" (24). Stein also painted the covers for a number of Edgar Rice Burroughs novels including *The Bandit of Hell's Bend* (24), *At the Earth's Core* (14), *The Eternal Lover* (14), *The Lad and the Lion* (17), *Pellucidar* (15), and *The Red Hawk* (25). He later did Hollywood graphic portrait art. Stein continued to illustrate well into his seventies and even did a cover illustration for *Astounding Stories* in 1942 when he was seventy-one. He died at age eighty-seven.

PUBLISHED WORK:

HC: *The Bandit of Hell's Bend* (25)

ASF: 1942 (11)

UK: 1939 (10)

STERANKO, JAMES (b. Nov. 5, 1938) American artist. Born in Reading, Pennsylvania, Steranko was an overachiever in all fields he entered.
He worked as a stage magician and escape artist and became close friends
with Walter Gibson, author of *The Shadow* (also an expert on stage magic
and a notable magician). Steranko also was a self-taught artist and worked
part time as an ad-agency art director.

In 1966, while working as a movie illustrator and doing agency work,
Steranko entered the comic-book field, creating three comic characters for
Harvey Publishing Co. The three books were not successful, but Steranko
continued to work in comics. He soon was doing art and stories for Marvel
Comics and became one of the most acclaimed artists and writers in the
comic field. While working for Marvel in the late 1960s, Steranko branched
out into the science fiction illustration field, painting a number of well-
received paperback covers.

When pressure from meeting deadlines forced Steranko to give up his
comic work, he formed his own magazine, *Comixscene,* later changed to
Mediascene, which covers the movie and entertainment field. Also during
this period, Steranko painted twenty-three covers for Pyramid/Jove Books
in their program of reprinting *The Shadow* in paperback. Still friends with
Walter Gibson, Steranko was a perfect choice to illustrate this character,
who was on the borderland of fantasy fiction. In recent years Steranko has
devoted all of his time to his magazine and has done very little illustrating.

PUBLISHED WORK:

HC: *Warlocks and Warriors*

PB: *Ace of the White Death* (70), *The Bat Staffel* (69), *The Black Master* (74), *Charg
Monster* (77), *Creeping Death* (77), *The Crime Cult* (75), *The Death Giver* (78), *Double
Z* (75), *Fingers of Death* (77), *The Ginger Star* (74), *Gray First* (77), *Green Eyes* (77),
Hands in the Dark (75), *The Hounds of Skaith* (74), *Iceworld* (73), *Infinity One* (70),
Infinity Three (72), *Infinity Two* (71), *Kelwin* (70), *Kings of Crime* (76, 78), *The Living
Shadow* (74), *Lord of Blood* (70), *Master of the Dark Gate* (70), *Masters of the Pit* (71),
The Mighty Barbarians (69), *The Mighty Swordsmen* (70), *The Mobsmen on the Spot*
(74), *Mox* (75), *Murder Trail* (77), *Police Your Planet* (75), *Prisoners of the Sky* (69),
Purple Aces (70), *The Reavers of Skaith* (76), *The Red Menace* (75), *Return to the Stars*
(70), *The Romanoff Jewels* (75, 77), *Shadowed Millions* (76, 78), *The Shadow's Shadow*
(77), *Shores of Tomorrow* (71), *The Silent Death* (78), *The Silent Seven (75), The
Unknown* (78), *Warlocks and Warriors* (71), *The Wealth Seeker* (78), *Weird Heroes #1*
(75), *Weird Heroes #2 (75), Weird Heroes #3* (76), *Weird Heroes #7* (77), *Zemba* (77)

AMZ: 1969 (9)

STERNBACH, RICK (b. 1951) American artist. Born in Bridgeport, Connecticut, Sternbach was brought up in nearby Stamford. He attended the University of Connecticut for three years and then dropped out to learn directly through working in the field. He had been interested in astronomical art since childhood, and much of his art has an astronomical flavor. His first published art was done for *Analog* in 1973. Since that time, he has painted covers for all of the major magazines in the field as well as most of the major paperback and hardcover publishers. He has been nominated for the Hugo Award four times, winning it in both 1977 and 1978.

In 1977 Sternbach worked for the Disney studios for nearly a year. He also did some work for the Jet Propulsion Laboratory. In 1978 he was hired by Paramount Pictures to work on the *Star Trek* film, and he moved to California with his wife to concentrate on film and television work. In late 1977 he worked on *Cosmos*, done by Carl Sagan for Public Television. Sternbach has continued producing book and magazine covers in both the science fiction and the astronomical art field and is probably one of the best-known artists in the space-art field.

Sternbach works primarily with the air brush but also uses ordinary brushes. Most of his paintings feature astronomical scenes, with people and machinery playing only a small part of the total picture.

PUBLISHED WORK:

HC: *The Avatar, Manseed* (82), *Ringworld* (77), *Ringworld Engineers, A World Out of Time* (76)

PB: *Breaking Earth* (81), *Destinies* (winter 81), *Futures Past* (82), *Sector General* (83), *Tales of Known Space* (75), *Wrong End of Time* (71)

ASF: 1973 (10); 1974 (2, 10); 1975 (4, 6, 9); 1976 (2, 7, 8, 9, 12); 1977 (5, 6, 10, 12); 1978 (1, 4); 1980 (12); 1981 (1); 1982 (7, 12)

CSF: 1977 (5)

F&SF: 1974 (2); 1976 (4, 7); 1977 (2, 6, 8); 1978 (5, 9)

GXY: 1974 (1, 2, 5, 6); 1977 (3)

IASFA: 1979 (summer)

IASFM: 1977 (spring, summer, fall); 1978 (1, 3, 5, 7, 9); 1981 (5, 7)

IF: 1974 (2, 4, 12)

STEVENS, LAWRENCE STERN (Dec. 4, 1886–Jan. 7, 1960). American artist. Stevens was famous in the science fiction field for the work he did under the pseudonym Lawrence. However, although he was responsible for all of the black-and-white illustrations that appeared under this name (as well as those that appeared under the name Verne Stevens), many of the paintings credited to him were done by his son Peter Stevens★.

Born on December 4, 1886, in New York State, Stevens, like his contemporary Joseph Clement Coll★, was trained as a newspaper illustrator.

This was in a period before photos could be easily printed on newsprint, and illustrators were trained to produce quick and accurate sketches of important events with near photographic accuracy, using line work and stipple, that would reproduce by standard printing procedures of the time.

In 1914 Lawrence was sent by one of the major newspapers to cover the war in Europe. During his stay there, he met a girl in London, got married, and settled down in England. It was there that his son was born.

Lawrence moved back to the United States in the late 1930s, shortly before the outbreak of war in Europe. There was no longer a market for newspaper illustration, but the booming pulp market needed artists. Lawrence was already in his late fifties but began working for Popular Publications. He started doing interior illustrations for western, detective, and romance pulps and used the same photographic style that he used for newspaper illustration. The crisp, detailed line work was perfectly suited for inexpensive pulp paper. Lawrence was incredibly fast compared to most other professional artists; he could complete a full-page, detailed, black-and-white illustration in only a few hours. He was a perfect fill-in artist for other artists who might fall behind on their deadlines or not complete an illustration.

In late 1942 Lawrence was approached by the editors of Popular Publications about doing artwork for their science fiction magazines. In November 1942 "Stephen Lawrence," actually Lawrence Sterne Stevens, was credited for the cover art for its *Super Science Stories*. However, the December 1942 cover of its *Astonishing Stories* was also credited to "Stephen Lawrence," actually, Stevens's son Peter. For the next ten years, covers appearing under the name "Lawrence" were done by one or the other Stevens.

At the same time, Stevens illustrated interiors for the Popular science fiction magazines. Virgil Finlay* had been drafted in late 1942, and his interiors for *Famous Fantastic Mysteries* were important to the success of the magazine. Whereas Stevens's style was different from Finlay's, his work had a similar photographic detail, and he was capable of drawing the same sort of beautiful women that graced Finlay's best illustrations. When Finlay returned to illustrating after the war, Stevens was so firmly entrenched as an artist for the Popular science fiction magazines that the two men shared art assignments for the rest of the life of the magazine.

Stevens also branched out to other magazines, producing some fine art for *Thrilling Wonder* as early as 1943. However, a vast majority of his art was done for the Popular chain.

Evidently, Stevens finally retired in the early 1950s when he moved to Connecticut. One of the finest interior artists ever to work in the science fiction field, he died unnoticed by the science fiction community in January 1960.

PUBLISHED WORK:

AMF: 1949 (19); 1950 (2, 10)

AMZ: 1951 (9, 12); 1952 (2, 3, 5, 7); 1968 (11)

ASH: 1942 (10); 1943 (2, 4)

FA: 1951 (7, 8, 12); 1952 (4)

FFM: 1943 (9, 12); 1944 (3, 6, 9, 12); 1945 (3, 6, 9, 12);1946 (2, 4, 6, 8, 10, 12); 1947 (2, 4, 6, 8, 12); 1948 (2, 4, 6, 10, 12); 1949 (2, 6, 8, 12); 1950 (4, 6, 8, 10); 1951 (5, 7, 10, 12); 1952 (2, 4, 6, 8, 10, 12); 1953 (2, 4, 6)

FN: 1948 (3, 7, 11); 1949 (3, 5, 7, 9); 1950 (1, 5, 7, 9); 1951 (1, 4, 6)

FSQ: 1950 (spring, summer, fall); 1952 (spring)

FUT: 1951 (3, 7)

OW: 1953 (7); 1955 (5, 11)

SF+: 1953 (12)

SS: 1946 (spring, summer); 1947 (7, 11); 1948 (1, 3, 5, 7, 9, 11); 1949 (1, 3, 5, 7, 9, 11); 95: (1, 5, 7)

SSS: 1942 (11); 1943 (2, 5); 1949 (1, 4, 7, 9, 11); 1950 (1, 3, 5, 7); 1951 (1, 4, 6)

TWS: 1945 (fall); 1946 (winter, summer, fall); 1947 (4, 6, 10); 1948 (2, 6, 8, 10, 12); 1949 (2, 4, 6, 8, 10, 12); 1950 (2, 4); 1951 (4, 6, 8, 10, 12)

UNI: 1953 (3); 1954 (4, 5, 8); 1955 (10)

STEVENS, PETER (b. 1920) American artist. An unknown name to most science fiction art fans, Stevens was one of the most popular cover artists of the late 1940s. He was one of the finest cover painters ever to work for the pulp magazines and produced hundreds of excellent paintings in all genres before moving on to fine art.

Stevens was born in London, England, the son of artist Lawrence Sterne Stevens★. His mother was also an artist. Stevens studied art at the Royal Academy of London, where he met his future wife, Diana. When World War II threatened, he and his family moved to the United States. In 1941, at age twenty-one, he began a long associataion with Popular Publications as a cover artist.

Popular was the leading pulp magazine publisher in the United States at this time and produced a huge line of magazines ranging from western to detective to science fiction. Stevens was soon doing covers for the detective and adventure magazines. Like his father, he was an astonishingly fast artist and was able to do one painting or more a week. Along with Raphael De Soto★, Stevens dominated the covers at Popular for the next ten years.

In 1942 Stevens's first science fiction magazine cover art appeared. However, it did not appear under his own name. The December 1942 issue of *Astonishing Stories* featured a cover by "Stephen Lawrence." To fans, this was the same artist who had just done the cover for the November issue of *Super Science Stories*. However, the November cover was painted by

Peter's father, Lawrence Sterne Stevens, who also was working for Popular. Thus both artists used the same pseudonym to do covers for two different magazines.

Stevens's father began doing interior illustrations for the Popular science fiction titles, taking up the slack left by the departure of Virgil Finlay★ to the army. Stevens, meanwhile, continued to paint covers for Popular outside the science fiction field. In late 1943 his father began handling the cover art for *Famous Fantastic Mysteries* along with most of the interiors. But his father was over fifty years old, and there was only so much work he could do. So in 1946 Stevens began doing some of the covers for FFM, with credit going to the catch-all name "Lawrence." For the next four years, Stevens's father did all of the black-and-white interiors credited to "Lawrence" and a few of the cover paintings. Stevens, too, did twenty paintings under the "Lawrence" name, paintings that were highly praised in the science fiction field and thought to be the work of his father.

As Popular's science fiction magazines faltered, the work load decreased and Stevens's father was able to resume most of his painting duties. Stevens then continued to do covers for Popular, even after it dropped its pulps and concentrated mainly on *Argosy*, which had become a slick men's oriented magazine. Stevens also contribued art to the *Saturday Evening Post*, *American Weekly*, and other magazines.

In 1959 Stevens's illustration for a Hugh Cave story,"The Mission," featuring a young island girl, Yolanda, received the most mail ever for any illustration done for the *Post*. It was a sign of things to come. Stevens turned to fine-art and portrait painting and became a successful gallery artist. The Stevenses live in New York State, where he designs theater scenery and is a pianist, composer, and licensed pilot.

PUBLISHED WORK:

AMF: 1949 (12)

ASH: 1942 (12)

FFM: 1946 (10); 1947 (4, 10); 1948 (4, 8, 10, 12); 1949 (2, 4, 6, 8, 10); 1950 (2)

FN: 1948 (9); 1949 (5, 7, 9); 1950 (1)

STINSON, PAUL (b. Sept. 5, 1953) American artist. Stinson has worked in the science fiction and fantasy field since the late 1970s. His earliest work appeared on science fiction calendars, but he soon branched out into book illustration.

PUBLISHED WORK:

HC: *Battlefield Earth* (83)

PB: *Jesus on Mars* (79), *Revenge of the Manitou* (79)

STONE, DAVID KARL (b. 1922) American artist. Born in Reedsport, Oregon, Stone served in World War II in the infantry, where he rose to the position of first lieutenant. He studied art at the University of Oregon and received the BA in fine arts. Afterwards, he studied at the Art Center at Los Angeles. For a year, he did sketchwork in remote areas of Mexico, maintaining a studio at Morelia, Michoacan, Mexico, and studying at the Universidad de Michoacan.

In 1949 Stone moved to New York, and on Valentine Day, 1952, he married his wife, Peggy. They have two daughters, Kelly and Jamie. His earliest science fiction artwork was done for *Galaxy* magazine in 1951, and he continued doing pulp illustrations for several years before leaving the science fiction field. Recently, he returned to science fiction, illustrating jackets for the Science Fiction Book Club.

Stone has had a varied career in illustration, producing advertising art, book-cover art, and magazine illustrations. He has designed several stamps for the post office and was commissioned to paint seventy portraits of the members of the International Aerospace Hall of Fame. His paintings are included in the permanent collection of the U.S. Air Force, the Smithsonian, and the Society of Illustrators. He served as president of the Society of Illustrators and has won numerous awards for his artwork.

PUBLISHED WORK:

HC: *Complete Enchanter* (75), *The Faded Sun: Kesrith*, *The Faded Sun: Kutah*, *Mission to Moulokin*, *The Stainless Steel Rat Wants You*

AMZ: 1952 (4, 6, 7); 1953 (4, 6)

BEY: 1954 (9)

FA: 1952 (6, 7, 10); 1953 (1)

FSQ: 1954 (winter)

FTC: 1952 (summer, fall, 11); 1953 (1, 3, 7, 11); 1954 (1); 1967 (7); 1968 (1); 1969 (4, 6, 8)

GXY: 1950 (10); 1951 (2, 4, 6, 8, 10, 11, 12); 1952 (1, 2, 4, 7, 11); 1953 (4, 10, 12); 1954 (2); 1955 (1, 4, 5)

GXYN: 1950 (1)

SS: 1954 (summer)

STOOPS, HERBERT MORTON (1888–May 19, 1948) American artist. Born in Utah, the son of a clergyman, Stoops was brought up in Idaho. He attended Utah State University and then went to work as a staff artist for the *San Francisco Chronicle*. He moved on to the *San Francisco Examiner* and then to the *Chicago Tribune*. While living in Chicago he attended the Art Institute of Chicago. In 1917 he enlisted in the army and served as first lieutenant in France with the First Division.

He began work as an illustrator after the war, doing both cover paintings and interior art for magazines. He produced some illustrations for *Colliers* and other slick magazines but is best remembered for his work for the major pulp magazines, especially *Bluebook*. He was a regular cover artist for that magazine for thirteen years and did many interiors for them as well, under both his own name and the pseudonym Jeremy Canon, which he used when doing black-and-white dry-brush illustrations. He served as president of the Artists Guild in New York and belonged to several other artist organizations. Stoops also held an honorary membership in the New York Association of Veterans of the French Foreign Legion.

In the science fiction-fantasy field, Stoops illustrated many of the fantastic adventure stories that ran in *Bluebook* including the Kioga series, "The New Stories of Tarzan" (twelve stories that formed the book *Jungle Tales of Tarzan*) and "Tarzan's Quest."

STOUT, WILLIAM (b. Sept. 19, 1949) American artist. Born in Salt Lake City, Utah, Stout decided in high school that he wanted to be a doctor. However, on switching schools in his junior year, he found his new school such a bad experience that he could not imagine attending school all the years required for a medical degree. He won a California State Scholarship and became an illustration major at the Couinard Art School, California Institute of the Arts. In lieu of homework, he was allowed to turn in professional work, so in his sophomore year Stout did the covers for the first four issues of *Coven 13* magazine.

Stout is married to an actress who is studying to be a nurse. Since 1972 he has had a number of different jobs in the art field and thus has had what he describes as a "pinball career" bouncing from job to job. His assignments have included doing the artwork for *The Dinosaurs*, a heavily illustrated book on prehistoric reptiles, illustrating *Dinosaur Tales* by Ray Bradbury, providing poster art for the movie *Wizards*, serving as concept designer for the remake of the film *Invaders from Mars*, and handling many other projects in the science fiction and comic-book field.

Stout was influenced by nineteenth-century children's book artists including Rackham, Dulac, Detbolt, and J. C. Lyendecker. Modern artists who had an impact on him include Frank Frazetta* and Mobius.

Stout works in both watercolors and oils and views each assignment as a problem to be solved. He uses watercolors for light or whimsical work, with oils for more thoughtful or deeper projects. In all cases, the artist believes the subject dictates the solution.

PUBLISHED WORK:

HC: *The Dinosaurs*

PB: *Dinosaur Tales, The Dinosaurs*

COVEN 13: 1969 (9, 11); 1970 (1, 3)

SULLIVAN, EDMUND JOSEPH (1869–April 17, 1933) British artist. This distinguished British artist was H. G. Wells's favorite among the many who illustrated his work in books and magazines. Sullivan's exceptionally vigorous pen-and-ink drawings contained inventive and often bizarre imagery that could be simultaneously witty and macabre. After studying with his father, artist Michael Sullivan, Edmund Sullivan soon became one of the most innovative and original of the black-and-white illustration artists of the 1890s.

Sullivan's brilliant series of illustrations for *A Story of the Days to Come* by H. G. Wells portrayed the world during the last decade of the twenty-first century. The illustrations were published in five issues of the *Pall Mall Magazine* in 1899, running from June through October of that year. Each installment of the novel featured four illustrations by Sullivan. His first piece showed "the great machine that had come flying through the air from America, " a huge airship with separate tiers of sails, each hundreds of feet wide. The "day's labor" in the installment titled "The Ways of the City" predated similar scenes in Fritz Lang's movie *Metropolis*. In 1903 Sullivan also illustrated another fantastic tale, "The Tomb of Sarah,"by F. G. Loring, in *Pall Mall Magazine*. In 1905 Sullivan returned to art for works of Wells, when he illustrated the first edition of *A Modern Utopia*.

Later in his career, Sullivan wrote books on art and lectured on book illustration and lithography at Goldsmith's College. He became president of the Art Worker's Guild in 1931 and died in April 1933.

PUBLISHED WORK:

HC: *A Modern Utopia* (05)

SUMMERS, LEO RAMON (June 9, 1925–Apr. 1, 1985) American artist. Born in Los Angeles, Summers served in World War II and, afterwards, attended the Burnley School of Art in Seattle for three years. Although he was to be an artist for the rest of his life, he was color blind.

Summers joined the Ziff-Davis chain in Chicago in 1951 and soon became art director for *Amazing* and *Fantastic Adventures*. During this period the company relocated its offices in New York, and Summers moved with them. In 1952 Ziff-Davis started a new magazine, *Fantastic*, a digest-sized fantasy magazine, with hopes of featuring higher quality fiction and graphics. Summers was made art director of that publication as well. The early issues of *Fantastic* were among the most attractive visually of all science fiction magazines. In early 1953 *Fantastic Adventures* was killed by Ziff-Daivs, and *Amazing Stories* went digest size. It also was attractively packaged and illustrated under Summers' direction. But sales were not up to expectations, and cost-cutting measures for *Fantastic* and *Amazing* were soon in the works, dropping both the level of fiction and art. Summers left both magazines in 1956.

After his work for Ziff-Davis, Summers became a freelance illustrator, producing both science fiction art, book illustration, and advertising art. He also did some movie poster art. Summers continued to live in New York City and worked for all of the major science fiction magazines. Late in his career, he branched out and did some black-and-white comic artwork. In 1975 he was stricken with a brain seizure, and brain surgery was done in 1979. He died of brain cancer in April 1985.

PUBLISHED WORK:

AMZ: 1949 (11); 1950 (1, 2, 3, 4, 5, 6, 7, 8, 9, 10, 11, 12); 1951 (2, 3, 5, 6, 7, 9, 10, 12); 1952 (4, 5, 7, 12); 1953 (4); 1956 (11, 12); 1957 (1, 2, 11); 1958 (3, 4, 5, 6, 7, 9, 12); 1959 (4, 6, 7, 8, 9, 10, 11, 12); 1960 (1, 2, 4, 5, 6, 8); 1961 (2, 3, 5); 1962 (1, 4, 7, 8, 9, 11, 12); 1963 (2, 3, 4, 5, 7,); 1966 (2); 1969 (1, 3)

ASF: 1959 (1, 2, 4, 5, 8, 9, 12); 1960 (1, 3, 10, 12); 1961 (1, 8); 1962 (10); 1963 (4, 5, 6, 7, 8, 9, 10, 11); 1964 (1, 2, 3, 6, 10); 1965 (2, 3, 8); 1966 (3, 5, 8, 9, 10, 12); 1967 (2, 3, 4, 8, 9, 10); 1968 (2, 4, 5, 6, 8, 9, 10, 11, 12); 1969 (1, 2, 3, 4, 5, 6, 7, 8, 9, 10, 11, 12); 1970 (1, 2, 7, 9, 11); 1971 (1, 2, 3, 5, 6, 8, 10, 11, 12); 1972 (1, 3, 4, 5, 6, 7, 8, 9, 10, 11, 12); 1973 (1, 2, 3, 4, 5, 6, 7, 8, 9, 10, 11, 12); 1974 (2, 3, 5, 6, 7, 8, 9, 10); 1975 (6)

DW: 1957 (2, 5, 8)

FA: 1949 (11); 1950 (1, 2, 4, 7, 9); 1951 (1, 4, 6, 7, 9, 11, 12); 1951 (1, 2, 3, 4, 5)

FTC: 1952 (summer, fall, 11); 1953 (1, 5, 9); 1957 (2, 3, 4, 5, 7, 8, 9, 10, 11); 1958 (2, 3, 4, 5, 7, 8, 9, 10); 1959 (1, 4, 6, 7, 8, 9, 10, 11, 12); 1960 (1, 2, 3, 4, 6, 7, 9, 10, 11, 12); 1961 (1, 2, 4, 5, 7, 8, 9, 10, 11, 12); 1962 (1, 2, 3, 4, 5, 6, 7, 8, 9, 10, 11); 1963 (1, 2, 4, 5, 8); 1966 (3); 1967 (7); 1968 (12); 1969 (2, 6)

IF: 1954 (8, 11, 12); 1955 (2)

SWEET, DARRELL (b. Aug. 15, 1934) American artist. Born in New Brunswick, New Jersey, Sweet had been interested in the art field since he was little more than three years old. He received the BFA in painting from Syracuse University in 1956. As to major influences, Sweet points to the Brandywine School (especially Wyeth and Pyle), the Italian Renaissance, and the Dutch Renaissance. He also believes he has much in common with the great western painters Russell and Remington.

Sweet was doing realistic illustration for Ballantine Books when Lester and Judy-Lynn Del Rey were brought in to revitalize the Ballantine Science Fiction line. Sweet got along well with the pair who wanted an artist capable of doing realistic, believable fantasy illustrations. His first science fiction painting was *A Midsummer's Tempest* for Ballantine. He has remained with the Del Rey line ever since.

A prolific and extremely talented artist, Sweet does about twenty-five paintings a year for Del Rey. To maintain production, he often has two or three things in process at the same time. He works with the art directors and editors as a team, believing this is the best approach. Many times one book will be in the reading stage, another in trial sketches, and a third in final art. Research is all important to him, and he believes that by the time he gets to the painting stage, "lots of the headaches are gone."

Sweet originally worked in oils when he began his career, but they took too long to dry. When acrylics became more stable, he moved to them. They allow a style similar to oils but enable him "to function as fast as my head works." He uses an academic approach to all of his work. He believes that his paintings must fill certain criteria to be successful and, in all cases, believes the most important thing is that the painting sell the book. "If the publishing house doesn't survive, neither do you."

Sweet has learned that there are very literal people in the genre who are particular about details. Deviating four or five centuries on costume is okay, but the weapons always have to be correct. Another important guideline he follows is: "Don't disappoint the reader." First read the book and nail it down before you start; let the art show the type of book it is to the customer.

Sweet always looks at the technical side of every painting. He plans for the typography involved and treats each painting as a poster, making sure it catches the customer's eye. Before any work leaves his studio, he judges it on two things: art quality and integrity.

Although he has no favorite piece, Sweet likes many of the works he has done illustrating Piers Anthony's *Xanth* novels. He considers the stories to be charming and finds that working on the books "is a joy to do."

Since he approaches his paintings as a worker instead of a fan, Sweet believes he would like to be known as a working artist with a "hell of a track record." Because of this attitude, he has not locked himself into any particular category but has tried to do art in everything from hardware to fantasy: "It pays to be flexible."

Sweet, his wife, Janet, and his twelve-year-old son Darrell Roger live in New Jersey.

PUBLISHED WORK:

HC: *Fantasy Worlds of Peter Beagle* (78), *Heechee Rendezvous* (84), *Unbeheaded King* (83), *Unforsaken Hiero* (83), *White Gold Wielder* (83).

PB: *And the Devil Will Drag You Under* (79), *Beyond the Blue Event Horizon*, *Blue Star*, *The Cache* (81), *Camber of the Heretic* (81), *Castle Roogna* (79), *Curse of the Witch Queen* (82), *Dark Is the Sun* (80), *Demons of Dancing Gods* (84), *Doomfarers of Cora-monde*, *End of the Matter* (77), *Exiles at the Wall of Souls* (78), *Gaian Expedient*, *Giants Star* (81), *Harpist in the Wind*, *Heechee Rendevous*, *Heir of Sea and Fire*, *Hieros Journey* (83), *Ilearth War* (78), *Infinitum of Go* (80), *Ladies of Mandrigyn* (84), *Lord Foul's Bane* (78), *Lure of the Basilisk*, *Momoirs of Alcheringia*, *Merlin's Godson* (76), *Night Mare* (83), *Ogre, Ogre* (82), *Orphan Star* (81), *Power and the Prophet*, *Power That Preserves* (78), *Prophet of Lamath*, *Quest of the Wall of Sould* (78), *Return of Nathan Brazil* (80), *Requiem for a Ruler of Worlds* (85), *Riddle Master of Hed*, *River of Dancing Gods* (84),

Roadmarks, St. Camber (79), *Sorcerer's Son* (79), *Star Beast* (78), *Starfollowers of Coramonde, Vengence of Dancing Gods* (85), *Wizard in Waiting, Wounded Land* (81)

SZAFRAN, GENE (b. 1941) American artist. Born in Detroit, Szafran attended the Art School of the Society of Arts and Crafts there. He worked as staff artist for several Detroit studios, preparing automobile ads as well as doing some freelance artwork. He moved to New York City in 1967, where he was in great demand as a freelance artist. He provided artwork for *Playboy, Fortune,* and a number of other magazines, as well as for numerous paperback covers. His science fiction art was distinctive, mostly surrealistic and often using only one or two colors. For a number of years, Szafran placed high on many science fiction reader polls as best artist. By the late 1970s health problems forced him from illustrating, just when he was at the peek of his popularity in the science fiction field.

PUBLISHED WORK:

HC: *Second Trip* (72)

PB: *Beastchild* (70), *Corridors of Time* (71), *David Star, Space Ranger* (71), *Day after Tomorrow, Goat without Horns* (71), *Revolt in 2100, Space for Hire* (71), *Swords against Tomorrow* (70), *A Time of Changes* (71), *Time Masters* (72), *Timestop* (70), *Trullion Alastor 2262* (73), *Waters of Centaurus* (72), *Wolfwinter* (72)

TERRY, WILLIAM E. (b. Dec. 11, 1921) American artist. Born in Galesburg, Illinois, Terry attended Colorado College and then entered the Marine Corps with the outbreak of World War II. His left arm was injured at Okinawa, and he spent some time in the hospital recovering. Afterwards, he returned to Colorado College to complete work toward a degree. Terry also received art training at the Colorado Springs Fine Arts Center. In the late 1940s he got his first job illustrating for the Ziff-Davis chain. He began freelancing in 1950 and illustrated westerns, textbooks, and some comic-strip art; he also did commercial and advertising art. Based in Chicago, Terry mainly worked for magazines published in that city, including *Other Worlds* and *Imagination.* Like many artists who worked in the SF field in the 1950s, Terry stated that he liked the field because of the freedom he had to draw what he wanted and the lack of editorial interference with his creative process. He served as art editor for *Imagination* from January 1955 through June 1958 and for *Imaginative Tales* from January through July 1955.

PUBLISHED WORK:

AMZ: 1948 (10, 12); 1949 (1, 2, 3, 4, 5, 6, 8, 9, 10, 11, 12); 1950 (1, 2); 1955 (11); 1967 (10)

FA: 1948 (11); 1949 (1, 3, 4, 5, 6, 7, 9, 11); 1950 (1, 2, 3)

FTC: 1968 (3)

IMG: 1950 (12); 1951 (2, 4, 6, 9, 11); 1952 (1, 5, 7, 9, 10, 12); 1953 (1, 2, 4, 5, 6, 7, 8, 9, 10, 11); 1954 (1, 2, 3, 4, 5, 6, 7, 8, 9, 10, 11, 12); 1955 (1, 2, 3, 4, 5, 6, 7, 10, 12); 1956 (2, 4, 6, 8, 10); 1957 (2, 12)

IMGT: 1955 (1, 3, 5, 7, 9, 11); 1956 (3, 5, 7, 9, 11); 1957 (1, 3, 7, 11)

OW: 1950 (1, 3, 5, 7, 9 10, 11); 1951 (1, 3, 5, 6, 10, 12); 1952 (3, 4, 6, 7, 8, 10, 11, 12); 1953 (1, 2, 4, 5, 6)

UNI: 1953 (1)

THEOBALD, RAY (?) British artist. Theobald specialized in mass-produced mediocre covers for the numerous publishers of low-level science fiction that flourished in England in the 1950s. He produced work that was commensurate with the low rates of pay offered by Curtis Warren Publications and John Spencer Publications. Yet he was a talented artist who could achieve striking effects when he took his time. His female figures could be remarkably erotic, as evidenced on the covers for *The Land of Esa* and *The Queen People*, both published by Curtis Warren in 1952.

Theobold did all types of cover art, including western, mystery, and gangster stories as well as fantasy and science fiction. When the paperback boom in England came to an end, he drifted into comics, often working as a "fill-in artist." Probably his best work in this genre was "Mystery in the Milky Way," published in the *Rick Random* series in 1956. Theobald had little feel for science fiction and obviously little knowledge of the hardware associated with the fiction. Although he did numerous paintings in science fiction, it was the least of his production in the illustration field.

PUBLISHED WORK (All British publications).

PB: *Death Dimension* (52), *Galactic Storm* (51), *Gyrator Control* (51), *Land of Esa* (52), *Liquid Death* (53), *Ominous Folly* (52), *Para-Robot* (52), *Pirates of Cerebus* (53), *Planetfall* (51), *Planet X* (51), *Space Line* (52), *The Queen People* (52), *Titan's Moon* (52), *Trans-Mercurian* (52) *Twilight Zone* (54), *The Uranium Seekers* (53), *Worlds Away* (53), *Zero Field* (52)

OUT OF THIS WORLD: 1954 (10)

SUPERNATURAL STORIES: (1, 6, 9, 12, 13, 14, 15, 16, 17, 18, 19, 20, 21, 22, 23 24, 25, 26, 27, 28)

TALES OF TOMORROW: 1954 (summer)

WONDERS OF THE SPACEWAY: 1953 (fall); 1954 (winter, spring)

WORLDS OF FANTASY: 1953 (fall); 1954 (summer)

Philip Harbottle

THEYEN, RICH (b. Jan. 17, 1960) British artist. Born in Battersea, London, Theyen was the son of an artist/picture restorer. He studied at the High Wycombe College of Art and Technology in 1976–1977 and took up the "punk" cult, which he introduced to his artwork.

Theyen's early work included two strips for the comic *2000 AD* annuals in 1979 and 1980. In 1981 a chance meeting with Sydney Jordan brought him regular work on the science fiction strips. Since story lines were so varied, he was able to indulge in his love of high tech and the macabre within the disciplined confines of a daily strip. His work has ranged from the mysteries of Easter Island to alien visitors on Mars to a recent skirmish with the dreaded Cthulhu dreaming in his house in R'yleh.

Richard Dalby

TILBURNE, ALBERT R. (?) American artist. A New York-based illustrator, Tilburne did a number of covers for *Weird Tales* when it moved its editorial offices to New York City in 1938. A pulp cover artist who had done work for *Short Stories* magazine (owned by the same company that bought *Weird Tales*), Tilburne showed little skill in fantasy illustration. Along with his covers for the pulp, he did the uncredited cover for the 1947 Avon paperback collection *The Lurking Fear* by H. P. Lovecraft, the first mass-market appearance of a Lovecraft story volume. Tilburne was a well-known western American artist.

PUBLISHED WORK:

PB: *The Lurking Fear* (47)

WT: 1938 (11); 1942 (7, 9, 11); 1943 (1, 3, 5, 7, 9, 11); 1944 (1, 3, 5, 7, 9, 11); 1945 (1, 3, 5, 7, 9, 11); 1946 (1, 3, 5, 7, 9, 11); 1947 (1, 3); 1951 (5R); 1952 (9R)

TILLOTSON, JOSEPH WIRT (?) American artist. Tillotson was a staff artist for the Ziff-Davis chain of magazines when it was based in Chicago. After the publisher moved from the city, he continued to do some work for the new science fiction magazines published by Ray Palmer and Bill Hamling, based in the Midwest. Tillotson was a prolific artist who published work under both his own name and the brush name "Robert Fuqua." He used the Fuqua name for only his color work, whereas his black-and-white illustrations appeared under both names.

The artist attended Boys High in Chicago, where he was a classmate of science fiction writer Earl Binder. When they met some years later, Tillotson remarked how much he enjoyed painting the cover for Binder's story *I Robot*. Binder was surprised to learn that Tillotson and Fuqua were the same.

PUBLISHED WORK:

AMZ: 1938 (10, 11, 12); 1939 (1, 2, 3, 4, 5, 7, 8, 9, 10, 12); 1940 (1, 2, 3, 4, 5, 6, 7, 9, 10, 11, 12); 1941 (1, 2, 3, 4, 5, 7, 8, 9, 10, 11); 1942 (1, 2, 3, 4, 5, 6, 7, 8, 9, 10, 12); 1943 (1, 2, 3, 4, 5, 6, 7, 8, 9, 11); 1944 (1, 3, 5, 9, 12); 1945 (3, 9, 12); 1946 (5, 6, 7, 8, 9, 11); 1947 (3, 5, 8, 9, 10, 11, 12); 1948 (1, 3); 1950 (6); 1951 (7); 1961 (4); 1966 (4); 1967 (10)

FA: 1939 (5, 11); 1940 (1, 2, 3, 5, 6, 8, 10); 1941 (1, 3, 5, 6, 7, 8, 9, 10, 11); 1942 (1, 2 with Harold McCauley★, 3, 5, 6, 7, 8, 9, 10, 11, 12); 1943 (2 4, 6, 7, 8); 1944 (2, 4); 1945 (4, 7, 12); 1946 (2, 11); 1947 (1, 3, 11, 12); 1948 (1, 2, 4, 5, 8, 9); 1951 (10)

FTC: 1966 (9); 1967 (3)

IMG: 1950 (10, 12); 1951 (2, 4, 6, 9, 11); 1952 (33); 1953 (6)

OW: 1950 (7); 1951 (6, 12); 1952 (1, 4, 6, 8, 12); 1953 (1, 3, 5); 1956 (6)

TIMLIN, WILLIAM MITCHESON (Apr. 11, 1892–1943) British artist. The creator of the most beautiful and valuable science fiction book published this century has remained a largely unknown, shadowy figure, never included in any other artist reference works. Timlin was born in Ashington, Northumberland, England, the son of colliery foreman Peter Timlin and Margaret (nee Mitcheson). The family immigrated to South Africa in the early 1900s. After the First World War, Timlin became a successful practicing architect and also became known for his distinctive style of fantasy painting, which equaled the best work of Arthur Rackham and W. Heath Robinson.

His masterpiece, *The Ship That Sailed to Mars: A Fantasy*, was published in a large royal quarto by George Harrap in November 1923 (the book itself was undated). It was finely bound in quarter vellum richly decorated with gilt. It contained forty-eight superb color plates by Timlin, alternated throughout with forty-eight leaves adorned with his fine calligraphic text. These pieces of art were all mounted by hand on grey matte paper. Two thousand copies of the book were produced in Britain, of which two hundred fifty were distributed in America by Stokes of New York (in 1924). The latter copies were sold at twelve dollars each but now are valued in the many hundreds of dollars.

The story can be interpreted as a fairy tale with slight mixtures of Tolkien and Burroughs, set on Mars. Among the best of the memorable paintings are *The Raising of the Tower*, *The Celebration*, and *The Temple*. The film rights to the book were sold in America, but the movie, which was to be called *Get off the Earth*, was never completed.

Timlin's later series of pictures, intended as plates for a book to be entitled *The Building of a Fairy City*, were never published as a collection, but some of these excellent designs, including *Fantasy and Triumphal Arch*, are available on postcards in South Africa.

The artist's pen-and-ink drawings for travel books, including *South Africa: Out of the Crucible* and many others in the same vein, are uninspired compared to his wonderfully imaginative work.

Timlin died at Kimberley in 1943.

PUBLISHED WORK:

HC: *The Ship That Sailed to Mars: A Fantasy* (23)

Richard Dalby

TIMMINS, WILLIAM (?) American artist. Timmins took over cover duties on *Astounding Science Fiction* in September 1942, when the war effort made it impossible for Hubert Rogers★ to contribute art to the magazine. Timmins was a reasonably competent artist, but his paintings were rarely exciting. They fit the more subdued nature of *Astounding*, which emphasized plot over fast action. However, many of the Timmins cover paintings were so bland that often they gave no hint that they illustrated SF stories. After the war, Timmins was slowly crowded off the covers by much better artists.

PUBLISHED WORK:

ASF: 1942 (9, 12); 1943 (1, 2, 3, 4, 5, 6, 7, 8, 9, 10, 11, 12); 1944 (1, 2, 3, 4, 5, 6, 8, 9, 10, 11, 12); 1945 (1, 2, 3, 4, 5, 6, 7, 8, 9, 10, 11, 12); 1946 (1, 2, 3, 4, 5, 6, 7, 8, 9, 10, 11); 1947 (1, 4, 7, 8, 9, 10); 1948 (4, 5, 6, 7, 8, 9); 1949 (2, 3); 1950 (12); 1961 (5R)

TINKELMAN, MURRAY (b. Apr. 2, 1933) American artist. Born in Brooklyn, Tinkelman attended the New York High School of Industrial Art. After serving in the army he returned to New York, where he studied at Cooper Union Art School for two years. He then switched schools and attended the Brooklyn Museum Art school under a Max Beckmann Scholarship and studied there under Reuben Tam. Originally planning to be a fine-arts painter, Tinkelman was unhappy with the commercialism in galleries and instead decided to be an illustrator. He joined the Charles Cooper Studio, a well-known group of illustrators in New York. When the studio dissolved, he freelanced and became one of the best-known artists working in illustration today.

Along with illustrating for every major magazine published, Tinkelman has served as a teacher and lecturer at Parsons School of Design and at Syracuse University, has lectured extensively throughout the United States on art and is a well-known art historian, and has lectured on the history of illustration on public television. He has won more than one hundred fifty major art awards, with more than seventy of them from the Society of Illustrators, and has illustrated jackets for every major hardcover and paperback publisher in the country. He has also done a series of illustrations for the National Park Service that have been shown in traveling exhibitions on the National Parks and are in the permanent collection of the Smithsonian. In the past few years he has been concentrating on western and rodeo art and has had a number of books collecting his art on these subjects published.

In the fantasy field, Tinkelman had his first illustration published in 1953 in the first issue of *Vortex* magazine. However, he is best known for his distinctive series of covers illustrating Ballantine Books reissue of H. P. Lovecraft's work. He also did a number of fine covers for reissues of John Brunner's books. Although not working on SF at this time, Tinkelman stated: "I look forward to working on another paperback series by an author of the stature and quality of H. P. Lovecraft or John Brunner."

As to how he illustrates, Tinkelman always reads the story to be illustrated and allows visual images to emerge. In his science fiction illustration career, he has never had to submit a sketch or had a correction on any of his pieces.

PUBLISHED WORK:

HC: *This Fortress World* (55)

TSCHIRKY, L. ROBERT (?) American artist. Tschirky studied anthropology at the University of Pennsylvania and the University of Chicago. He served as a research assistant at the University Museum in Philadelphia. Working in archaeology, he traveled to many of the major archaeological sites in the Mediterranean countries and Mexico.

A longtime science fiction fan, Tschirky was a member of the Philadelphia SF Society. In late 1946 four members of that group began Prime Press, a small-press publisher. Keeping everything local, art for most of the Prime Press hardcovers was done by friends of the group. Tschirky, not a full-time artist, produced competent but uninspired illustrations for the books he worked on.

PUBLISHED WORK:

HC: *And Some Were Human* (48), *Homunculus* (49), *Incomplete Enchanter* (50), *Lest Darkness Fall* (49), *Nomad* (50), *Solitary Hunters & the Abyss* (48), *The Torch* (48), *Venus Equilateral* (47), *Without Sorcery* (48)

TURNER, HARRY (?) British artist. Turner was a prominent Manchester fan active as an artist in the prewar fanzines such as *Novae Terrae* (later titled *New Worlds*). During the war he edited *Zenith*, which was beautifully illustrated by the artist. His first professional work was done for Walter Gilling's magazine *Tales of Wonder*, which was published from 1937 through 1942. This work was primarily small black-and-white story illustrations, akin to woodcuts, all of which were highly derivative of the work of American artist Frank R. Paul★.

Of a much higher standard were Turner's drawings for Newnes's *Fantasy* published in 1938–1939. Turner was introduced to the rival magazine's editor by John Russell Fearn. The outbreak of the war put an end to the magazine after its third issue, thus destroying a potential market.

Turner's first color art was for *Tales of Wonder* in 1940, and a section of the cover—showing a futuristic city—was reprinted as a dustwrapper by World's Work Publisher in 1944.

In 1950 Turner painted a cover and did several interiors for Gilling's *Science Fantasy*. His style was visually striking, having developed into a semi-impressionistic mode. His strong black-and-white story illustrations became a regular feature of *Nebula Science Fiction* from 1954 through 1959.

PUBLISHED WORK (All British publications).

HC: *The Golden Amazon* (44)

PB: *Thrilling Stories* (46)

NEB: 1954 (8, 10, 11); 1955 (12, 13, 14); 1956 (15, 16, 17); 1957 (20, 21, 22, 23, 24, 25); 1958 (26, 27, 31)

NEW FRONTIERS: 1947

ScF: 1950 (summer, winter)

TALES OF WONDER: #1

Philip Harbottle

TURNER, RONALD (b. 1924) Britist artist. Turner's intererst in science fiction was first awakened by H. G. Wells and films such as *Flash Gordon* and *Things to Come*. During World War II he saw active service overseas and survived a close encounter with a V.2 rocket.

After the war, Turner became a technical artist at Odhams studios. He began doing freelance work as Ronald Turner for Scion Ltd., starting with comic strips.

Turner's interest in science fiction secured him a commission to paint the paperback cover of *Operation Venus* by John Russell Fearn, published in 1950. His second cover, for *Annihilation*, also published in 1950, was outstanding and contributed to the success of the *Vargo Statten* paperback line. It showed a rocket ship blasting into space to escape a doomed Earth wracked by electrical storms. It typified Turner's covers: dramatic, realistic, beautifully colored, and featuring an accurate depiction of the story. After that Turner was in constant demand by several publishers. His depictions of Earth as seen from space in works such as *Black Bargain* in 1954 were done with such realism that they seemed to be based on photographs. When asked how he produced such outstanding covers, Turner stated, "I imagine it was a combination of John Russell Fearn's imagination and descriptive capacity and my own interest in the subject matter."

After 1955 Turner switched to comic strips and became famous for the *Rick Random* series as well as for his artwork for *The Daleks* on television channel 21. In 1985 Turner returned to the comic field, creating *Nick Hazard*, a science fiction strip hero whose continuities are based on John Russell Fearn stories. He is now working on the very popular IPC strip *Dan Dare*.

Married, with two grown sons who share his hobby of repairing old cars, Turner has inherited the mantle of the late Frank Hampson* as Britain's leading science fiction illustrator.

PUBLISHED WORK (All British titles and magazines).

PB: *2,000 Years On* (50), *Alien Virus* (55), *Anjani the Mighty* (51), *Annihilation* (50), *Before the Beginning* (54), *The Black Avengers* (53), *Black Bargain* (53), *The Catalyst* (51), *City of No Return* (54), *Cosmic Exodus* (53), *The Cosmic Flame* (50), *Deadline to Pluto* (51), *The Devouring Fire* (51), *Dimension of Illion* (55), *The Dissentizens* (54), *Doomed Nation of the Skies* (53), *Dynasty of Doom* (53), *The Dyno-Depressant* (53), *The Eclipse Express* (52), *Enterprise 2115* (54), *Exile from Jupiter* (54), *Exit Life* (53), *The Extra Man* (54), *The Frozen Limit* (54), *Fugitive of Time* (53), *The G-Bomb* (52), *The Genial Dinosaur* (54), *The Gold of Akada* (51), *The Grand Illusion* (53), *The Hand of Havoc* (54), *The Hell Fruit* (53), *The Hell Planet* (54), *Home Is the Martian* (54), *I Came—I Saw—I Wondered* (54), *I Fight for Mars* (53), *I Spy* (54), *Inferno* (50), *The Inner Cosmos* (52), *Jupiter Equilateral* (54), *Laugher in Space* (52), *The Lie Destroyer* (53), *The Living World* (54), *The Lonely Astronomer* (54), *The Magnetic Brain* (53), *The Man from Tomorrow* (52), *Man of Two Worlds* (53), *The Master Must Die* (53), *The Master Weed* (54), *Menace from the Past* (54), *The Micro Men* (50), *Mission to the Stars* (54), *Moons for Sale* (53) *The Multi-Man* (54), *Nebula X* (50), *The New Satellite* (51), *Odyssey of Nine* (53), *One Thousand Year Voyage* (54), *The Petrified Planet* (51), *Pioneer in 1990* (53), *Planetoid Disposals* (53), *The Purple Wizard* (53), *The Renegade Star* (51), *The Resurrected Man* (54), *Scourge of the Atom* (53), *Slave Traders of the Sky* (54), *Slaves of the Spectrum* (54), *Space Hunger* (53), *Space Puppet* (54), *Space Warp* (52), *Spawn of Space* (51), *The Star Seekers* (53), *The Sun Makers* (50), *A Time Appointed* (54), *The Time Bridge* (52), *Tormented City* (53), *Ultra Spectrum* (53), *Vassals of Venus* (54), *Wanderer in Space* (50), *Wealth of the Void* (54), *Zero Hour* (53)

FUTURISTIC SCIENCE STORIES: 1952 (winter, spring)

OUT OF THIS WORLD: 1955 (winter)

TALES OF TOMORROW: (3, 4, 6)

VARGO STATTEN/BRITISH SF MAGAZINE: (4, 5, 10, 11, 12)

WONDERS OF THE SPACEWAYS: (2, 3, 4)

WORLDS OF FANTASY: 1952 (4, 9)

Philip Harbottle

UTPATEL, FRANK (Mar. 4, 1905–July 12, 1980) American artist. A native of Wisconsin, Utpatel was a friend of August Derleth and Mark Schorer and began illustrating the weird fiction of his friends. He was an infrequent contributor to *Weird Tales* in the 1930s. H. P. Lovecraft was impressed by Utpatel's work, and the artist illustrated the only book by Lovecraft published during the author's lifetime, *The Weird Shadow over Innsmouth* (1936). Utpatel remained friends with Derleth and illustrated a number of books for Arkham House. He prepared numerous jackets for this weird-fiction publishing company and produced artwork for Arkham's sister company, Mycroft and Moran. At the same time, Utpatel became well known as a Wisconsin regional artist, with work in the Whitney Museum, the Art Institute of Chicago, and the Library of Congress. He was well known in the art field for his fine woodcuts. Utpatel died soon after completing illustrations for the Collected Solar Pons stories by August Derleth.

PUBLISHED WORK:

HC: *Always Come Evening* (57), *Collected Poems of H. P. Lovecraft* (63), *The Dark Brotherhood* (66), *The Dark Château* (51), *The Dark Man and Others* (63), *The Feasting Dead* (54), *A Hornbook for Witches* (50), *The Inhabitant of the Lake and Less Welcome Tenants* (64), *Nightmare Need* (64), *Nine Horrors and a Dream* (58), *Over the Edge* (64), *The Phantom Fighter* (66), *Poems for Midnight* (64), *Poems in Prose* (65), *Portraits in Moonlight* (64), *The Quick and the Dead* (65), *Someone in the Dark* (41), *Something Breathing* (65), *Spells and Philtres* (58), *Tales of Science and Sorcery* (65), *The Travelling Grave and Other Stories* (48), *The Weird Shadow over Innsmouth* (36), *Whispers* (77), *Whispers 2* (79)

WT: 1932 (6, 8, 9); 1934 (6); 1936 (1, 4, 6, 8); 1937 (4)

VALIGURSKY, EDWARD I. (b. Oct. 16, 1926) American artist. Born in New Kensington, Pennsylvania, Valigursky graduated from high school in 1944 and immediately entered the U.S. Navy, serving until 1946. After his discharge he studied at the Art Institute of Chicago and the American Academy of Arts. He graduated from the Art Institute of Pittsburgh, taking the five-year course in illustration and advertising.

In 1952 Valigursky became associate art director for Ziff-Davis publishing in New York. At Ziff-Davis he soon became a regular illustrator for their two science fiction magazines, *Amazing* and *Fantastic Adventures*. In 1953 he became art director for Quinn Publishing Company, which published *IF* magazine. After working for Quinn for two years, he went into freelance illustration and has remained a freelance artist ever since.

Valigursky was one of the major paperback artists of the 1950s. In addition to producing a great deal of magazine art for *Fantastic* and *Amazing*, he painted hundreds of paperback covers. His art, along with that of Ed Emshwiller*, dominated the Ace science fiction line of the 1950s and 1960s. Valigursky was a fine technical artist, and his robots were among the best ever painted in the science fiction field; his hardware was always impressive and realistic. At the same time, he was capable of creating believable people. His humans were not as stylized or flashy as those of many of the artists working in the field but were much more believable.

In advertising, Valigursky did artwork for Avco, Goodyear, Esso, Piper Aircraft, Bell Telephone, Shell Oil, the Air Force, The Air National Guard, and many other clients. His exceptional paintings of aircraft made him a natural for the many companies associated with the aviation field.

Besides illustrating magazine science fiction, Valigursky contributed to many popular magazines including *True, Argosy, Saga, Collier's, Popular*

Mechanics, and *Popular Science*. He was known for his aviation and space illustrations outside as well as in the science fiction field. He left the science fiction field after many years to pursue the much more lucrative nongenre illustration market.

Five paintings done by Valigursky are on permanent exhibit in the Pentagon, and he has won numerous awards from National Artists Groups as well as the National Association of Industrial Arts.

Valigursky's name is not as well known as that of other science fiction artists like Emshwiller, Jack Gaughan★, and Kelly Freas★, although he was nearly as prolific as any of them. However, unlike the other artists, Valigursky did not sign his paintings. Although many of the illustrations for magazine covers were identified, only a few of Valigursky's science fiction paperback covers were labeled. His best covers, such as the cover illustration for Clifford Simak's novel *City*, was not identified, and thus many fans never knew the identity of one of the dominant science fiction illustrators of the late 1950s. Valigursky's excellent machinery-oriented illustrations served as the inspiration for many of the science fiction artists who grew up in the 1960s. On a few illustrations, he used the name William Rembach.

PUBLISHED WORK:

HC: *Best from F&SF* 7 (58)

PB: *100th Millenium, Across Time, Angry Espers, Ballad of Beta–2 Blue Atom, Changling Worlds, City, Cosmic Checkmate, Cosmic Computer* (64), *Crashing Suns* (65), *Doomsday Eve, Earth Gods Are Coming, Galaxy Primes, Genetic General, Key Out of Time* (63), *Last Hope of Earth, Lest We Forget Thee Earth, Life with Lancelot, Lunar Eye, Man Called Destiny, Martian Missile, Mayday Orbit, Mechanical Monarch, Our Man In Space* (65), *Outside the Universe, Plague Ship, Plot against Earth, Prodigal Sun, Rim of Space, Secret Martians, Ship from Outside, Siege of the Unseen, Sioux Spaceman, Sons of Ganymede, Starhavan, Sun Saboteurs, To the Tombaugh Station, Touch of Infinity, Trouble on Titan* (67), *Wizard of Lihn*

AMZ: 1951 (8, 10, 11, 12); 1952 (1, 2, 3, 4, 5, 6, 7, 8, 10, 11); 1953 (6, 7); 1954 (11); 1955 (1, 3, 5, 7, 9, 11, 12); 1956 (1, 2, 3, 4, 5, 6, 7, 8, 9, 10, 11, 12); 1957 (1, 2, 3, 4, 5, 6, 7, 8, 9, 10, 11); 1958 (1, 2, 3, 4, 5, 6, 7, 8, 9, 10, 11, 12); 1959 (4, 5); 1960 (1, 2, 5); 1961 (1); 1966 (10)

DW: 1957 (2, 8)

FA: 1951 (9, 10, 11); 1952 (1, 2, 3, 9)

FTC: 1952 (summer); 1955 (4, 6, 8, 12); 1956 (2, 4, 6, 8, 10, 12); 1957 (2, 3, 4, 5, 6, 8, 9, 10, 11, 12); 1958 (1, 2, 5, 6, 9); 1959 (3, 4, 6, 8, 10, 12); 1967 (11)

IF: 1953 (3, 5, 7, 9, 11); 1954 (1, 3, 4, 5, 6, 7, 8, 9, 10, 11, 12); 1955 (1, 2, 3, 4, 8, 10)

PS: 1952 (1)

SS: 1955 (winter)

VALLA, VICTOR (?) American artist. Valla had wanted to be an artist since the age of ten. He received degrees in painting, illustration, and print-making from the Rochester Institute of Technology and the University of Illinois. After teaching for a year at Rochester, he was awarded a grant to study in Paris at the Printmaking Workshop of Stanley Hayter. At present, he teaches graphic design and illustration at Kean College in New Jersey. He has received many awards for his illustrations and has received Gold Medals for illustration from the Art Directors Club of New Jersey for two years in a row.

At present, Valla uses a combination of inks, dyes, the air brush, and casein, often with collage. He has also done work on canvas on board. He has two methods of painting. When strong characters are involved, he tries to personify them by using movie or television stars as models for the pictures he constructs. He tries to pick actors who are strongly defined and thus would fit the type of person used in the story.

When he believes that mood in a book is paramount, he strives to use symbolism and color to convey the feeling of the story. "If one can create a feeling of dread, gloom, anxiety, conflict, depression, awe, or danger by other than obvious symbols or literal images, the whole tone of the book or story is conveyed. . . . That, for me, is the challenge of science fiction art."

PUBLISHED WORK:

HC: *The 1974 Annual World's Best SF* (75)

PB: *Dark Man* (72)

VALLEJO, BORIS (?) American artist. Born in Lima, Peru, Vallejo was the son of a successful lawyer. He originally wanted to be a concert violinist and studied the violin for seven years but was never satisfied with his music, thinking that he could not reach the perfection he desired. Thus he turned to medicine and took two years of premed training. At the same time, his skill in art was starting to emerge. He studied graphic design at the National School of Fine Arts in Peru, winning a scholarship. He also won a Gold Medal for his work and at sixteen was offered a scholarship to study art in Florence, Italy.

Instead of accepting the scholarship, Vallejo moved to the United States in 1964. He spoke no English and had few connections. Starting out with eighty dollars and a portfolio of art, Vallejo luckily ran into some fellow Peruvians who helped him. He soon got a job working in the advertising department for a chain store. After spending six months at its Hartford office, he returned to New York, where, at the company's New York Office, he met Doris Maier, who was to become his wife and sometime collaborator on a number of books.

After two years of advertising work, Vallejo became a freelance artist. He did mostly fashion art but also other work including Christmas-card illustrations. During the late 1960s he began reading the monster magazines being published by Warren Publications and decided to try the type of art being used there. After selling a cover to *Eerie* magazine in 1971, he soon was providing art for Warren on a regular basis. Marvel Comics, which wanted to establish itself with the same type of magazines, featuring painted covers (with black-and-white comic stories inside), then began asking for paintings by Vallejo. It was working for Marvel that helped establish his reputation.

Marvel had been publishing comic-book adventures of Conan the Barbarian, based on the character created by Robert E. Howard, for several years. In the early 1970s the company brought out a black-and-white magazine also featuring Conan comic adventures. Vallejo was asked to do some of the early covers. His paintings for *The Savage Sword of Conan* were universally acclaimed as the finest Conan paintings since those done by Frank Frazetta★. Not only was Conan well executed, but the monsters, demons, and beautiful girls that filled the paintings were similarly well done. Vallejo's muscular heroes, a reflection of the artist's own interest in bodybuilding, were compared favorably with Frazetta, and many fans hailed him as the "next Frazetta." With Frazetta so popular that he could pick and choose his assignment, art directors began using Vallejo's art for books that years before would have been illustrated by the now much more expensive Frazetta.

Vallejo's first paperback cover painting was done for Edgar Rice Burrough's novel *I am a Barbarian* published in 1975; within a short time Vallejo was concentrating almost exclusively on paperback and hardcover covers. His fame grew rapidly as a result of the much greater exposure he received from the many covers he was doing. Although he primarily worked in the fantasy field, he also did romance covers, gothics, and historical covers.

When Ballantine Books reissued the first seven Gor novels in 1976, Vallejo was chosen as the artist. Again, the covers attracted a great deal of attention. His men were the stuff heroic fantasy novels thrived on, but his women were even more popular. They were the stuff of adult fantasies. Boris was also selected when Ballantine decided to reissue all twenty-four Tarzan novels. The art attracted so much notice that Ballantine did a Tarzan calendar using many of the illustrations as well as a new piece used as a centerfold. The sales of the calendar were so good that Workman Publishing began issuing Vallejo's calendars every year, reprinting some of his best art. Sales of these calendars in the fantasy field were topped only by the Frazetta calendars, again attesting to Vallejo's fan following.

In 1978 Vallejo's career made another transition when Del Rey Books published *The Fantastic Art of Boris Vallejo* in a lavish hardcover and softcover format. The book reprinted more than forty of his best paintings and featured a very flattering text by Lester Del Rey. Now fans who knew Vallejo only by his artwork were able to read about the man and his work. More important, it attached a name to the art. As with Frank Frazetta, the publication of a collection of his art in book form gave Vallejo art an importance beyond just being book covers. However, the book did not have the impact on his career that the Frazetta collections had on Frazetta's. By now, there were too many artbooks about fantasy artists, and none of them generated the attention that the first Frazetta art collection did. His breakthrough came on his next book.

Mirage signaled a new phase in Vallejo's career. Published in 1982, it originally was planned as a portfolio of erotic art that grew beyond the initial concept. Motivation for the collection was a growing frustration with the censorship and limitations imposed on paperback and book art. Full female nudes were rarely ever used, and paintings were often retouched to make sure that they fit certain editorial standards of decency. Vallejo's desire to do art the way he wanted pushed him to do so. The portfolio concept was to have featured only black-and-white studies, but when he began doing paintings as well, it made the original plan of private publishing unfeasable. Del Rey Books was contacted, but Ballantine took the entire project, which featured thirty-two new color paintings, a number of detailed pen-and-ink sketches, and an interview with the artist on his purpose in doing the paintings.

The book was unique in the fantasy field in that the paintings were all erotic fantasies done specifically for the collection and not published anywhere else. Doris Vallejo wrote a series of short erotic poems to go with the art. Even the principle model used for the paintings, Danielle Anjou, was listed and thanked. *Mirage* stood on its own, not as a reprint collection of art but as a portfolio of all-new and strikingly different Vallejo art. The book sold extremely well. Like the Frazetta collections, which introduced many thousands of new collectors to the artist, *Mirage* widened Vallejo's appeal beyond the science fiction marketplace. More than *The Fantastic Art of Boris Vallejo*, it served as a breakthrough for the artist.

It was followed in 1984 with *Enchantment*, featuring more erotic paintings, this time with each accompanied by an erotic short story by Doris Vallejo. Although Vallejo still does book and paperback cover art, it seems that his career has taken a major turn as a result of the popularity of these collections of erotic art, but only time can measure the impact of these publications on his future.

Although Vallejo is an accomplished artist in pen and ink or pencils, most of his works are paintings. He works in oils and usually uses models, often himself or his wife. Beginning a work, he always does a preliminary sketch of the entire piece in pencil. Next he prepares illustration board by giving it two coats of gesso. Line work, done from photos, is traced on the board in pencil. He then does some preliminary work in acrylics, usually as a base for shadows using shades of brown. After that the painting is given a glaze in oils diluted with turpentine. When the glaze dries, he works in oils, doing one figure at a time until the painting is completed. The combination of oil and glaze gives his paintings a shine and glow that makes his people seem more lifelike, and the entire paintings almost take on a life of their own.

PUBLISHED WORK:

HC: *Day of Damnation* (84), *Enchantment* (84), *The Fantastic Art of Borris Vallejo* (78), *Matter for Men* (83), *Mirage* (82), *Techniques of Art* (85)

PB: *Angry Ghost* (77), *Assassin of Gor* (75), *Atlan* (78), *Beasts of Tarzan* (77), *Behind the Walls of Terra* (77), *Berserker Man* (78), *Berserker Planet* (80), *Best of Leigh Brackett* (77), *Boss of Terror* (76), *Broken Sword* (77), *Captive of Gor* (76), *Cheon of Weltanland* (83), *Conan of Aquilonia* (77), *Conan the Wanderer* (77), *Davy* (74), *Demon in the Mirror* (77), *Demon Night* (82), *Dragon* (78), *Dragon and the George* (76), *Dreamsnake* (79), *Earth Magic* (78), *Eternal Champion* (78), *Flight of the Horse* (73), *Flying Sorceror* (76), *Gateway* (78), *Gateways in the Sand* (76), *Godsfire* (78), *A Guide to Barsoom* (76), *High Couch of Silistra* (77), *A Private Cosmos* (77), *Hostage for Hinterland* (76), *I am a Barbarian* (75), *Ice Schooner* (78), *Imaro* (79), *In the Moons of Borea* (78), *Jungle Tales of Tarzan* (77), *Kings Daughter* (79), *Magic Goes Away*, *Maker of Universes* (77), *Mortal Gods* (79), *Mountain Monster* (76), *Mutiny on the Enterprise* (83), *Nomads of Gor* (76), *Of Men and Monster*, *Outlaw of Gor* (75), *Priest Kings of Gor* (77), *Tarzan at the Earth's Core* (77), *Roar Devil* (77), *Secrets of Synchronicity* (77), *Shapechangers* (83), *Son of Tarzan* (77), *Space Guardian* (78), *Spawn of the Swinds* (78), *Spotted Men* (77), *Tarnsman of Gor* (75), *Tarzan and the Ant Men* (77), *Tarzan the Invincible* (77), *Tarzan and the Castaways* (75), *Tarzan and the City of Gold* (77), *Tarzan Lord of the Jungle* (76), *Tarzan and the Forbidden City* (77), *Tarzan and the Foreign Legion* (77), *Tarzan and the Golden Lion* (77), *Tarzan Triumphant*, *Tarzan and the Jewels of Opar* (77), *Tarzan and the Lion Man* (77), *Tarzan of the Apes* (77), *Tarzan and the Lost Empire* (77), *Tarzan the Magnificent* (77), *Tarzan the Terrible* (77), *The Return of Tarzan* (77), *Tarzan the Untamed* (77), *Tarzan's Quest* (77), *Through the Reality Warp* (76), *To Walk the Night* (76), *Web of Wizardry* (78), *When Hell Laughs* (82)

MISC: Boris Vallejo Fantasy Calendar 1980, 1981, 1982, 1983; The Tarzan Calendar (1979)

VAN DER POEL, W. I., JR. (?) American artist. Van der Poel served as art director for *Galaxy Science Fiction* from its first issue through June 1960. He also served in that same capacity for *Galaxy's* short-lived fantasy companion *Beyond*. In the late 1950s he was art director for Gnome Press and designed most of their covers. When Gnome abandoned full-color illustrated covers due to costs, Van der Poel designed a number of artistic line-work illustrations that were used for covers on the later Gnome series.

PUBLISHED WORK:

HC: *Agent of Vega* (60), *Bird of Time* (60), *Coming Attractions* (57), *Dawning Light* (58), *Drunkards Walk* (61), *Invaders from the Infinite* (60), *Path of Unreason* (59), *Phil-*

osophical Corps (61), *Purple Pirate* (60), *SF 58* (58), *SF 59* (59), *They'd Rather Be Right* (57), *Unpleasant Profession of Jonathan Hoag* (60), *Vortex Blaster* (60)

VAN DONGEN, HENRY RICHARD (?) American artist. Van Dongen had two careers in science fiction, each of them successful. In 1950 he entered the science fiction magazine field with his cover painting for the September 1950 issue of *Super Science*. He soon progressed from doing art for lesser magazines like *Super Science* and *Worlds Beyond* to the premier magazine of the time, *Astounding Science Fiction*. His first cover for that magazine was August 1951, and within a short time he became one of the mainstays of the publication, sharing cover and interior art duties with Frank Kelly Freas.* Van Dongen continued to work on *Astounding* until late in 1961, when he left science fiction for the commercial-art field. This was the end of his first career in science fiction.

In 1975 Lester Del Rey began work on an illustrated book on science fiction art. In assembling the book, Del Rey contacted Van Dongen for permission to reprint one of his early covers. In passing, the editor mentioned to the artist that he would be interested in seeing new work from him. By coincidence, Van Dongen was without any assignment at the time and contacted Ballantine Books (where Del Rey worked) about a cover assignment. Van Dongen's new work producing art for paperback covers was well received when it began appearing, and he soon was doing numerous covers for both Del Rey and DAW Books.

Van Dongen was a capable artist who could do both realistic people and believable aliens. His covers for *Astounding* were much more subdued than most of the art appearing on other science fiction magazines, and they gave the publication a much more dignified appearance. His recent paperback artwork featured some exceptional alien creations and demonstrated that the artist had not lost any of his talent in his years away from the science fiction field.

PUBLISHED WORK:

PB: *Beneath the Shattered Moon* (77), *Best of Edmond Hamilton* (77), *Best of Eric Russell* (78), *Best of Hal Clement* (79), *Best of James Blish* (79), *Best of John W. Campbell* (76), *Best of Lester del Rey* (78), *Best of Murray Leinster* (78), *City of the Chasch* (79), *The Dirdir* (79), *Doomtime* (81), *The Fluger* (79), *Garments of Caean* (80), *Jungle of Stars* (76), *Midnight at the Wall of Souls* (77), *One on Me* (80), *Panorama Egg* (78), *The Pnume* (79), *Siege of Wonder* (77), *To Keep the Ship*, *Voice out of Ramah* (79)

AMF: 1950 (4)

ASF: 1951 (8, 10, 11, 12); 1952 (1, 2, 3, 5, 6, 8, 9, 10, 11, 12); 1953 (1, 2, 4, 5, 6, 7, 8, 9, 10, 11, 12); 1954 (1, 2, 3, 4, 5, 6, 7, 9, 10, 11, 12); 1955 (1, 2, 3, 4, 5, 6, 7, 8, 9, 11, 12); 1956 (1, 2, 3, 4, 5, 6, 7, 8, 9, 10, 11, 12); 1957 (1, 2, 3, 4, 5, 6, 7, 8, 9, 10, 11, 12); 1958 (1, 2, 3, 4, 5, 6, 7, 8, 9, 10, 11, 12); 1959 (1, 2, 3, 5, 6, 7, 8, 11, 12); 1960 (1, 2, 3, 5, 7, 9, 10, 11, 12); 1961 (1, 2, 4, 5, 6, 7, 9, 10, 11); 1980 (9); 1981 (7); 1982 (1, 3, 5, 6, 10, 11, 12)

GXY: 1963 (12)

SFA: 1952 (11); 1953 (5, 9)

SpSF: 1953 (2, 7)

SSS: 1949 (9); 1950 (3, 5, 7, 8, 11); 1951 (1, 8)

WB: 1951 (1, 2)

VELEZ, WALTER (?) American artist. Born in Harlem, Velez was brought up in the South Bronx. He always wanted to be an artist and as a child was a fan of Frank Frazetta★. He studied at the School of Visual Arts and also spent a great deal of time studying the Old Masters at numerous museums. "My real teachers were Da Vinci and Michelangelo," said the artist.

Velez painted his first science fiction paperback cover in 1978, but it was in 1979 that he first had an impact on the field. His cover for *Thieves World* from Ace Books captured the mood of that book and helped make the series it started one of the most popular in recent science fiction publishing history. Although Velez has done a number of other science fiction covers, he is noted in the field primarily as the cover artist for eight *Thieves World* paperbacks and hardcovers.

Velez is a strong believer in artistic integrity. He believes in his work and strives for constant perfection in it. Fortunately, some years back he met Jill Bauman★, who at the time was studying to be an artist. Bauman was impressed by Velez's work and apprenticed to him, serving also as his agent. Since Velez can be undiplomatic, Bauman serves as a perfect intermediary between the artist and his clients.

Along with science fiction, Velez has done cover art for Video Discs (including *Dracula*); magazine covers for *Scholastic Magazine*, *TV Guide*, *Marvel Comics*, *Starlog Magazine*, and *Creative Computing*; and movie promotion materials.

PUBLISHED WORK:

HC: *Cross Currents* (84), *Lord Darcy* (83), *Myth Adventures* (3), *Sanctuary* (82)

PB: *Birds of Prey* (78), *The Borribles* (79), *The Bug Wars* (79), *Cat Karina* (82), *Daughter of Witches* (82), *Dawning Light* (82), *Defiant Agents* (80), *Dream Master* (81) *Exiles Trilogy* (79), *Face of Chaos* (83), *Falcon of Eden* (80), *Galactic Derelict* (82), *Golden Man* (79), *Jamie the Red* (83), *Machines That Kill* (84), *Magic in Ithkar* (84), *Monster Paper Dolls* (84), *Moon of Three Rings* (80), *Moon's Fire-Eating Daughter* (84), *Myth Conceptions* (84), *Myth Directions* (84), *New Voice III* (79), *Phase Two* (79), *Sanctuary* (80), *Sargasso of Space* (81), *SeeTee* (78), *Seventh Tower* (83), *Shadow Magic* (83), *Shatterday* (81), *Shrouded Planet* (82), *Silverlock* (78), *The Steel, the Mist, and the Blazing Sun* (79), *Steel Tsar* (82), *Storm Season* (82), *Tales from the Vulgar Unicorn* (80), *Thieves World* (79), *Time Traders* (80), *Timescope* (80), *Tin Woodman* (81), *Winds of Altair* (82), *Wings of Omen* (84), *Zero Stone* (80)

VESTAL, HERMAN (?) American artist. A Fiction House staff artist, Vestal worked for all of the pulps published by that chain. He was a black-and-white interior artist who used clean, sharp lines for maximum effect. Like many of the artists working for the chain, his art showed strong influences from comic art, although he contributed only minor strips to the Fiction House Line. Vestal was also a boys' book illustrator in the 1950s.

PUBLISHED WORK:

2CSAB: 1951 (summer, winter); 1952 (spring, summer); 1953 (spring)

PS: 1947 (spring, summer, fall, winter); 1948 (fall); 1949 (summer, fall, winter); 1950 (summer, 11); 1951 (1, 3, 5, 7, 9, 11); 1952 (1, 3, 5, 7, 9); 1953 (1, 3, 5, 11);1954 (5, summer, fall); 1955 (summer)

TOPS: 1953 (spring)

VISKUPIC, GARY (b. 1944) American artist. Born in Brooklyn, Viskupic attended Cooper Union and illustrated the school magazine, *At Cooper Union*. Later, he attended the University of Illinois and has since done illustrations for the university's Depot Press. Growing up in the 1950s, Viskupic was strongly influenced by the science fiction movies of the day, particularly *Invasion of the Body Snatchers* and *It Came from Outer Space*.

Viskupic does conceptual art for the editorial pages of *Newsday*, for which he has served as chief illustrator for several years. He also is contributing artist to *Car and Driver* magazine and has done a great deal of freelance illustration for magazines ranging from *Business Week* to *Psychology Today*. He is also involved in poster design. Most of his science fiction art has been done for the Science Fiction Book Club.

The artist has won numerous awards in the art and graphics field. His work has been exhibited in shows throughout the world as well as at the Bicentennial Poster Exhibition sponsored by the Smithsonian.

PUBLISHED WORK:

HC: *The Best of C. M. Kornbluth, City, Flashing Swords #4* (77), *The Day of the Triffids, Slan, The Starchild Trilogy*

VON HOLST, THEODOR (Sept. 3, 1810–Feb. 12, 1844) British artist. Born in London of Livonian descent, Von Holst exhibited his first picture at the Royal Academy in 1827 and continued to show his work there until his premature death seventeen years later. He was strongly influenced by Henry Fuseli, whose pupil he became, and whose peculiarities he copies in his own work. At the age of twenty one Von Holst became the first artist to illustrate Mary Shelley's *Frankenstein*, which is considered by many historians in the science fiction field as the first modern science fiction novel.

Later works by Von Holst included "The Apparition to the Second Lord Lyttelton" and "The Raising of Jairus's Daughter." He died in London in February 1844.

PUBLISHED WORK:

HC: *Frankenstein: or, The Modern Prometheus* (1831)

Richard Dalby

WALOTSKY, RON (b. 1943) American artist. Born in Brooklyn, Walotsky attended the School of Visual Arts in New York City and graduated with his degree in 1966. Interested in surrealistic art, he got into science fiction illustration "because it was the closest way for me to paint the type of work I enjoyed and get paid for it." About when he was selling his first paintings to *Fantasy & Science Fiction*, he was also breaking into the poster field, producing posters for Dream Merchants, Third Eye, and a number of other poster companies. He quickly became known in and out of the SF field for his strong imagery, and he was soon doing work for most of the major hardcover and paperback publishers.

Walotsky's work is not limited to the science fiction field. His versatility had him painting album covers and dust jackets for fiction and nonfiction best-sellers and providing a great deal of magazine art for publications such as *Viva*, *Penthouse*, *Scholastic*, and the *New York Times Sunday Edition*.

Walotsky has taught art at Sullivan County Community College. His art has been exhibited in galleries in New York, in the Museum of Modern Art, and at the U.S. Cultural Center in Paris. Among his best-known pieces is the painting *Eclipse* done for Data General to symbolize the Eclipse Family of computers produced by that firm.

Walotsky works only in acrylics. For book covers, he does part of the work by hand and part by air brush or uses some combination of the two. He usually will read the manuscript, present one or two sketches to the art director, and then work up the sketch to one to three times the repro size.

Ron Walotsky lives with his son, Lennon, by the ocean in New York. His most recent project involves a series of limited-edition prints of some of his most popular works along with new pieces done strictly for the collectors market.

PUBLISHED WORK:

HC: *40 Thousand in Gehenna, Annals of the Time Patrol, Blooded on Arachne, Catacomb Years, Chrome, Lord Valentine's Castle, Millennium, The Fires of Paratime, Titan, Where Time Winds Blow*

PB: *The ABC's of SF, Apocalypse, The Black Flame* (79), *The Blue Star, Casselee, Chaining the Lady, Chy-Une, Cloak of Aesir* (72), *Cluster, Conan the Defender, Conan the Invincible, Conan the Unconquered, Creatures of Light and Darkness, Dark Stars, Dark Symphony* (70), *Doomsday Exhibit, Doorways in the Sand, The End of the Dream, England Swings, The Eternal Man, Guns of Avalon, Hand of Oberon, Haunted Earth* (73), *Infinity Five* (73), *Infinity Four* (72), *Kirlian Quest, Living Way Out, Lord of Light, The Lost Continent, Magic of Atlantis* (70), *The Man in the Maze, Man of Two Worlds, Men Inside* (73), *Mute, Nine Princes in Amber, Omnivor, Options, Orn, Overlay* (72), *Ox* (76), *Pig World* (73), *The Realms of Tartarus, Robots Have No Tails* (73),

The Shores Beneath, Sign of the Unicorn, Strange Ecstasies, Strange Tomorrows (73), *The Sword Swallower, Teenocracy, Ten Million Years to Friday* (71), *Thousand Star, Transmigration, Understanding MU, Unreal People* (73), *Venus Plus X, Vergan, Viscous Circle, Voices from the Sky, The World of SF*

F&SF: 1967 (5, 8); 1968 (2, 6, 10); 1969 (3, 8, 10); 1970 (3, 7); 1971 (2, 5, 7, 8); 1972 (1, 6, 7, 12); 1973 (11, 12); 1974 (3, 7, 12); 1975 (6); 1976 (2, 12); 1977 (1, 12); 1978 (7); 1979 (1, 11); 1980 (12); 1981 (2, 5, 12); 1982 (6); 1983 (2); 1984 (2)

WARD, LYND (1905–1985) American artist. Ward spent most of his life in New Jersey and was known as one of America's premier wood engravers. However, he also painted three huge murals for the Methodist Building of Evanston, Illinois; collaborated with his wife May McNeer on a number of children's books; and has placed art in numerous museums. He illustrated a number of books for the Heritage Book Club and the Limited Edition Book Club. Among his many awards were the Caldecott Medal and the Library of Congress Award.

Ward spent four years at Columbia University, studying the theory of design and art history. Afterwards, he was a special student at the State Academy for Graphic Arts in Leipzig, Germany, where he studied with Hans Mueller, Alois Kolp, and George Mathey. Much of Ward's early fame came from his novels without words, books done without text and entirely illustrated by wood engravings. The first two were *God's Man* and *Madman's Drum*, published in 1929 and 1930. Both were fantastic works.

Ward did illustrations for a number of books that were fantasy oriented, but his most famous work in the fantastic literature field was a series of sixty illustrations for the major ghost-story anthology *The Haunted Omnibus* published in 1937. He used a technique unlike any of his other styles in the illustrations for this book. In a letter to noted fantasy art collector Gerry de la Ree, in 1974, Ward described his thoughts on *The Haunted Omnibus* illustrations: "I felt that a technique that would emphasize darkness was preferable to a straight forward drawing with pencil, pen or brush. At the same time, it was necessary, because of the fact the book would be printed by letterpress, to have illustrations that could be reproduced by line-cut. . . . To solve this problem, . . . I experimented with a technique somewhat similar to mezzotint, one of tonal techniques that etchers or line engravers sometime use. I started with a tool called a moulette, which is a small pear-shaped instrument rotating freely on an axle that is attached to a handle. The pear-shaped head of the moulette is covered with tiny irregular projections, which when rotated back and forth, with considerable pressure will make tiny indentations in the material being prepared. In this case, celluloid.

"When the moulette has been run back and forth over the surface of the celluloid sufficiently, the celluloid will be roughened and its surface will consist of thousands of tiny pricked holes. At this point, the surface is painted with a coating of black paint. . . . When dry, this surface is ready to be worked on.

"Using a small knife or razor blade, the subject is developed out of the solid black surface of the celluloid by scraping. Light scraping will result in a gray, because the tiny holes in the celluloid have been filled with black paint—the scraping removes the black from the spaces between the holes and the holes remain black. This produces a gray, as do the dots in an ordinary halftone.

"More scraping reduces the size of the black dots and increases the amount of white resulting in lighter gray. And if the dots are scraped off completely, a white results."

Ward's work for the book remain among the classic studies of horror and fantasy art in the field. Not only were the illustrations unique in their composition, but each piece captures the essence of weirdness and supernatural feeling displayed in the fiction. The art is among the finest ever done for fantasy fiction. Notable among many fine illustrations are cuts for "Where Their Fire Is Not Quenched," "The White People," and "The Horla."

As a well-known and highly regarded mainstream artist who illustrated fantasy as well as classical novels, Ward had a strong influence on the science fiction and fantasy field in the 1940s and 1950s. He was a major figure in the history of fantasy illustration.

PUBLISHED WORK:

HC: *Beowulf* (39), *The Cadaver of Gideon Wick* (34), *Faust* (30), *Frankenstein* (34), *God's Man* (29), *The Haunted Omnibus* (37), *Madman's Drum* (30), *The Motives of Nicholas Holtz* (36)

WARHOLA, JAMES (b. Mar. 16, 1955) American artist. One of the many young excellent science fiction artists, Warhola was born in Pittsburgh, Pennsylvania. He attended Carnegie-Mellon University and received the BFA in design in 1977.

While still living in Pittsburgh, Warhola developed an interest in science fiction and comic art. He traveled to New York City for various comic-art shows and was strongly influenced by the science fiction art he saw on display. He lost much of his interest in comic art when he found that the work was too limited for what he wanted to do—paint in oils.

Warhola moved to New York the day after his graduation in May 1977. He did commercial art for several art studios while freelancing during the evenings. He worked as an art designer and designer for several years before going into illustration full time.

In New York Warhola studied at the Art Students League for two years with Jack Faragasso*. Since then he has worked five years with Michael Aviano in polishing his style.

Warhola's first published art was done for *Questar* magazine, which printed his first professional work for "The Enforcer" in 1980. The work for *Questar* helped him build up a portfolio, which landed him his first assignment for a paperback cover: *The Book of Philip Jose Farmer*, one of his favorites, featuring Farmer surrounded by characters from his story while typing on a Martian Landscape.

The artist was influenced by the golden age of illustrators, including Norman Rockwell and N. C. Wyeth, and works primarily in oil. In doing an illustration, he reads the manuscript thoroughly, sometimes two or three times to make sure he understands all the details. He treats every cover as a design problem, working from the question: "What would best represent the book." He then works up sketches for review by art directors. Warhola strongly believes that the final cover has to look good on the stands. It must be "pleasing to sell," in his words. Having done a great deal of design work, he is familiar with the viewpoint of the art director and tries to satisfy both his client and himself.

PUBLISHED WORK:

PB: *Battlestar Galactica #11* (86), *Battlestar Galactica #12* (86), *Bear Creek Legends* (86), *The Bloody Sun*, *The Book of Philip Jose Farmer* (82), *City of Darkness*, *Creature Feature Film Guide*, *Dr. Futurity*, *Great Ghost Stories*, *The Harp and the Blade*, *Homonculus* (86), *The Last Dream* (86), *Long Twilight*, *Magic for Sale*, *Man in the High Castle*, *Master of Space and Time* (86), *The Med Series* (83), *Mercy Man*, *Monsters You Never Heard Of*, *Neuromancer*, *Nightflyers*, *Persistence of Vision*; *Planet Savers* (80), *Sagard the Barbarian Series #1, 2, 3, 4*, *Suicide Inc.*, *Sword of Aldones* (80), *Time Piper*, *World Wreckers*, *Worlds Apart*

WENZEL, PAUL E. (?) American artist. A cover artist who worked for a short period from 1958 through 1964, primarily for the *Galaxy* science fiction magazine chain, Wenzel did eleven covers, none of them very distinguished. He was best at astronomical paintings, but too often, he did action scenes with poorly executed humans and mediocre aliens. Green and orange dominated most of his action covers.

PUBLISHED WORK:

FTC: 1963 (12)

GXY: 1958 (11); 1961 (6); 1968 (6)

IF: 1961 (3, 9); 1962 (9); 1963 (9); 1964 (10); 1967 (2, 6); 1968 (3)

SpTr: 1958 (9, 11)

WOT: 1964 (4)

WESSO, H. W. (1894–?) American artist. Wesso was the professional name of Hans Waldemer Wessolowski, a German-born artist who moved to the United States in 1914 and worked for many years as a magazine and pulp illustrator. Educated at the Berlin Royal Academy, he worked his way through school doing cartoon work. After moving to the United States he worked as a magazine illustrator for most major publications. His first science fiction artwork was done in 1929 for *Amazing Stories*, before which time he had never read a story in the field.

A great traveler, Wesso covered 256,000 miles by water in two years and traveled around the world twice. Favorite artists included Dean Cornwall, Raleigh, and McClelland Barclay.

Wesso was one of the most influential artists of the 1930s. Most of his paintings were done in watercolors, which gave his paintings a greater clarity and brighter color range than the oils used by most other pulp artists. He was not afraid to illustrate gruesome monsters and was noted for his spectacular bug-eyed monsters. He was a talented artist, able to paint people as well as monsters, a talent that many of the early science fiction illustrators lacked.

PUBLISHED WORK:

AMZ: 1929 (9, 10, 11, 12); 1930 (1); 1968 (2); 1972 (9)

AQ: 1929 (fall); 1930 (winter, spring, summer, fall); 1931 (winter, spring, summer, fall); 1932 (winter, spring, fall)

ASF: 1930 (1, 2, 3, 4, 5, 6, 7, 8, 9, 10, 11, 12); 1931 (1, 2, 3, 4, 5, 6, 7, 8, 9, 10, 11, 12); 1932 (1, 2, 3, 4, 5, 6, 9, 11); 1933 (1, 3, 10, 11); 1934 (1); 1936 (1, 2, 4, 7, 8, 9, 10, 11, 12); 1937 (1, 2, 3, 4, 5, 6, 7, 8, 9, 10, 11, 12); 1938 (1, 2, 3, 4, 5, 6, 7, 8, 9, 10, 11, 12); 1939 (1, 2, 3, 4, 5, 6, 7, 8, 9, 10, 11)

ASH: 1942 (3)

CF: 1940 (winter, spring, summer, fall); 1941 (winter, spring, summer, fall); 1942 (summer); 1943 (winter)

DYN: 1939 (2, 4)

FTC: 1973 (7)

MSS: 1939 (2)

SS: 1939 (1, 5, 9, 11); 1940 (5, 7, 11); 1941 (1, 3, 7, 11); 1942 (1, 3, 7)

SSS: 1942 (8)

ST: 1931 (9,11); 1932 (1, 3, 6, 10); 1933 (1)

StrS: 1939 (4, 6, 8, 10); 1940 (10, 12)

TWS: 1937 (6, 8, 10, 12); 1938 (2, 4, 6, 8, 10, 12); 1939 (2, 4, 6, 8, 10, 12); 1940 (1, 3, 4, 5, 6, 7, 8, 9, 10, 11, 12); 1941 (1, 3, 4, 6, 12); 1942 (2, 4, 6, 8); 1943 (fall)

UK: 1939 (10, 11)

WHELAN, MICHAEL (b. June 29, 1950) American artist. In little more than ten years, Whelan has risen to the position of one of the most dominant forces in modern science fiction art. A multiple-award winner at all of the major science fiction conventions, he is one of the few artists whose name is proudly proclaimed on many of the paperbacks and hardcovers he illustrates to help boost sales. His art routinely brings the highest prices ever garnered at science fiction art auctions, and each major sale sets a new record over the last major Whelan painting. He is one of the major artists who turned science fiction paperback and book illustration away from the surrealism of the 1960s and early 1970s and back to the garish pulp-style illustration of the early eras.

Whelan was born in Culver City, California, the son of Nancy and William Whelan. He was one of three children, his sisters being Lorie and Wendy. His father is an aerospace engineer, and so the family moved frequently when he was young, mostly to the California and Colorado area. He first encountered science fiction and fantasy art at the age of three when he discovered his father's science fiction magazines. He maintained this interest in science fiction and in art all through school and, during his high school years in Colorado, took summer classes at Phil Stel's Rocky Mountain School of Art in Denver.

In 1968 Whelan graduated from Oak Grove High School in San Jose, California, and enrolled at San Jose State University to study art and the biological sciences. Wanting to prepare himself for a "real career," he began as a premed major. To help finance his education, Whelan worked as an aide in the college's Anatomy/Physiology Lab. There he worked as a medical illustrator and anatomical model maker and helped prepare cadavers for anatomy classes. Whelan also did illustrations for the *Journal of Bone and Joint Surgery*. Under the guidance of M. D. Stewart and Dr. R. F. Brose, Whelan was encouraged to concentrate on art as his major. Lacking a strong interest in chemistry, he stopped his studies of the human body after completing his classes in neuroanatomy and neurophysiology. He instead made plans to become an illustrator.

In 1973 Whelan graduated as a president's scholar with a BA with great distinction in painting. He enrolled soon after at The Art Center College of Design in Los Angeles. He perfected his skills at the school and after nine months, his instructors thought he was ready for commercial illustration. Whelan left the school and went to New York. His first paperback commission soon followed, from Donald Wollheim at DAW Books.

In 1975 Whelan started working for both DAW and Marvel Comics. By March he had been approached by Ace Paperbacks as well and began doing art for that company. He started turning out numerous covers for both companies, his art attracting immediate attention for its powerful, heroic images and forceful use of color. He soon was one of the most popular artists working in the field. With each assignment, he became known as "the definitive" artist for that series of books. His paintings for H. Beam Piper's *Little Fuzzy* novels were popular fan favorites and helped boost the sales of the novels. At the 1976 World Science Fiction Convention, a large display of his paintings attracted major attention from both fans and professionals.

Late in that year DAW books began reissuing Michael Moorcock's *Elric* series with new covers by Whelan. The artist, who already was noted for his fantasy art, received unanimous acclaim for his interpretation of the series of six paperbacks, and the paintings were proclaimed as among the finest ever done in the swords–and–sorcery field.

In 1977 Whelan began producing art for Ballantine/Del Rey Books. His artwork for the Del Rey line attracted even more attention, especially his paintings for the Anne McCaffrey series of *Dragonriders of Pern* novels. His painting for *White Dragon* attracted national attention since the book made the best-seller list. In 1978 Whelan did a series of wraparound covers for Del Rey's reissues of the Edgar Rice Burroughs *Mars* series, and again fan response was unrestrained enthusiasm.

In 1979 Donning Books published *Wonderworks*, a collection of the best of Whelan's work with commentary by the artist. The book immediately sold out and went back to press. It has remained in print ever since and has sold more than twenty thousand copies in trade paperback. Soon Whelan began his own company, producing limited graphics of some of his most popular works. Along with handling his book and magazine assignments, Whelan also illustrated a number of rock album covers.

With each assignment, Whelan rose a little higher in the science fiction field until he was at the top of his profession. Major novels routinely had his covers. Important science fiction works featuring art by Whelan included *Friday, Foundation's Edge, 2010: Odyssey Two, The Robots of Dawn,* and *Job: A Comedy of Justice.* His art attracted such attention outside the science fiction field that he was specifically asked to do the cover for the Jackson's album, *Victory.*

Whelan's current projects include production art for a science fiction film as well as involvement in the Society of Illustrators first SF Show. He is married to Audrey Price, and with their daughter, Alexa, they live in Connecticut.

During the past five years, Whelan has dominated the art awards in the science fiction and fantasy field. He won the Hugo Award in 1980, 1981, 1982, 1983, and 1984 and also won The World Fantasy Award as Best Artist of the Year in 1983.

Whelan summed up his own feelings as an illustrator in his introduction to *Wonderworks* (1979). "A good artist is a good communicator.... The resulting creation must convey something to its audience.... Ultimately, not only must the artist communicate the thrust of someone else's ideas to a significant number of people, he also must do this in a manner consistent with the author's vision, while doing best not to miscommunicate his own. ... There's the irresistible challenge of creating a vital and expressive piece of art out of the inherent difficulties in commercial illustration."

Whelan primarily works in color, although he has done a few pieces in pen and ink. He paints with acrylics on masonite or canvas board. Like many artists working in the science fiction field today, he first submits a rough color sketch, makes a full-size drawing in pencil, and then does his painting.

PUBLISHED WORK:

HC: *Bearing an Hourglass* (84), *The Fuzzy Papers* (76), *Job, A Comedy of Justice* (84), *On a Pale Horse* (83)

PB: *Agent of the Terran Empire* (80), *All My Sins Remembered* (78), *Amazons* (79), *Amazons Cauldron II* (82), *Anackire* (83), *Bane of the Black Sword* (77), *The Bloody Sun* (75, 80), *Brother Assassin* (78), *Bunduki* (76), *Chessmen of Mars* (79), *City* (76), *Day of the Klesh* (79), *Diadem from the Stars* (76), *Dragonflight* (78), *Dying for Tomorrow* (76), *Earthchild* (77), *Elric at the End of Time, Elrick of Melnibone* (76), *Empire* (81), *Enchantress of World's End* (75), *Ensign Flandry* (79), *Federation* (81), *Fighting Man of Mars* (79), *First Cycle* (82), *Flandry of Terra* (79), *The Florians* (76), *For Love of Mother Not* (83), *Friday* (83), *Fuzzies and Other People* (81), *Fuzzy Bones* (81), *Fuzzy Sapiens* (76), *Gameplayers of Zan* (76), *Gate of Ivrel* (75), *Gods of Mars* (79), *Hecate's Cauldron* (82), *Horn Crown* (81), *Immortal of World's End* (76), *In the Green Star's Glow* (76), *John Carter of Mars* (79), *Krozair of Kregan, Lamarchos* (77), *Land Leviathan* (74), *Last Amazon, Little Fuzzy* (75), *Llana of Gathol* (79), *Lord Kalvan of Otherwhen* (76), *Lou of the Witch World* (80), *Man of Gold* (84), *The Man Who Counts* (77), *Master Mind of Mars* (79), *Mention My Name in Atlantis, Nifft the Lean* (82), *Night Face* (77, 81), *Nor Crystal Tears* (82), *Paratime* (81), *Perigrine* (78), *The Planet Savers* (76), *Princess of Mars* (79), *Question and Answer* (77), *Red as Blood* (83), *Renegade of Kregen* (76), *Sailor on the Seas of Fate* (76), *Stone in Heaven* (79), *Storm Queen* (78), *Stormbringer* (77), *Swords and Ice Magic* (77), *Swords of Mars* (79), *Synthetic Men of Mars* (79), *Thuvia, Maid of Mars* (79), *Tides of Kregan, Time and Again* (76), *Transition of Titus Crow* (75), *Tree of Swords and Jewels* (83), *The Trouble with Tycho* (76), *Ultimate Enemy* (79), *Under the Green Star's Spell* (76), *The Vanishing Tower* (76), *Volkhavaar* (77), *Warlord of Mars* (79), *Weird of the White Wolf* (77), *Well of Shiuan* (77), *When the Waker Sleeps* (75), *Whetted Bronze* (78), *White Dragon* (78), *Wildebloods Empire* (77), *With Friends Like These* (77), *World without Stars* (77), *Years Best Horror #3* (75), *Years Best Horror # 5* (77), *Years Best Horror #6* (78), *Years Best Horror #7* (79), *Years Best Horror #8* (80), *Years Best Horror #9* (81), *Years Best Horror #13* (85)

WHITE, TIM (b. Apr. 1952). British artist. Born in Erith, Kent, White studied at Medway College of Art from 1968 to 1972. Much of the work he produced during this time was fantasy oriented. After leaving college, he spent two years working for a number of advertising studios. In 1974 he received his first book-cover commission, for Arthur C. Clarke's *The Other Side of the Sky*. This launched his career as a full-time freelance illustrator.

Since that time, White has done more than one hundred fifty cover paintings, along with many other works including record-jacket and magazine illustrations. Among his most notable cover paintings are the works he did for the Christmas 1975 edition of *Science Fiction Monthly* and *The Visual Encyclopedia of Science Fiction* published in 1977 by Pan Books.

Now regarded as one of Britain's finest science fiction illustrators, White combines superlative detail with a largely figurative approach to his work and creates a totally realistic image of his landscape of the imagination. A collection of his work, *The Science Fiction and Fantasy World of Tim White*, was published by New English Library in 1981.

PUBLISHED WORK (All British editions).

HC: *The Darkness on Diamondia* (75), *The Man with the Thousand Names* (75)

PB: *Brain Wave* (76), *City of the Sun* (79), *Critical Threshhold* (79), *Death To Those Who Watch* (77), *Dying Inside* (79), *Eater of Worlds* (76), *Enemy within the Skull* (76), *The Fires of Lan Kern* (80), *The Fog* (75), *Gather Darkness* (79), *Glory Road* (78), *The Heaven Makers* (80), *Icerigger* (75), *Jewel of Jarhen* (76), *The Light Fantastic* (79), *Lord of the Spiders* (79), *Man Who Sold the Moon* (79), *The Moon Is a Harsh Mistress* (77), *Not before Time* (77), *The Number of the Beast* (80), *The Other Side of the Sky* (74), *Out of My Mind* (80), *Perilous Planets* (80), *The Rain Goddess* (76), *Revolt in 2100* (77), *Salem's Lot* (76), *Santaroga Barrier* (79), *A Scent of New-Mown Hay* (75), *Seetee Alert* (76), *The Space Machine* (80), *Star Light Star Bright* (79), *Stopwatch* (75), *Strange Invaders* (77), *Stranger in a Strange Land* (78), *Thorns* (78), *Through a Glass Darkly* (77), *UFO UK* (80), *Unpleasant Profession of Jonathan Hoag* (76), *The Witling* (78)

Richard Dalby

WILSON, GAHAN (b. Feb. 18, 1930) American artist. In the fantasy art field, only Frank Frazetta★ may be known to more people than Wilson. Emerging from a cult favorite in *Playboy*, Wilson has become one of the best-known and most recognized cartoonists in modern America. There are few people who cannot immediately identify his work or remember some ghoulish panel he drew. Along with providing art for *Playboy* and other magazines, Wilson has worked on a long-running Sunday comic feature and has written some fiction much in the same vein as his cartoons. In the fantasy field he also designed the bust of H. P. Lovecraft that is awarded each year to the winners of the World Fantasy Awards. He has edited a number of collections of horror fiction and writes a regular column for *Twilight Zone* magazine. He is a descendent of P. T. Barnum and the nephew of a lion tamer. He and his wife, journalist Nancy Winters, live in New York.

Of his youth, Wilson wrote, "Born in Evanston, Illinois, a gothic town full of mansions where scary old ladies slowly turned into witches, died, and were eaten by their cats or dogs or both before intimidated servicefolk could bring themselves to break in on their privacy. I wanted to be a cartoonist as far back as I can remember. I recently came across some drawings saved by my parents done when I was a tiny kid and even back then I was drawing skeletons, space ships, etc., and on one of the drawings, written in a mother's loving hand, it says: HORRIBLE MONSTER COMES TO KILL US ALL."

Wilson attended several commercial art schools during high school vacation but soon realized they taught only surface techniques. He enrolled in the Art Institute, taking its four-year fine-arts course. He was the first student ever to admit on his application that he wanted to be a cartoonist.

Influences included Chester Gould's villains in Dick Tracy, W. C. Fields, the Marx Brothers, Boris Karloff and Bela Lugosi, Goya, H. P. Lovecraft, *Weird Tales*, M. R. James, *The New Yorker*, radio serials, George Gross, The Shadow, Oz, Daumier, and Betty Boop. More than anything else, Wilson found life itself focusing the direction of his work: "Essentially I started out basing my cartoons rather heavily on classic fantasy, the Gothics new and old, but I found that life about me as reported in the news and as viewed from day to day was considerably more bizarre than anybody admitted and commonly weirder than made up monstrosities. What was Dracula compared to Hitler? And had Frankenstein come up with anything near as sinister as Love Canal? So my stuff had become, willy nilly, without my really intending it, more political, more of a social commentary than I'd set out to make it."

Wilson's first professional sale was a cartoon sold to Ziff-Davis for $7.50. He sold to the chain reasonably regularly, and from Ziff-Davis, it was only a short step to *Collier's*. Sales to *Playboy* followed. As the magazine's popularity grew, so did Wilson's. With his increased popularity, his market expanded, until cartoons by Wilson were appearing in every major American magazine that ran humorous illustrations. Advertising illustrations with the unique Wilson touch also helped increase the artist's visibility. Beginning in 1964 he contributed a long series of cartoons to *Fantasy & SF* magazine.

As to how he constructs his cartoons, Wilson stated, "A cartoon is a mold of literary and plastic art forms—take away the caption and the picture doesn't work; take away the picture and the caption doesn't work—I approach it from both orientations at once. My usual tactic in making up a cartoon idea is to select a specific theme or even a particular object and stick with it until I have produced an idea based on it. It is important to keep your deals with yourself in creativity. I work with pen (crow quill) and ink and use traditional watercolors, finding them highly flexible, and I just plain like them, having something of the same reverential feeling for them as, I am told, the Chinese traditionalist painter has for his ink block."

As to his favorite piece, Wilson tries to be proud and happy with each drawing before he sends it out. Future plans include a novel as well as some short stories, films, and a radio venture. In all his pursuits, he remains one of the most creative and innovative people in the fantasy art scene.

As with Frank Frazetta and Charles Addams★, Wilson's importance rests not only in the quality of his work but in the acceptance it has gained in modern American tastes. Like Addams before him, Wilson enabled people to laugh at horror and thus accept it. The rash of horror movie spoofs owe a great deal of their content to the creatures that inhabit the Wilson cartoons, and many modern horror writers have been consciously or subconsciously influenced by his light and irreverent approach to the genre. Wilson's cartoons have helped bring the monsters of the past into the present, from out of the decaying castle into the modern office building.

PUBLISHED WORK:

HC: *And Then We'll Get Him* (78), *The First World Fantasy Awards, Gahan Wilson's America* (84), *Gahan Wilson's Cracked Cosmos, Gahan Wilson's Favorite Tales of Horror, Gahan Wilson's Graveside Manner* (66), *I Paint What I See* (71), *Is Nothing Sacred* (82), *The Man in the Cannibal Pot, Nuts, Playboy's Gahan Wilson, The Weird World of Gahan Wilson*

AMZ: 1954 (3)

F&SF: 1964 (4, 6, 7); 1965 (1, 5, 6, 7, 8, 9, 10, 11, 12); 1968 (3, 8); 1969 (1); 1980 (1)

WOOD, STANLEY LLEWELLYN (1866–1928) British artist. A prolific magazine illustrator, Wood was known for his familiar bucking broncos and macho heroes with large jutting chins. He illustrated innumerable boys' adventure stories, but he is probably best known for his drawings, which accompanied the popular and long-running adventures of Captain Kettle at the turn of the century. Among the many books he illustrated were *The Arabian Nights Entertainments* (1890 and 1901) and his own volume *Ten Little Sausages* in 1915.

Born in Monmouthshire, England, on the Welsh border, Wood spent his childhood and early adult life in the United States. During the 1880s he had a tough, adventurous life on the western plains. He camped, rode, worked, and lived the life of a cowboy in the cattle ranges of Texas and southern California. All of his rifles, saddles, pistols, cartridge belts, and horses were drawn from real life. So were many of the adventures he illustrated, although it is not recorded if he actually encountered any creatures like the prehistoric "Monster of Lake Lamatrie."

Wood's best imaginative science fiction illustrations were commissioned by C. Arthur Pearson for the series *Stories of Other Worlds* by George Griffith, which appeared in *Pearsons Magazine* from January through June 1900.

PUBLISHED WORK:

HC: *Dr. Nikola* (1896)

MISC: "The Monster of Lake Lamatrie" (*Pearsons Magazine*, August 1899), "Stories of Other Worlds" (*Pearsons Magazine*, January through June 1900)

Richard Dalby

WOOD, WALLACE A. (June 17, 1927–Nov. 2, 1981) American artist. Born in Menzhga, Minnesota, "Wally" Wood was a self-taught artist, although he did attend the Minneapolis School of Art as well as Burne Hogarth's Cartoonists and Illustrators School for short periods. He broke into the comic-strip field as a letterer, and his first comic art appeared in 1949. He worked on newspaper strips as well as for a number of different comic book companies. In 1951 he became one of the major artists for the EC Comics line, handling many of their best science fiction comics.

While he was working for EC, Wood first tried his hand at science fiction illustration, doing a small amount of work for *Planet Stories* in 1953. However, he did not continue to work for the SF magazines at the time in part because of his many comic-book commitments. When EC folded its comic line in 1956, he branched out into many different areas. He had already been contributing a great deal of art to EC's *Mad* and continued to do so. He also began preparing advertising art and syndicated comic-strip art; he worked on comic books for nearly all of the major comic publishers. At the same time, he returned to the science fiction field and provided art for the Galaxy chain of magazines: *Galaxy*, *IF*, *Worlds of Tomorrow*, and *Galaxy Novels*.

Wood primarily did interior illustrations, although he also contributed a small number of excellent cover paintings. His interiors were done in gouache, giving them a depth and feel that most other magazine art could not match. He made very effective use of greys, blacks, and white in his art, and the picture seemed to leap out of the pages. His interiors were among the finest that appeared in the science fiction magazines of the 1950s and early 1960s. Years of working for science fiction comics had given him an excellent feel for the material, and his monsters were spectacularly monstrous, his heroes heroic, and his beautiful women unbelievably lush. However, he left the science fiction field when the comic-book field experienced a surge in publishing in the 1960s. In late 1981 Wood committed suicide.

Wood is remembered in the science fiction field not only for his excellent illustrations but also for his EC comic art. His science fiction stories for EC more than any other work are considered the best-illustrated science fiction comic art ever done and are masterpices of fine illustration. For the many science fiction fans and professionals who grew up in the 1950s, Wood symbolized the best in science fiction comics.

PUBLISHED WORK:

HC: *Colonial Survey* (57), *Return of Conan* (57), *Shrouded Planet* (57), *Survivors* (58), *Undersea City* (58)

PB: *Address: Centauri* (58), *The Forever Machine* (58), *Mission of Gravity* (58), *Twice in Time* (58)

AMZ: 1958 (2)

GXY: 1957 (9, 10, 11, 12); 1958 (2, 3, 4, 5, 6, 7, 8, 9, 10, 11, 12); 1959 (2, 4, 6, 8, 10, 12); 1960 (2, 4, 6, 8, 10, 12); 1961 (6, 12); 1962 (12); 1963 (6, 8, 10); 1965 (10, 12); 1966 (2); 1967 (8)

IF: 1959 (7, 9); 1960 (1, 3, 5, 9, 11); 1961 (7); 1965 (9); 1966 (5, 6, 7); 1967 (8, 11); 1968 (11, 12)

PS: 1953 (1, 9); 1954 (summer)
SF: 1959 (5)
WOT: 1963 (3, 6, 8, 12)

WOODROFFE, PATRICK (b. 1940) British artist. Born in Halifax, Yorkshire, Woodroffe was the son of an engineer. Against his inclinations, he studied for a degree in modern languages and graduated in French and German from Leeds University in 1964. During this period he produced a number of drawings that were exhibited at the Institute of Contemporary Arts in 1966. He taught French and German for eight years, rearing a family and painting in his spare time, but it was not until 1972 that he sold any of his work. He soon decided to become a freelance illustrator.

His early paintings were very much influenced by Bosch, Dali, surrealism, and the Viennese school of "fantastic realism." Since his style was so specific, he was often told that he should write his own books to incorporate the pictures.

A successful exhibition at the Covent Garden Gallery in London in 1972 was followed by his first commission for a book-cover design. This was from Pan Books for Fred Pohl's *Day Million*. He soon was much in demand, booked up for months in advance, working for most British paperback publishers as well as several in the United States.

Mike Jarvis, art director for Quartet Books, commissioned Woodroffe to paint most of the Michael Moorcock covers, and Woodroffe became well known as the premier Moorcock artist. Most of his paintings are done in acrylic, gouache, crayon, ink, and marbling.

Like many other British fantasy artists, Woodroffe turned to record jackets for another line of work. His first record sleeve was for *Ross* in January 1974. It was soon followed by many others including *Bandolier* (1975), *Greenslade* (1975), and *Sad Wings of Destiny* (1976).

Woodroffe prefers working in the record field because of the format, which allows the artist to work in the same size, obviating the need for reduction. He finds the people producing the music very appreciative of his work, whereas it is unusual even to hear from the authors of the paperbacks he illustrates.

He has always been more at home with mythological than technological imagery, although he is equally adept at both. "Nothing delights me more than to invent new animal species, to exaggerate their characteristics, to combine them to make hybrids of chimarae" (*Mythopoeikon*).

His best "fantasies, monsters, nightmares, daydreams" have been collected in *Mythopoeikon* (1977). This book was followed seven years later by *Hallelujah—Anyway*, a collection of illustrated lyrics.

PUBLISHED WORK:

PB: *A for Andromeda* (75), *The Best of Isaac Asimov* (73), *The Best of John Wyndham*, *The Best of Robert Heinlein*, *Billion Year Spree* (74), *The Broken Sword* (73), *The Bull and the Spear, Burn Witch Burn, Continuum One, A Cure for Cancer, Dangerous Visions 1 (73), Dangerous Visions 2 (73), Day Million (72), Day of Wrath, The Door into Summer, Dwellers in the Mirage, The English Assassin, The Face in the Abyss, The Face of Heaven, A Feast Unknown, The Forever War, The Gray Prince, The Green Hills of Earth, The Guns of Avalon (73), Hallelujah-Anyway (84), In the Kingdom of the Beasts, The Jagoon Pard (75), The Judgment of Eve, The Moon Pool, Mythopoeikon (77), Neq the Sword, The New Adam, Nine Princes in Amber (73), The Oak and the Ram, One-Eye, Our Haunted Planet, The Sailor on the Seas of Fate, The Satyr's Head, Seven Footprints to Satan, The Sleeping Sorceress, Sos the Rope, The Still Small Voice of Trumpets (75), The Sword and the Stallion, Tales of Ten Worlds, To Your Scattered Bodies Go, Trullion Alastor 2262, Var the Stick, Waldo (74), The Warlord of the Air*

Richard Dalby

WOOLHISER, JACK (?) American artist. Son of artist Harvey Woolhiser, Jack Woolhiser was born in New York City. An early inspiration was the art of Chesley Bonestell★, whose work Woolhiser discovered on covers of science fiction magazines. Woolhiser attended Pratt Institute and since graduation has worked as a freelance artist and illustrator, doing paintings and interiors for most leading magazines. He is married and the father of four children.

Woolhiser enjoys doing science fiction illustration for several reasons. "In science fiction, the artist has a sense of freedom that is not matched in any other form of realistic commercial art. I find it extremely exciting because of the possibilities" (*The New Visions*, 1952). He is fascinated by spaceships and the imagination they require. The combination of present reality and future fantasy, Woolhiser believes, produces wonderful possibilities and exciting concepts.

PUBLISHED WORK:

HC: *Best of Leigh Brackett* (77), *The Faded Sun: Son' Jir, Riddle of Stars, Three Hanish Novels, Three from the Legion*

PB: *Agent of Vega* (62)

WURTS, JANNY (b. Dec. 10, 1953) American artist. Born in Bryn Mawr, Pennsylvania, Wurts had been interested in space and the fantastic since childhood. She attended Hampshire College, where she studied astronomy and art, and graduated in 1975 with a BA in creative writing and illustration. She also attended Moore College of Art for one semester, continuing course work there. In college she worked as a lab assistant at the Hampshire College Astronomy Department, where she acquired technical experience that has helped make her astronomical paintings more realistic.

Since graduation, Janny has freelanced as a fantasy and SF illustrator as well as doing wildlife illustrations and graphic designs. She has done advertising illustration and design for a wide range of clients including the

American Bankers Association, Fortress Press, Mayfair Games, and Defenders of Wildlife.

Wurts's studio is in Frazer, Pennsylvania, on the farm of author and naturalist Daniel P. Mannix. Her illustrations were used in Mannix's novel *The Wolves of Paris*, and she often sketches his collection of animals.

In rendering a painting, she always reads the book to be illustrated, unless the art was bought from her portfolio. She works predominantly in oils, although she has used air brush and acrylic for high-tech illustrations. Sketches are done in acrylic to save time. An average painting takes around four weeks. She illustrates whatever the publishers offer that agrees with her style, interest, and schedule. She tries to do one sketch based on suggestions given by the art director and one that is her own idea.

A popular science fiction convention artist, Wurts also has had a number of her paintings done as prints and used for greeting cards. A great deal of her SF work has been for Mayfair Games.

Recently, Wurts has translated her interest in science fiction into print. She has had two novels, *Stormwarden* and *Sorcerer's Legacy*, published by Ace Books and is working on more fiction. She states, "I expect to be active in the field as writer and illustrator for a number of years to come."

PUBLISHED WORK:

HC: *Bug Jack Barron* (83), *A Case of Conscience* (82), *Wolves of Paris* (77)

PB: *Best SF of the Year 13* (84), *Brisingamen* (84), *Dragons of Darkness* (81), *Father to the Stars* (80), *Sorceror's Legacy* (85), *Spellstone of Shaltus* (79), *Stormwarden* (84), *Though All the Mountains Lie Between* (80)

FTC: 1980 (10)

YATES, CHRISTOPHER (b. Apr. 19, 1948) British artist. Yates studied at Epsom College of Art from 1964 to 1969. His first cover, *Nebula Award Stories 2*, published in 1970, was accepted by Panther Books only six months after Yates finished art school. A number of British paperback science fiction cover assignments followed, including some book illustrations for Arrow Publishers. Yates's own book, *How to Interpret Your Dreams*, was published by Marshall Cavendish in 1976.

Yates's specialty is producing startling, eye-catching covers by using scientific methods, usually creating complex photographic collages based on double-exposed color transparencies. Objects rescued from junk shops, including glass ornaments, appeared on several early covers in different forms. He also has illustrated a number of prize-winning record jackets.

PUBLISHED WORK (All British books).

PB: *Creatures of Light and Darkness*, *The Electric Crocodile*, *Elric of Melnibone*, *The Jagged Orbit*, *Nebula Award Stories 2* (70), *Rogue Moon*, *The Winds of Gath*

Richard Dalby

YOST, JAMES (?) American artist. One of the more prominent new artists doing work for the Science Fiction Book Club, James Z. Yost lives and works in New York City. Of his views on science fiction, Yost wrote that "people is what science fiction is really about, not laser-ray guns, quantum mechanics, and interstellar spaceships. These are just the props and stage upon which science fiction is acted. The beauty of *good* science fiction is that it gets to the heart, to the essence of human drama, and lets it unfold free from all the Tedious Limitations of the 'real' world" (The New Visions, 1982).

PUBLISHED WORK:

HC: *Forerunner*

Science Fiction Art: What Still Exists

As of early 1987 there were no major holdings of science fiction art in public or private institutions in the United States. There has been talk for several years of establishing a science fiction museum, which among its major exhibits would have a collection of science fiction art, but this project remains in the discussion stages. The U.S. Air and Space Museum of the Smithsonian has a large collection of original "space art," but the title refers primarily to astronomical art, even though many pieces have been donated or done on consignment by SF artists covered in this volume.

Science fiction art is in the hands of individuals. Through the efforts of science fiction fans and collectors of genre material, art that otherwise would have been lost is still in existence. However, since most fans are not eager to broadcast what valuable items are part of their collections, providing a detailed listing of major holdings of original art is nearly impossible. Instead, this appendix is intended to provide a general historical overview of what actually exists in terms of original artwork done for science fiction books and magazines. Although there have been other studies on SF art, no previous attempt has been made to establish what originals made their way into private hands.

During the past fifteen years, science fiction art shows at conventions have grown to huge proportions, with most artists working in the field exhibiting and selling their own work. Because of this fact, this appendix concentrates on the period before the liberation of modern artists from company control. In present-day science fiction, original art is returned to the artist, and through secondary sales, the artist is able to obtain more money for his painting. This was not always the case. The history of science fiction art is part of the history of pulp publishing in America. It is not a story of fairness or consideration for the artists' wishes.

1

Although some fantasy and science fiction art exists from before the advent of the pulp magazines, such pieces normally fall into the category of rare nineteenth- and early twentieth-century art and were rarely available or collected by science fiction fans. Harry Clarke art does exist as do pieces by Lynd Ward and other famous mainstream artists whose work drifted into the domain of science fiction, but such art is offered for sale by major galleries and its outside the scope of this survey.

It was in the pulps that science fiction art first became available to the general fan and collector. The pulp magazines were run in a manner to maximize profits. Stories were bought on an all-rights basis in most cases, with monies for reprints going directly to the publisher instead of the author. When the author was popular enough to dictate his own terms (and all-rights contracts were never considered), reprint rights were split with the publisher and detailed agreements over dramatic and film rights were built into every contract. However, in the art field, contracts were much simpler. Magazines of the period bought all rights to the art and kept the originals as well. Only under special arrangements were the actual illustrations or paintings returned, and even then, this was done with extreme reluctance by the companies. The general feeling was that the paintings were a part of the magazine and belonged to the publisher. The artist was producing a work for hire and had no claim upon the actual finished piece.

At the same time, the pulp publishers did not have enough storage space for all of the artwork they accumulated, so paintings were either destroyed, sold, or, in many cases, given away. *Adventure* magazine in the teens and twenties would run a mail auction every year for cover paintings featured on the magazines. Minimum bid was fifteen dollars, and anyone was able to enter. That there was rarely much demand for the art was evidenced by the fact that prospective bidders were told in advance that a minimum bid would usually win the desired piece.

At Street & Smith, art illustrating cover stories was often offered to the authors of the work at the price the company had paid for the painting. Otherwise, the originals were kept in basement storage rooms. From time to time, art was even reused. The cover for the first issue of *The Shadow* pulp magazine was a reprint of the original cover for an issue of *The Thrill Book*, published years before by Street & Smith. When the company was sold to Conde Nast in 1959, an art appraiser went through the original paintings owned by the company and pulled out the pieces by known mainstream artists (primarily N. C. Wyeth, who illustrated some early pulp covers). The rest of the art was given away to any Street & Smith employees who wanted it.

One of the first authors to express interest in all of the paintings illustrating his work was Edgar Rice Burroughs. Burroughs made an effort to obtain a number of the originals used to illustrate his stories, especially those that appeared in hardcover form. Edgar Rice Burroughs, Inc., today owns one of the finest collections of early originals used to illustrate Burroughs's work, including many exceptional pieces by J. Allen St. John. As was often the case, the art usually was not bought from the artist but from the publishers of the volumes. Most of the early St. John paintings were done for the A. C. McClurg Company of Chicago.

St. John did obtain some of his paintings by visiting the publisher and asking for a number of the pieces to be returned. Unfortunately, by that time, some of the paintings illustrating Burroughs novels had already vanished. The publisher evidently made no attempt to keep track of art in its vaults, and either employees took paintings for decoration or various department heads gave away paintings to friends or major customers of the company. Among the numerous missing major St. John paintings are the oils done for *The Beasts of Tarzan*, *The Son of Tarzan*, *Jungle Tales of Tarzan*, *Tarzan the Untamed*, *Tarzan the Terrible*, *Tarzan and the Lion Man*, *Tarzan and the Ant Men*, *Tarzan at the Earth's Core*, *The Mucker*, *The Cave Girl*, *The Mad King*, *The Outlaw of Torn*, *The Monster Men*, and *The Land That Time Forgot*. Possibly, many of these paintings were given to people in the Chicago area (where the publisher and artist were both located), but diligent searching for more than fifty years by collectors has yet to turn up one of these pieces.

Edgar Rice Burroughs later went into the publishing business himself and thus was able to buy the originals used to illustrate his books with a minimum of effort. After Burroughs's death, his company, Edgar Rice Burroughs, Inc., continued to buy both new and old originals used to illustrate the Burroughs novels. Much of the art owned by the estate can be seen in the massive three-volume set, *The Edgar Rice Burroughs Library of Illustration* (1976–1985), published by Russ Cochran.

Most originals done for the Munsey magazines *Argosy* and *All-Story* that related to science fiction stories disappeared over the years. However, some paintings still exist. In 1986 Robert Weinberg bought from an East Coast art dealer a painting used for *My Lady of the Nile*, a 1921 fantasy serial published in *Argosy* magazine. At present, this is the oldest known *Argosy* cover in private hands.

Otis Adelbert Kline was given a number of paintings used for his serial novels in *Argosy*, and his family retained the art for a number of years before selling the paintings to a collector and literary agent in Georgia. Among the existing *Argosy* paintings were the covers for *Maza of the Moon* and *Outlaws of Mars*. Other Paul Stahr and Robert Graef original paintings from the Munsey pulps are also in private collections, but none of the other paintings are from science fiction stories.

Munsey was bought by Popular Publications in late 1942. All files, bound volumes, and other property owned by the publisher was taken over by Popular. However, no paintings were included in the transaction: they had either been destroyed or given away before the final deal was made.

2

When *Weird Tales* began publication in 1923, the editors used the least expensive art available. This policy slowly changed over the years, with rates rising as the magazine became more successful. However, as with all other pulps, *Weird Tales* kept all of the originals done for its stories. Farnsworth Wright, who served as editor from 1924 through 1940, was extremely generous with the artwork done for the magazine. For example, whenever he wrote to Greye La Spina, one of the regular writers for the pulp in the 1920s, Wright made sure to send along several interior illustrations that had graced her recent works. Most of these originals were later obtained by Robert Weinberg from the family of Mrs. La Spina.

E. Hoffmann Price described, in a memoir published in 1973, how he visited Wright in his offices in 1927 and was presented with the cover painting illustrating his story "The Infidel's Daughter." Over the years, Wright gave Price a number of original illustrations for his stories that appeared in *Weird Tales*. Jack Williamson, in his autobiography, related that Wright offered to send him the two St. John paintings done for Williamson's novel *Golden Blood* but that he could not accept them because he had no place in his modest cabin to keep the art. The title painting for the novel later turned up in a Chicago bookstore and was bought by Russ Swanson, who still owns the piece. The other cover painting disappeared.

Otis Adelbert Kline, who was given a number of cover paintings from *Argosy* for his novels, was also given several *Weird Tales* covers. Two of these paintings, a St. John cover illustrating *Buccaneers of Venus* and a C. C. Senf painting for *Tam, Son of the Tiger*, were given by the Kline family to a Chicago bookstore to sell. The St. John painting was bought by a Chicago collector who has since sold it to an art dealer in Atlanta. The Senf painting probably was sold, but its current whereabouts are unknown. The paintings were priced at one hundred dollars each.

Wright sent Edmond Hamilton numerous interior pieces of art that illustrated his stories. Seabury Quinn also collected as many originals as he could that illustrated his Jules de Grandin stories. Manly Wade Wellman was yet another *Weird Tales* author who was given a number of interiors that went with his work in that magazine.

Margaret Brundage's pastel chalk paintings were extremely fragile and were kept under glass for safekeeping. There is no record of Wright giving any of these paintings to authors, yet Brundage never was given back any of her art. In 1970 the Gallery Bookshop of Chicago sold nearly a dozen of her paintings, still in perfect condition, under glass, to an Illinois collector. The paintings since have been distributed throughout the fantasy field.

One of the Brundage paintings was a cover for *Oriental Stories*, the short-lived 1930s companion magazine to *Weird Tales*. Wright did give the first cover painting for that magazine to author Frank Owen, whose story was illustrated by the piece. The second cover painting was discovered by Robert Weinberg at the Gallery Bookshop in the early 1970s. Both paintings were done by Donald Von Gelb. Another *Oriental* cover later turned up in 1985, again in the possession of the Gallery Bookstore, and was sold to a Kansas City collector. All of the art was evidently bought by the owner of the bookstore in the 1930s from a major fan and collector of *Weird Tales* who had obtained the material from Farnsworth Wright.

3

No artwork from *Amazing Stories* during the early days when it was published by Hugo Gernsback is known to exist. Gernsback was noted for being close with his money, so it is doubtful that any of Frank R. Paul's artwork was returned to him. Instead, the art was probably destroyed or lost during the change in ownership of the magazine in 1929. Gernsback went on to publish *Science Wonder Stories* and *Air Wonder Stories* that same year. Again, none of the art was offered for sale. However, in 1953 SF historian Sam Moskowitz was working for Gernsback Publications, editing its magazine *SF+*. On leaving the New York offices late one night, Moskowitz spotted a stack of large paintings in garbage drums waiting for the next day's pickup. Upon inspection, he discovered nearly a dozen very large-size Frank R. Paul original paintings done for the Wonder pulp chain. The art had been kept in storage for years until the owners of the chain decided it was taking up too much room. Without any thought, they decided to throw away all of the pieces. Moskowitz rescued the art, many paintings of which were among Paul's finest work and dated from 1929. A number of them were published in science fiction calendars edited and published by Moskowitz in the 1970s.

By the middle 1930s Gernsback had relented somewhat, and original paintings made their way into a newly developing science fiction fandom. The July 1935 *Wonder Stories* featured a Paul cover, and readers were asked to write a story about it. The prize was the cover painting itself. This painting surfaced again in the early 1970s when it was offered for sale by a West Coast book store. A number of other Paul paintings were donated to the early science fiction conventions of the 1940s.

Clayton Magazines entered the science fiction and fantasy field with *Astounding Stories* in 1930 and *Strange Tales* in 1931. None of the art done for these magazines seems to have survived the bankruptcy of this chain in 1933.

Street & Smith took over *Astounding Stories* when the magazine folded in March 1933. As mentioned earlier, the company believed in keeping all of the artwork used in its magazines. Official policy was to hold onto the art unless the artist specifially asked for it back. Most of these paintings were kept in basement storage areas where they were largely forgotten by the owners. From time to time, art was given to authors by John W. Campbell, Jr., who became editor of *Astounding* in 1938. Among such paintings given away was the cover done for *Galactic Patrol* by E. E. Smith (painted by H. W. Wesso) and Hubert Rogers's original for *The Stolen Dormouse* by L. Sprague de Camp. Charles Schneeman did ask for his art back, and many of his black-and-white illustrations for classic stories from *Astounding SF* in the early 1940s are in the possession of his family. Edd Cartier was also able to obtain a number of his original interiors for *Unknown*.

However, the Cartier painting for *Lest Darkness Fall* used for the December 1939 cover of *Unknown*, which featured the story, was given by Campbell to the author, L. Sprague de Camp. During the Korean conflict, de Camp donated the original to a science fiction auction to raise money to send SF books to soldiers. The art was bought by an Ohio collector, who kept it for many years before selling it to the Book Sail in California. Given the small number of paintings ever to appear in *Unknown*, it seems likely that this is the only existing color piece from that magazine.

The First World Science Fiction Convention was held in New York in 1939. Since most of the major publishers were located in the city, a number of editors attended. In an attempt to raise money for the convention expenses, an auction was held featuring items donated to the convention by the editors as well as by other attending authors and artists. A number of original pieces of art by Paul, Virgil Finlay, and other major artists of the day were sold. Prices were astonishing. Originals by Finlay were sold for a dime. Sometimes several pieces were sold for a quarter. Paintings went for a dollar or two. Art was considered an interesting bit of science fiction memorabilia but nothing more.

Ziff-Davis, who took over publication of *Amazing* in 1938, maintained its headquarters in Chicago. Fans in that city found original art easy to obtain by a visit to the offices of the magazines. Ray Palmer, editor of the science fiction line, was notoriously generous about giving away original art. A long-time fan himself, Palmer rarely returned art to his artists. Nor did the staff artists, working long hours for low pay, expect their paintings back.

Earl Korshak, a well-known collector of the time, visited Palmer in his offices and was given a St. John cover painting that he had admired. Frank Robinson, who worked as an office boy for Ziff-Davis, was also given a

St. John *Amazing* cover in 1943. Both paintings remain in existence in private collections.

When the Second World Science Fiction Convention was held in Chicago, Palmer donated a huge number of originals. Front- and back-cover art by Paul, McCauley, Fuqua, and other major artists were all made available to convention members for exceptionally low prices. Among the paintings donated to that convention were "The Blue Tropics" by Frank R. Paul from *Fantastic Adventures*, April 1940, which was sold for $1.00; "Cat Women of Ganymede," a back cover from *Amazing*, also by Paul, which sold for $3.50; and the first cover for *Fantastic Adventures* by Robert Fuqua.

Other publishers also donated art. A Virgil Finlay painting for *Famous Fantastic Mysteries* illustrating the novel *Darkness and Dawn* was sold for five dollars. Ted Dikty, who served as auctioneer at the convention, remembered offering a handful of Virgil Finlay originals for ten or fifteen cents to a crowd of largely uninterested science fiction fans.

Palmer continued to give away cover and interior art throughout his reign as editor of *Amazing Stories* and *Fantastic Adventures*. In the late 1940s, a collector on the West Coast offered for sale a number of original paintings from the Ziff-Davis pulps. They included works by Robert Gibson Jones, Malcolm Smith, Frank R. Paul, and J. Allen St. John. In the late 1960s an art dealer in New Orleans turned up ten paintings from the 1940s by Robert Gibson Jones, including the original cover art for *The Court of Kublai Khan*, *You're All Alone*, *Lavender Vine of Death*, and *Forgotten Worlds*. In 1986 a back-cover painting by Frank R. Paul for the February 1940 *Fantastic Adventures* was found by a collector at a flea market in the Chicago suburbs. It seems likely that a number of other paintings from the Ziff-Davis magazines are hidden away in attics throughout the Midwest.

4

Virgil Finlay was one of the few artists who was wise enough to request his art back from publishers. This is not to say that all of his art was returned, but he did get a number of pieces. Hannes Bok also asked for his art, but, again, it was more due to luck than to any ethical considerations when the illustrations were returned to the artist.

The Standard chain did not return art done for its magazines during the 1940s. Thus original art from *Startling Stories*, *Thrilling Wonder*, and *Captain Future* magazines is virtually nonexistent. Popular Publications believed in keeping all of the art used in its magazines, and with the exception of Finlay, few artists for that chain's magazines ever received any of their art. Although some of Finlay's art was kept by Popular, much of it was returned to him.

The editors at Popular were not as generous as Ray Palmer, but a number of originals from its magazines made it into the hands of collectors. At least three Lawrence Sterne Stevens covers for *Super Science Stories* painted in

1949 and 1950 were sold at conventions, as was a Henry Van Dongen painting done for the same magazine. A number of Finlay paintings also were sold, including the cover for "The Metal Monster" done for the August 1941 issue of *Famous Fantastic Mysteries* and the Finlay painting for "The Crystal Circe" done for the June 1942 issue of *Astonishing Stories*.

In the late 1940s the editor of *Famous Fantastic Mysteries*, the leading Popular Publications pulp, depended on several well-known collectors to help her select obscure fantasy and science fiction novels for the magazine, which published a reprint novel in each number. These collectors were not paid any fee, but at least one of them was sent cover paintings by Lawrence Sterne Stevens and Virgil Finlay as a form of noncash payment. In this manner, the originals for *Burn Witch Burn* illustrated by Finlay and for *Conquest of the Moon Pool* and *Dwellers in the Mirage* illustrated by Lawrence Sterne Stevens found their way into private collections.

Planet Stories had an unusual way of disposing of art. The letter column in *Planet* was active, with many fans commenting in every issue. Readers were asked to vote on their favorite letter, and the three letter writers chosen in each issue were given their choice of an original piece of art from the pulp. A number of pieces by Bok and Leydenfrost were given away to fans in this manner.

In the early 1950s magazines continued to keep art whenever possible. A number of artists, however, realized the resale value of their own work and began requesting the originals back. Kelly Freas was able to obtain many of his early pieces from various publishers, although a number of illustrations apparently disappeared forever. Again the artist had to make a request for the art to be returned. This remained the policy of Street & Smith and many other magazines of the time; *Galaxy* and *If* made it a practice never to return originals. Art was still treated as an extra perk for the company. A photographer friend of the president of Street & Smith was given three paintings as a present, including an Emsh original for *Exploration Team* by Murray Leinster. John W. Campbell kept a Henry R. Van Dongen painting for a favorite *Astounding* cover hanging on the wall of his office for years before finally returning it to the artist.

Often art was lost through sheer disinterest. When Fiction House went out of business in the late 1960s, all of the original art stored in its warehouse was burned. The workers at the warehouse saved the comic art since they had heard that such material was valuable, but they saw no reason to keep any of the science fiction art. Fortunately, a number of Freas covers had been rescued by the artist many years before and ended up in the hands of private collectors. In even a more unusual twist of fate, Freas bought two *Planet Stories* covers by Allen Anderson when he visited the offices of Fiction House to discuss his own artwork. The two pieces owned by Freas are the only known paintings in existence by this forgotten artist.

At *Other Worlds*, a Ray Palmer publication, art was returned on request but otherwise was donated to science fiction conventions. At *Imagination* and *Imaginative Tales*, published in Chicago by William Hamling, cover art was routinely donated to conventions or given to fan gatherings in the city. Literally dozens of paintings by Malcolm Smith, Harold McCauley, and William Terry were bought by fans in the 1950s. Only Hannes Bok asked for his art to be returned.

5

The small-press publishers of the 1940s and 1950s were only a little better than the magazine chains in their dealings with artists. Art was sometimes returned, but often the originals were donated to conventions, or frequently, the publisher kept the originals. Sometimes, the artists actually gave the publishers permission to keep the art or asked for a small extra sum if the publisher wanted to keep the originals. In the late 1970s Martin Greenberg of Gnome Press sold a large number of original cover paintings and interiors from the Gnome Press series. Earle Korshak paid extra so that he could keep many of the originals used in Shasta Books, which he had cofounded. Fantasy Press donated most of its cover art to science fiction conventions. Art from the major hardcover publishers of the period rarely turned up and was probably returned to the artists or destroyed.

Paperback houses evolved in the same marketplace as did the pulps, and in a sense paperbacks are the children of the pulp field. The ethics of publishing remained the same. Art for covers was rarely returned unless the artist specifically asked for the originals back, and even then, the publishers did not always comply. Most major publishers accumulated stacks of paintings, which they kept stored in poorly ventilated, dirty, damp warehouses in the New York City area.

From time to time, realizing the futility of such holdings, a major company would let go of its stock of original paintings. In 1970 the publisher of *Galaxy*, *IF*, *Worlds of Tomorrow*, and *Beyond* offered paintings and interiors for sale at very low prices. A number of excellent paintings by Ed Emsh, Wally Wood, Virgil Finlay, and other artists were bought by knowledgeable collectors, but most of the art remained unsold. In 1975 Robert Weinberg and Victor Dricks contacted James L. Quinn, the publisher of the magazines, about that art. Hundreds of pieces, both interior and full color, were still available, and the two art dealers took much of it on consignment. Although Weinberg and Dricks sold a number of pieces, a lot of material was returned to Quinn and is presumably still in storage somewhere.

In 1978 Ace Books released all of the original paintings collecting dust in its New York warehouse. A number of science fiction paintings had been given away by editors at Ace, and some of the art had actually been returned to the artists. Still, more than five hundred science fiction paintings were offered for sale by dealers Ray Walsh, Doug Ruble, and Robert Weinberg working in conjunction with the publisher. More than a hundred excellent paintings by Emsh were sold, as well as dozens of originals by Ed Valigursky and Kelly Freas, among many others. The original *Lord of the Rings* paintings by Jack Gaughan were also part of that immense offering. The average price for a classic painting by Emsh or Valigursky was less than $150.

More recently, Pyramid Books released more than a thousand paintings in all fields to a Florida-based art dealer. Included were several dozen early science fiction paintings by Emsh, Schoenherr, Engel, and Jeff Jones.

6

Virgil Finlay and Hannes Bok were among the few artists who consistently asked for their art. When Finlay needed money for cancer treatments, he contacted well-known book dealer and art collector Gerry de la Ree and asked him to sell the originals Finlay had accumulated over the years. In 1969 and 1970 de la Ree sold hundreds of Finlay black-and-white illustrations as well as a number of paintings. It was probably the largest single offering of quality art ever conducted in the science fiction field.

During the 1950s Hannes Bok sold many of the originals he had painted for book and magazine covers of the previous decade. At the time, he had difficulty in finding a market. Science fiction fandom was a small group, and science fiction art was considered a novelty, not something of much value. Most of Bok's originals went to close friends whom he contacted by letter. As is often the case, since the artist's death, his work has increased in value far beyond the prices he was able to obtain when he needed the money.

Fortunately, the science fiction field is reasonably unique. It is a small world unto itself, having developed primarily from the pulp ghetto of the 1930s. Art that was given to collectors or authors usually stayed in the field. When the owner decided to sell a piece, the art was offered to other collectors and not placed in the general art marketplace. Even when an author or collector died, his family usually knew enough about his hobby to sell the items to other collectors. Since the 1940s fans have been able to advertise unwanted items in magazines. In this manner, many of the originals donated to science fiction conventions or given away to individuals have surfaced again and again in fandom.

In 1940 the front cover of the first issue of *Fantastic Adventures* (May 1939) by Robert Fuqua was sold at auction at the Second World Science Fiction Convention. In the March 1948 issue of *Fantasy Advertiser*, the piece was offered for sale at $3.50. In 1932 the painting surfaced in New York State when it was sold to a local book dealer by the relative of a science fiction fan who had just died. Several months later the painting was sold to Robert Weinberg for $350.00. Weinberg later sold it to a collector in Michigan for

$450.00. Since that collector has recently lost interest in science fiction art, the piece will probably surface again in the coming years.

The Virgil Finlay painting for "Darkness and Dawn" from *Famous Fantastic Mysteries* was sold to a Pennsylvania fan at the Second World Science Fiction Convention for $5. Many years later the fan sold it to Camille Cazedessus, Jr., a well-known art collector, for $50. It was later offered in *Graphic Gallery # 7* in 1976 for $900 and sold immediately.

Many paintings in the hands of private collectors have similar histories. Although it is unfortunate that the original artists rarely benefited from the sale of their works, at least the paintings have survived. Without the interest of a small number of fans, it seems likely that few examples of early science fiction art would exist today.

Art Awards

Because so many art shows are held each year at various major regional conventions and a number of professional and semiprofessional societies also give out medals and awards, the listings below are limited to the two awards generally regarded as the most prestigious in the SF field.

THE HUGO AWARDS

Named after science fiction pioneer Hugo Gernsback, the Hugo Awards are given each year by the World Science Fiction Convention and are determined by a vote of the membership in the convention. Because of the limited size of the voting group (many of whom often do not vote), decisions often reflect fan biases. In general, they are a good indication of the popularity of the winner. The following list includes just the art winners.

The Awards began in 1953. That was the only year that separate awards were given for interior and cover artists. All future art awards were designated only for best artitst. There were no Hugo Awards in 1954 and no art award was given in 1957.

1953: Best Cover Artist, tie between Ed Emshwiller and Hannes Bok; Best Interior Artist, Virgil Finlay

1955: Frank Kelly Freas

1956: Frank Kelly Freas

1958: Frank Kelly Freas

1959: Frank Kelly Freas

1960: Ed Emshwiller

1961: Ed Emshwiller
1962: Ed Emshwiller
1963: Roy G. Krenkel
1964: Ed Emshwiller
1965: John Schoenherr
1966: Frank Frazetta
1967: Jack Gaughan
1968: Jack Gaughan
1969: Jack Gaughan
1970: Frank Kelly Freas
1971: Leo and Diane Dillon
1972: Frank Kelly Freas
1973: Frank Kelly Freas
1974: Frank Kelly Freas
1975: Frank Kelly Freas
1976: Frank Kelly Freas
1977: Rick Sternbach
1978: Rick Sternbach
1979: Vincent Di Fate
1980: Michael Whelan
1981: Michael Whelan
1982: Michael Whelan
1983: Michael Whelan
1984: Michael Whelan
1985: Michael Whelan
1986: Michael Whelan

Beginning in 1967 a separate Hugo was awarded to the Best Fan Artist. As many winners later went on to become professionals in the science fiction art field, this listing is included as well:

1967: Jack Gaughan
1968: George Barr
1969: Vaughan Bode
1970: Tim Kirk
1971: Alicia Austin
1972: Tim Kirk
1973: Tim Kirk
1974: Tim Kirk

1975: Bill Rotsler
1976: Tim Kirk
1977: Phil Foglio
1978: Phil Foglio
1979: Bill Rotsler
1980: Alexis Gililand
1981: Victoria Poyser
1982: Victoria Poyser
1983: Alexis Gilliland
1984: Alexis Gilliland
1985: Alexis Gilliland

THE WORLD FANTASY AWARDS

Given each year by the World Fantasy Convention, these awards are chosen by a panel of five judges. The preliminary ballot is also selected by the same judges, who nominate several artists. Two other nominees for the final ballot are selected by members of two previous conventions who vote on their choices. This system thus combines the concept of a popular vote along with a quality panel selection in producing the final ballot. The following are winners of the Best Artist Award:

1975: Lee Brown Coye
1976: Frank Frazetta
1977: Roger Dean
1978: Lee Brown Coye
1979: Tie between Alicia Austin and Dale Enzenbacher
1980: Don Maitz
1981: Michael Whelan
1982: Michael Whelan
1983: Michael Whelan
1984: Stephen Gervais
1985: Edward Gorey

Bibliography

1987 SF Calendar. Los Angeles: Bridge Publications, 1986.

Achilleos, Chris. *Sirens*. London: Paper Tiger, 1986.

Aldiss, Brian. *Science Fiction Art*. New York: Bounty Books, 1975.

American Paperback Calendar, 1982. Brownwood, Tex: American Paperback Institute, 1981.

Bails, Jerry, and Ware, Hames. *Who's Who of American Comic Books*. Detroit: Jerry Bails, 1973.

Ballantine, Betty. *Fantastic Art of Frank Frazetta*. New York: Peacock Press, 1975.

————. *Fantastic World of Gervasio Gallardo*, New York: Peacock Press/Bantam Book, 1976.

————. *Frank Frazetta, Book Two*. New York: Peacock Press, 1977

————. *Frank Frazetta, Book Three*. New York: Peacock Press, 1978.

————. *Frank Frazetta, Book Four*. New York: Peacock Press, 1980.

Barr, George. *Upon the Winds of Yesterday*. West Kingston, R.I.: Donald Grant, 1976.

Barson, Michael. "Avon Artists Unmasked." *Paperback Forum #1*. New York: Paperback Forum, 1984.

"Bogeyman." *Family Circle*. Newark, N.J.: Family Circle, Inc., August 26, 1938.

Boris Vallejo Fantasy Calendar, 1980. New York: Workman Publishing Co., 1979.

Boris Vallejo Fantasy Calendar, 1981. New York: Workman Publishing Co., 1980.

Boris Vallejo Fantasy Calendar, 1982. New York: Workman Publishing Co., 1982.

Boris Vallejo Fantasy Calendar, 1983. New York: Workman Publishing Co., 1982.

Brooks, C. W. *Revised Hannes Bok Checklist*. Newport News, Va.: Ned Brooks, 1974.

Cartier, Dean. *Edd Cartier: The Known and the Unknown*. Saddle River, N.J.: Gerry de la Ree, 1977.

"Chris Achilleos Interview." *Dr. Who Magazine #114*. London: Marvel Comics, July 1986.

de la Ree, Gerry. *Fantasy Collectors Annual, 1974*. Saddle River, N.J.: Gerry de la Ree, 1974.

————. *Fantasy Collectors Annual, 1975*. Saddle River, N.J.: Gerry de la Ree, 1975.

Del Rey, Lester. *Fantastic Science-Fiction Art, 1926–1954*. New York: Ballantine Books, 1975.

Di Fate, Vincent. "The Dark Side of Surrealism." *Starship*. New York: Algol Press, Summer 1979.

————. "An Interview with John Schoenherr." *Algol*. New York: Algol Press, Summer-Fall 1978.

————. "Sketches." *Algol*. New York: Algol Press, Summer 1976.

————. "Sketches." *Algol/Starship*. New York: Algol Press, Winter 1978–79.

————. "Sketches." *Starship*. New York: Algol Press, Spring 1979.

Dricks, Victor. "Ronald Clyne: A Portrait." *Xenophile #18*. St. Louis: Nils Hardin, October 1975.

Elliott, Jeffrey. "The Fantasy Art of Rowena Morrill." *Threshold of Fantasy #2*. Sunnyvale, Calif.: Fandom Unlimited Enterprises, 1986.

Elson, Peter, and Moore, Chris. *Parallel Lines*. New York: Dragons Dream, 1981.

Fenner, Arnie. "Richard Corben Profile." *Fantasy Review*. Boca Raton, Fla.: Florida Atlantic University, June 1985.

Frane, Jeff. *Seventh World Fantasy Convention Program Book*. Berkeley, Calif.: Seventh World Fantasy Convention, 1981.

Frank Kelly Freas: A Portfolio. Chicago: Advent Publishers, 1957.

Freas, Kelly. *Frank Kelly Freas: The Art of Science Fiction*. Norfolk, Va.: Donning, 1977.

Gerrold, David. *SF Yearbook #1*. New York: Starlog Press, 1979.

"Graves Gladney Speaks." *Duende #1*. North Quincy, Mass.: Odyssey Publications, April 1975.

"Graves Gladney Obituary." *Duende #2*. North Quincy, Mass.: Odyssey Publications, Winter 1976–77.

"Graves Gladney Obituary." *Xenophile #22*. St. Louis: Nils Hardin, March 1976.

Heroic Fantasy Calendar 1979. Woodland Hills, Calif.: Earth Art Graphics, August 1978.

Hildebrandt, Greg. *From Tolkien to Oz*. Parsippany, N.J.: Unicorn Books, 1985.

Hill, M. C. "James Steranko by M. C. Hill." *Paperback Quarterly*. Brownwood, Tex.: Paperback Quarterly, Spring 1981.

"Interview with Graves Gladney." *Whizzard #4*. St. Louis: Marty Klug, Summer 1974.

"Interview with Graves Gladney." *Whizzard #5*. St. Louis: Marty Klug, January 1975.

"Interview with Jon D. Arfstrom." *Etchings & Odysseys #3*. Madison, Wisc.: Strange Co., 1983.

"Interview with Kelly Freas." *Paperback Quarterly*. Brownwood, Tex.: Paperback Quarterly, Summer 1980.

"James Bama Interview." *Doc Savage and Assoc.* Florrissant, Mo.: George Rock, February 1982.

Jones, Bruce, and Eisen, Armand. *Sorcerors*. New York: Ballantine Books, 1978.

Jones, Peter. *Solar Wind*. New York: Perigee Books, 1980.

Miller, Ian. *Secret Art*. Holland: Dragons Dream, 1980.

Miller, Ron. *Space Art*. New York: O'Quinn Studios, 1978.

———. *Space Art*. New York: Starlog Magazines, 1978.

Miller, Ron, and Durant, Frederick C., III. *Worlds Beyond: The Art of Chesley Bonestell*. Norfolk, Va.: Donning Books, 1983.

Moskowitz, Sam. Science Fiction Calendar, 1977. New York: Charles Scribner & Sons, 1976.

Mugnaini, Joseph. *Joseph Mugnaini: Drawings and Graphics*. Metuchen, N.J.: Scarecrow Press, 1982.

Murray, Will. "The Unknown Unknown." *Xenophile #42*. St. Louis: Nils Hardin, September 1979.

"New Doc Savage Artist." *Doc Savage Club Reader*. Berwyn, Ill.: Bronze Men of Berwyn, 1974.

The New Visions. Garden City, N.Y.: Doubleday & Co., 1982.

Nicholls, Peter. *The Science Fiction Encyclopedia*. Garden City, N.Y.: Doubleday, 1979.

Papalia, William. "John Newton Howitt." *Xenophile #33*. St. Louis: Nils Hardin, July 1977.

Petaja, Emil. *Showcase of Fantasy Art*. San Francisco: SISU, 1974.

"Pulp Cover Dean—Rafael De Soto." *Cartoonist Profiles # 50*. Fairfield, Conn.: Cartoonist Profiles, June 1981.

Reed, Walt, and Reed, Roger. *The Illustrator in America, 1880–1980*. New York: Madison Square Press, 1984.

Robert Schulz Memorial Exhibition. New York: Grand Central Art Galleries, 1980.

Schreuders, Piet. "Rudolph Belarski." *Paperback Forum #1*. New York: Paperback Forum, 1984.

Schreuders, Piet. "Paperbacks U.S.A." San Diego: Blue Dolphin Books, 1981.

SF Calendar 1980. Garden City, N.Y.: Doubleday & Co., 1980.

Skeeters, Paul W. *Sidney H. Sime: Master of Fantasy*. Pasadena, Calif.: Ward Ritchie Press, 1978.

Summers, Ian. *The Art of the Brothers Hildebrandt*. New York: Ballantine Books, 1979.

Thorpe, Dickson. "Norman Saunders." *Echoes #18*. Seymour, Tex.: Fading Shadows, April 1985.

Trojan, William. "Ace SF Specials." *SF Collector #5*. Calgary, Alberta, Can.: Pandora's Books, September 1977.

Tuck, Donald H. *Encyclopedia of Science Fiction & Fantasy*. 3 vols. Chicago: Advent, 1974–83.

Tymn, Marshall B., and Ashley, Mike, eds. *Science Fiction, Fantasy, and Weird Fiction Magazines*. Westport, Conn.: Greenwood Press, 1985.

Virgil Finlay. West Kingston, R.I.: Donald Grant, 1971.

"Walter Baumhofer Interview." *Doc Savage Club Reader #9*. Berwyn, Ill.: Frank Lewandowski.

Weinberg, Robert. "Collecting Fantasy." *Fantasy Newsletter*. Penfield, New York: Fantasy Newsletter, October 1981.

Whelan, Michael. *Wonderworks*. Norfolk, Va.: Donning, 1979.

Worlds of Fantasy Calendar 1976. New York: Peacock Press, 1975.

Yesterday's Lily. Holland: Dragons Dream, 1980.

Index of Biographical Entries

Index

(For the sake of practicality, this index does not cover books listed in the bibliographical entries for each artist. Magazine listings are indexed. The bibliography and introductory material also is not covered in the index. Films are denoted as such only when there is the possibility of confusion with a book or story with the same title.)

About the Author

ROBERT WEINBERG is the author of *The Weird Tales Story*, *Annotated Guide to Robert E. Howard*, and several hundred articles published in books and magazines. He has edited nearly fifty collections of stories from the science fiction and fantasy magazines, and won the World Fantasy Award (1978) for his contributions to the field of fantastic fiction scholarship.